# IT-Based Management:
# Challenges and Solutions

Luiz Antonio Joia
Brazilian School of Public and Business Administration,
Getulio Vargas Foundation and
Rio de Janeiro State University, Brazil

 **IDEA GROUP PUBLISHING**

Hershey • London • Melbourne • Singapore • Beijing

EL CIDA-GULF COT
UNIVERSITY LIBRARY

| | |
|---|---|
| Acquisition Editor: | Mehdi Khosrowpour |
| Managing Editor: | Jan Travers |
| Development Editor: | Michele Rossi |
| Copy Editor: | Beth Arneson |
| Typesetter: | LeAnn Whitcomb |
| Cover Design: | Integrated Book Technology |
| Printed at: | Integrated Book Technology |

Published in the United States of America by
Idea Group Publishing (an imprint of Idea Group Inc.)
701 E. Chocolate Avenue
Hershey PA 17033-1240
Tel: 717-533-8845
Fax: 717-533-8661
E-mail: cust@idea-group.com
Web site: http://www.idea-group.com

and in the United Kingdom by
Idea Group Publishing
3 Henrietta Street
Covent Garden
London WC2E 8LU
Tel: 44 20 7240 0856
Fax: 44 20 7379 3313
Web site: http://www.eurospan.co.uk

Library of Congress Cataloging-in-Publication Data

IT-based management : challenges and solutions / [edited by] Luiz Antonio Joia.
    p. cm.
  Includes bibliographical references and index.
    ISBN 1-59140-033-3 (cloth) -- ISBN 1-59140-075-9 (ebook)
    1. Knowledge management. 2. Information technology--Management. I. Joia, Luiz
Antonio.

  HD30.2 .I85 2002
  658.4'038--dc21

                                                              2002068793

British Cataloguing in Publication Data
A Cataloguing in Publication record for this book is available from the British Library.

# IT-Based Management: Challenges and Solutions

Luiz Antonio Joia
Brazilian School of Public and Business Administration,
Getulio Vargas Foundation and
Rio de Janeiro State University, Brazil

**IDEA GROUP PUBLISHING**

Hershey • London • Melbourne • Singapore • Beijing

| Acquisition Editor: | Mehdi Khosrowpour |
| Managing Editor: | Jan Travers |
| Development Editor: | Michele Rossi |
| Copy Editor: | Beth Arneson |
| Typesetter: | LeAnn Whitcomb |
| Cover Design: | Integrated Book Technology |
| Printed at: | Integrated Book Technology |

Published in the United States of America by
    Idea Group Publishing (an imprint of Idea Group Inc.)
    701 E. Chocolate Avenue
    Hershey PA 17033-1240
    Tel: 717-533-8845
    Fax: 717-533-8661
    E-mail: cust@idea-group.com
    Web site: http://www.idea-group.com

and in the United Kingdom by
    Idea Group Publishing
    3 Henrietta Street
    Covent Garden
    London WC2E 8LU
    Tel: 44 20 7240 0856
    Fax: 44 20 7379 3313
    Web site: http://www.eurospan.co.uk

Library of Congress Cataloging-in-Publication Data

IT-based management : challenges and solutions / [edited by] Luiz Antonio Joia.
    p. cm.
  Includes bibliographical references and index.
   ISBN 1-59140-033-3 (cloth) -- ISBN 1-59140-075-9 (ebook)
   1. Knowledge management. 2. Information technology--Management. I. Joia, Luiz Antonio.

HD30.2 .I85 2002
658.4'038--dc21

                                    2002068793

British Cataloguing in Publication Data
A Cataloguing in Publication record for this book is available from the British Library.

**IGP**

# *NEW* from Idea Group Publishing

# IT-Based Management: Challenges and Solutions

# Table of Contents

## Section IV: IT-Based Logistics and Accounting

# Preface

Information technology (IT) has revolutionized the way in which organizations are run. Despite the fact that old paradigms are still used in business administration, IT has changed the ground rules of strategic management, marketing, logistics, organizational design, human resource management, accounting and so forth. The old strategic models developed during the industrial era are things of the past and it would be unwise not to take into account the role the Internet has had in marketing frameworks. It is also impossible to ignore organizational architectures, mainly virtual and process-based ones or even not to appreciate that logistics and supply chain management have to be innovated within the context of information technology.

Concepts like learning organization, intellectual capital, knowledge management, performance evaluation, e-commerce and the like rely heavily on the possibilities offered by information technology.

We are still deploying management theories developed for an industrial-based world in companies, despite living in a knowledge economy where intangibility is the actual path for sustainable success and gaining a competitive edge.

Every facet of management must be reappraised by academics, researchers and practitioners—from strategy to logistics, from marketing to accounting and from organizational design to personnel management, to name but a few. We should accept and appreciate the turmoil and shake-up IT has created for companies around the world and the resulting need these companies have to find new *modus operandi* and business models.

The main scope of this book is to show how IT has created a new mandate for management as a whole and for all its ramifications, in order to develop new business models and frameworks based on the important role IT has in these fields of knowledge.

Hence, a given chapter of this book will tackle the role and impact of IT on strategy as well as the resulting new models to be used in this context, while another may examine marketing in similar fashion. In this manner we will have given at least a small glimpse of the major transformations IT has brought about in the way corporations need to be managed, as well as propose new models based on the pervasive role IT exercises in the current business arena.

This book was developed for a hybrid audience, i.e.:

- Executives and practitioners keen to understand the impact of IT on their business models, as well as seeking for a new mandate for management that takes into account the pervasive role of information technology within their competitive boundaries;
- Academics who want to exchange ideas about new management frames of reference regarding the influence of information technology and try to innovate their fields of research using IT as an enabler; and also

- MBA students who want to compare and analyze both old and new paradigms based on the deployment of information technology within companies.

There are several books that analyze the overriding need to rethink management, but only a few address information technology as a main enabler in this endeavor.

As can be appreciated, one book would be insufficient to encompass all these issues; consequently, only the most relevant chapters addressing different facets of management were chosen by both the reviewers and the editor to compose this volume.

This book contains 16 chapters, gathered under four section headings according to the field of knowledge addressed. Section 1 analyzes IT-Based Strategy; Section 2 analyzes IT-Based Organizational Design and Behavior; Section 3 analyzes IT-Based Marketing and Retailing; and, finally, Section 4 analyzes IT-Based Logistics and Accounting.

Section 1—IT-Based Strategy—addresses how corporate and business strategies have been challenged by information technology, as well as how it can be used to increase the competitiveness of companies.

Section 2—IT-Based Organizational Design and Behavior—features chapters that present new organizational architectures made possible by information technology, in addition to other issues it influences in terms of organizational behavior, such as managerial responsibility, workspace design, etc.

Section 3—IT-Based Marketing and Retailing—analyzes strategic marketing management enhanced by IT. By the same token, the evolution of retailing as a whole, as well as in specific industries, and the role of IT in this improvement are also presented in a couple of chapters.

Finally, Section 4—IT-Based Logistics and Accounting—includes chapters showing how information technology has created new *modus operandi* for the logistics and accounting realms within the business arena.

Naturally, the idea of grouping chapters together into sections was to make the book more readable, though there will clearly be cases where chapter topics overlap. Hence, some chapters might be classified into more than one single section. This shows that management is merely a single field of knowledge and also that a systemic view of all its facets is paramount for a better understanding of the behavior of companies in their competitive arenas.

# Acknowledgments

The editing of a book is a collective project, where all the players have an important role. Hence, I would like to thank all the authors who believed in this project since its inception and gave their best effort for the success of this publication. I would also like to thank the team at Idea Group Publishing, namely, Prof. Mehdi Khosrow-Pour, Ms. Jan Travers and Ms. Michele Rossi, for their commitment and responsiveness for the successful completion of this book. And, last but not least, I would like to thank the Brazilian School of Public and Business Administration of the Getulio Vargas Foundation, where I have served as an associate professor, and Rio de Janeiro State University, where I have served as an adjunct professor, for the support shown to me.

This book is dedicated to my wife Lucia and my lovely daughters Cecilia and Elisa for their support, love and respect.

Luiz Antonio Joia

# Section I

# IT-Based Strategy

## Chapter I

# Information Systems Requirements in Support of the Firm's Portfolio of Knowledge-Driven Capabilities

David W. Birchall
Henley Management College, UK

George Tovstiga
ABB Process & Business Consultants, ABB Switzerland Ltd

## ABSTRACT

*Organisations, whether within knowledge-intensive high technology sectors or in more traditional manufacturing and utility industries, are recognizing the significance of knowledge as a competitive weapon. All firms possess a wealth of knowledge assets which enable them to function and develop. Whilst some of this knowledge is made explicit in the form of best practice procedure manuals, meeting minutes, working papers, patents and other means, much of the knowledge within the organisation remains tacit. This tacit knowledge is held by individuals and may well be embedded in their working practices, but it includes knowledge both about the internal functioning of the operation and knowledge about the environment in which the organisation exists and which could contribute to its development. Even though this tacit knowledge is often largely unrecognized it does lie at the roots of the firm's competitive base.*

*Indeed, the future of the firm is very much tied up in these knowledge-driven competencies which form the collective knowledge to which the firm has access. Information systems have been recognised as playing a role in the process of making this tacit knowledge more explicit, in its storage and later accessibility. Information systems have a role in generating new knowledge by supporting the creative and problem solving processes. Additionally, information systems knowledge will be a key competence that will be embedded into new products and services, into processes for production and delivery. Making these knowledge-driven competencies or capabilities more recognizable and establishing their positioning in relation to the strategic thrust of the business are essential if organisations are to be in a position to leverage their internal assets for long-term benefit. Without this strategic understanding, many organisations will fail to develop their information systems strategy to support the long-term needs of the business.*

*In this chapter the authors develop a methodology for utilizing a strategic capabilities positioning matrix for integrating the information systems opportunities and needs into the strategic direction of the organisation, thus forming the basis for developing the information systems strategy.*

# INTRODUCTION

Knowledge management has come to the fore as organisations begin to appreciate the impact of the connected economy. There is little doubt that many organisations have recognised the importance of knowledge in being a vital source of competitive advantage; knowledge of technologies and their application in products and services, knowledge of customers and their needs, knowledge of the supply market. As pointed out in an earlier article (Birchall & Tovstiga, 2000), knowledge in a firm manifests itself primarily in the firm's competencies and capabilities. The authors adopted the meaning attached by Hamel (1994) to capabilities, i.e., rather than being seen as single, discrete skills or technologies, they comprise bundles of constituent skills and technologies that create disproportionate value for the customer, differentiate its owner from competitors and allow entrance to new markets. Where the firm has superior capabilities to its competitors it has the potential to gain competitive advantage.

Capabilities are actually the result of an accumulation of learning over time. Moreover, it is the knowledge content of competencies and capabilities that is tacit, i.e., that which remains hidden and hence uncodified, rather than the explicit form of knowledge, which underlies the firm's real basis of competitive advantage. A truly *key* or *core* capability, one that provides a clear basis for competitive differentiation to the firm, will, for a disproportionate part, consist of knowledge in a highly tacit form.

This feature of a capability carries a number of important implications for competitive differentiation. One of these has to do with the ease with which a capability can be replicated, transferred or lost to a competitor. Our premise is that a high *degree of tacitness* is an effective barrier to diffusion of knowledge. From the external perspective, this represents a protective mechanism; for the owner firm's internal operations, extracting and sharing this tacit knowledge amongst those who can add value to it represents a challenge to be overcome.

A firm cannot actively "manage" core capabilities—and at the aggregate level, core competencies—if there is uncertainty and a lack of consensus with respect to what those capabilities actually are. The clarity of a firm's definition of its portfolio of capabilities and the degree of consensus within the firm on that definition are rudimentary tests of the firm's capacity to manage one of its key determinants of competitiveness.

In an earlier article, the authors (Birchall & Tovstiga, 2000) proposed a methodology for establishing the firm's key capabilities. This involves a focus on key processes and, for each, the identification of a set of capabilities, their selection and classification according to their competitive impact (maturity) and competitive position (firm's position of strength with respect to the particular capability). In the methodology the authors use the *degree of tacitness* as an indicator of the firm's position of strength with respect to a particular capability; the greater the degree of tacitness, as postulated earlier, the more the capability represents a unique competitive feature of the firm.

In the first part of the chapter we examine the nature of capabilities, their identification and impact. We then go on to look at the makeup of the capabilities portfolio and its mapping. A methodology is then introduced to aid the mapping of IS future opportunities and requirements to then be the basis of a capabilities identification process.

# CAPABILITIES – THEIR NATURE, IDENTIFICATION AND IMPACT

The firm's key competencies by definition will have the greatest impact on the important key success factors of the firm's industry. Because the firm's capabilities are based on a large and diverse set of mostly knowledge-based discrete activities, skills and disciplines embedded within the organization's value creating processes and routines, their identification and delineation are major challenges. But this is a pre-requisite to the implementation of a competitive strategy through exploiting key competencies.

In developing an understanding of the relative position of capabilities to the firm's competitive position there needs to be a fundamental understanding of *key success factors* for the business, factors which must be established in relation to the *external* competitive environment in which the firm operates. The firm's capabilities are the *internal* competitive activities which form the basis of the firm's competitiveness with which the firm can deliver in line with the key industry success factors.

Organisational boundaries are often based around collections of similar competence such as professional groupings. Business processes, on the other hand, normally cross organisational boundaries and in an extended form may cross inter-organisation boundaries. They depend on a wide range of interconnecting capabilities for successful operation. From the perspective of strategic impact these business processes and in turn their embedded capabilities can be categorized on a scale from those which are simply supporting to those which are truly "key" in a strategic sense. This is illustrated in Figure 1.

Knowledge-driven capabilities (Hamel, 1994) can be classified as:

- **Market-Interface Capabilities** – which include selling, advertising, consulting, technical service.
- **Infrastructure Capabilities** – which focus on internal operations such as management information systems or internal training; these are largely invisible externally.
- **Technological Capabilities** – these are technical capabilities that directly provide support to the firm's product or service portfolio; these may be further subdivided into:
  - *applied science capabilities (large "R" & small "d")*
  - *design and development capabilities*
  - *manufacturing capabilities.*

Capabilities in all categories can be equally powerful for the firm; however, technology-related capabilities appear to the authors to be particularly important because they often have the potential for initiating a reorientation with respect to the firm's approach to innovation, i.e., they can impact on multiple dimensions of the product or service, bringing about radical innovation. Hence the emphasis put by the authors on technology-related capabilities rather than Hamel's categorization into functionality-related capabilities.

In trying to develop a map of those capabilities which are key to the firm, a general list of capabilities that support the key processes has to be compiled. From this list those capabilities that have a major impact on the key success factors and clearly go beyond a merely supportive role in the firm, probably numbering no more than 10 capabilities, should be carefully reviewed.

Leonard-Barton (1995) provides a useful checklist-type test for screening truly "core" capabilities: Core or strategic capabilities comprise at least four interdepen-

*Figure 1: Strategic positioning of a firm's capabilities (adapted from Leonard-Barton, 1995, p. 4)*

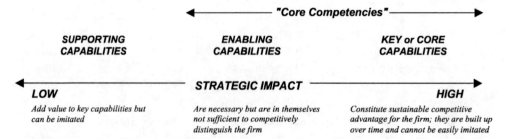

dent dimensions. Two of these may be thought of as *dynamic knowledge reservoirs* or *competencies,* and two of which are more *knowledge controlling* or *knowledge channeling* mechanisms:

1.  **People-Embodied Knowledge and Skills.** In addition to knowledge of techniques specific to the firm, this includes industry specific as well as scientific and professional knowledge. The knowledge within the capability is both in-depth and broad in that there is a deep understanding in narrow areas but enough understanding of the interfaces between the specific and the general to make it possible to relate the in-depth knowledge to its wider application and thus cultivate new or improved applications. The firm-specific knowledge is generally the least codified and therefore the most difficult to replicate and hence transfer.

2.  **Physical/Technical Systems.** People-embodied knowledge gets embedded into processes such as manufacturing layouts and configurations, and software. This embedded knowledge remains even after the originators have moved on. The rationale for the system may well be forgotten and the knowledge on which it was based may well have become tacit in nature as a result. But it remains accessible to the organization as a result of it having been embedded into systems.

3.  **Managerial Systems.** Managerial systems can include formalized procedures, e.g., for decision making. But they also include the many implicit ways of managing organizations which seem to be part of the fabric and are learned over time by working within the firm and passed on from one group to another.

4.  **Culture, Values and Norms.** The dominant values and norms can be seen as the glue that underpins the organization and determines how it functions. No two organizations are alike. Often the dominant culture was set by the founders of the business and in many organizations has been enduring. Even when organizations are envied for the particular characteristics of its culture it is impossible to copy and replicate. Some organizations clearly have a culture which fosters innovation–typified by encouraging experimentation, openness, no-blame, learning from experience. We all recognize that it is extremely difficult to transform an organization which has always been a follower, a me-too, into an industry leadership position.

All core capabilities will exhibit elements of all four dimensions, though not likely in equally distributed proportions. The authors assert that the *people-embodied knowledge and skills* dimension of a core capability will be a substantial element in any core capability. All of the capabilities in this category will, however, have a major impact on the firm's key success factors.

It is then possible to classify these capabilities in relation to their competitive impact. These capabilities can be classified as to whether they are emerging, pacing, key or base, as shown in Table 1.

Having identified a number of key capabilities and classified them according to competitive impact, the next step is to assess the firm's competitive position in relation to each capability. We propose a classification based on the organization's

*Table 1: Classification of capability according to competitive impact*

| Competitive Classification | Competitive Impact of Capability |
|---|---|
| **I.   EMERGING** | • Has not yet demonstrated potential for changing the basis of competition. |
| **II.  PACING** | • Has demonstrated its potential for changing the basis of competition. |
| **III. KEY or CORE** | • Is embedded in and enables products/processes.<br>• Has major impact on value-added stream (cost, performance, quality, and enables proprietary position. |
| **IV.  ENABLING - BASE** | • Necessary (enabling) but confers only minor impact on value-added streams; common to all competitors; commodity status (base). |

*Table 2: The strategic positioning matrix*

| Degree of Control (competitive position) | Competitive Impact | | | |
|---|---|---|---|---|
| | Emerging | Pacing | Core | Enabling/Base |
| **Strong** | | | | |
| **Neutral** | | | | |
| **Weak** | | | | |

degree of control over the capability. Control can result from ownership of or exclusive rights to intellectual property. It can also result from strong brand recognition and reputation. But as pointed out earlier, we contend that strong control is more likely to result from the extent to which the capability is based on implicit knowledge which is not easily explicated, imitated nor acquired. It is also apparent as the result of the firm's ability to exploit these capabilities. Table 2 shows a matrix for positioning capabilities according to both competitive impact and competitive position; as will be shown further on, this matrix provides a useful framework for mapping the firm's portfolio of capabilities.

# THE CAPABILITIES PORTFOLIO AND ITS DEVELOPMENT

For each of the organization's key processes a portfolio of key capabilities can be established. These are capabilities over which the firm has a high level of control and which are in the range of core to pacing. So the firm is likely to have a series of key capabilities as illustrated in Figure 2.

Where capabilities fall outside those defined as key, the organisation is faced with a series of dilemmas. Where capabilities are base, they are easily replicated by

*Figure 2: Strategic positioning matrix*

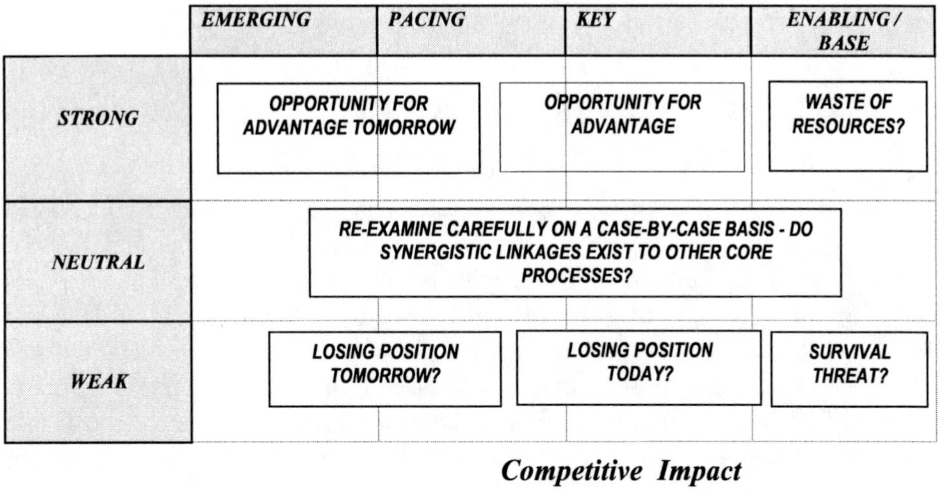

| | EMERGING | PACING | KEY | ENABLING / BASE |
|---|---|---|---|---|
| **STRONG** | OPPORTUNITY FOR ADVANTAGE TOMORROW | | OPPORTUNITY FOR ADVANTAGE | WASTE OF RESOURCES? |
| **NEUTRAL** | RE-EXAMINE CAREFULLY ON A CASE-BY-CASE BASIS - DO SYNERGISTIC LINKAGES EXIST TO OTHER CORE PROCESSES? | | | |
| **WEAK** | LOSING POSITION TOMORROW? | | LOSING POSITION TODAY? | SURVIVAL THREAT? |

**Competitive Impact**

others and therefore offer no competitive advantage. As these are likely to already be available from a number of alternative sources, rather than reinforcing them internally, other strategies might be more appropriate, e.g., buying in or outsourcing. However, where control of a base technology is high, exploitation of the capabilities may be achieved through offering services to third parties and hence new value streams created, particularly if cost advantage can be gained.

Emerging technologies create tomorrow's opportunities and wealth. Where control is weak but the capability is considered essential for long-term well-being, means should be sought to secure a stronger position, e.g., strategic partnerships, license agreements, reinforcement of the core team, acquisition. But given that often new products and services are the result of bringing together a wide range of technological capability it is unlikely that the organisation will be in a position to establish strong internal capability in all areas, so choices will have to be made based on risk assessment. One key capability for sustaining development in many organisations is the ability to integrate technology developed by others and the management of relationships with suppliers so as to secure adequate control. Grant (1996) and Boisot (1998) emphasise the importance of the firm as a knowledge integrator of the knowledge created internally and/or acquired through means such as strategic alliances. This capability is particularly in evidence in the case of virtual organisations.

The firm's emerging technologies can be the source of novel and radical change if capabilities are built around them. As one moves to the other end of the spectrum to base capabilities, incremental cost-reducing refinements may be the only feasible innovative strategy unless these base capabilities can be combined with some stronger capabilities to reorientate products and services. However, whilst emerging technologies might well have the potential to radically change an industry, it is recognised that to do so will probably first require major organisational transformation. So the possession and recognition of capabilities will not automatically result in strong innovative behaviour.

# INFORMATION SYSTEMS AND THE CAPABILITIES PORTFOLIO

Information systems can support all three categories of capability identified earlier, i.e., *market-interface, infrastructure and technological,* and may well be central in the firm's ability to deliver. Information systems, for the purposes of this paper, are to be thought of as technologies, broadly defined, which enhance and enable the generation, codification and transfer of the knowledge which in turn is embedded in the firm's core capabilities. It is essential that a thorough and systematic review of both the current contribution and the potential impact of the firm's information systems is carried out. The sub-methodology proposed here is designed to support this review.

Zack (1999) contends that a firm's strategic IS-supported knowledge processing can be segmented into two broad classes: *integrative* and *interactive*. Each of these addresses different knowledge management objectives. Together, however, the two approaches provide a broad set of knowledge-processing capabilities which support both the firm's well-structured repositories for managing its store of *explicit* knowledge while enabling interaction to integrate the firm's repositories of *tacit* knowledge.

*Integrative IS applications* represent flows of sequential knowledge into and out of the firm's knowledge repositories. This mode represents knowledge primarily in the explicit form; it is more precisely and formally articulated although removed from the original context of creation or use. The repository becomes the primary medium for knowledge exchange; members of a knowledge community are provided with a place for contributing their knowledge and views.

*Interactive IS systems*, on the other hand, focus primarily on supporting social interaction among individuals holding the firm's tacit knowledge. Here, the repository is merely a by-product of interaction and collaboration. Its content is dynamic and emergent. Distributed learning and electronic discussion space-based form are examples of this mode.

In relation to the strategic positioning matrix we postulate that information systems can serve six specific purposes which are a mix of integrative and interactive in nature:

1.   IS to assist in the process of establishing the portfolio of key capabilities, e.g., group decision-support systems. Specifically, IS can be used very effectively to tap into and externalize portions of the firm's stock of tacitly held knowledge, knowledge held by individuals in the form of experience, insight and relational understanding.

2. IS can be an integral part of a capability, e.g., global engineering design utilizing CAD and ICT.
3. IS can support the development of the capability, e.g., intelligent agents seeking out information to support R&D, GroupWare to support new knowledge generation.
4. IS can enable the exploitation of the capability, e.g., data mining to establish new customer needs; knowledge distribution.
5. IS developments can create radically new opportunities for product/service development and hence become part of an emerging capability. Here we are thinking of developments which lead to a reorientation of the base capabilities perhaps in conjunction with other technology breakthroughs.
6. IS can provide the link to an elaborate external network of suppliers, distributors, commerce services providers and customers and thereby generate value for end customers and for the firm itself. Increasingly, IS is playing an important role as firms participate in networked and fluid collections of businesses that are characteristic of the emerging network economy.

In relation to the portfolio of key capabilities, it is likely that most capabilities, being bundles of constituent skills and technologies, will include elements of IS serving one or more of the purposes described by Laudon and Laudon (1998, p. 41, and based on Anthony, 1965). Whilst IT is largely commoditised, as are many IS applications, it is the unique combination of overall skills, knowledge and technologies which will provide competitive advantage. These skills and knowledge, as in other areas of capability, are going to include a major degree of tacitness. It is the unique way in which the firm chooses to embed information systems into its operations that will result in competitive advantage or otherwise. One of the key challenges of the firm in this context has to do with how it can maximize the impact of its integrated IS on the firm's stock of tacit knowledge.

Another matrix, Table 3, offers the means for recording the contribution of IS in relation to each key capability. We suggest that the Laudon framework (1998) could be used to identify specific systems. Having established the current position, the next step in the analysis is to identify developments in IT/IS and superimpose those which are seen as having the potential to dramatically change the rules whether in the product, service offering, or delivery processes. Use might be made of

Table 3: The information systems (IS) contribution matrix

| CLASSIFICATION OF PURPOSE | IS CONTRIBUTION | | |
|---|---|---|---|
| | Supporting | Enabling | Key |
| Assisting in identification | | | |
| Integral to capability | | | |
| Supporting development of capability | | | |
| Enabling exploitation | | | |
| Creating new opportunities | | | |
| Link to external business network | | | |

Foresight Programmes (e.g., the UK's DTI Foresight Programme) and techniques such as Technology Roadmapping.

The next step proposed is to identify the capabilities needed to support the processes, which will be largely tacit. The framework in Table 4 can be used to identify the dimensions of the capabilities needed to support the existing and potential IT/IS applications. Through undertaking a systematic appraisal, the gap between the opportunity afforded by emerging and pacing IT/IS and the current level of overall capability can be estimated. The language now exists to integrate these perspectives into the wider review of capabilities described earlier.

Once the current and potential contributions to the strategic portfolio matrix have been established, alternative actions for the firm, in relation to information systems design and development, will depend upon the relative position of the capability on the matrix as described earlier. It is recognised that many organisations have significantly reduced their in-house IT capability, opting rather to outsource these services. This may leave them vulnerable in relation to innovation based on IT/IS developments as pointed out by Lacity and Hirschheim (1995) based on their study of 14 cases of outsourcing: "Most participants felt that long-term contracts restrict their ability to exploit new technologies because the contract centers on delivering the same services and technologies defined in the baseline year. Moreover, it restricts a company's flexibility to move quickly to exploit new business opportunity." The lack of innovation resulting is explained by Earl (1996) as "loss of the innovative capacity to create new ways of providing IT services and of exploiting IT for the client business because those with the entrepreneurial flair are no longer connected to those with specialist knowledge of technology development."

In this situation the links to external organisations with expertise in such areas as IT futures and the establishment of partnerships with leading IT developers may be needed to ensure the firm's next generation product development and service capability to maintain competitive position. The emerging technologies present the

*Table 4: Dimensional breakdown of capabilities*

| CLASSIFICATION OF PURPOSE | DIMENSIONS OF CAPABILITY | | | |
|---|---|---|---|---|
| | *Knowledge & Skills* | *Culture* | *Management Systems* | *Technology* |
| *Assisting in identification* | | | | |
| *Integral to capability* | | | | |
| *Supporting development of capability* | | | | |
| *Enabling exploitation* | | | | |
| *Creating new opportunities* | | | | |
| *Link to external business network* | | | | |

greatest challenge, as the opportunities they offer will not be obvious, even to those developing the technologies. The use of interdisciplinary team-working, including those from a wide range of technical and functional backgrounds, is widely recognised as an important mechanism for unlocking such potential.

If the potential offered by information systems technology is to be fully utilized those responsible for the development of the infrastructure and systems need to be party to the analysis of the firm's strategic capabilities and fully involved in its development. Through this process there could be a more effective integration of business IT and broader technology strategy. It could result in what Goodman and Lawless (1994) describe as "synergistic" innovation, where the innovation is based on a significant interdependence amongst several functional areas. This leads to "next generation" products and services in contrast to "functional" innovation, which improves one element of the product only.

It is clear that the adoption and absorption of emerging technology is key to long-term competitive advantage but progress in this is influenced by many factors in addition to the recognition and development of related capabilities. Access to the technology is just one of these. Examples of the internal mechanisms that influence the organization's absorptive capacity are the transfer of knowledge across and within subunits; the structure of communication between external environment and the firm, i.e., the centralization of the interface function; a broad and active network of internal and external relationships; and cross-functional interfaces (Cohen & Levinthal, 1990). Some firms are clearly much better able to implement information systems and extract added value than others are. This is particularly the case where major transformative possibilities exist. But the capability in integrating technologies into new or enhanced products is possibly the one capability out of the whole range which is likely to make a difference.

# CONCLUSIONS

A methodology has been presented which has been designed to support a review of knowledge-driven capabilities within a firm at a strategic level. The methodology enables integration into the firm's value creating processes including technological advances in the area of IT/IS.

The authors contend that much of the knowledge that is the basis of competitive advantage is implicit rather than explicit and embedded in the firm's capabilities. But in order to leverage these capabilities there needs to be a consensus around what constitutes these key capabilities.

The methodology presented focuses attention on those capabilities which are the basis of the key success factors for the firm within its specific industrial or commercial sectors. In reviewing the capabilities which underpin these key processes, a review of the firm's degree of control over these assets and their contribution to competitive advantage is the basis of a mapping process.

A range of IT/IS technologies and skills contribute to the firm's capabilities and to the strategic management of these. It is shown how a well-integrated IT/IS system can play a critical role in the explication of the firm's tacit knowledge, knowledge which if left untapped represents lost potential competitive opportunity for the firm. The key challenge remains in how to maximize the impact of the firm's IT/IS toward unlocking, bringing to the surface, and ultimately sharing its tacit knowledge—the firm's ultimate source of competitive advantage.

# REFERENCES

Anthony, R. N. (1965). *Planning and Control Systems: A Framework for Analysis*. Cambridge, MA: Harvard University Press.

Birchall, D. W. & Tovstiga, G. (2000). Methodology for identifying and assessing the strategic impact of a firm's portfolio of knowledge-driven capabilities. In A. A. Thomson, & A. J. Strickland (Eds.), *Crafting and Executing Strategy: Text and Readings*. New York: Irwin/McGraw-Hill.

Boisot, M. (1998). *Knowledge Assets*. Oxford, England: Oxford University Press.

Cohen, W. M. & Levinthal, D. A. (1990). Absorptive capacity: A new perspective on learning and innovation. *Administrative Science Quarterly*, *35*(1), 128-152.

Earl, M. J. (1996). The risks of outsourcing IT. *Sloan Management Review*, *37*(3), 26-33.

Goodman, R. A. and Lawless, M. W. (1994). *Technology and Strategy*. Oxford, England: Oxford University Press.

Grant, R. M. (1996). Prospering in dynamically competitive environments: Organizational capability as knowledge integration. *Organizational Science*, *4*(4), 375-387.

Hamel, G. (1994). The concept of core competence. In Hamel, G. and Heene, A. (Eds.), *Competence-Based Competition*. New York: John Wiley & Sons.

Lacity, M. C. and Hirschheim, R. (1995). *Beyond the Information Systems Outsourcing Bandwagon*. New York: John Wiley & Sons.

Laudon, K. C. and Laudon, J. P. (1998). *Essentials of Information Systems* (3rd ed.). Englewood Cliffs, NJ: Prentice Hall.

Leonard-Barton, D. (1995). *Wellsprings of Knowledge–Building and Sustaining the Sources of Innovation*. Boston: Harvard Business School Press.

Zack, M.H. (1999). Managing codified knowledge. *Sloan Management Review*, *40*(4), 45-59.

## Chapter II

# Competitive Strategies and Global Management: Linking With Technology

Mingfang Li
California State University, USA

## ABSTRACT

*Competitive strategies remain a central topic of research in strategic management. Recent conceptual developments and practices reveal possible additional types of competitive strategies due to the advances in information as well as manufacturing technologies. This paper proposes a conceptual extension of the generic strategies originally developed by Michael Porter (1980) to include additional competitive approaches as various combinations and extensions of the original four. Furthermore, this paper applies the extended model of competitive strategies to global strategic management to present a number of propositions. Contributions, limitations and future research are considered.*

## INTRODUCTION

Central to the study and practice of strategic management are three research streams related to various aspects of company strategy. They are, respectively, product-market scope (Ansoff, 1965; Goold, Campbell, & Alexander, 1994; Mintzberg, 1988), global management gestalts (Bartlett & Ghoshal, 1998; Harzing, 2000; Leong & Tan, 1993; Prahalad & Doz, 1987), and competitive approaches (Campbell-Hunt, 2000; Da Silveira, Borenstein, & Fogliatto, 2001; Mintzberg, 1988; Porter, 1980, 1985). The product-market scope question focuses on the extent of diversification, synergistic connections among multiple businesses within the same corporation, and the role of the corporate headquarters (Ansoff, 1965; Goold et al., 1994; Mintzberg, 1988; Rumelt, Schendel, & Teece, 1994). The global management gestalts or typologies identify critical challenges which multinational enterprises must confront, namely, whether they are pressures for globalization, pressures for localization, need for worldwide learning and innovation, or the combination of all three challenges, and propose strategic solutions as, respectively, global, multi-local, international and finally transnational (Bartlett & Ghoshal, 1998; Boudreau, Loch, Robey, & Straud, 1998; Harzing, 2000; Leong & Tan, 1993). The competitive approaches or generic strategies (Campbell-Hunt, 2000; Da Silveira et al., 2001; Porter, 1980; Reitsperger, Daniel, Tallman, & Chismar, 1993) are concerned with specific competitive orientations a business would adopt from the list of four—cost leadership, differentiation, cost-based focus, and differentiation-based focus—and possibly other variations and extensions.

The notion of fit, a central assumption in strategic management, would suggest that the competitive environment, company strategy, organizational structure and processes, and resources and capacities need to be meshed together in a coordinated and coherent manner (Bartlett & Ghoshal, 1998; Lengnick-Hall & Wolff, 1999; Miles & Snow, 1978). There exists however a considerable gap between the research in corporate and global strategy areas and that in competitive strategies (Campbell-Hunt, 2000; Da Silveira et al., 2001). While there have been strong and ongoing research activities in the corporate and global strategy areas, the extant literature on competitive strategies is comprised essentially of Porter's original conception in 1980 and some limited conceptual extensions and empirical studies primarily conducted in 1980s and early 1990s.

As Campbell-Hunt (2000) summarizes in an extensive review and a meta-analysis of competitive strategy research, the bulk of the empirical studies focused on the existence of empirical archetypes of competitive approaches and their resemblance to the four types Porter (1980, 1985) conceived and the performance impacts of different competitive approaches empirically derived. Conceptual formulation in the meantime centers on Porter's prediction that differentiation and cost leadership strategies are fundamentally incompatible, and any attempt at combining these two would lead to a "stuck in the middle" predicament, labeled as the so-called incompatibility hypothesis (cf., Corsten & Will, 1994). A number of authors suggest however that developments in advanced manufacturing technologies coupled with increasingly widespread application of information technologies would enable businesses to pursue a successful combination of both, leading to the so-called compatibility hypothesis (Corsten & Will, 1994, 1995; Lei, Hitt, & Goldhar, 1996; Reitsperger et al., 1993). Furthermore, there are ways to combine broad scope and focus orientation together successfully (Evans & Wurster, 1997; Schlie & Goldhar, 1995). Finally, mass customization has become one of the emerging competitive approaches (Boynton, Victor, & Pine, 1993; Da Silveira et al., 2001; Gilmore & Pine, 1997; Goldhar & Lei, 1995; Lampel & Mintzberg, 1996; Pine, 1993).

While these empirical efforts and conceptual extensions are important, several major limitations in the extant literature point at the need for further work in this important area. First of all, most empirical studies assessing the existence of competitive strategy archetypes focused primarily on various functional aspects identified in Porter's (1980) original conception. New developments in advanced manufacturing technologies and information technologies (Evans & Wurster, 1997; Lei et al., 1996) and the convergence of manufacturing and service technologies (Schlie & Goldhar, 1995) were not accounted for. Even though Campbell-Hunt's (2000) extensive meta-analyses revealed a variety of archetypes that were not included in Porter's parsimonious competitive strategy typology (1980), it is difficult to assess the overall significance of some of those archetypes because of the possible omission of various functional aspects closely related to new technologies such as agile manufacturing and information. Conceptual extensions considering the impact of those technological advances seem to focus on some limited aspects of competitive strategy combinations. Theoretical formulations of the impact of technology on strategic management often either focus on a number of other issues rather than competitive strategies per se or are fragmented. As a result, the research in this area has not only failed to keep up with new developments in technologies but also failed to match with conceptual and empirical work in other related strategy research streams, specifically, corporate strategies and global strategic gestalts.

This is unfortunate. First of all, developments in manufacturing and information technologies have had profound impacts on all aspects of economic activities (cf., Boudreau et al., 1998; Groth, 1999; Grover, Fiedler, & Teng, 1997; Henderson & Venkatraman, 1993; Molloy & Schwenk, 1995; Sampler, 1998; Segars & Grover, 1994). Given the central position of strategies in guiding firms in their domain definition and navigation activities (Andrews, 1971; Mintzberg, 1988; Porter, 1980, 1985), an improved understanding of the impact of technologies on various strategies will lead to more effective strategic management. Secondly, as indicated earlier, competitive strategies are one of the three central elements of company strategy; an improved understanding of the relationship between technologies and competitive strategies will also help us link competitive strategies with other strategic aspects so that companies may be able to combine three strategic elements effectively to deal with environmental challenges and to organize their firms accordingly.

This paper therefore aims at (a) extending the competitive strategy model in light of the emergence of manufacturing and information technologies and the convergence of manufacturing and service technologies and (b) identifying potential connections between this extended model and global management considerations. This paper is organized as follows. First we review basic models dealing with competitive strategies and global management. Next we review basic conclusions derived from empirical studies on competitive strategy and summarize findings from literature on the impact of technology on strategic management. Building on these bases this paper then presents an extended conceptual model of competitive strategies and links it with global management considerations. The final section considers the potential contribution of, the practical significance of, and future studies related to the model developed in this paper.

# CONCEPTUAL BASES

## Competitive Strategy

Porter, in his seminal work on analyzing competitive landscapes, proposed a parsimonious typology of four competitive strategies (1980, 1985). This typology was organized into a conceptually elegant framework of sources of competitive advantage (cost leadership and differentiation) and market scope (broad and focused) to host the four strategies, namely, cost leadership, differentiation, and focus based on cost and differentiation, respectively. Several important predictions stemmed from this framework. First of all, Porter predicted that businesses that adhere to one of these pure types would outperform those that do not. A closely related assumption of this prediction is the existence of businesses that configure their resource bases according to the typology. Secondly, after assessing the resource requirements, Porter predicted that effective competitive approaches should be those pure types instead of various hybrids. Businesses that attempt to achieve multiple advantages would, according to this prediction, get "stuck in the middle" and suffer poor performance as a consequence.

Clearly this theorization was plausible at the time when advanced manufacturing technologies and information technologies had not had a pervasive influence on business activities and operations. In general, cost leadership strategy requires substantial economies of scale, stability of production or operation to facilitate learning-based cost reduction, tight cost control process and reporting structure, product design for easy manufacturing, and low-cost distribution system. Differentiation strategy, on the other hand, depends on marketing ability; product innovation and creativity; coordination among key functional areas including R&D, marketing, and product development; highly skilled labors; and cooperation from channels (Grimm & Smith, 1997; Porter, 1980, 1985). Both variations of the focus strategy will depend on the above respective resources directed at the particular strategic target market and a keen understanding of the unique market segment.

Since the resource requirements for cost leadership and differentiation strategies are diametrically different, Porter formulated what some authors termed the "inconsistency hypothesis" (cf., Corsten & Will, 1994). Essentially, businesses that attempt to achieve a combination of cost and differentiation advantages would not be able to deal effectively with the conflicting resource requirements and as a consequence would not be able to outperform those that pursue one of the pure strategy types. As summarized in a later section, empirical research of Porter's theoretical formulation focused on (1) identifying the existence of these strategic approaches in practice, (2) evaluating their performance implications, and (3) exploring the necessity, feasibility and even desirability of hybrid forms of competitive approaches.

# Corporate Product-Market Scope or Diversification Strategy

One of the major topics of strategic management has been the product-market scope of a corporation and resultant managerial challenges (Ansoff, 1965; Chandler, 1962; Goold et al., 1994; Rumelt, 1974; Rumelt et al., 1994). From a resource development and utilization point of view, competitive advantages at various businesses are believed to form the basis for corporate scope determination (Porter, 1987). This reasoning is consistent with the resource-based-view thinking on appropriate corporate scope (Palich, Cardinal, & Miller, 2000). Core competences developed in various businesses ought to be leveraged and utilized in a synergistic fashion (Hamel & Prahalad, 1994; Palich et al., 2000). Other researchers also suggest that the corporate headquarters should make a maximum useful contribution—or providing parenting advantage—by identifying heartland businesses or those critical businesses which a corporation truly depends on for its survival and development, and guiding core competence development and leveraging on an on-going basis (Goold et al., 1994). The headquarters is believed to be able to exercise four types of influences. They are stand-alone influences, linkage influences, central services and functions, and finally corporate developments.

# Global Strategic Gestalts

Most firms competing in today's global markets are believed to fit into one of the three dominant organizational forms: global, multi-local, or international (Bartlett & Ghoshal, 1998; Harzing, 2000; Leong & Tan, 1993). The specific form chosen is believed to be a function of the critical strategic challenge each firm faces: the need to globalize (products), the need to localize (markets), or the need to specialize (functions) through innovation and learning.

Firms pursuing global strategies aim at achieving greater economies of scale and global efficiency by producing standardized products for a worldwide market. Firms emphasizing local responsiveness follow a multi-local strategy that seeks to be sensitive to variations in local tastes and preferences. These firms tend to develop a complete set of value creating activities in respective countries and geographic regions; they provide differentiated products and apply differing marketing approaches appropriate for each local market. Finally, firms pursuing an international strategy would transfer their home country innovations and unique skills to new markets where indigenous competitors lack such capabilities.

Each of these approaches effectively deals with one critical strategic challenge. Those challenges, respectively, are global power and efficiency, local sensitivity and responsiveness, and innovation and diffusion. Today's global business environment has been described as posing all three challenges simultaneously. The integrative solution proposed for dealing with all three challenges is the transnational strategy. The transnational strategy may provide an effective way to embed global power and efficiency, local responsiveness and differentiation, and specialized worldwide innovation and learning within one strategic organizational form. Many firms are believed to be evolving into the transnational strategic form (Bartlett & Ghoshal, 1998; Boudreau et al., 1998; Harzing, 2000; Leong & Tan, 1993).

Clearly, corporate strategy or the extent of diversification will play a key role in influencing global strategies by enabling a corporation to position its various businesses on a global scale in order to utilize resources, explore markets, and more importantly initiate strategic moves to deal with competition. On the other hand, global strategic leadership focusing on corporate renewal will influence the extent and nature of the diversification move. Thus, we can summarize the connection between diversification and global strategies as global strategic positioning (from corporate to global) and corporate renewal (from global to corporate strategy). Earlier on we summarized the connection between business and corporate strategy as core competence building in heartland businesses (from business to corporate strategy) and parenting advantage (from corporate to business strategy) through linkage influences and central services and functions.

The links between business strategy and global strategy are of interest in this study. We identify the requisite variety of competitive approaches (from global to business) and worldwide innovation and diffusion of effective competitive approaches (from business to global strategies) as two crucial linkages. The interconnections among three strategies are depicted in Figure 1. After considering conceptual extensions to the competitive strategy typology, we will discuss the global management implications by focusing on the requisite variety and worldwide innovation and diffusion of effective competitive approaches. To do so, it is necessary to review the transaction-cost-based assessment of global strategies.

## A Transaction-Cost-Based Model of Global Management

The eclectic model of international production (Dunning, 1980) suggests that *ownership* of unique resources and capabilities, *location* based advantages, and *internalization* of key organizational activities (OLI) are important factors when

*Figure 1: Strategy triangle*

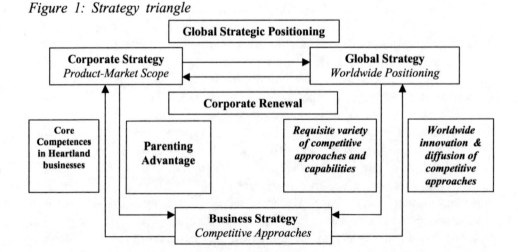

considering global investments. A reformulation of this paradigm (Rugman & Verbeke, 1992) stated these issues in transaction cost terms. According to these authors, a firm may possess *firm-specific advantages* that are either *non-location bound* or *location bound*. Country or *location specific advantages* may come from home country, or host country, or both. According to this model, transnational corporations need to combine home and host country location specific advantages with both non-location bound and location bound firm specific advantages.

Location bound sources of competitive advantages are important when considering geographical clusters within each competitive approach may be reasonably standardized. Competitive practices especially developed for different regions will respond well to local differentiation (Bartlett & Ghoshal, 1998), and utilizing those within a region will help create business ecosystems at a more localized level (Lengnick-Hall & Wolff, 1999; Porter, 1998; Stacey, 1996). Non-location bounded sources of competitive advantages provide hints for worldwide diffusion of various effective competitive practices, important for companies to utilize their resources on a greater scale. Furthermore, combining home country advantages and host country advantages allows cross-pollination of effective practices and possibly developing new competitive approaches (Bartlett & Ghoshal, 1998).

# EXTENSIONS TO COMPETITIVE STRATEGY STUDY
## Conclusions From the Extant Literature

A major comprehensive review of the literature on competitive strategies provides several important findings (Campbell-Hunt, 2000). Instead of repeating various issues identified in the literature in detail, the following summary highlights important conclusions and research directions. According to this review, the empirical literature related to the typology proposed is comprised of three major topics. They are identifying major dimensions of competitive strategies, examining the existence of empirical archetypes resembling Porter's pure competitive types, and finally assessing the performance implications.

First of all, meta-dimensions of competitive strategy as Campbell-Hunt (2000) identified include marketing, sales, quality reputation, product innovation, operations, and market scope. These dimensions captured various indicators rather well. However, it is difficult to discern any marked influence of advanced manufacturing technologies and information technologies in these dimensions and their respective indicators. This is a potential pitfall of the existing studies that essentially mapped strategic dimensions based on the original theoretical model formulated years ago when information technologies and advanced manufacturing technologies were yet to become a topic of strategic importance on a broader scale.

Empirical archetypes of competitive strategies, rather than confirming Porter's competitive strategies, reveal some interesting insights. First of all, there are a number of types that were not characterized in the theoretical formulation. Secondly, several are hybrid forms. Campbell-Hunt (2000) identified several types. They include *cost economy, focused quality economy, sales leadership, broad quality and sales leadership, innovation and operations leadership,* and *focus quality leadership.* As several authors already suggested, a number of factors such as the nature of industry might become important considerations when selecting competitive approaches, and businesses may decide the best approach appropriate for their own situations (e.g., Da Silveira et al., 2001; Reitsperger et al., 1993).

In probing the third topic, the performance implication of competitive strategies, Campbell-Hunt (2000) reached the conclusion that there exists significant doubt whether firms pursuing the pure types Porter proposed will outperform others that might pursue hybrid strategies. Clearly the jury is still out on this important topic. This is probably true since the extant empirical literature has not captured well the impact of information and advanced manufacturing technologies on innovative competitive approaches, and as such it may not be informative regarding this important issue. In the meantime scholars from a number of fields explored the influence of information and advanced manufacturing technologies on firm strategy, mainly through conceptual developments and case studies.

## Several Findings From Conceptual Extensions

One important direction of research focused on the competitive necessity, possibility and desirability of combining cost leadership and differentiation strategies (Corsten & Will, 1994, 1995). Researchers point out that competitive pressures are so intense nowadays that companies are constantly raising the bar on the minimum threshold of quality level Porter emphasized when he proposed the cost leadership strategy (Porter, 1980; Schlie & Goldhar, 1995). At the same time, applications of advanced manufacturing technologies such as CAD, CAM and CIM have enabled firms to achieve efficiency and quality variations simultaneously (Corsten & Will, 1994, 1995). Furthermore, the convergence between manufacturing and service technologies has further bridged the gap between cost leadership and differentiation competitive approaches (Schlie & Goldhar, 1995). Together, competitive pressures, applications of advanced manufacturing and information technologies, and convergence of manufacturing and service technologies make it desirable and possible for firms to combine cost leadership and differentiation strategies.

Another direction of research relates to the market scope question. Instead of selecting either a broad market or a focused market segment, businesses may be able to exploit advantages of both by using the so-called multi-niche strategy (Schlie & Goldhar, 1995). Versioning of digital products would be an example of this approach (Grover & Ramanlal, 2000; Shapiro & Varian, 1998). Clearly, this approach combined reach (larger scale) with richness (uniqueness of each segment; Evans & Wurster, 1997) successfully.

In addition, mass customization has been viewed as another new strategy (Da Silveira et al., 2001; Gilmore & Pine, 1997; Mascarenhas, Baveja, & Jamil, 1998; Pine, 1993). Customers are of course looking for ever-increased value and performance. Mass customization, as a strategic approach, allows firms to produce an increasing variety of products or services while at the same time reducing their costs. This strategy ought to provide the basis for faster response, creation of best value solutions, and higher degree of flexibility to serve new customers and segments with future innovations. A growing set of advanced technological, marketing and distribution capabilities is necessary for this strategy so that firms can produce products or deliver services to smaller and smaller segments while simultaneously lowering their unit costs (Da Silveira et al., 2001; Lei et al., 1996). The rise of advanced manufacturing technology, the rapid use of modular product design techniques, the growth of the Internet as a distribution channel, and market segmentation tools and techniques such as data mining and data warehousing form the backbone of this new strategy. The necessary organizational arrangements and human resources are additional conditions for the successful implementation of this strategy (Lei et al., 1996; Vickery, Droge, & Germain, 1999).

Successful implementation of these new strategies depends not only on employing advanced manufacturing and information technologies but also changes in organizational structure and processes. For example, Corsten and Will (1994, 1995) suggest that it will require work groups to supplement CAD, CAM and CIM in operation in order to pursue cost leadership and differentiation hybrid strategy. Goldhar and Lei (1995) clearly identified the need for understanding changes in information flow, knowledge use and organizational structure due to the adoption of advanced manufacturing and information technologies in organizations. This reasoning is clearly an extension of Porter's assessment of resource requirements for each type of strategy. As companies contemplate the use of more sophisticated competitive approaches, they need to assess carefully the feasibility of implementing these approaches. On the basis of these empirical research and conceptual extensions, we now turn to the extended model of competitive strategy types and link it to global management.

# COMPETITIVE STRATEGY TYPES AND GLOBAL MANAGEMENT
## An Extended Model of Competitive Strategy Types

Briefly stated, the summary of the extant literature on competitive strategy suggests that there might exist other types in addition to the basic types proposed earlier, and the performance implications of these strategies remain unclear at best. In the meantime the conceptual extensions proposed moved beyond the basic four types to include other possibilities. Putting these extensions into perspective, we propose other types as illustrated in Table 1. This extended model essentially used the original dimensions of competitive advantage and market scope. By adding the combination of cost leadership and differentiation advantage on the one hand and the multi-niche scope approach on the other, we produce a set of nine possible competitive strategy types. While earlier studies may have focused on one of the additions outlined above without clear deliberation of the other, in this model we clearly identified the possibility that companies might pursue a cost leadership and differentiation combination based on broad or focused market scope, and that companies might pursue a multi-niche strategy based on either cost leadership or differentiation. Clearly, we proposed in this model mass customization as embedding all the key strategic elements of cost leadership, differentiation and forever increasing segmentation.

There are important reasons to propose this extension. First of all, we suggest the possibility of a variety of combinations of competitive approaches. By identifying these possible types of competitive approaches it will be possible for researchers to probe the resource implications. Secondly, we suggest that each strategic type identified in this model might be a useful prescription depending on firm and industry characteristics and competitive environments in different locals. There clearly is no ideal strategy until one considers both internal and external factors. This proposition becomes even more evident once we start to consider the challenging tasks of global management when firms need to tailor their competitive approaches based on local conditions of the area in which they are operating and sources of competitive advantages as delineated earlier (Rugman & Verbeke, 1992).

## Linking With Global Management

Transnational strategy is believed to be the emerging model that will allow firms to deal with all three challenges (globalizing, localizing, and worldwide innovation and diffusion) effectively. For this model to be successful contributions from national organizations will be crucial. For national organizations to successfully contribute to the global enterprise, they must have higher potential of location specific advantages for MNE's competitiveness and greater contribution to firm-specific development, that is, to be strategic leaders in Bartlett and Ghoshal's (1998) conception of the roles of subsidiaries. Collectively, however, businesses in various locations will need to make useful contributions to the MNE, and the MNE headquarters will also need to make contributions to the businesses resided in many geographic locations. As highlighted in Figure 1, the linkage from global strategy to business strategy is *requisite variety of competitive approaches*, and the linkage from business strategy to global strategy is *worldwide innovation and diffusion of effective competitive approaches*.

*Table 1: An extended typology of competitive approaches*

| | Market Scope Approach | | |
|---|---|---|---|
| **Basis of Advantage** | *Broad* | *Focus* | *Multi-niche* |
| *Simultaneous Advantage* | *Simultaneity* | *Focused Simultaneity* | **Mass Customization** |
| *Differentiation* | **Differentiation** | **Differentiation-Focus** | *Multi-niche Differentiation* |
| *Cost Leadership* | **Cost Leadership** | **Cost-Focus** | *Multi-niche Cost Leadership* |

# Requisite Variety of Competitive Approaches

**Dynamic Fit.** Strategy represents a fit between a firm's internal environment and its external environment on an ongoing basis (Itami, 1987). From the transaction cost model (Rugman & Verbeke, 1992), we know that firm-specific advantages may be location bound or non-location bound. Consider many national organizations; each might be developing its unique advantages, and among these advantages some might be location bound and others not. How each national organization can develop unique competitive advantage and how this advantage may be transferred to other national organizations are important research topics (Kostova, 1999). Besides transnational transfer of competitive advantage there is the question of developing homegrown advantage. That topic may relate to the specific conditions of the country or region as well. As discussed above, different strategies require different resource configurations and organizational processes. The more complex the hybrid strategy, the more important it is to rearrange organizational processes and structure. In the context of transnational enterprises, it is important to consider if a national organization can successfully employ a particular strategy.

The external condition, in this case, may be captured along two main dimensions. One is infrastructure, such as communication, transportation and information technology facilities in a local area. Another is institutional, i.e., the basic practices, beliefs and other factors that govern business undertakings. Scholars suggest the specific characteristics of product market, capital market, labor market, governmental regulations and contract enforcement to be important institutional factors (Aoki, 2000; Khanna & Palepu, 1997; Li, Li, & Tan, 1998; Whitley, 1999). Considering these issues would help understand the potential applicability of different competitive strategic approaches outlined in Table 1. While different countries or regions may be able to gain infrastructure advantage by leapfrogging (Brezis, Krugman, & Tsiddon, 1993; Trauth, 1999), development of institutional environment often takes much longer (Aoki, 2000; Khanna & Palepu, 1999; Scott, 1995; Whitley, 1999). It is therefore necessary to consider both.

*Proposition: Each competitive strategy type might be appropriate given specific firm characteristics and environmental factors.*

**Strategic Complexity of Competitive Approaches.** While it is already challenging when one considers the appropriate competitive strategy for each national or local organization, it will be more so when one considers the totality of national organizations in a transnational enterprise. Surely each national organization needs to consider its competitive approach according to the resources and capabilities it owns and its external conditions. But from a more holistic point of view it is important to see a variety of competitive approaches simultaneously being practiced at different national organizations. A transnational corporation will need to experiment with different strategies and test their applicability to other settings. Stated simply, transnational organizations need to build requisite variety in terms of competitive approaches employed by their national organizations.

*Proposition: Strategic complexity of competitive approaches will enable transnational firms to perform better.*

## Organized Worldwide Learning and Diffusion of Competitive Approaches

Well, in addition to asking what national organizations can do for the transnational firm, it is necessary to ask what the transnational company headquarters can do for its national organizations. That is an important task indeed. It is necessary to consider the roles of headquarters in terms of parenting advantage (Goold et al., 1994). This consideration perhaps would bridge several roles of corporate headquarters including stand-alone influence, and linkage influences.

**Information Technology Facilitated Worldwide Diffusion.** Transnational corporations, faced with multiple challenges of globalizing, localizing, and worldwide innovation and diffusion, need to consider their responsibilities seriously (Bartlett & Ghoshal, 1998). Effective deployment of information technology to facilitate worldwide innovation and learning then becomes an important consideration (Boudreau et al., 1998). E-commerce, interorganizational systems (IOS), intranet, and extranet are all useful tools for effective worldwide innovation and diffusion of competitive approaches.

As suggested earlier, transnational enterprises need to pursue both home country and host country based advantages and combine both location bound and non-location bound sources of advantage. Worldwide diffusion of innovations at various locations would require an assessment of the applicability of those innovations at different places and a consideration of creating and enhancing the regional ecosystem (Lengnick-Hall & Wolff, 1999; Porter, 1998; Stacey, 1996). This task requires corporate involvement as well.

*Proposition: Information technology investment to facilitate collaboration and learning will enable transnational firms to perform better.*

**Headquarters Guided Competence Leveraging.** In addition to encouraging innovation and learning from national organizations, the transnational headquarters has the important task of competence leveraging. Goold et al. (1994) emphasized the value-added of the corporate headquarters. These authors identified four ways to do so. They are stand-alone influence through executive appointments, budgeting, performance review and strategic guidance; linkage influence, essentially facilitating the realization of synergistic connections among multiple business units within the same corporation; central services and functions to improve resource utilization; and finally corporate development.

Identifying the appropriate scope within which effective competitive approaches can be applied relates to linkage influence. Benchmarking and diffusion of best practices are effective management processes as long as appropriate boundaries for those best practices can be clearly identified. After all, being best depends on the local circumstance and internal characteristics. For that reason, the corporate headquarters needs to assume yet another value-added role, facilitating international organization learning by identifying similar external conditions and therefore national organization clusters.

*Proposition: Transnational firms facilitating innovation diffusion by identifying applicable conditions will perform better.*

# CONCLUSIONS AND DISCUSSIONS

This article synthesized various research streams regarding competitive strategy and integrated them into the framework of a strategy triangle—corporate, global and competitive strategies. While plenty has been said about corporate and global strategies, the research on competitive strategies stagnated after some initial work (Campbell-Hunt, 2000). In the meantime, the development and application of advanced manufacturing technologies and information technologies, and the convergence between manufacturing and service technologies met with the competitive pressures of a forever increasing need to deliver values to increasingly segmented customer groups (Boudreau et al., 1998; Da Silveira et al., 2001; Gilmore & Pine, 1997; Pine, 1993). All these factors call for extending the original framework of competitive strategy and furthermore identifying the linkage between competitive strategies and global management. This paper synthesized the extant conceptual extensions and empirical research to propose a model of competitive approaches that includes a number of hybrid strategies in addition to the pure types Porter (1980) identified. Certainly various approaches were identified in a fragmented body of literature. This paper synthesized those together into this conceptual model.

Furthermore, the current paper suggests that competitive approaches need to fit with firm characteristics, industry conditions, and external environment conditions each national organization confronts, and that the transnational corporation should actively develop a portfolio of strategic approaches to enhance its war chest in terms of overall competitiveness. In addition, the headquarters should assume the central responsibility of leveraging informational resources to encourage diffusion of innovation and more importantly to evaluate the framework within which to transfer innovative competitive practices.

Challenges are plenty, and so are opportunities. The real issue is if corporations will develop a consistent scheme to align the key elements in the strategy triangle (Figure 1), manage to harmonize those elements, and motivate subsidiary organizations to contribute to the knowledge base of the whole corporation and learn from the experience of other best-practice businesses.

More challenges are coming to researchers. First, it would be useful to identify the boundary condition for various competitive approaches identified in this paper. Each strategy must be matched with resources and market conditions. It is reasonable to assume that the ever-expanding significance of fixed cost will favor mass customization. But at the same time one may find industries where variable costs might still be a crucial consideration. For example, in the knowledge-intensive service industry, delivering highly customized service may involve largely variable costs. This probably would explain in part the lack of systematic coverage on service industry mass customization (Da Silveira et al., 2001). In addition, some industries are by nature producing a generic output. To what extent can the firms in these industries pursue other variations of strategic types?

Secondly, it would be useful to develop an inventory of resource requirements for different strategic types, with provision for potentially meaningful business practices that were not anticipated before. As a starter, various applications of advanced manufacturing technologies, MIS practices such as data warehousing and data mining for versioning purpose, integration of information technologies and advanced manufacturing technologies, and utilization of service technologies in manufacturing process and vice versa ought to be included in the resource consideration.

Extending this line of inquiry to global management, it would be useful to identify the characteristics for a cluster of firms where best practices can be diffused and study the optimal scope for strategic complexity and most importantly assess their performance implications.

# REFERENCES

Andrews, K. R. (1971). *The Concept of Corporate Strategy*. Homewood, IL: Richard D. Irwin.

Ansoff, H. I. (1965). *Corporate Strategy: An Analytic Approach to Business Policy for Growth and Expansion*. New York: McGraw-Hill.

Aoki, M. (2000). *Information, Corporate Governance, and Institutional Diversity: Competitiveness in Japan, the USA, and the Transitional Economies* (S. Jehlik, Trans.). Oxford, England: Oxford University Press.

Bartlett, C. A. & Ghoshal, S. (1998). *Managing Across Borders: The Transnational Solution* (2nd ed.). London: Random House Business Books.

Boudreau, M.-C., Loch, K. D., Robey, D. and Straud, D. (1998). Going global: Using information technology to advance the competitiveness of the virtual transnational organization. *Academy of Management Executive, 12*(4), 120-128.

Boynton, A. C., Victor, B. and Pine, B. J., II. (1993). New competitive strategies: Challenges to organizations. *IBM Systems Journal, 32*, 40-64.

Brezis, E. S., Krugman, P. R. and Tsiddon, D. (1993). Leapfrogging in international competition: A theory of cycles in national technological leadership. *American Economic Review, 83*, 1211-1219.

Campbell-Hunt, C. (2000). What have we learned about generic competitive strategy? A meta-analysis. *Strategic Management Journal, 21*, 127-154.

Chandler, A. D., Jr. (1962). *Strategy and Structure*. Cambridge, MA: MIT Press.

Corsten, H. and Will, T. (1994). Simultaneously supporting generic competitive strategies by production management: Supportive concepts of information technology and work organization. *Technovation, 14*, 111-120.

Corsten, H. and Will, T. (1995). Integrated production concepts: Structural reasons for superior competitive performance. *Management International Review*, *35*, 69-88.

Da Silveira, G., Borenstein, D. and Fogliatto, F. S. (2001). Mass customization: Literature review and research directions. *International Journal of Production Economics*, *72*, 1-13.

Dunning, J. H. (1980). Toward an eclectic theory of international production: Some empirical tests. *Journal of International Business Studies*, *11*, 9-31.

Evans, P. B. and Wurster, T. S. (1997). Strategy and the new economics of information. *Harvard Business Review*, *75*(5), 70-82.

Gilmore, J. H. and Pine, B. J., Jr. (1997). The four faces of mass customization. *Harvard Business Review*, *75*(1), 91-101.

Goldhar, J. D. and Lei, D. (1995). Variety is free: Manufacturing in the twenty-first century. *Academy of Management Executive*, *9*(4), 73-86.

Goold, M., Campbell, A. and Alexander, M. (1994). *Corporate-Level Strategy: Creating Value in the Multibusiness Company*. New York: John Wiley & Sons.

Grimm, C. M. and Smith, K. G. (1997). *Strategy as Action: Industry Rivalry and Coordination*. Cincinnati, OH: South-Western College.

Groth, L. (1999). *Future Organizational Design: The Scope for the IT-Based Enterprise*. Chichester, England: John Wiley & Sons.

Grover, V., Fiedler, K. D. and Teng, J. T. C. (1997). Corporate strategy and IT investments. *Business and Economic Review*, *43*(3), 17-22.

Grover, V. and Ramanlal, P. (2000). Playing the e-commerce game. *Business and Economic Review*, *47*, 9-14.

Hamel, G. and Prahalad, C. K. (1994). *Competing for the Future*. Boston: Harvard Business School Press.

Harzing, A.-W. (2000). An empirical analysis and extension of the Bartlett and Ghoshal typology of multinational companies. *Journal of International Business Studies*, *31*, 101-120.

Henderson, J. C. and Venkatraman, N. (1993). Strategic alignment: Leveraging information technology for transfering organizations. *IBM Systems Journal*, *32*(1), 4-16.

Itami, H. (1987). *Mobilizing Invisible Assets*. Cambridge, MA: Harvard University Press.

Khanna, T. and Palepu, K. (1997). Why focused strategies may be wrong for emerging markets. *Harvard Business Review*, *75*(4), 41-51.

Khanna, T. and Palepu, K. (1999). The right way to restructure conglomerates in emerging markets. *Harvard Business Review*, *77*(4), 125-134.

Kostova, T. (1999). Transnational transfer of strategic organizational practices: A contextual perspective. *Academy of Management Review*, *24*, 308-324.

Lampel, J. and Mintzberg, H. (1996). Customizing customization. *Sloan Management Review*, *38*, 21-30.

Lei, D., Hitt, M. A. and Goldhar, J. D. (1996). Advanced manufacturing technology: Organizational design and strategic flexibility. *Organization Studies, 17,* 501-523.

Lengnick-Hall, C. A. and Wolff, J. A. (1999). Similarities and contradictions in the core logic of three strategy research streams. *Strategic Management Journal, 20,* 1109-1132.

Leong, S. M. and Tan, C. T. (1993). Managing across borders: An empirical test of the Bartlett and Ghoshal (1989) organizational typology. *Journal of International Business Studies, 24,* 449-464.

Li, S., Li, M. and Tan, J. J. (1998). Understanding diversification in a transition economy: A theoretical exploration. *Journal of Applied Management Studies, 7,* 77-94.

Mascarenhas, B., Baveja, A. and Jamil, M. (1998). Dynamics of core competencies in leading multinational companies. *California Management Review, 40*(4), 117-132.

Miles, R. E. and Snow, C. C. (1978). *Organizational Strategy, Structure, and Process.* New York: McGraw-Hill.

Mintzberg, H. (1988). Generic strategies: Towards a comprehensive framework. In R. Lamb & P. Shivastava (Eds.), *Advances in Strategic Management (Vol. 5,* pp. 1-68). Greenwich, CT: JAI Press.

Molloy, S. and Schwenk, C. R. (1995). The effects of information technology on strategic decision making. *Journal of Management Studies, 32,* 283-311.

Palich, L. E., Cardinal, L. B. and Miller, C. C. (2000). Curvilinearity in the diversification-performance linkage: An examination of over three decades of research. *Strategic Management Journal, 21,* 155-174.

Pine, B. J. (1993). *Mass Customization: The New Frontier in Business Competition.* Boston: Harvard Business School Press.

Porter, M. E. (1980). *Competitive Strategy: Techniques for Analyzing Industries and Competitors.* New York: Free Press.

Porter, M. E. (1985). *Competitive Advantage: Creating and Sustaining Superior Performance.* New York: Free Press.

Porter, M. E. (1987). From competitive advantage to corporate strategy. *Harvard Business Review, 65*(3), 43-59.

Porter, M. E. (1998). Clusters and the new economics of competition. *Harvard Business Review, 76*(6), 77-90.

Prahalad, C. K. and Doz, Y. L. (1987). *The Multinational Mission: Balancing Local Demands and Global Vision.* New York: Free Press.

Reitsperger, W. D., Daniel, S. J., Tallman, S. B. and Chismar, W. G. (1993). Product quality and cost leadership: Compatible strategies? *Management International Review, 33,* 7-21.

Rugman, A. M. and Verbeke, A. (1992). A note on the transnational solution and the transaction cost theory of multinational strategic management. *Journal of International Business Studies, 23,* 761-771.

Rumelt, R. P. (1974). *Strategy, Structure, and Economic Performance*. Cambridge, MA: Harvard University Graduate School of Business Administration.

Rumelt, R. P., Schendel, D. and Teece, D. J. (1994). *Fundamental Issues in Strategy: A Research Agenda*. Boston: Harvard Business School Press.

Sampler, J. L. (1998). Redefining industry structure for the information age. *Strategic Management Journal*, *19*, 343-355.

Schlie, T. W. and Goldhar, J. D. (1995). Advanced manufacturing and new directions for competitive strategy. *Journal of Business Research*, *33*, 103-114.

Scott, W. R. (1995). *Institutions and Organizations*. Thousand Oaks, CA: Sage.

Segars, A. H. and Grover, V. (1994). Strategic group analysis: A methodological approach for exploring the industry level impact of information technology. *Omega*, *22*, 13-34.

Shapiro, C. and Varian, H. R. (1998). Versioning: The smart way to sell information. *Harvard Business Review*, *76*, 106-114.

Stacey, R. D. (1996). Emerging strategies for a chaotic environment. *Long Range Planning*, *29*(2), 182-189.

Trauth, E. M. (1999). Leapfrogging an IT labor force: Multinational and indigenous perspectives. *Journal of Global Information Management*, *7*, 22-32.

Vickery, S., Droge, C. and Germain, R. (1999). The relationship between product customization and organizational structure. *Journal of Operations Management*, *17*, 377-391.

Whitley, R. (1999). *Divergent Capitalisms: The Social Structuring and Change of Business Systems*. Oxford, England: Oxford University Press.

**Chapter III**

# From Strategic Management to Strategic Experimentation: The Convergence of IT, Knowledge Management, and Strategy

V. K. Narayanan
Drexel University, USA

Mari W. Buche and Benedict Kemmerer
University of Kansas, USA

## ABSTRACT

*The new competitive landscape of the 21st century is forcing organizations to move away from traditional conceptualizations of strategy formulation towards an approach of strategic experimentation. The central objective of this chapter is to articulate the requirements that will be placed on IT as organizations move toward strategic experimentation. We base our central argument in contingency theory, which has postulated that to maximize organizational effectiveness, the IT infrastructure must be congruent with organizational structure and processes. Strategic experimentation requires different IT and knowledge management tools to support it than the ones currently prevalent. Information technology, knowledge management, and strategy formulation will have to coevolve for strategic experimentation to fulfill its promise. Each will have to change while maintaining its fit with the other two elements. This gives a renewed mandate for a strategic role of IT in organizations, a role that is central to organizational success.*

Over the last decade, developments in information technology (IT) and strategic management have become increasingly intertwined in two major ways. First, advances in information technology and associated business processes (CAD, CAM, CIM, MIS, to name a few) have enabled an ever-increasing pace of product and process innovation, leading to a "hypercompetitive environment" (D'Aveni, 1994). Second, this new competitive landscape is forcing organizations to move away from traditional conceptualizations of strategy formulation towards an approach labeled "strategic experimentation." Still in its infancy and hence only partially practiced in many organizations, the emergent approach relies on knowledge management and enabling information technologies. It has, in turn, renewed the mandate for a strategic role of IT in organizations. Thus, as we enter the 21$^{st}$ century, the merging of the roles of strategy formulation and IT is fast becoming a major requirement for the competitiveness and success of the modern corporation.

The central objective of this chapter is to articulate the requirements that will be placed on IT as organizations move toward strategic experimentation. We base our central argument in contingency theory, which has postulated that for organizational effectiveness, the IT infrastructure should be congruent with organizational structure and processes. During the 1980s, the IT infrastructure changed to keep pace with the evolution of strategy formulation; indeed, the present "state of the art" IT infrastructure has emerged to support the dominant mode of strategy formulation—"strategic management"—practiced in large corporations. However, the hypercompetitive environments of the late 1990s have made it necessary for organizations to move towards a strategic experimentation mode, which requires different knowledge management tools to support it than the ones currently prevalent. We will argue that some fundamental changes in IT infrastructure are needed to support these knowledge management tools.

The plan of this chapter is as follows. First, we define key terms and introduce contingency theory as the root theory of our argument. Second, we articulate the concept of strategy and discuss its use of knowledge and information. Third, we focus on the role of IT and knowledge management in traditional strategic management approaches. In the fourth section we go on to argue that technological and environmental shifts increasingly require a new approach to strategic planning. This "strategic experimentation" approach is highlighted in the fifth section, setting the stage for our discussion of strategic experimentation's knowledge management and information technology requirements. We conclude with some thoughts on the developments in IT that are needed to enable this evolution towards strategic experimentation.

# THEORETICAL BACKGROUND
## Clarification of Terms

*Information technology*. When discussing technology, people often use the terms information systems and information technology interchangeably. While in some contexts the differences are relatively insignificant, we choose to differentiate between the two. For the purposes of this chapter, information technology is defined as the physical equipment (hardware), software, and telecommunications technology, including data, image and voice networks, employed to support business processes (Whitten & Bentley, 1998). The overarching plan for IT deployment within an organization is called the IT architecture. Technology infrastructure refers to the architecture, including the physical facilities, the services, and the management that support all computing resources in an organization (Turban, McLean, & Wetherbe, 1996).

*Knowledge management.* The meaning of the term "knowledge" has been the subject of much debate in the literature, especially in relation to data and information. We adopt the view that data are objective, explicit pieces or units, information is data with meaning attached, and knowledge is information with an implied element of action. Davenport and Prusak (1998) offer the following definition:

> Knowledge is the fluid mix of framed experience, values, contextual information, and expert insight that provides a framework for evaluating and incorporating new experiences and information. It originates and is applied in the minds of knowers. In organizations, it often becomes embedded not only in documents or repositories but also in organizational routines, processes, practices, and norms. (p. 5)

Knowledge management is "a set of business practices and technologies used to assist an organization to obtain maximum advantage from one of its most important assets—knowledge," (Duffy, 2000, p. 62). In other words, it is the process of actively capturing, sharing, and making use of what is known within the organization. IT often facilitates knowledge management initiatives by integrating repositories (e.g., databases) and indexing applications (e.g., search engines), and user interfaces. Davenport and Prusak (1998) note that knowledge management involves, in addition, traditional management functions: building trust among individuals, allocating resources to knowledge management initiatives, and monitoring progress of the initiatives.

Knowledge management leverages the prevailing IT infrastructure; in turn, the IT infrastructure is typically designed to meet organizational requirements. The dominant prescriptions have flowed from contingency theory, which is the foundation for our argument.

## Contingency Theory

Dating back to the mid-1980s, the information systems community has relied upon prescriptions from contingency theory for the design of IT infrastructures. Originally developed in organization theory (see Narayanan & Nath, 1993, for a historical review), contingency theory, when applied to information systems, asserts that organizations are interpretation systems: They continuously scan their environment for information (Daft & Weick, 1984), interpret the information, and take action based on their interpretation, learning over time from their experiences. The right type and amount of information will reduce uncertainty and ambiguity as decision makers analyze their environments. Thus the thrust of IS design should be to match the type of information to the level of uncertainty present in a given situation (Daft & Lengel, 1984).

Organizations generally have an abundance of data and information; their challenge is to make intelligent use of the data to solve business problems by reducing uncertainty and dealing with equivocality (lack of clarity or problem definition; Daft & Lengel, 1986). In other words, in situations of high uncertainty, the very richest information is necessary. For example, if a problem is complex, a face-to-face meeting is suggested as most effective. Therefore, according to the theory, better fit between the IT infrastructure and organizational structure and processes leads to superior organizational performance. Research studies have recently tested this hypothesis, with findings partially supporting the premise (e.g., Keller, 1994). The general rule of thumb is for the organization to use the simplest technology available that will satisfactorily meet the decision makers' needs (Warner, 2001).

We will argue that IT, following contingency theory, has successfully evolved to support the strategy creation process as presently practiced. But, since strategy creation processes are themselves undergoing fundamental transformation, IT will also have to evolve further.

# THE CONCEPT OF STRATEGY AND THE ROLE OF KNOWLEDGE

The concept of "strategy" explicated in strategic management is one of marketplace strategy, i.e., winning in the marketplace against competitors, entrenched or incipient. To quote Fahey and Randall (2001), for example, "to enjoy continued strategy success, a firm must commit itself to outwitting its rivals" (p. 30). A large body of literature on strategic management has persuasively argued that effective strategy creation and execution are central to a firm's performance (e.g., Covin, Slevin, & Schultz, 1994; Wisner & Fawcett, 1991). Strategy creation involves both formulating goals—defined in terms of external stakeholders rather than operational milestones—and crafting the strategic means by which to accomplish these goals (Hofer & Schendel, 1978). The means typically include business scope, competitive posture, strategic intent, and the organizational mechanisms for implementation.

Strategy creation processes are distinct from operational decision processes in several ways. First, strategic decisions involve irreversible commitment of substantial resources (Grant, 1996). Second, they have consequences that are removed in time and not clearly discernible. Third, and perhaps most important to our purpose, they represent "messy" problems (Mason & Mitroff, 1973). That is, the decision context is characterized by incomplete and ambiguous stimuli, contradictory and sometimes vaguely felt data, and partially controllable contexts. The decision makers in strategic situations have to interpret and make sense of this messy data and chart the firm's course into the future.

Without a doubt, strategy makers use several sources of explicit or codifiable knowledge while they craft and implement a strategy. To facilitate strategy creation, firms typically employ several complementary approaches: competitive intelligence systems (e.g., Codogno, 1999; Hilmetz & Bridge, 1999; Martinsons, 1994), market research that focuses on customer surveys and behavior (e.g., Denny, 1998; Sterling & Lambert, 1989), and financial modeling and related knowledge bases of the impact of decisions on financial and human resources (e.g., McAleer & Wightman, 1993; Farin, 1991; Asch, 1991; Mockler & Dologite, 1988).

In addition to explicit data or information in the "objective" sense, the decision makers involved in strategy creation rely heavily on the subconscious tacit knowledge (Nonaka, 1991) they have accumulated over the years. This includes judgment, intuition, well-reasoned conjecture, and individual cognitive maps (Dutton, Fahey & Narayanan, 1983). Tacit knowledge is highly subjective, uncodified, and shaped by the individuals' past experiences. It may include predictions of competitive behavior based on the intimate knowledge of the actors in competitor organizations, of how consumers and distribution channels may respond based on vaguely articulated past experience, or even an intuitive assessment of how the internal organization may execute a strategy.

In practice, the process of strategy creation has often taken the form of strategic planning. Comprehensive strategic planning (Gluck, Kaufman, & Walleck, 1978) has historically been practiced in large corporations: A celebrated example is the use of scenarios by Royal-Dutch Shell ("The Worldwide Search for Oil," 1975). It typically consisted of several sequential stages of decision making involving diagnosis, alternative development, evaluation and choice, and implementation. In each step, the strategic planners emphasized deliberate juxtaposition of "objective data" and careful analysis, with top management judgment, thus highlighting the role of tacit knowledge.

The conjunction of explicit and tacit knowledge, indeed the emphasis on tacit knowledge, has fueled an evolution of our conception and practice of strategic planning over the years. Writing in the '70s, Gluck et al. (1978) identified four phases of evolution: budgeting, long-range planning, strategic planning, and strategic management. Each phase of evolution incorporated the lessons from the earlier phases but also took into account the emerging realities faced by corporations. Gluck (1985) noted that during the 1980s the "strategic management" phase represented the cutting edge of practice in the world. We will first examine the role of IT and knowledge management in the (now) traditional "strategic management" phase for comparison purposes.

# THE ROLE OF KNOWLEDGE MANAGEMENT AND IT IN TRADITIONAL STRATEGIC PLANNING

Traditionally, the focus of IT infrastructure was to capture the knowledge of experts in a centralized repository (Davenport & Prusak, 1998; Grover & Davenport,

2001). The users of technology approached the repository with a specific purpose, i.e., to obtain knowledge—or more often, simple data—in a narrowly defined domain (Broadbent, Weill, & St. Clair, 1999). Most of the knowledge contained in databases was characteristically explicit and historical (e.g., competitor pricing, market share), and the infrastructure served to facilitate functional decision making or to automate routine tasks (as in reengineering).

Consequently, IT originally played a significant, yet ultimately limited role in the strategy creation process because of its initial emphasis on codified knowledge and explicit databases. Management information systems (MIS) arguably generated information that was only moderately applicable to strategy creation, as noted in early writings on the linkage between MIS and strategic planning (e.g., Lientz & Chen, 1981; Shank, Boynton, & Zmud, 1985; Holmes, 1985). As indicated in our earlier discussions of the information demands of strategic decision making, the complex and ambiguous problem-solving contexts confronted by strategic planning require rich media interaction and tacit information exchange beyond the scope of traditional MIS (Daft & Lengel, 1986).

The active management of knowledge was similarly underdeveloped. Despite the fact that strategic decision makers emphasized the role of tacit knowledge (albeit using other terms such as "judgment"), the actual importance of knowledge was not explicitly recognized. Formalized knowledge management (Davenport & Prusak, 1998) with its associated terminology and tools is a recent development and, as such, did not traditionally inform the strategic planning process.

## Recent Advances

However, IT and knowledge management have not remained stagnant. The shifts that have taken place in IT infrastructures over the last decade have brought them closer to the creators of strategy; indeed, IT and knowledge management are enablers in the contemporary strategic management practice. Table 1 compares traditional with "state-of-the-art" IT infrastructures to illustrate this point. The basic focus of IT infrastructure is moving from the functional work unit to a process orientation. Whereas computer systems were once the focal point, the new infrastructure is network-centric, with an emphasis on business knowledge (Nidumolu, Subramani, & Aldrich, 2001; Broadbent, Weill, & St. Clair, 1999). For example, traditional search engines utilized rule-based reasoning to identify elements matching specific search criteria; the "state-of-the-art" knowledge management systems employ case-based search techniques to identify all relevant knowledge components meeting the user's request (Grover & Davenport, 2001). It now takes into account contexts that include cross functional experts and knowledgeable on a wide variety of potentially relevant issues. Additionally, there is greater emphasis on the integration of infrastructure with structure, culture (Gold, Malhotra, & Segars, 2001), and organizational roles (Davenport & Prusak, 1998). In many ways, the newer IT infrastructures have enabled marshalling of explicit knowledge throughout the organization to speed up strategy creation and implementation.

*Table 1: A comparison of traditional and state-of-the-art infrastructures*

| | Traditional Infrastructure | State-of-the-Art Infrastructure |
|---|---|---|
| **A. Components of IT Infrastructure** | | |
| Focus | Functional unit. | Processes. |
| Approach | Computer-centric and technology-oriented. | Network-centric and process-oriented. |
| Purpose | Facilitate batch processing; process simplification; codification and uncertainty reduction. | Facilitate transactions across unit boundaries; promote process innovation; personalization and communication; encourage exploration. |
| Structural Characteristics | Static and formal structure, with separate, functionally independent legacy systems. | Dynamic and flexible structure; distributed systems, including firm-wide integration. |
| Physical Equipment | Desktop computers; local area networks (LAN) and wide area networks (WAN). | Mobile and wireless computer capabilities, e.g., laptops and cellular phones. |
| **B. Types of Knowledge Management Supported** | | |
| Type of Knowledge | Emphasizes systems knowledge; explicit; narrow domain. | Emphasizes business knowledge; broad domain. |
| Implementation of Knowledge Management | Projects. | Integration of knowledge management with business processes. |
| Knowledge Infrastructure | Fragmented knowledge repositories. Deliberate structure development. | Fluid exchange of knowledge and communities of practice (collaboration). Emergent structure. |
| Search Mechanism | Rule-based search engines. | Case-based search criteria. |

Strategic management was a response to the environment of the 1980s. Since then, Gluck's work has not been updated and few have highlighted the emerging landscape of strategic planning. In the following, we will discuss the environmental developments that have altered the context for strategy creation processes.

# THE CHANGING ORGANIZATIONAL ENVIRONMENT

The 1990s witnessed a revolution in information and telecommunications technologies, bringing in their wake radical changes in organizational environments. For example, Fahey and Randall (2001) identify several concrete marketplace changes: product proliferation, technology convergence, breakdown of industry boundaries, and global competition, among others. Michael Hammer (in Pink, 2001) notes the transition of technologies that lie at the core of information systems: from mainframe computing to personal computers, the Internet, various intranets, and eventually, to extended networks across linked businesses. As we noted in our introduction, the competitive landscape created by rapid technological change has recently been described as "hypercompetition" (D'Aveni, 1994).

The changes in organizational environments—both intensified competition and the possibilities opened up by technological developments—have created three major imperatives for organizations: time compression, globalization, and technology integration (Narayanan, 2001). In addition, the increased environmental dynamism also contributes to an increase in the degree of uncertainty confronted by strategic managers, calling into question traditional planning practices.

Thus, the environmental changes and the potential for business process transformation triggered by technology are altering the traditional strategic planning processes outlined by Gluck (1985). During the 21st century, a new type of strategy creation process is evolving which we term "strategic experimentation." With this evolution, the relationship between strategy creation, knowledge management, and IT is undergoing a profound shift. In the remainder of the chapter we elaborate on this transition to strategic experimentation, describe the emerging roles of knowledge management and IT, and outline a set of theoretical and practical implications.

# FROM STRATEGIC MANAGEMENT TO STRATEGIC EXPERIMENTATION

Throughout all four phases of strategic planning documented by Gluck et al. (1978, 1980), including their final phase of "strategic management," three implicit assumptions have remained largely unchanged:

1. There is one guiding strategic vision, derived from the analysis of the current and future internal and external environment.
2. This vision is translated into one strategic initiative (or very few initiatives) that involve large parts of the organization.
3. The strategic initiative is implemented with the aim of maximum impact, i.e., using significant resources to ensure its success.

In its most extreme form, this relatively sequential approach to strategy creation and execution leads to the identification of the one winning strategy that has the highest probability of success; thus, it is logical to commit the maximum available resources to its implementation in order to further increase this probability. The goal is to obtain a sustainable competitive advantage vis-à-vis the firm's rivals. Uncertainty is reduced ex ante using analytical forecasting techniques as well as market research. This approach to planning seems to have been effective during the 1980s when the environment was moderately dynamic, and as a consequence firms faced limited uncertainty.

In contrast, firms today often face high velocity environments (Bourgeois & Eisenhardt, 1988; Eisenhardt, 1989). In high tech industries, for example, market participants frequently confront great uncertainty over technological possibilities, consumer preferences, and viable business models. This high level of ambiguity often results in a situation where (a) traditional methods of ex ante uncertainty reduction (e.g., market research) fail, and (b) the costs and risk of the traditional "big bet" strategic management approach begin to outweigh its advantages in terms of focus, decisiveness, and concentrated resource commitment. It is in this situation that the emerging strategic experimentation approach holds significant promise.

Strategic experimentation (Brown & Eisenhardt, 1998; McGrath, 1998; McGrath & MacMillan, 2000) draws on real-options reasoning (e.g., McGrath, 1997), discussions of exploration vs. exploitation (March, 1991), as well as trial-and-error learning (e.g., Van de Ven & Polley, 1992). Companies engaging in strategic experimentation continually start, select, pursue, and drop strategic initiatives before launching aggressively those initiatives whose value is finally revealed (McGrath & MacMillan, 2000, p. 340). Strategic initiatives thus serve as low-cost probes (Brown & Eisenhardt, 1998) that enable discovery learning about product technology and market preferences. They also serve as a stepping stone option for future competitive activity in that particular product-market domain. The role of the strategic manager is to administer a portfolio of strategic initiatives which represent an appropriate mix of high and low uncertainty projects and to maximize the learning from these real options (McGrath & MacMillan, 2000).

Table 2 highlights a number of key differences between the traditional strategic management and the strategic experimentation approach. While strategic experimentation is to some extent the logical extension of the strategic management philosophy, it represents a fundamentally different view of the practice of strategic planning and the path to competitive advantage. Movement is emphasized over position in this approaches. Thus, competitive advantage is viewed as temporary at best, and hence, innovation and learning are considered crucial to success. The spirit of strategic experimentation is perhaps hinted at by Jack Welch, the (now retired) legendary chairman and CEO of General Electric, who in a 1999 interview told the *The Wall Street Journal* that every acquisition GE makes has

> […] a perfect plan, but we know that 20 or 30% will blow up in our face. A small company can only afford to make one or two bets or they go out of business. But we can afford to make lots more mistakes, and in fact, we have to throw more things at the walls. The big companies that get into trouble are those that try to manage their size instead of *experiment with it [italics added]*. (Foster, 2001, p. A18)

*Table 2: Comparison of approaches: Strategic management and strategic experimentation*

| | Strategic Management | Strategic Experimentation |
|---|---|---|
| Premise/Goal | Seek sustainable competitive advantage. | Seek disruption and temporary competitive advantage. |
| Focus | Single core strategic initiative. | Portfolio of initiatives. |
| Resource Commitment for Each Initiative | High. | Mostly low, higher for more mature initiatives. |
| Role of Uncertainty | Uncertainty is reduced ex ante, e.g., through market research or futurism. | Uncertainty is reduced ex post by direct experience through small-scale experiments with real-options character. These then reduce uncertainty for new or revised strategic initiatives. |
| Role of Knowledge | Fact-based, explicit knowledge is used to identify opportunities and to reduce uncertainty over the outcome of strategic initiatives. Decision makers' tacit assumptions also play a role. | Experiential knowledge is discovered stepwise through a series of experiments. |
| Role of IT | Supply and analyze explicit knowledge. | Support acquisition of experiential, tacit knowledge; sensemaking support. |
| Environmental Context | Slow-paced, low uncertainty. | Fast-paced, high uncertainty. |
| Planning Time-Frame | Usually long. | Usually short. |

Strategic experimentation is especially appropriate for high velocity environments such as emerging product markets with high uncertainty surrounding both technology and customer preferences (e.g., the early personal digital assistant (PDA), Internet appliance, and satellite-based telephony markets). Here, low-cost probes can be very effective in gaining knowledge and reducing uncertainty while minimizing exposure to the results of faulty assumptions. To illustrate, when Apple introduced its Newton handheld computer (see Case Vignette 1), it followed a traditional paradigm of immediately launching a highly complex product, with heavy marketing support, in order to gain a sustainable first-mover advantage. Although the market did not yet exist, sales expectations were built on market research. In contrast, the strategic experimentation approach would have implied a small-scale launch of one (or potentially even multiple) simple version(s) with limited resource commitments in order to learn from the market reaction. Subsequently, that learning experience would be used as input for future products.

# THE ROLE OF IT AND KNOWLEDGE MANAGEMENT IN THE ERA OF STRATEGIC EXPERIMENTATION

Since "strategic experimentation" represents the cutting edge of ideas in strategic management, we should expect significant advances in tool development and utilization in the next few years. These advancements will enable firms to move the idea towards normal organizational practice. Knowledge management is critical in strategic experimentation, at the core of which lie innovation, experimentation, and learning. Therefore, it is not surprising that many of the tools currently being developed have emerged from the knowledge management field. IT can accelerate the development of strategic experimentation by designing infrastructures that accommodate the new knowledge management demands imposed by this new mode of planning.

We develop the above argument in three steps: (a) identifying the requirements for implementing strategic experimentation, (b) summarizing the knowledge management tasks to fulfill these requirements, and (c) discussing the imperatives the knowledge management tasks generate for the IT infrastructure. Our arguments are summarized in Table 3.

## Functional Requirements of Strategic Experimentation

Strategic experimentation necessitates four major functions to be performed by an organization: (a) rapid decision making, (b) integration of learning from experiments, (c) diffusion of learning across organizations, and (d) managing a portfolio of strategic experiments.

1. *Rapid decision making.* Recall that the need for strategic experimentation was triggered by the emergence of hypercompetitive environments, where rapid decision making is a major requirement for success (Eisenhardt, 1989; Nadkarni & Narayanan, 2001). At the strategic level, decision making relies on tacit knowledge that incorporates the judgment and experience of top-level executives. Thus, the ability to quickly marshal tacit knowledge in all phases of decision making is a central requirement in strategic experimentation. At a minimum, this involves embedding urgency and speed in three activities: development of pathways or scenarios to the future, identification of failures,

*Table 3: Knowledge management and IT requirements in the era of strategic experimentation*

| Strategic Experimentation Challenge | Knowledge Management Tool | Benefits and Outcomes | Examples of IT Tools / Applications in Current Use | Future Development Needed |
|---|---|---|---|---|
| Rapid decision making | Visualization tools | Reduces decision time by allowing rapid visualization and prototyping as a basis for feasibility and go/no-go decisions. | Rapid Prototyping, Computer-Aided Design, CASE Tools | Real time display |
| | Group decision facilitation tools | Reduces decision time by allowing users to share knowledge asynchronously or in real time using rich media independent of geographic location. | Group Support Systems (GSS), MS NetMeeting, Lotus Notes | Advanced multimedia and communication capabilities |
| | Knowledge representation | Intervention to identify individual mental models and to promote development of shared assumptions and goals. | Decision Explorer | Repository of mental models to promote knowledge sharing |
| Rapid integration of learning from experiments | Decision histories | Learning requires the understanding of the original situation as well as the assumptions, goals, and reasoning behind the decision to initiate the strategic experiment. | Relational Databases, Decision Support Systems (DSS) | Qualitative databases |
| | Group brainstorming and decision support | Capture and integration of knowledge from a wide variety of members involved with the experiment. | GSS Using Rich Media, Decision Explorer | Multimedia enhanced communication facilitation |
| | Shared communication platforms | Enable efficient exchange of information and collaboration on individual documents and applications. | Electronic Mail, NetMeeting, Workflow Management Systems, GSS, Lotus Notes | Open platforms – integrating multiple communications systems |
| Diffusion of learning from experiments throughout the firm | Knowledge maps or networks | Represent who knows what; allow rapid access to experts and expertise. | Databases | Dynamic expertise coordination |
| | Repositories of case histories (learning histories) to identify relevant precedent that sheds light on a particular problem | Compiles chronology of events and decisions; enables access to case histories; facilitates distribution of knowledge. | Case-Based Expert Systems, Intranets, DSS | Case-based and focused search engines |
| Management of a portfolio of experiments | Tools for monitoring experiment status | Provides continuous feedback about both qualitative and quantitative performance of strategic experiments. | DSS, Content Analysis Applications | Neural networks |

and investment of resources in potential blockbuster strategies if, and when, they become apparent.

2.  *Integration of learning from experiments.* Organizational learning, another core concept in strategic experimentation, requires that appropriate learning be distilled from each experiment. This orientation combines decision making and learning: Initiatives judged to be failures are not merely weeded out, nor are successes viewed simply as alternatives to be financially backed. Rather, failures become occasions for discovering root causes, and successes are opportunities to identify best practices.

3.  *Diffusion of learning.* In addition, organizational learning has to be diffused throughout the organization. Since formal organizational channels may stifle transmission of tacit knowledge, diffusion may require interactions among "communities of practice" (Grover & Davenport, 2001; Davenport & Prusak, 1998). An organizational architecture, incorporating relevant tools and IT infrastructure, has to be designed to support these interactions.

4.  *Managing a portfolio of strategic experiments.* Unlike in previous eras, strategic experimentation requires maintenance and management of a portfolio of initiatives. This has three major implications. First, the knowledge base for decisions must be broader and richer, simply due to the increase in the number of initiatives. Second, the knowledge base becomes much more complex, since the initiatives themselves differ in terms of the mix of tacit and explicit knowledge. In essence, newer initiatives are likely to be more dependent on tacit knowledge, whereas mature ones can be augmented by explicit knowledge. Finally, and flowing from the above, the sheer number of people involved in the process will be larger, given that specialized pockets of tacit knowledge would have developed around specific strategic initiatives.

Taken together, these four functions have brought about the need for tools that can accelerate acquisition, assembly, and processing of tacit knowledge, which is likely dispersed throughout the organization.

## Knowledge Management Tools

As detailed above, during the strategic experimentation phase, the key purpose of knowledge management is not one of uncertainty reduction and process simplification, but one of rapid decision making, integration of learning from strategic experiments, diffusion of learning, and managing a portfolio of experiments (cf., Broadbent, Weill, & St. Clair, 1999). Table 3 also displays the key knowledge management tools that have evolved to support strategic experimentation. As shown in the table, the tools facilitate:

1.  *Rapid decision making* with the help of tools designed to promote collaborative work in groups. Current tools support visualization and prototyping, group decision facilitation, and knowledge representation. Each method attempts to reduce the time needed for a group to progress from problem identification to solution implementation. These tools help to coordinate the use of data, systems, tools, and techniques to interpret relevant information in order to take action (Little, Mohan, & Hatoun, 1982).

2. *Rapid integration of learning from experiments* using learning histories (Roth & Kleiner, 1998), group brainstorming, and shared communication platforms.

3. *Transmission of learning* through knowledge maps identifying the experts in specific areas and repositories of case histories. These systems are evolving to include dynamic updating of repositories and focused search tools to reduce information overload.

4. *Managing portfolios of experiments*, currently through DSS and other rich data applications including cognitive mapping, which can be used to capture both knowledge and feedback.

In Case Vignette 2, we have summarized a Cap Gemini Ernst & Young methodology, that (while much more general and not explicitly designed for this purpose) illustrates how some of the knowledge management tools are able to support a specific strategic experiment. During the era of strategic experimentation, organizations will have to learn to do similar strategic experiments on an ongoing basis. Thus, knowledge management tools will be called on to perform four interrelated functions: to customize knowledge for specific decisions on a recurring basis, to connect communities of practice, to assist the simultaneous processing of explicit and tacit knowledge, and to embed speed in decision making.

Since some tools designed to accomplish customization — that have already found their way into practice — originated with IT professionals, they are built upon existing IT infrastructures. For example, the state-of-the-art knowledge management systems that employ case-based search techniques to identify all relevant knowledge components meeting the user's request (Grover & Davenport, 2001) were developed by IT professionals. However, many of the tools detailed in Table 3 have emanated outside the IT field. For example, knowledge representation tools that capture tacit and explicit knowledge have emerged from decision sciences (Eden & Ackermann, 2000) and managerial cognition (e.g., causal mapping, see Narayanan & Fahey, 1990; Nelson, Nadkarni, Narayanan & Ghods, 2000; Kemmerer, Buche & Narayanan, 2001). Similarly, the tacit knowledge transfer among communities of practice is enhanced by telecommunications technologies (e.g., videoconferencing). The potential advancement of tools that have not originated with IT can be enhanced by further evolution of IT infrastructures in organizations, a point to which we now turn.

## Needed Developments in the IT Infrastructure

As Davenport and Prusak (1998) state, "knowledge projects are more likely to succeed when they can take advantage of a broader infrastructure of both technology and organization" (p. 155). This is as true in strategic experimentation as it is in typical knowledge management projects. Cap Gemini Ernst & Young's ASE is a case in point: It uses a combination of IT and process tools to facilitate the rapid integration of explicit and tacit knowledge and supports knowledge exchanges through rich media visualization tools as well as knowledge repositories that supply the needed explicit knowledge. In the end, such integrated organizational, IT, and knowledge management tools are needed to implement fast sense making in organizations (Boland, Tenkasi, & Te'eni, 1994).

Knowledge characteristics of strategic experimentation and the application of knowledge tools detailed above impose additional requirements on the IT infrastructure over and beyond those in the strategic management phase. Consider how each of the following functions can be enhanced by IT infrastructure development:

1.   Future advances can significantly reduce the time expended in solution development through real time displays and expand opportunities for geographically dispersed collaboration. Also, advanced multimedia and communication capabilities would increase the benefits of GSS and DSS tools.

2.   Learning from experiments can be enriched by qualitative database construction, multimedia enhancements to communication applications, and open platforms to permit the sharing of knowledge over various communication channels, including wireless media.

3.   Today, diffusion is hampered by information overload that has intensified competition for the user's attention (Hansen & Haas, 2001). To solve the problem, search tools should include separate parameters for content, rationale, and purpose of the query in order to isolate salient responses. Additionally, knowledge repositories must be maintained to ensure the contents are accurate and of high quality. Also, maintenance that is currently provided by intermediaries (Markus, 2001) might be performed faster by automated systems.

4.   Expert systems or neural networks may be developed to manage and track portfolios, promoting reuse of the knowledge captured.

From our discussion, the significant implication for IT infrastructure is the need for technology integration (Narayanan, 2001), i.e., integration with other technologies and disciplines. We can identify two fundamental thrusts of technology integration:

1.   IT infrastructure should exploit the potential for integration with other hard technologies such as telecommunications to enhance the organizational capacity for speed and carrying capacity for tacit knowledge.

2.   IT should seek to interface with decision sciences to embed AI-based processing tools and with cognitive theorists to capture the tacit knowledge pervasive in organizations.

# CONCLUSIONS AND IMPLICATIONS

We have argued that the technological changes of the 1990s have ushered in the need for strategic experimentation as the metaphor for planning practice. Strategic experimentation involves (a) maintaining a portfolio of strategic thrusts, (b) rapid decision making so that successful experiments are backed and failures are weeded out quickly, (c) learning from both successes and failures, and (d) diffusion of both explicit and tacit knowledge throughout the relevant segments of an organization. This phase requires fundamental shifts in our view of knowledge management, including its significance, use, and tools. Finally, we have argued that the shift to strategic experimentation requires fundamental shifts in the development of IT infrastructure. Instead of developing in relative isolation to other disciplines, IT should focus on technology integration by working in close collaboration with telecommunication technologies, artificial intelligence community, and managerial cognition scholars.

Information technology, knowledge management, and strategy formulation will have to coevolve for strategic experimentation to fulfill its promise. Each will have to change while maintaining its fit with the other two elements. In our opinion this gives a renewed mandate for a strategic role of IT in organizations, a role that is central to organizational success.

## Case Vignette 1

*Traditional Strategic Management in an Uncertain Environment:*
*The Apple Newton*

Apple launched its Newton PDA in August 1993, a first major entry into an emerging market full of technological and marketing uncertainties. Apple had made large-scale investments into the development and marketing of the Newton, launching it with great fanfare. However, the product was a flop and was ultimately discontinued in 1998. Several reasons can help explain this failure: At the time of launch, the demand for handheld computers was still very small and would not take off until years later. Similarly, technological challenges (e.g., handwriting recognition) were as yet largely unresolved, despite claims to the contrary. Finally, what consumers wanted from a PDA was far from clear, and a dominant design exemplifying typical product category attributes had not yet evolved. In the end it was the much less advanced, smaller, simpler Palm that would define the PDA mass market. Given the uncertain environment in 1993, a strategic experimentation approach would have probably been more appropriate than a traditional strategic management approach. Early sales numbers—encouraging by other standards—were seen as a failure due to Apple's high resource commitments, encouraging a threat rigidity response of persistence and incremental improvements. In contrast, a less costly and high profile launch would have allowed Apple to declare initial sales a conditional success. It could then have exploited its first-mover advantage by leveraging the insights it had gained about consumer needs and technological challenges to launch another, completely redesigned product into an environment with less uncertainty and risk. As it turned out, it was another company—Palm Inc.—that learned from Apple's mistakes and, in essence, appropriated the rents of Apple's failed experiment. (Sources: Bower & Christensen, 1995; Gore, 1998; Hamel, 2001)

## Case Vignette 2

*Using IT to Support Strategic Experimentation: CGEY's Accelerated*
*Solutions Environment*

Cap Gemini Ernst & Young's Accelerated Solution Environment (ASE) is an integrated combination of group process, physical environment, and technology that supports rapid problem solving and strategy making for complex issues. The ASE combines behavioral process components with IT-based support tools and infrastructures. In 2-3 day ASE events, IT is used in the form of intranet support, online research options, document libraries, documentation of key sessions and session outcomes, graphic support, rapid prototyping, and simulation and modeling tools. The ASE is an example of a new tool that uses IT in a way capable of supporting strategic experimentation. First, it uses IT to improve the speed of decision making, which is key to strategic experimentation that confronts rapidly changing environments and multiple decision points due to its incremental real-options logic. Second, the ASE focuses on creativity, facilitating the exchange of tacit knowledge while also providing necessary explicit knowledge. Thus, IT moves from simply providing the inputs for decision processes to facilitating the individual and collective sense making processes of decision makers. Real-time documentation functions, in addition to supporting the current decision process, also provide a documentary basis to later understand the history and rationale behind decision outcomes achieved. This knowledge is necessary for individuals and firms to be able to extract the maximum possible learning from the strategic experiments conducted. As an integrated process and information tool that can accommodate multiple stakeholders, ASE supports the rapid creative formulation of strategic experiments as well as the integration of the tacit experiential learning from these experiments. It also aids in the translation of such knowledge into new experiments and initiatives.

## ACKNOWLEDGMENT

The authors thank the Fulbright Alumni Initiatives Program for an award supporting the PhD seminar in Knowledge Management that led to the formulation of this chapter. The proposal for the chapter was written when the first author was the director of the Center for Management of Technology at the University of Kansas.

## REFERENCES

Asch, D. (1991). Financial planning as a strategic tool. *Accountancy, 107*, 106-109.

Boland, R. J., Jr., Tenkasi, R. V. & Te'eni, D. (1994). Designing information technology to support distributed cognition. *Organizational Science, 5*, 456-475.

Bourgeois, L. J., III, & Eisenhardt, K. M. (1988). Strategic decision processes in high velocity environments: Four cases in the microcomputer industry. *Management Science, 34*, 816-835.

Bower, J. L. & Christensen, C. M. (1995). Disruptive technologies: Catching the wave. *Harvard Business Review, 73*, 43-53.

Broadbent, M., Weill, P. & St. Clair, D. (1999). The implications of information technology infrastructure for business process redesign. *MIS Quarterly, 23*, 159-182.

Brown, S. L. & Eisenhardt, K. M. (1998). *Competing on the Edge: Strategy as Structured Chaos*. Boston: Harvard Business School Press.

Codogno, E. (1999). Getting CI from internal sources. *Competitive Intelligence Magazine, 2,* 21-23.

Covin, J. G., Slevin, D. P. & Schultz, R. L. (1994). Implementing strategic missions: Effective strategic, structural and tactical choices. *Journal of Management Studies, 31,* 481-505.

D'Aveni, R. A. (1994). *Hypercompetition: Managing the Dynamics of Strategic Maneuvering*. New York: The Free Press.

Daft, R. L. & Lengel, R. H. (1984). Information richness: A new approach to managerial behavior and organization design. In B. M. Staw and L. L. Cummings (Eds.), *Research in Organizational Behavior (Vol. 6,* pp. 191-233). Greenwich, CT: JAI Press.

Daft, R. L. & Lengel, R. H. (1986). Organizational information requirements, media richness and structural design. *Management Science, 32,* 554-571.

Daft, R. L. & Weick, K. E. (1984). Toward a model of organizations as interpretation systems. *Academy of Management Review, 9,* 284-295.

Davenport, T. & Prusak, L. (1998). *Working Knowledge: How Organizations Manage What They Know*. Boston: Harvard Business School Press.

Denny, N. (1998). Listening to your customer is vital. *Marketing, 11*(12), 18.

Duffy, J. (2000). The KM technology infrastructure. *Information Management Journal, 34,* 62-66.

Dutton, J. E., Fahey, L. & Narayanan, V. K. (1983). Toward understanding strategic issue diagnosis. *Strategic Management Journal, 4,* 307-323.

Eden, C. & Ackermann, F. (2000). Mapping distinctive competencies: A systemic approach. *Journal of the Operational Research Society, 51,* 12-20.

Eisenhardt, K. M. (1989). Making fast strategic decisions in high-velocity environments. *Academy of Management Journal, 32,* 543-576.

Fahey, L. & Randall, R. M. (2001). *The Portable MBA in Strategy* (2nd ed.). New York: John Wiley & Sons.

Farin, T. A. (1991). Computer modeling: How to play "What If?" *Credit Union Executive, 31,* 26-28.

Foster, R. (2001, September 10). The Welch legacy: Creative destruction. *The Wall Street Journal,* A18.

Gluck, F. W. (1985). A fresh look at strategic management. *Journal of Business Strategy, 6*(2), 4-19.

Gluck, F. W., Kaufman, S. P. and Walleck, S. (1978, October). The evolution of strategic management. *McKinsey Staff Paper*.

Gluck, F. W., Kaufman, S. P. and Walleck, S. (1980). Strategic management for competitive advantage. *Harvard Business Review, 58*(4), 154-161.

Gold, A. H., Malhotra, A. and Segars. A. H. (2001). Knowledge management: An organizational capabilities perspective. *Journal of Management Information Systems, 18,* 185-214.

Gore, A. (1998). Feet of clay: The Newton's death should be a lesson for Apple. *Macworld, 15*(5), 19.

Grant, R. M. (1996). Toward a knowledge-based theory of the firm. *Strategic Management Journal, 17,* 109-122.

Grover, V. and Davenport, T. (2001). General perspectives on knowledge management: Fostering a research agenda. *Journal of Management Information Systems, 18,* 5-21.

Hamel, G. (2001). Inside the revolution: Smart mover, dumb mover. *Fortune, 144*(4), 191-195.

Hansen, M. T. and Haas, M. R. (2001). Competing for attention is knowledge markets: Electronic document dissemination in a management consulting company. *Administrative Science Quarterly, 46,* 1-28.

Hilmetz, S. D. and Bridge, R. S. (1999). Gauging the returns on investments in competitive intelligence: A three-step analysis for executive decision makers. *Competitive Intelligence Review, 10158,* 4-11.

Hofer, C. W. and Schendel, D. (1978). *Strategy Formulation: Analytical Concepts.* St. Paul, MN: West.

Holmes, F. W. (1985). The information infrastructure and how to win with it. *Information Management Review, 1*(2), 9-19.

Keller, R. T. (1994). Technology-information processing fit and the performance of R&D project groups: A test of contingency theory. *Academy of Management Journal, 37,* 167-179.

Kemmerer, B., Buche M. W. and Narayanan, V. K. (2001, August). *Deriving revealed causal maps from non-traditional source documents: Challenges and methodological extensions.* Paper presented at the Academy of Management Annual Meeting, Washington, D.C.

Lientz, B. P. and Chen, M. (1981). Assessing the impact of new technology in information systems. *Long Range Planning, 14*(6), 44-50.

Little, J. D., Mohan, L. and Hatoun, A. (1982). Yanking knowledge from the numbers: How marketing decision support systems can work for you. *Industrial Marketing, 67,* 46-56.

March, J. G. (1991). Exploration and exploitation in organizational learning. *Organization Science, 2,* 71-87.

Markus, M. L. (2001). Toward a theory of knowledge reuse: Types of knowledge reuse situations and factors in reuse success. *Journal of Management Information Systems, 18,* 57-93.

Martinsons, M. G. (1994). A strategic vision for managing business intelligence. *Information Strategy: The Executive's Journal, 10*(3), 17-30.

Mason, R .O. and Mitroff, I. I. (1973). A program for research on management information systems. *Management Science, 19,* 475-487.

McAleer, E. and Wightman, S. (1993). The use of micro computers in corporate planning: A research note. *IBAR, 14,* 127-135.

McGrath, R. G. (1997). A real options logic for initiating technology positioning investments. *Academy of Management Review, 22,* 974-996.

McGrath, R. G. (1998). Discovering strategy: Competitive advantage from idiosyncratic experimentation. In Hamel, G., Prahalad, C. K., Thomas, H. and O'Neal,

D. (Eds.), *Strategic Flexibility: Managing in a Turbulent Environment* 351-370. Chichester, England: John Wiley & Sons.

McGrath, R. G. and MacMillan, I. (2000). *The Entrepreneurial Mindset.* Boston: Harvard Business School Press.

Mockler, R. J. and Dologite, D. G. (1988). Developing knowledge-based systems for strategic corporate planning. *Long Range Planning, 21,* 97-102.

Nadkarni, S. and Narayanan, V. K. (2001, August). *A comparative analysis of the influence of cognitive frames on organizational performance in high and low velocity industries.* Paper presented at the Academy of Management Annual Meeting, Washington, D.C.

Narayanan, V. K. (2001). *Managing Technology and Innovation for Competitive Advantage.* Englewood Cliffs, NJ: Prentice Hall College Division.

Narayanan, V. K. and Fahey, L. (1990). Evolution of revealed causal maps during decline: A case study of admiral. In A. S. Huff (Ed.), *Mapping Strategic Thought*, pp. 107-131. London: John Wiley & Sons.

Narayanan, V. K. and Nath, R. (1993). *Organization Theory: A Strategic Approach.* Burr Ridge, IL: Irwin.

Nelson, K. M., Nadkarni, S., Narayanan, V. K. and Ghods, M. (2000). Understanding software operations support expertise: A causal mapping approach. *MIS Quarterly, 24,* 475-507.

Nidumolu, S. R., Subramani, M. and Aldrich, A. (2001). Situated learning and the situated knowledge web: Exploring the ground beneath knowledge management. *Journal of Management Information Systems, 18,* 115-150.

Nonaka, I. (1991). The knowledge-creating company. *Harvard Business Review, 79,* 96-104.

Pink, D. H. (2001, September). Who has the next big idea? *Fast Company,* 108-116.

Roth, G. and Kleiner, A. (1998). Developing organizational memory through learning histories. *Organizational Dynamics, 27,* 43-60.

Shank, M. E., Boynton, A. C. and Zmud, R. W. (1985). Critical success factor analysis as a methodology for MIS planning. *MIS Quarterly, 9,* 121-129.

Sterling, J. U. and Lambert, D. M. (1989). Customer service research: Past, present, and future. *International Journal of Physical Distribution & Materials Management, 19*(2), 2-23.

Turban, E., McLean, E. and Wetherbe, J. (1996). *Information Technology for Management.* New York: John Wiley & Sons.

Van de Ven, A. H. and Polley, D. (1992). Learning while innovating. *Organization Science, 3,* 92-116.

Warner, F. (2001, September). He drills for knowledge. *Fast Company,* 186-191.

Whitten J. L. and Bentley, L. D. (1998). *Systems Analysis and Design Methods* (4th ed.). Boston: Irwin/McGraw-Hill.

Wisner, J. D. and Fawcett, S. E. (1991). Linking firm strategy to operating decisions through performance measurement. *Production & Inventory Management Journal, 32,* 5-11.

The worldwide search for oil. (1975). *Business Week,* 2366, 38-44.

## Chapter IV

# Strategic Information Systems: The Concept of Alignment

Theodorou Petros
Public Power Corporation, Greece

## ABSTRACT

*Certain contingencies of business environment raise the importance of alignment in the explanation of tactics with strategic implications. Alignment is an important aspect that has to be examined in all multivariate and normative models. In this paper, the Information Technology (IT) alignment is examined along with business strategy and structure, while taking into account environmental contingencies. The concept of alignment raises the strategic role of information technology through the integration of business and IT strategy. Most of the firms nowadays cannot capture the strategic role of IT and underestimating its value as persisting only on financial valuation. In this work, an attempt has been made to fill out this lack of strategic estimation by the use of the alignment model. A taxonomy of strategic information technology applications is presented and an integration of IT with business strategy and structure is attempted in order to create competitive advantage.*

## INFORMATION TECHNOLOGY AND STRATEGIC ALIGNMENT

The concept of alignment has been widely examined in strategy and organizations theory literature, underlying the contingency theories and constituting the groundwork of management of technology and strategy information systems. Strategic alignment and fit have been among the top concerns of business executives

(Rodgers, 1997; Brancheau, Janz & Wetherbe, 1996) and the core concept in the normative models, having desirable performance implications. Alignment according to literally means an arrangement of groups or forces in relation to one another. The determination of those forces is an important aspect of strategic alignment research. The following aggregate variables are commonly found in many alignment models: environment uncertainty, business structure, information technology (IT) and business strategy. Among those variables, Miles and Snow (1984) determine strategy as the basic alignment mechanism and organizational structure and management processes as the internal arrangements. In the classical school of strategy, environment has the most important role as the determinant of alignment; structure should follow the alterations of environment while the role of IT is collateral. Strategy should follow environment and determine the structural form according to variations; IT should follow strategy as well. In contrast, Mintzberg and Quinn (1996) proposed a bottom-up view that is free of the "environmental biased" (Theodorou, 1997). The alterations that originated, either in the internal or in the external environment of the business, create the need to exercise a flexible strategy. Practical experience suggests that those variables—which should be aligned—are interrelated in a multidimensional way usually for the sake of simplicity. A simple bivariate approach is used among: environment↔strategy, structure↔strategy, IT↔strategy, and IT↔structure. It is worthwhile to mention that strategy creation and strategic alignment have two dimensions (Horovits, 1984; Reich & Benbasat, 1999), the intellectual (interrelated IT and business plans) and the social dimensions (understanding and commitment of participants); among these the first will be examined.

Nowadays enterprises face increased uncertainty as the external environment becomes volatile. Volatility increases in a positive way along with supply and demand variability. Enterprises proceed with process reengineering and restructuring in order to achieve higher performance. Elements of internal structure like intermediate inventory, equipment maintenance, absenteeism, etc. (Theodorou, 2000) increase uncertainty and thus the need for flexibility. Firms in order to keep pace with competition need a flexible internal structure. The variations from which the need for flexibility emerges are the following: demand variability, supply variability, process variability, product variability, workforce variability, and equipment variability (Theodorou, 1996a). As the need for flexibility increases and as the enterprises attain the rest of strategic priorities like cost and quality, the role of IT will be increased drastically until its strategic importance for the achievement of competitive and distinctive advantage, will be recognized. Information technology as part of internal structure proved capable to affect strategy and create competitive advantage. IT is not a mere collection of bolts and nuts due to the programming capabilities of microprocessors; thus, it has a direct effect on business structure as an important contributor that increases flexibility. The flexibility of structure enables enterprises to take advantage of IT's full potential in order to bypass environmental uncertainty. Just-in-time responding to environmental changes is critical for the survival of the synchronous enterprise in a highly competitive environment. IT and structure fit are of strategic importance. Internal structure and external environment should fit as well.

Alignment is more an ongoing process and not a stable state. In strategic management, no strategy is universally superior, irrespective of the environmental or organizational context (Venkatraman, 1989). The flexibility of structure to follow demand and produce in low cost and high quality is a strategic matter of a long-term investment. Strategic alignment enables enterprises to avoid oversimplification while targeting at competitive and distinctive advantages that assist in dominating competition. Strategy should be aligned with environment if competitive advantage is to be attained from the strategic issues of cost, flexibility, dependability and quality. Under that concept, business strategy should evolve while taking into account the impact of IT. On the other hand, if information technology is applied without taking into account the strategic targets then only operational benefits will be created without any impact on competitive advantage.

Electronic point-of-sales (EPOS) can just in time inform the warehouse for the deduction of materials, and a material requirements planning system (MRP) can process the request for order; furthermore, a B2B electronic commerce solution can complete the request for order. Moreover, imagine an automated warehouse with AGVs like the one in Benetton, which automatically load and unload the materials. All the systems previously mentioned do not have only operational benefits, but at strategic level what was achieved was the completion of two ultimate strategic targets: to deliver just in time the product and to create dependability upon the customer.

Thus, it is easy to understand that strategic alignment is a problem with multiple dimensions: Environmental uncertainty, business structure, IT, and business strategy are the main determinants (Figure 1).

Aside from the previously mentioned variables, we could refer to business culture, managerial knowledge/processes and individual roles, which are substantial determinants of the alignment model.

Alignment among business strategy and IT should consider among other contingencies the impact of industry and competitive change (particularly under the influence of IT and the generic strategies in the strategy portfolio), the strategic changes induced by IT that affect the reengineering of internal and external value chains, and the IT capabilities that shift or expand the business domain and scope.

*Figure 1: Strategic alignment is a problem with multiple dimensions*

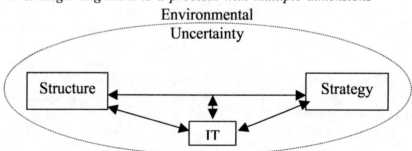

*Figure 2: Research framework*

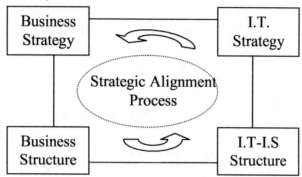

Management in the '90s research framework (Morton, 1991) illustrates the various aspects of the firm that have to be considered in the alignment process but without any reference to external environment (Figure 2).

In this model the upper two boxes define strategic fit by looking at the IT potential to shape and support business strategy, and the lower two boxes define alignment at the organizational level by looking at organizational infrastructures and processes. According to this model four perspectives of alignment arise: the strategy execution, the technology, the competitive potential and the service level. Furthermore four alignment mechanisms are identified: value management, governance, technological and organizational capability.

Misfit and misalignment are reasons why many IT applications are not meeting up to the expectations or not meeting the needs of a company. In the following paragraphs a bivariate approach will be used in order to examine strategy, structure and IT alignment, but before that a brief presentation of SIS applications will be made.

# STRATEGIC INFORMATION SYSTEMS APPLICATIONS

First we will explore IT applications in general and afterwards we will consider the rest of the determinants of strategic alignment in relation to IT. There are three main groups if we want to present and classify IT from both a hard and a soft perspective (Theodorou, 1996a):
1.  Flexible engineering design automation
2.  Flexible manufacturing automation
3.  Flexible administrative planning and control automation

## Flexible Engineering Design Automation (FEDA)

FEDA refers mainly to products' design automation. This kind of automation includes technologies and techniques such as computer-aided design (CAD), computer-aided engineering (CAE), solid modeling (SM) and finite element analysis

(FEA).

*Computer-Aided Design* is comprised basically of computer graphics. It was initiated in MIT around 1963 and consisted of a sketch pad system which was composed of a cathode ray tube (CRT) and a TX2 computer. Later on the evolution of personal computers had as a consequence the mass diffusion of such applications. CAD is distinguished in 2D and 3D. The three-dimensional CAD has evolved in the following stages: wireframe, surface modeling, solid modeling. We can find CAD applications in engineering design, electronic design, architectural design, cartography and clothes design (Wheelwright, 1987).

*Computer-Aided Engineering* systems allow the calculations for the tolerance, durability, dimensions and physical properties of materials like structural, thermal, and magnetic characteristics. Solid modeling belongs to the class of CAE systems as long as it allows algorithmic calculations besides design. These computations concern geometric paradoxes and check for possible alterations of the manufacturing materials, etc. The elements obtained by this technique are volume, mass, gravitational centre, rotational radius etc. According to the geometric model definition, the solid modeling systems can be assigned into three classes: constructive solid geometry (CSG), boundary representation (B-rep), and hybrid aspects of the above two. In the CAE category, along with solid modeling, the finite element analysis (FEA) can be found. Finite element analysis is used to compute the breaking point of the material and thermoelectric conductance as well as other elements of the modeled product.

Generally the existing tendency is to incorporate all the above-mentioned techniques and technologies into CAD. Indeed most of the CAD programs incorporate in modules the above-mentioned methods.

## Flexible Manufacturing Automation (FMA)

The basic scope of this kind of IT application is machine programming. Techniques and technologies of this kind include numerical control (NC), direct numerical control (DNC), computer numerical control (CNC), robots, flexible manufacturing systems (FMS), automated guided vehicles (AGVs), automated storage/retrieval systems (AS/RS).

The basic concept of *NC/DNC/CNC* is to control and program the way the machine tool functions through numerical code. This technology was introduced in 1940 by J. T. Parsons and was developed since in the MIT laboratories. The first demonstration of the NC prototype was held in 1952. Communication with tool machines was initially through punched tapes, NC cards. In 1968 the cards were abolished and direct connections between computers and machines were achieved (DNC), but the cost of direct numerical control was high and the size was comfortless. In DNC a computer controls a number of machines through direct connection in real time. In principle one large computer can be used to control more than 100 separate machines. In DNC there are two alternative system configurations; one is called behind-the-tape-reader and the second, the specialized machine control unit. Around 1970 DNC was replaced by computer numerical control (CNC) because of size, cost, and the trend toward downsizing in computers. Those systems were applied in industry, making possible the use of separate computers for each tool machine that comprised computer numerical control (CNC). In computer numerical control once the punched card is entered it is stored in memory. The difference between NC and CNC is that in the second case each machine is connected separately to onboard microprocessors. Computer numerical control machine programming is accomplished in 3 steps: part programming, main programming, post programming. APT is the most famous programming language for numerical control.

*Robots and NC* machines appear to have a lot in common. The basic difference is that robots are programmed in real time with stored instructions in their memory, and they are human-like because of their arms. Most robots have one of the following configurations: polar coordinate, cylindrical coordinate, jointed arm, and Cartesian coordinate. There are six basic motions which provide the robot with the capability to move: vertical traverse, radial traverse, rotational traverse, wrist swivel, wrist bend and wrist yaw. The common methods by which robots can be programmed are manual method, walk-through method, lead-through and off-line programming. Computer controlled robots require a language which, in addition to the previously mentioned methods, can program the robots' motion. Famous robot programming languages are VAL and APT. Robots are used in transportation, loading/unloading, welding, etc.

*Flexible manufacturing systems (FMS)* consist of a group of processing stations interconnected by means of an automated material handling and storage system and controlled by an integrated computer system. FMS were introduced around 1967 but the cost of the investment limited their installations. By 1981 the FMS population was 25 in USA, 40 in Japan and 50 in Europe, and by the beginning of 1985 the estimated number of installations worldwide was 300 (Groover, 1987; Groover & Zimmers, 1984).

*Automated guided vehicle systems (AGVs)* are systems for the transport or transfer of materials and tools which function autonomously on a program path

*Automated storage/retrieval systems (AS/RS)* aim to store and retrieve materials in a fast and accurate mode, preindicated according to need. AGVs are used in these systems, which are also referred to as pickup and deposit stations.

## Flexible Administrative Planning and Control Automation (FAPC)

In this category we incorporate computer applications used in accounting, logistics, warehouse management, management of stocks, quality control, etc. Also in FAPC we include the management of information systems (MIS) and decision support systems (DSS), which use inputs from the applications mentioned above and use various techniques and models to help management decisions on various aspects. Other systems in this category are the following: electronic data interchange (EDI), electronic point-of-sales (EPOS), optimized production technology (OPT), group technology (GT), material requirements planning (MRP I), manufacturing resource planning (MRP II; Vlahopoulou, Manthou & Theodorou, 1996; Nakane, 1986), just in time (JIT), computer-aided production planning (CAPP), shop floor control (SFC), factory data collection systems (FCS), data acquisition systems (DAS), computer-aided quality control (CAQC), concurrent engineering (CE), etc.(Nakane & Hall, 1991).

*Materials requirement planning (MRP)* is a computational technique that converts the master production schedule (MPS) into a detailed schedule for the raw materials. The detailed schedule identifies the quantities of each raw material and also indicates when each item must be ordered and delivered so as to meet the MPS. That system concentrates on setting priorities for dependent demand products and it appears to work best for companies with mass production assembly lines. Generally MRP assumes unlimited capacity in all work centers, whereas in reality some work centers always behave as bottlenecks. However when MRP is used as an integrated system that has capacity planning, shop floor control and a link with the financial system of the company then we are talking about manufacturing resource planning (MRP II). MRP II is an operational and financial system for all facets of the business including sales, production, engineering, cash flows, etc.

*Just in time (JIT)* is an approach for providing smoother production flows and making continual improvements in processes and supplied products. Just in time attempts to reduce work in process inventories, lead times and setup times. That system emphasizes small lot sizes and requires short lead times, which it translates into small inventories at every stage. Just in time is a pull system because the user of raw and intermediate materials pulls the parts or subassemblies from the suppliers.

*Optimized production technology* calculates the near optimum schedule and sequence of operations for all work centres of a manufacturing company into account priorities and capacities. Optimized production technology (OPT) attempts to maximize the use of critical resources and minimize the work in process inventories and manufacturing lead times. This approach determines priorities for each operation using a weighted function of various criteria like best product mix, due dates, safety stock and bottleneck machines. OPT breaks down a total production plan into separate stages and searches for the best possible detailed schedule. The system takes into account scores of factors that control production efficiency, plant capacity, work in progress, setup times, substitutions, overlapping among process batches, subcontracts and safety stocks. The program plots these factors on a graph and determines a near-optimum combination.

*Group technology* is a manufacturing philosophy in which similar parts are identified and grouped together to take advantage of their similarities in manufacturing and design. Similar parts are arranged into group families. The efficiencies achieved by such a system are reduced setup times, lower in-process inventories, better scheduling, improved tool control and the use of standardized process plans. There are three main methods for grouping parts into families:

a)    The methods based on part design attributes
b)    The methods based on part manufacturing attributes
c)    Hybrid of the above-mentioned methods

Most small-medium sized enterprises (SMEs), when implementing a part classification and coding system, elect to purchase a commercially available package rather than develop their own. Three types of part classification systems are widely known:
a)    Opits system
b)    MICLASS system
c)    CODE system

*Computer-aided production planning and computer-aided process planning* automatically generates the manufacturing operation sequence based on the characteristics of a given part. A CAPP system offers the potential for reducing the routine clerical work of manufacturing engineers. At the same time, it provides the opportunity to generate production routings which are rational, consistent and optimal. Two alternative approaches to computer-aided process planning have been developed and these are retrieval-type CAPP systems and generative CAPP systems. Retrieval-type CAPP systems use parts classification and coding and group technology as a foundation. The Generative CAPP systems create an individual process plan from scratch through computer, automatically and without human assistance. The computer through various techniques will create a final plan for manufacturing. Inputs to the system would include a comprehensive description of the workpart and some form of part code number. The generative CAPP system synthesises the design of the optimum process sequence, based on an analysis of part geometry, materials and other factors which would influence manufacturing decisions.

*Shop floor control (SFC)* includes systems that establish a direct connection between computers and manufacturing operations for the purpose of monitoring the manufacturing process. SFC systems are not control systems in the sense of automatic feedback control or computer process control because humans still play an important role in the control loop. The purpose of that system is to generate information by which the middle management can make decisions on effective factors management and implementation of the master schedule. The functions of SFC classified by Raffish are the following:
a)    Priority control and assignment of shop orders
b)    Maintain information on work in process for MRP
c)    Monitor shop-orders status information
d)    Provide production output data for capacity control purposes
      The SFC consists of three steps which are:
a)    Order release
b)    Order scheduling
c)    Order progress

*Factory data collection system (FDC)* provides data for monitoring order progress. These data are submitted to the order progress module for analysis and generation of work-orders status reports and exception reports.

*Data acquisition systems (DAS)* imply an online system that collects data for direct communication to a central computer.

*Computer-aided quality control (CAQC)* is comprised of computer-aided inspection (CAI) and computer-aided testing (CAT). The objectives of CAQC are to improve product quality, to increase productivity in the inspection process and to increase productivity and reduce lead times in manufacturing. In many respects computer-aided quality control represents a significant departure from the traditional quality control methods.

We summarize the previously mentioned ITs in Table 1 according to the criterion of usage (Theodorou, 1996a).

Kathuria and Igbaria (1997) present a different taxonomy of IT mainly in relation to business processes. Those systems are design for manufacturability (DFM), make to stock (MTS), capacity planning using overall factors for less products variety (CPOF), just in time inventory (JIT), reorder point (ROP), assembly line balancing (ALB), quality control (QC), quality engineering (QE:Taguchi methods), continuous review systems (Q_R), computer-aided design (CAD), make to order (MTO), quality planning (QP), quality function deployment (QFD), assemble to order (ATO), capacity bills procedures (CBP), capacity requirements planning (CRP), materials requirement planning (MRPI), optimized production technology (OPT), sequencing scheduling (S-Sched), distribution requirements planning (DRP) and resource profiles (RP). These techniques and technologies are presented according to business functions alignment in Table 2.

Nowadays most IT applications are integrated in platforms that use large database systems, encompassing from warehouse computerization to Web servers that support B2B and B2C TCP/IP applications. Those systems are known as

*Table 1: Previously mentioned ITs*

| FLEXIBLE DESIGN AUTOMATION | FLEXIBLE MANUFACTURING AUTOMATION | FLEXIBLE ADMINISTRATIVE AUTOMATION |
|---|---|---|
| CAD | NC/DNC/CNC | MIS/DSS |
| CAE: FEA, SM | ROBOTS | OPT |
| | FMS | MRP I,II |
| | AGVs | JIT |
| | AS/RS | EDI |
| | | EPOS |
| | | GT |
| | | SFC |
| | | CAPP |
| | | CAQC |

*Table 2: Techniques and technologies*

| IT Applications by Functional Area | | | | | | |
|---|---|---|---|---|---|---|
| Design | Demand Management | Capacity Planning | Inventory Management | Shop Floor | Quality Management | Distribution |
| DFM | MTS | CPOF | JIT/ROP | ALB | QC/QE | Q_R |
| DFM/CAD | MTO | | JIT | ALB | QC/QP/QFD | |
| | ATO | CBP/CRP | MRPI/OPT | S_SCHED | | DRP |
| CAD | MTO/MTS | RP/CPOF | OPT/ROP | S_SCHED/ALB | QP/QFD | DRP |

enterprise resource planning (ERP) and management resource planning systems (MRP II). The functionality of those systems provides enterprises with the ability to craft the platform upon specific needs. Moreover the modularity of those systems enables firms to invest in specific applications that can be further upgraded in the future and integrated with complementary applications. Those integrated systems have the advantage that they can handle, transfer and filter information in every side of the firm. Most times, information can be lost or has such a size that it needs too much time to handle. In the case of ERP systems, information is filtered and can be accessed using neural networks anytime and from anywhere. Moreover advanced neural and expert networks and techniques such as intelligent data mining can search easily and provide inputs in intelligent decision support systems, thus minimizing the processing time of transforming data to useful information.

Generally what is important for success, regardless of the system's advances, is what was already mentioned: strategic alignment and fit. Employees' commitment, top management support and generally an organic and flexible structural form aligned with top management's strategic targets are prerequisites for successful utilization of IT applications.

# STRATEGY AND IT ALIGNMENT

An important aspect of strategy and IT alignment was to correspond the strategic content with IT capabilities; in other words, match IT to strategic objectives and see how they are affected. That topic is basically examined in strategic information system literature where matrix models are developed in order to determine strategic alignment.

Porter's (1979, 1980, 1985, 1986, 1987) work comprised the basis for the development of strategic information systems even though it is more familiar in strategic management literature. Neumann (1994), in his book about strategic information systems (SIS), denotes that Porter's model of five forces is the framework of frameworks. Specifically, regarding the strategic objectives, Porter attempted a generalization of specific strategic targets, the so-called generic strategies, which are cost, differentiation and focus (niche) strategies. Furthermore, Wiseman (1998) extended that logic by adding the strategic targets of alliance, growth and innovation.

Generally business strategy should take into account IT in order to attain opportunities that increase the competitive advantage. Competitive advantage from IT can be derived by taking into account the opportunities that can be exploited from the five forces model, e.g., how can the firm build barriers to entry, build switching costs, change the basis of competition, change the balance of power in supplier relationships and generate new products. Moreover, the sustainability issue raised the importance of business strategy and IT integration. Strategic information systems literature tried to explain alignment among strategy and IT with the use of matrix models. Synnot (1987) made a composition of Boston Consulting Group matrix and Porter's generic strategies in order to identify IT strategic options and achieve strategic alignment. A well-known model for the attainment of strategic opportunities criticized for oversimplification is the strategic grid matrix developed by McFarlan (1984). The empirical research of Hirschheim (1982) indicates that regardless of the "simplicity problem" an important benefit that arises is that the model forms the basis for a dialogue among management; thus helping consensus and agreement, which is a significant part of social alignment. An important upgrade of the strategic grid was made by Ward (1987), who extended the hermeneutic capability of the model by incorporating IS/IT planning. In Figure 3, a composition of the strategic grid and the Ward extension is presented.

The vertical axis represents the degree of business strategy and IT alignment. The upper part of vertical axis represents higher integration among IT and strategic targets. The horizontal axis represents the degree of IT diffusion inside the organization. The more we move to the left the higher the dependence of business on IT. The upper left part of the four-quadrant box indicates a firm with high dependence on IT and high strategy↔IT alignment. In that case the hypothesis is that the firm achieved operational benefits from IT use and is looking to exploit new opportunities in order to attain sustainability. Competitive advantage has been created from IT use and the enterprise is trying to maintain the distance from the competitor (sustainability of competitive advantage). In the opposite side, lower right is a firm that has not aligned business and IT strategy and the only benefit is operational, with a small increase in efficiency rates.

Based on this matrix, Parson (1983; see Ward, Griffiths & Whitmore, 1994 p. 251) discussed alignment among generic and IT strategies. Parson's generic IS/IT strategies are the following six: centrally planned, leading edge, free market,

*Figure 3: Composition of strategic grid and Ward extension matrix*

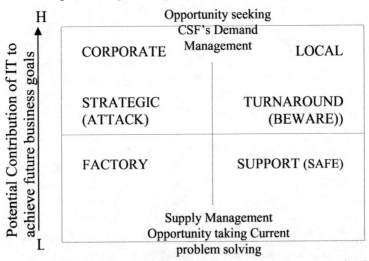

*Figure 4: Central planned strategy*

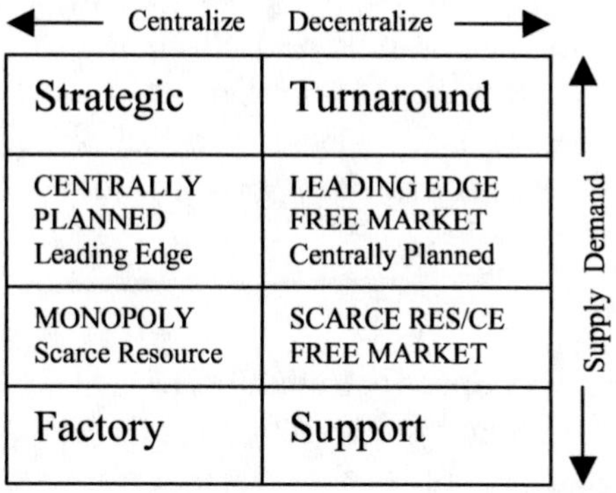

monopoly, scarce resource and necessary evil. As can be seen in Figure 4, the diagram, full alignment and fit, can be achieved only in centrally planned strategy.

The strategic objectives in capitals are the ideal strategies that best fit and those in lowercase are the less effective. The conclusion is that an organization will need to adopt a full range of generic strategies if it is to manage an extensive portfolio. Central planning is a demand management strategy; in contrast, monopoly is a supply management approach, and both lead to strong centralization and control. Free market and leading edge are demand management approaches obviously decentralized. Scarce resource is a supply management strategy and is mainly decentralized (Ward et al., 1994). Best alignment among IT and business strategy or best-fit IT strategy is presented in capital letters. Moreover, Parson attempts a classification of IT applications according to the organization's functions and Porter's generic strategies.

In Table 3, an integration of the Boston Consulting Group matrix (BCG) with the strategic grid, Ward's and Parson's generic IT strategies are presented.

In Table 3, IT strategies are sorted in term of importance according to the best-fit criterion (Parson, 1983). Moreover, taking into account the strategic movement of a firm over Boston matrix (BCG), we can conclude that the movement over strategic grid can be the following: Strategic→Factory→Support, with a free move to any segment from the turnaround point.

*Table 3: Boston Consulting Group (BCG) matrix*

| BCG | Business Strategy | Parson's IT Strategies | Strategic Grid |
|---|---|---|---|
| Star | Invest | 1. Leading Edge<br>2. Centrally Planned | Turnaround |
| Wildcat | Examine | 1. Centrally Planned<br>2. Leading Edge<br>3. Free Market | Strategic |
| Dog | Divest | 1. Scarce Resource<br>2. Monopoly<br>3. Free Market<br>4. Necessary Evil | Support |
| Cash Cow | Milk | 1. Monopoly<br>2. Scarce Resource | Factory |

An important set of generic strategies is also found in manufacturing strategy literature. Based on the distinction made by Skinner (1985, p. 78, 80, 88), Swamidass and Newell (1987), Adam and Swamidass (1989), and Swink and Way (1995), strategy is determined by priorities and priorities determine the strategic direction. According to Skinner (1969), Buffa (1984) and Wheelwright (1984), the basic strategic priorities in ascending order of importance are:

1.    Cost
2.    Quality
3.    Flexibility
4.    Dependability (Delivery Speed or Reliability)

This rank of manufacturing priorities reflects the order that an enterprise should follow for the achievement of competitive advantage overcoming the "trade-off" of the "focused factory" (Skinner, 1974) and going further to the cumulative model. For instance the firm who wants to achieve the target of flexibility must first accomplish the low-cost dimension and after that, the quality target. Moreover, the previous priority list is the one that the Japanese companies followed (Nakane, 1986; Nakane and Hall, 1991; De Meyer et al., 1989). Additionally to this list, Giffi, Roth and Seals (1990) add innovation and customer service as the 5th and 6th priorities. The dimensions of cost and price are no longer first in order as the importance of other dimensions like quality and innovation increases in today's environment. Furthermore Hill (1993, p. 45) put on the following five priorities: color range, product range, design, brand image, and technical support. Ferdows and De Meyer (1990), in their "sand-cone" model, adopt a different prioritization of manufacturing dimensions, putting quality before dependability, flexibility as a third priority and at the end cost. Swink and Way (1995) accept the same order. According to Hall (1987), quality becomes the first goal, second comes dependability, followed by cost and at the end flexibility. We observe a slight difference between Ferdows, De Meyer and Hall in the order of the last two priorities, flexibility and cost. Hall and Nakane (1990) add to the previous list another two dimensions: company's culture that precedes quality and innovation as the 6th dimension. Noble (1997) change Hall's progression, with a distinction among dependability and delivery that comes after and including innovation at the end. Regarding Skinner's prioritizing, Chase et al. (1992) believe that service is a fifth dimension unrelated to dependability and 5th in order. Some studies have focused on quality only (Adam, 1994; Flynn et al., 1994) while others have focused on productivity as a criterion for prioritizing (Hayes & Clark, 1985; Schmenner, 1988, 1990, 1991; Noble, 1997).

To reach business and corporate goals, supportive cost, time, quality and flexibility goals must be developed (Skinner, 1969). These manufacturing goals are achieved and sustained by a "pattern of decisions" (Hayes & Wheelwright, 1984) that it has to be alignment with business as well as IT strategy targets. According to Skinner (1985), these priorities integrate manufacturing and business strategy. Skinner (1996) contends that one of the major problems in implementing strategic objectives was a proven inability of management to step back and assess the coherence of their strategies. Skinner (1996) endorses that the insufficient research on the process of strategy making has held back the adoption of manufacturing strategy ideas.

Moreover, manufacturing priorities as well as practices differentiate across countries. International differentiation has been the subject of study by Reitspergen and Daniel (1990) for USA and Japan, Vastag and Whybark (1994) for USA and Europe, and Hall and Nakane (1990) for USA and Japan. Finally, Miller et al. (1992) have done an exhaustive comparison of the manufacturing priorities and action programmes of firms in American, European and Pacific Rim countries.

Research projects on the manufacturing priorities and how they are formed in different countries have been made by Horte et al. (1991,1987), who explored Sweden; Belgium by Gelders et al.(1994); Singapore by Ward's et al. (1995); Japan by Nakane (1986); and more recently India by Nagabhushana and Shah (1999). An interesting and integrative approach proposed by De Meyer (1998) relatively to the manufacturing priorities and action plans in Europe. That research held on a long-term horizon of 10 years.

Finally an attempt has been made in international manufacturing to identify various barriers to the management of international operations (Klassen & Whybark, 1993; Ferdows et al., 1986).

As can be seen from the literature review, the generic business and IT strategies have been split up into more than five competitive priorities and those priorities can be further split up into many tactics (for a more detailed analysis, see Theodorou, 1996b). Discussion will be based on the basic priorities of cost, quality, flexibility, dependability and innovation (Theodorou, 1997). In Table 4, IT technologies and priorities are aligned according to the business functions (Kathuria & Igbaria, 1997).

As can be seen, IT applications are determined in a broad sense based on Cooper and Zmud's (1990) approach. Moreover Kathuria and Igbaria (1997) in this matrix correlate organizations' structure (from a functional view) with strategic priorities and IT, bypassing the limits of a two-dimensional approach.

Thus, cost strategy is mainly aligned with IT systems like design for manufacturability (DFM), make to stock (MTS), capacity planning using overall factors for less products variety (CPOF), just in time inventory (JIT), reorder point (ROP), assembly line balancing (ALB), quality control (QC), quality engineering (QE:Taguchi methods) and continuous review systems (Q_R). Quality strategy is mainly aligned with DFM, computer-aided design (CAD), make to order (MTO), JIT/ALB/QC/QP, quality planning (QP) and quality function deployment (QFD). Flexibility is aligned with assemble to order (ATO), capacity bills procedures (CBP), capacity requirements planning (CRP), materials requirement planning (MRP I),

*Table 4: IT technologies and priorities*

| Priorities | IT Applications by Functional Area | | | | | | |
|---|---|---|---|---|---|---|---|
| | Design | Demand Management | Capacity Planning | Inventory Management | Shop Floor | Quality Management | Distribution |
| Cost | DFM | MTS | CPOF | JIT/ROP | ALB | QC/QE | Q_R |
| Quality | DFM/CAD | MTO | | JIT | ALB | QC/QP/QFD | |
| Flexibility | | ATO | CBP/CRP | MRP I/OPT | S_SCHED | | DRP |
| Dependability | CAD | MTO/MTS | RP/CPOF | OPT/ROP | S_SCHED/ALB | QP/QFD | DRP |

*Table 5: Flexibility and IT applications alignment with variability*

| EXTERNAL FLEXIBILITY | | INTERNAL FLEXIBILITY | | | |
|---|---|---|---|---|---|
| | | VARIABILITIES | | | |
| DEMAND | SUPPLY | PROCESS | PRODUCT | WORKFORCE | EQUIPMENT |
| CAD | MRP I,II | FMS | CAD | ROBOTS | OPT |
| CAE, FEA | JIT | NC/CNC | GT | FMS | FMS |
| EDI | EDI | AGVs | EDI | AGVs | SFC |
| EPOS | AS/RS | OPT | CAE | AR/RS | NC/CNC |
| CE | CAQC | GT | CE | NC/CNC/DNC | CAPP |
| | | SFC | | | |
| | | CE | | | |
| | | CAPP | | | |
| | | CAQC | | | |

optimized production technology (OPT), sequencing scheduling (S-Sched) and distribution requirements planning (DRP). Finally dependability is aligned with CAD, MTO/MTS, CPOF/OPT/ROP/SEQ/SCHED/ALB/QP/QFD/DRP and resource profiles (RP).

Among strategic targets, flexibility has the highest priority and as already mentioned has the highest importance for alignment with external (environmental) and internal (business structure) variabilities. That importance is higher in the case of discrete production systems because of the complexity of the production process. In Table 5, flexibility and IT applications alignment with variability is presented (Theodorou, 1996a).

It should be mentioned that those technologies are not panacea and they cannot solve problems on their own; in the opposite, problems arise from their adoption. They only support people and organizations structured with flexibility that can take just-in-time action. Thus, only if this technology is aligned with people can it be put to work; otherwise, the utilization of the systems can be very poor with no effect on efficiency. In most studies about MRP II researchers recognize that the impact of IT on performance increases as the level of utilization increases. Those levels of utilization are nothing else than the levels of alignment among IT and business structure. If operational alignment has been achieved, then greater strategic benefits can be attained. The movement among domains in the model of Luftman (1996) explains that alignment according to the service level creates operational benefits and alignment according to competitive potential creates competitive advantage.

# STRUCTURE AND IT ALIGNMENT

The theme of fit and alignment is central to any contingency model developed by organization theorists. Structure should be aligned with environment, taking advantage of IT capabilities. The plan is to shape a structure that is flexible enough in order to respond quickly to environmental threats and opportunities. Flexibility enables structure to interface with environmental uncertainty while taking advantage of IT potential.

Venkatraman's (1989) statistical conceptualization "opened" the field of empirical research in testing strategic alignment, introducing the concepts of moderation, mediation, matching, covariation, profile deviation and gestalt. Ivary (1992) refers that the mediation perspective dominates in research but omits the criterion of performance. Fiedler, Grover and Teng (1996) attempted a taxonomy of IT in relation to structure without a performance criterion. Brown and Magill (1994) refer to the gestalts approach for the identification of the form of centralization. Furthermore, Bergeron, Raymond and Rivard (2001) found that moderation and matching perspective confirm the performance implications for the structure↔IT pair under the strategic IT management approach.

Generally, it can be seen that the prevailing concepts in structure-IT fit are the matching, mediation and moderation perspectives. Those concepts, according to Raymond, Pare and Bergeron (1995), can be presented as follows:

Matching: ((structure↔IT)→Performance)

Mediation: (IT→structure→Performance)

Moderation: (IT→(structure→Performance))

Theodorou (1997), based on a performance criterion and using structural variable analysis, determined IT-structure fit using the moderate perspective for certain contingencies and concluded that the matching approach confirms that high performing organizational subunits matched a decentralized and differentiated structure with nonroutine (flexible) technology. Once the firm makes strategic choices on IT, matching structures must be defined if the resulting performance is to be high (Raymond et al., 1995). If structure is to be defined in a more detailed mode, then the main structural variables and parameters should be determined. Organisation theory and design define structure using structural dimensions and structural variables. The following structural dimensions were determined by Pugh, Hickson, Hinings and Turner (1968): degree of standardisation, degree of routines, formalisation of procedures, specialisation of roles, stipulation of behaviour, concentration of authority and line control of workflow. Pugh et al. used these dimensions for empirical, classification purposes and derived seven structural forms. Generally, it can be observed that the exact form and number of the structural dimensions are not universally accepted (Sanchez, 1993; Rich, 1992). Thus, some researchers adopted a more generic definition of structural dimensions and progress in a more detailed level as they define structural variables. The definition of Blackburn and Cummings (1982) is based on this generic concept. They define structure by the following three core structural dimensions: complexity, formalisation and centralisation (Robbins, 1990). Hage (1965) early made that distinction and referred that those structural characteristics can vary in their presence from high to low, thus, proposing a qualitative construction for the measurement of those core dimensions. Furthermore, Burton and Obel (1995) add to the previous list the following three dimensions: configuration, coordination and control. A different viewing angle is proposed from the organisational information processing theory; communication, coordination and cooperation are the essential structural dimensions (Stock & Tatikonda, 2000). Edmondson and Moingeon (1990) and Moingeon, Ramanantsoa, Metails and Orton

(1998) referred organisational learning as another important determinant of organisation structure. Organisational learning determines how a firm develops its capabilities and competencies over time (Eden & Spender, 1998). Miller (1987) underlined the new capabilities which the role of information technology brings over the previously mentioned dimensions. Furthermore, Miller as well as Raymond et al. (1995) underlined the importance of structural sophistication due to information technology applications.

Structural variables determine the general parameters of structural design. The research of Blackburn and Cummings (1982), Reimann (1974), Mintzberg and Quinn (1996), Parthasarthy and Sethi (1992), and Theodorou (1997, 2000) defines general sets of structural variables. The alignment of those variables with IT capabilities has a direct effect on performance and the structural effectiveness. According to the previous discussion, a general set of structural parameters that fulfil the analytical purposes of this study are the following: formalisation, complexity, centralisation, coordination-cooperation, control and reward system. The structural parameters help to determine the form of structure in order further to detect IT-structure alignment. The structural form that better fits to specific IT sophistication is determined using a performance criterion. Structural parameters interrelated and the effect of IT on each of them cannot be detected univocally. The effect of IT on centralization needs to be examined moderating formalization. IT can have a positive effect on centralization when formalization is kept at low levels. Moreover, if conclusions are to be drawn, other contingent variables have to be detected like size, environment, strategy, etc.; but for simplicity, IT alignment will be detected ceteris paribus. Ceteris paribus, a positive effect of IT on the complexity parameter can be detected. The main characteristics of IT, the reprogramming capability and the capacity to adapt according to circumstances, raise the importance of the sophistication of those systems referred by Miller (1987) and Raymond et al. (1995). Sophistication generates the need for the flexible specialized employee that is capable of having wider tasks and doing wider part of work, without the need of supervision. Thus, complexity increases parallel to IT sophistication when the span of control narrows and vertical differentiation increases. Self-managing teams and empowerment were the key words for restructuring and business process reengineering. As Morton (1995) denotes, "production and coordination are two of the key activities of an organization … and since these are affected in a major way by information technology it is obvious to rethink how best to put the organization together." Regarding the formalization parameter, a positive effect may exist as well. Formalization relates to the presence of rules manuals and job descriptions that are not compatible with flexible specialized employees. Control mechanisms rely on cooperation and flexible quality standards. Low formalization is an efficient coordination device when the firm operates under uncertainty and production is not based on standard procedures. Coordination is relied on cooperation among flexible specialized employees who have to be in contact without formalized procedures. Thus, ceteris paribus, IT has a negative effect on formalization. Centralization in the same logic is positively affected by information technology. Low centralization increases performance (Gonvidarajan, 1986). Cooperation is the main control device that accomplishes coordination in flexible specialized employee. Flexible specialization permits employees to give solutions immediately to the problems that arise, and decentralization is a prerequisite in order to act. As cooperation substitutes for direct control, decentralization of authority increases. Structure and IT fit may increase efficiency and performance. The more the firm's operation is based on IT, the higher the effect of fit on efficiency. Moreover, a given level of information processing requirements should be matched to a given level of information processing capacity in order to achieve effective task outcome (Stock & Tatikonda 2000).

What can be derived from the discussion above is that structure is aligned with IT when it is decentralized, with low formalization and flexible specialized employees. Of course certain contingencies regarding the uncertainty of the environment as well as the size of the enterprise play an important role but do not change the conclusions regarding the structural parameters. Moreover nowadays, nearly most of the enterprises act under an uncertain environment that requires flexibility. Even the most rigid organizations like the army need a more organic and flexible structure. Regarding the contingency of the size, under the unbundling and downsizing perspective, the "small" tends to be a common target.

IT and structure fit can be achieved under the concurrent engineering perspective. According to that approach, functional integration and interdepartmental cooperation (structural variables that determine certain parameters and structural form) are prerequisites for increased performance that is generated by structure alignment with advanced CAD/CAM applications. The model of matrix structure emerged with no rigid and divisional forms. Galbraith (1994) discussed about the trade-offs among functional divisional and matrix structure. Quinn (1992) refers to the following new forms: starbust, cluster, networked, and internal market form and concludes that most organizations have to learn living with change, indicating that structure should be adaptive and aligned with environment and IT. The subject of interest is the flexible, organic form or learning organization, with system thinking, personal mastery, mentality, shared vision and team learning (Morton, 1995). That type of organization is capable for alignment and fits to environmental variability taking advantage of IT potential. Mintzberg and Quinn (1996) refer to the entrepreneurial, simple, mature, diversified, professional, innovative organizational forms and ad-hocracy. The empirical research of Drago (1998) proved that the previous structural forms are more common than hybrid structures and that the simple structured firm seems to be the best performing. Furthermore, Drago (1999) studied empirically the effect of organisational domains on complexity/simplicity and has found that the effect is contingent on the dimensions of the domain. Thus, product diversification was found to lead to greater strategic simplicity and greater performance when firms are nondiverse. Core and distinctive competences have to be examined carefully in order not to lead to oversimplification.

Finally, the size of the firm plays an important role as well. The small and lean enterprise with an organic structure is more flexible that the large one. That is why outsourcing became of primary importance for large organizations. Moreover, the culture of the organization is also an important contingency for IT and structure alignment. Fit needs increased flexibility and dependability as JIT response to market fluctuations is a strategic matter.

# STRATEGY, STRUCTURE AND IT ALIGNMENT

In the mass production model,[1] the enterprise set cost as its primary priority (Theodorou, 1996b). Companies targeted high profitability and efficiency. Thus, price competition becomes the primary objective. In contrast, innovation and quality priorities due to the structure of mass production have a positive impact on cost and finally increase the product's price; because of this trade-off, those manufacturing priorities were overlooked (Hayes & Wheelwright, 1979a, 1979b). Nowadays the mass production model proved highly inefficient especially under a dynamic environment (where high demand diversification is present) and the mass customization model seems to be his successful descendant. In this model the belief of cost and quality trade-off is bypassed. One of the reasons why the mass production model became obsolete was its inflexible character (Theodorou, 1996b; Kenney & Florida, 1993). Moreover, high inventory for the sake of security resulted in excess capacity and rigidity and increased the defectiveness in production. Nowadays, the diversification in demand forced enterprises to increase the range of production. Models are produced in high variability but in fewer quantities. The need for variability increases the need for production flexibility. In this environment, competitive advantage increases as the ability of production to accomplish the needs of diversified market niches increases. Thus, market-focused production and mass customization is established as a standard model with high functional integration among production and marketing departments. Just-in-time production drastically decreases inventory levels. In this model IT proved to be a basic ingredient of structure for the attainment of flexibility and dependability in order to overcome the variability of internal and external environments. In Table 6, alignment is presented among environment variability, production functions and IT applications.

Furthermore, Victor et al. (in Luftman, 1996) resume previously mentioned business models in Figure 5.

*Table 6: Environment variability, production functions and IT applications*

| | VARIABILITIES | | | | | |
|---|---|---|---|---|---|---|
| | DEMAND | SUPPLY | PROCESS | PRODUCT | WORKFORCE | EQUIPMENT |
| | CAD | MRP I,II | FMS | CAD | ROBOTS | OPT |
| | CAE, FEA | JIT | NC/CNC | GT | FMS | FMS |
| | EDI | EDI | AGVs | EDI | AGVs | SFC |
| IT | EPOS | AS/RS | OPT | CAE | AR/RS | NC/CNC |
| | CE | CAQC | GT | CE | NC/CNC/DNC | CAPP |
| | | | SFC | | | |
| | | | CE | | | |
| | | | CAPP | | | |
| | | | CAQC | | | |

*Figure 5: Business model*

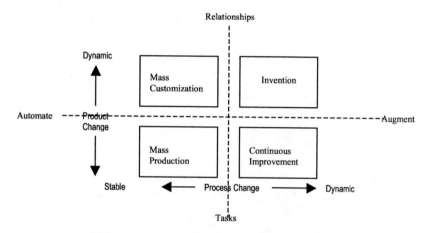

From Figure 5, it can be understood that IT alignment can be achieved in relation to the effect of IT on deskilling and formalizing employees' tasks and relationships. In mass production, hard automation and centralisation do not permit cross-boundary communication. Infrastructure is centred on the concepts of stability and control. Cost becomes the primary objective and alignment is achieved by hard automation, which leads to deskilling workers and standardizing processes. In the invention model, organic structure permits alignment with dynamic environment with frequent variations. IT has to be reprogrammed according to the needs, and flexibility becomes the primary objective. Collaboration among employees helps to bypass uncertainty. In the continuous improvement model, IT alignment is achieved by augmenting tasks and enhancing people's knowledge and skills. Information can be shared horizontally across the functions of the organization. IT is aligned with product and quality teams for most enterprise functions. In the model of network or mass customisation, IT also automates the relationships between modular processes in order to help the creation of virtual teams according to needs and augments knowledge and skills.

Generally the organization's structure should be aligned with environment. The more the environment is dynamic, the more the organization is tending to be organic. A stable environment leads to a cost-based strategy that dictates hard automation with a formalized and stable production process. Under that environment, the strategic target of an IT system is to reduce cost and centralize information as decision making is concentrated on the upper levels of the organization. The opposite effects are found in a firm that operates in an unstable and uncertain environment. Flexibility is the most appropriate strategic target as well as quality and dependability. IT, in order to be aligned, should permit flexibility of operation, diffusing information in all levels of the organization according to needs. Decentralized systems and client-server architecture are aligned with such an environment. Further competitive advantage can be gained with wide area applications that affect the whole industry. In such an environment where change is frequent, the importance of alignment is much greater, as realignment is required in order to achieve sustainability of advantage.

# ENDNOTE

1 Further details on production models are given in Kenney and Florida (1993).

# REFERENCES

Adam, E.E. & Swamidass, P.M. (1989). Assessing operations management from a strategic perspective, *Journal of Management, 15*(2), pp. 181-203.

Adam, E.E. (1994). Alternate quality improvement practices and organization performance, *Journal of Operations Management, 12*, pp. 27-44.

Bergeron, F., Raymond, L. & Rivard, S. (2001). Fit in strategic information technology management research: An empirical comparison of perspectives. *Omega, 29*, 125.

Blackburn, R. & Cummings, L. (1982). Cognitions of work unit structure. *Academy of Management Journal*, December, 836.

Brancheau, J. C., Janz, B. D. & Wetherbe, J. C. (1994). Key issues in information systems management. *MIS Quarterly*, March, 59-84.

Brown, C. V. & Magill, S. L. (1994). Alignment of the IS function with the enterprise: Toward a model of antecedents. *MIS Quarterly, 18*(4), 371-403.

Buffa, E. S. (1984). *Meeting the Competitive Challenge: Manufacturing Strategy for U.S. Companies.* Homewood, IL: Dow Jones-Irwin.

Burton, R. & Obel, B. (1995). *Strategic Organizational Diagnosis and Design.* Kluwer Academic.

Chase, R.B., Kumar, K.R. & Youngdahl, W.E. (1992). Service based manufacturing: the service factory, *Production and Operations Management, 1*(2), pp. 175-84.

Cooper R.B. & Zmud R.W. (1990). Information Technology Implementation Research: A Technological Diffusion approach, *Management Science, February*, pp. 123-139

De Meyer, A. (1998). Manufacturing Operations in Europe: Where Do We Go Next, *European Management Journal, 16*(3), pp.262-271.

De Meyer, A., Nakane, J., Miller, J.G. & Ferdows, K. (1989). Flexibility: The next competitive battle - The manufacturing futures survey, *Strategic Management Journal, 10*, pp. 135-144.

Drago, W. A. (1998). Mitzberg's Pentagon and organizational positioning. *Management Research News, 21*(4/5), 30.

Drago, W. A. (1999). Simplicity/Complexity as a Dimension of Strategic Focus: Effect on Performance in Different Organisational Domains, *22*(7), 12.

Eden, C. & Spender, C. (1998). *Managerial and Organizational Cognition.* Thousand Oaks, CA: Sage.

Edmondson, A. & Moingeon, B. (1990). *When to Learn How and When to Learn Why: Appropriate Organizational Learning Processes as a Source of Competitive Advantage.* Thousand Oaks, CA: Sage.

Ferdows, K. & De Meyer, A. (1990). Lasting improvements in manufacturing performance: in search of a new theory, *Journal of Operations Management, 9*(2), pp. 168-84.

Ferdows, K., Miller, J.G., Nakane, J. & Vollmann, T.E. (1986). Evolving global manufacturing strategies: projections into the 1990s, *International Journal of Operations & Production Management, 6*(4), pp.6-16.

Fiedler, K. D., Grover, V. & Teng, J. T. C. (1996). An empirically derived taxonomy of information technology structure and its relationship to organizational structure. *Journal of Management of Information Systems, 13*(1), 9-34.

Flynn, B.B., Schroeder, R.G. & Sakakibar, S. (1994). A framework for quality management research and associated measurement instrument, *Journal of Operations Management, 11*, pp. 339-66.

Galbraith, J.R. (1994). *Competing with Flexible and Lateral Organizations,* Addison-Wesley.

Gelders, L., Mannaerts, P. & Maes, J. (1994). Manufacturing strategy, performance indicators and improvement programmes, *International Journal of Production Research, 32*(4), pp. 797-805.

Giffi, C., Roth, A.V., & Seal G. (1990). *Competing in World Class Manufacturing: America's 21st Century Challenge.* Homewood, IL: Business One Irwin.

Gonvidarajan. (1986). Decentralization strategy and effectiveness of SBU in multi-business organizations. *Academy of Management Review, 11*(4), 844.

Groover, M. P. (1987). *Automation, Production Systems, and Computer Integrated Manufacturing.* Englewood Cliffs, NJ: Prentice Hall.

Groover, M.P. & Zimmers, E.W. (1984). *CAD/CAM: Computer-Aided Design and Manufacturing.* Englewood Cliffs, NJ: Prentice Hall.

Hage, J. (1965). An axiomatic theory of organizations. *Administrative Science Quarterly,* December.

Hall, R.W. (1987). *Attaining Manufacturing Excellence.* Homewood, IL: Dow Jones-Irwin.

Hall, R.W. & Nakane, J. (1990). *Flexibility: Manufacturing Battlefield of the '90s: Attaining Manufacturing Flexibility in Japan and the United States,* Wheeling, IL: Association for Manufacturing Excellence.

Hayes, D.R. & Wheelwright S. C. (1984). *Restoring Our Competitive Edge.* New York, NY: John Wiley & Sons.

Hayes, R.H. & Clark, K. B. (1985). Exploring the sources of productivity differences at the factory level. In K. B. Clark, R. H. Hayes, & C. Lorenz (Eds), *The Uneasy Alliance: Managing the Productivity-Technology Dilemma,* Boston, MA: Harvard Business School Press.

Hayes, R. H. & Wheelwright, S.C. (1979a). Link manufacturing process and product life cycles. *Harvard Business Review, 57*(1), 133-140.

Hayes, R. H. & Wheelwright, S. C. (1979b). The dynamics of product-process life cycles. *Harvard Business Review, 57*(2), 127-136.

Hill, T. (1993). *Manufacturing Strategy, The Strategic Management of the Manufacturing Function* (2nd ed.), London, England: The Macmillan Press Ltd. London Business School.

Hirschheim, R. A. (1982). *Information Management Planning in Organizations.* (LSE Working Paper).

Horovits, J. (1984). New perspectives on strategic management. *Journal of Business Strategy*, Winter, 19-33.

Horte, S.A., Borjesson, S. & Tunalv, C. (1991). A panel study of manufacturing strategies in Sweden, *International Journal of Operations & Production Management, 11*(3), pp. 135-44.

Horte, S.A., Lindberg, P. & Tunalv, C. (1987). Conference paper: manufacturing strategies in Sweden, *International Journal of Production Research, 25*(11), pp. 1573-86.

Iivary, J. (1992). The organizational fit of information systems. *Journal of Information Systems, 2*(1), 3.

Kathuria R. & Igbaria M. (1997). Aligning IT applications with manufacturing strategy: an integrated framework. *International Journal of Operations & Production Management, 17*(6), pp. 611-629.

Kenney, M. & Florida, R. (1993). *Beyond Mass Production: The Japanese System and Its Transfer to the U.S.* Oxford, England: Oxford University Press.

Klassen, R.D. & Whybark, D.C. (1993). Barriers to the management of international operations, *Journal of Operations Management, 11*, pp. 385-96.

Luftman, J. N. (1996). *Competing in the Information Age.* Oxford.

McFarlan, F. W. (1984). Information technology changes the ways you compete. *Harvard Business Review*, May-June, 98-103.

McFarlan, F. W., McKenney, J. L. & Pyburn, P. (1983). The information archipelago–Plotting a course. *Harvard Business Review*, Jan/Feb.

Miles, R. E. & Snow, C. C. (1984). Fit, failure and the hall of fame. *California Management Review, 26*(3), 10-28.

Miller, D. (1987). Strategy making and structure: Analysis and implications of performance. *Academy of Management Journal, 30*(1), 7.

Miller, J.G., Meyer, A.D. & Nakane, J. (1992). *Benchmarking Global Manufacturing.* Homewood, IL: Irwin.

Mintzberg, H. & Quinn, J. B. (1996). *The Strategy Process.* Englewood Cliffs, NJ: Prentice Hall.

Moingeon, B., Ramanantsoa, B., Metails, E. & Orton, D. (1998). Another look at strategy-structure relationships. *European Management Journal 16*(3), 297.

Morton, S. M. (1991). *The Corporation of the '90's Information Technology and Organizational Transformation.* Oxford.

Morton, S. M. (1995). Emerging organizational forms: Work and organization in the 21st century. *European Management Journal, 13*(4), 339.

Nagabhushana T.S. & Shah J. (1999). Manufacturing priorities and action programmes in the changing environment. An empirical study of Indian industries, *International Journal of Operations & Production Management, 19*(4), pp. 389-398.

Nakane, J. (1986). *Manufacturing Futures Survey in Japan, A Comparative Study 1983-1986*. Tokyo: Waseda University, System Science Institute.

Nakane J. & Hall R.W. (1991). Holonic Manufacturing: Flexibility-The competitive battle in the 1990s, *Production Planning and Control, 2*, pp. 2-13.

Nakane, J., Hall, R. W. & Holonic, J. (1991). Manufacturing: Flexibility–The competitive battle in the 1990s. *Production Planning and Control, 2*, 2-13.

Neumann, S. (1994). *Strategic Information Systems, Competition Through Information Technologies*. New York: Macmillan.

Noble, M. (1997). Manufacturing Competitive Priorities and Productivity: An Empirical Study, *International Journal of Operations and Production Management, 17*(1), pp.85-99.

Parsons, G. (1983). Information Technology: A New Competitive Weapon, *Sloan Management Review*, Fall.

Parthasarthy, R. & Sethi, P. (1992). The impact of flexible automation on business strategy and organizational structure. *Academy of Management Review, 17*(1), 86-111.

Porter, M. (1979). How Competitive Forces Shape Strategy, *HBR*, Mar.-April.

Porter, M. (1980). *Competitive Strategy: Techniques for Analysing Industries and Competitors*. New York: Free Press.

Porter, M. (1985). *Competitive Advantage*. New York: Free Press.

Porter, M. (1986). *Competition in Global Industries*. Boston: Harvard Business School Press.

Porter, M. (1987). From Competitive Advantage to Corporate Strategy, *HBR*, May-June, pp.43-59.

Pugh, D., Hickson, D., Hinings, C. & Turner, C. (1968). Dimensions of organizations structure. *Administrative Science Quarterly*, June, 7.

Quinn, J.B. (1992). *Intelligent Enterprise: A Knowledge and Service Paradigm for Industry*. New York: John Wiley & Sons.

Raymond, L., Pare, G. & Bergeron, F. (1995). Matching information technology and organizational structure: An empirical study with implications for performance. *European Journal of Information Systems, 4*(3).

Reich, B. H. and Benbasat I. (1999). Factors that influence the social dimension of alignment between business and information technology objectives. *MIS Quarterly*.

Reimann, B. C. (1974). Dimensions of structure in effective organizations: Some empirical evidence. *Academy of Management Journal*, December, 693-708.

Reitspergen, W.D. & Daniel, S.J. (1990). Dynamic manufacturing: a comparision of attitudes in the USA and Japan, *Management International Review, 30*(3), pp. 203-16.

Rich, P. (1992). The organizational taxonomy: Definition and design. *Academy of Management Review, 17*, 758.

Robbins, S. (1990). *Organization Theory: Structure Designs and Applications.* Englewood Cliffs, NJ: Prentice Hall.

Rodgers, L. (1997). Alignment revisited. *CIO Magazine*, May 15.

Sanchez, J.C. (1993). The long and thorny way to an organizational taxonomy. *Organizational Studies, 14*, 73.

Sayer, A. (1986). New developments in manufacturing: The just-in-time system. *Capital and Class, 28*, Spring.

Schmenner, R.W. & Rho, B.H. (1990). An international comparison of factory productivity, *International Journal of Operations & Production Management, 10*(4), pp. 16-31.

Schmenner, R.W. (1988). Behind labor productivity gains in the factory, *Journal of Manufacturing & Operations Management, 1*(4), pp. 323-38.

Schmenner, R.W. (1991). International factory productivity gains, *Journal of Operations Management, 10*(2), pp. 229-54.

Skinner, W. (1969). Manufacturing: Missing Link in Corporate Strategy, *HBR*, May-June, pp 136-145.

Skinner, W. (1974). The focused factory, *HBR, 52*(3), pp. 113-21.

Skinner, W. (1985). *Manufacturing: the Formidable Competitive Weapon.* New York: Wiley.

Skinner, W. (1996). Manufacturing strategy on the 'S' curve, *Production and Operations Management Journal, 5*(1), pp. 3-13.

Stock, G. N. and Tatikonda, M.V. (2000). A typology of project level technology transfer processes. *Journal of Operations Management, 18*, 719-723.

Swamidass, P.M. & Newell, W.T. (1987). Manufacturing Strategy, Environmental Uncertainty and Performance: A Path Analytic Model, *Management Science, 33*(4), April, pp. 509-522.

Swink M. & Way, M.H. (1995). Manufacturing Strategy: Propositions, Current Research, Renewed Directions, *International Journal of Operations & Production Management, 15*(7), pp. 4-26.

Theodorou, P. (1996a). Flexible manufacturing and the IT applications: The manufacturing strategies map. *2nd ALPS Euroconference*. Bologna.

Theodorou, P. (1996b). The restructuring of production in SME: The strategy of manufacturing flexibility. In I. Siskos, K. Zoupouidis and K. Pappis (Eds.), *The Management of SME*. University Publications of Kreta.

Theodorou, P. (1997). *Restructuring, structure strategy and information technology alignment.* Unpublished doctoral dissertation, University of Macedonia, Thessaloniki, Greece.

Theodorou, P. (2000). Structural design fit in garment production: A neural network approach. *Proceedings of the 2nd European Conference on Intelligent Management Systems in Operations*. Operational Research Society University of Salford 3-4 July.

Vastag, G. & Whybark, D.C. (1994). American and European manufacturing practices: an analytical framework and comparisions, *Journal of Operations Management, 12*, pp. 1-11.

Venkatraman, N. (1989). The concept of fit in strategy research: Toward verbal and statistical correspondence. *Academy of Management Review, 14*(3), 423.

Vlahopoulou, M., Manthou, V. and Theodorou, P. (1996). The implementation and use of material requirements planning system in Northern Greece: A case study. *International Journal of Production Economics, 45*(1-3), August, 187-193.

Ward, J. M. (1988). Information systems and technology: Applications portfolio management–An assessment of matrix-based analysis. *Journal of Information Systems, 3*(3), December.

Ward, J. P. (1987). Integrating information systems into business strategies. *Long Range Planning, 20*(3), 19.

Ward, J. P., Griffiths, P. and Whitmore, P. (1994). *Strategic Planning for Information Systems*. New York: John Wiley & Sons.

Ward, P.T., Duray, R., Leong, G.K. & Sum, C.C. (1995). Business environment, operations strategy, and performance: an empirical study of Singapore manufacturers, *Journal of Operations Management, 13*, pp. 99-115.

Wheelwright, S.C. (1984). Manufacturing strategy: defining the missing link, *Strategic Management Journal, 5*, pp. 77-91.

Wheelwright, S. C. (1987). Reflecting corporate strategy in manufacturing decisions. *Business Horizons*, February, 57-66.

Wiseman, C. (1998). *Strategic Information Systems*. Homewood, IL: Irwin.

# Section II

# IT-Based Organizational Design and Behavior

Chapter V

# Managerial Responsibility and IT: How Does the Use of Information Technology Change the Way Managers Have to Think and Realize Responsibility?

Bernd Carsten Stahl
University College Dublin, Ireland

## ABSTRACT

*The purpose of this paper is to analyse the relationship between management, responsibility and information technology. It is shown that there are structural similarities between the three terms that facilitate addressing normative issues in the management of IT through the use of the concept of responsibility. That means that responsibility seems to be a perfect choice for dealing with ethical, moral, and legal problems arising from IT. However, there is also another aspect, the fact that the use of IT can pose a threat to managerial responsibility ascriptions. The paper aims at clarifying the nature of these threats and opportunities. The knowledge about them should help managers maximise their chances of successfully discharging their responsibilities in IT.*

# INTRODUCTION

Responsibility is probably one of the most important and defining notions for managerial work. Every manager is responsible for his or her company, department, etc. More specifically, she has responsibility for the quality of the product or service. The responsibility also extends to employees, customers, and the general public. Furthermore, most managers would probably say that they feel responsibility for their personal lives, their families and a general responsibility as a member of society and a citizen of their state.

This short list shows that responsibility is a many-facetted notion containing numerous roots and meanings. The different sorts of responsibility have always been prone to conflicts and are an old source of moral and legal problems. Nowadays the use of computers and information technology has added a whole new order of magnitude to the potential for responsibility but also to its possible problems. The purpose of this article is therefore to investigate how the use of information technology influences the manger's capacity to assume responsibility. Not surprisingly we will come to the conclusion that the increasing use of IT opens new avenues for responsibility but at the same time poses new threats. Threats and opportunities, however, are not equally distributed. Opportunities are often clearly visible and frequently talked about. IT is a tool that allows greater measures of control and of knowledge about the organisation. Managers can respond better and quicker, which facilitates the discharge of responsibility. The threats, on the other hand, are frequently hidden in conditions and assumptions of IT that seem so natural to us that they are rarely discussed. Management has to take these threats seriously because they can endanger the legitimacy of the use of IT and in some case even the legitimacy of management. In this paper we will demonstrate that IT promises to facilitate management work. Good management, however, that looks at more than just the immediate financial bottom line will in many cases become harder to achieve than it used to be.

In order to give this demonstration, the paper will address several points. In a first step we will show that management and the notion of responsibility are closely related on several levels. In the following section, we will introduce information technology and its impact on management on the one hand and responsibility on the other hand. In a last section we will discuss the feedback between the three terms and take a look at the pros and cons of managerial responsibility as they result from IT.

# MANAGEMENT AND RESPONSIBILITY

In this section we will give a brief overview of the notion of responsibility, followed by a definition of management. We will demonstrate that management should pay attention to ethical matters and continue to show that management and responsibility are closely related for several reasons.

## Responsibility

Even though most managers would probably say that they know their responsibilities and that they have no problem seeing what exactly the term means in their day-to-day work, the notion is anything but clear. The term originally stems from the judicial realm, where it stands for the answer that the accused has to give to the judge. This points to the etymology of the word, the answer, which can be found in several languages such as the English *respons[(e)ibility]*, the French *respons[(e)abilité]* or the German (Ver)*Antwort*(ung) (cf., French, 1979, p. 210; Etchegoyen, 1993, p. 45; Lenk, 1991, p. 64). This stem of the notion pointing towards the "answer" is one important clue leading us to possible meanings.

Apart from the purely formal property of aiming at an answer, responsibility has several other possible meanings. It can stand for causality as in "the storm is responsible for the damage" (cf., Johnson, 2001, p. 174). In most cases, however, the use of the term wants to convey something more than just causality. It is generally used to ascribe something to somebody, which brings us to the dimension of responsibility. These are the subject (who is responsible?), the object (what is the subject responsible for?) or the instance (who does the subject have to answer to?) (cf., Bayertz, 1995, p. 15f; Höffe, 1995, p. 23; van Luijk, 1990, p. 41). Responsibility has the purpose of ascribing the object of responsibility to the subject.

This in turn refers to the communicative structure of responsibility. The ascription of responsibility can have several meanings. It can stand for the construction of a causal relationship as mentioned before. Related to this but different is the meaning of responsibility at which we take a closer look here, the ascription of moral judgements to someone or something on account of the results of their action. This process of ascription can in turn be realised in different ways. It can be done reflexively as in "I take full responsibility for the actions of the company" or transitively as in "you are responsible for the actions of the company." There are also two different temporal aspects, which have to be taken into account. Responsibility can be attributed *ex post* for facts, actions, or deeds that lie in the past or *ex ante* for facts that are still to come. One last distinction that needs to be mentioned is the fact that there are different sorts of responsibility apart from causality. There are legal responsibility, moral, task responsibility and a whole host of others. For the purposes of this article we will concentrate on the moral aspect of responsibility, which is the most comprehensive type since it comprises at least some aspects of all the other types.

The last detail of a theory of responsibility that needs to be discussed here is its objectives. When we ascribe responsibility to someone or something this can be motivated by several different ideas. In a classical, Old Testament sort of viewing things, responsibility can be seen as a means for retribution or revenge. This may in many cases still be the prime motivation but few of us would admit to it, and especially in management contexts it does not seem to be relevant. Apart from a theory of responsibility as a sentiment (Wallace, 1996) its most generally agreed-upon objective is the ascription of consequences with the express purpose of producing sanctions. These sanctions can be positive or negative in character but in most discussions the emphasis is put on the negative ones, on punishment. Sanctions can be moral, such as blame, or legal, such as prison sentences. Why do we sanction or punish? Again, there might be the motivation of revenge or retribution. More generally accepted today, however, is the idea that sanctions are a means for the production of some sort of social good. In a classical utilitarian view, punishment is meant to deter rational potential perpetrators from committing negative acts by offering them an incentive to refrain from committing them. This is what is usually referred to as the "economy of threats." If the expected value of a deed is negative, and the actor is able to recognise that, then sanctions and thus responsibility fulfil their purpose (cf., Hart, 1968, p. 40; Wallace, 1996, p. 54; De George, 1999, p. 64).

The idea of sanctions as an incentive for intended behaviour is certainly compatible with management's responsibilities. In economic contexts, however, the negative side is less important than the positive side. Managers are supposed to fulfil their roles and if they fail to do so they may be subject to punishment, blame, loss of reputation, etc. More importantly, there are many incentives in management that lead to positive performance. Among them are high remuneration, respect, reputation, power, etc. The distribution of these positive and negative sanctions is only possible on the basis of the ascription of actions and results to individuals. Responsibility is thus a central theme of management.

While it is important to management, the term responsibility also brings with it several problems. The short enumeration of different facets of responsibility given so far demonstrates that it is a difficult notion which lends itself to misunderstanding due to its many meanings (i.e., legal, moral, role, family responsibility for the past or future, assumed or ascribed, etc.). It is therefore important to find out whether there are some characteristics that bind these different meanings together. In fact there are some such characteristics. The three that we want to mention here are the openness of the notion, its proximity to action and its consequentialist character. Openness stands for the fact that the notion of responsibility, unlike many traditional moral systems, does not prescribe clear-cut duties but that its communicative character and its property of being a social process lead to its being intrinsically open and dependent on the perception of a specific case (Kaufmann, 1995, p. 88). Proximity to action stands for the supposition that the use of the notion responsibility will lead to practical consequences. This is often seen in contrast to most traditional ethical terms, which seem to lead to philosophers' discussions but not to an improvement of life. Proximity to action is certainly not evenly distributed over all different kinds of responsibility, but it stands to reason that in some cases, notably in legal responsibility, results do follow from the ascription (cf., Goodpaster & Matthews 1982, p. 133). The sanctions that were introduced as a central objective of responsibility are the most important aspect of practical consequences. The third combining point of most ascriptions is the fact that responsibility looks at the consequences of actions as a base for their judgement. Being responsible or being held responsible always points towards the factual or expected outcomes of an action.

## Management

One can hold two possible views of managers (cf., Korte, 1999, p. 140). The first one is the managerial functions approach that describes the processes and functions in organisations such as planning, organisation, leadership, control. The other view is the managerial role approach that concentrates on the persons who fulfil management tasks and their characteristics. We will mainly concentrate on the latter approach because this is where individual morality and responsibility are to be found.[2]

There are several reasons why managers might want to act morally. The first and most common reason is probably private morality. Most of us think of ourselves as moral beings and it would require a serious amount of schizophrenia to be a moral citizen, husband, and father while being an immoral manager. The other reason that is of more interest here is that there seems to be an increasing social awareness of morality of company decisions. Managers must appear open to new developments and knowledge (Galbraith, 1998, p. 141) and business ethics is one of them. The idea that "good ethics is good business" is now widely recognised. "Ethics is a prime requisite for long-term success in whatever we are trying to accomplish" (Ferguson, 1994, p. 10). If one accepts this then it is clear that managers have to adopt the idea of morality and to act accordingly. A large part of the academic discipline of business ethics deals with the question of how managers can do that. One suggestion as to how management can take moral matters into account that has been widely discussed lately is the stakeholder approach to management. The idea is that all of the relevant stakeholders of a firm and a specific decision are included in the process of decision making (cf., Donaldson & Preston, 1995; Gibson, 2000; Hendry, 2001; Kujala, 2001, p. 236; Ulrich, 1998). This, of course, is a task for management and a rather difficult one. We will not discuss the stakeholder approach in more detail but suggest that it is a good example of managerial morality discharged by responsibility. Considering the parties that are affected means that one has to communicate with them, that one has to answer their question, thus that one is responsible. If one accepts that managers should act morally, whatever the reason, then one must ask how this can be realised. A frequent answer to this is that they should be responsible. At this point it makes sense to ask why responsibility as a moral notion might appeal to management.

## Why Managers Can Relate to Responsibility

We believe that the affinity of management to responsibility is a direct result of some structural similarities between the term responsibility and the way managers in modern corporations work. The three characteristics of responsibility as we have seen are: openness, affinity to action, and consequentialism.

All three of these points can explain the appeal of the notion to businesspeople because they point in directions that management usually feels comfortable with. The openness is certainly a defining feature of management because the very nature of managing jobs is that they cannot be confined by strict delineations but change constantly with changes in markets, the firm, organisations, competition, etc. An affinity for action is another point that would strike most managers as sympathetic since activity is seen as one of the hallmarks of good and successful management. In order to survive in today's business environment a business not only has to have the openness to react to new and unexpected challenges but it also has to take the initiative and initiate change in the direction it wants. Also, the consequentialist orientation appeals to management, which is demonstrated by the fact that managers often point out that in the end only the bottom line counts. In the world of commerce, results tend to be of more importance than intentions, and this may be one of the reasons why a similar course would appeal to managers in the field of ethics. Responsibility as a social construction based on communication is furthermore a figure of thought that mirrors the daily work experience of managers of most levels. Modern management is an activity that consists mainly of communication with superiors, employees, colleagues, customers, competition, the general public, etc. It is mostly based on teamwork where only the successful moderation of the team can lead to promising results.

So far we have seen why responsibility is a notion with relevance in management. It describes some of the definitions of management rather well while at the same time being a term which reflects the ancient problems of ethics and morality. It facilitates a translation of traditional thoughts into the modern world of business. But what does this have to do with information technology?

# THE IMPACT OF IT ON MANAGEMENT AND RESPONSIBILITY

Information technology (IT) is another term that is hard to define. A purely technical definition such as "all technologies whose base is digital circuits and microelectronics" (cf., Zerdick et al., 2001, p. 111) is certainly too narrow. More fitting but also more difficult to handle are definitions of the following kind:

Information technology is the tangible means by which information is manipulated and carried to its ultimate users. An information system is a collection of information and information technology—including hardware, software, people, data, and procedures—designed to deliver services intended to improve a social system. (Mason, Mason & Culnan, 1995, p. 80)

Information technology has developed to such extend in the world of business that it is in many cases hard to distinguish between the two. Computer and information systems can be found in all functional areas, on all levels of management and in businesses of all sizes. IT is an important tool used by most managers to fulfil their tasks. IT is more than just a tool. It reflects the structure and organisation of a company. On the other hand it stabilises these same structures and holds them in place (cf., Rolf, 1998, p. 46ff). IT is more than a tool of management also in the sense that its common form prejudices a certain sort of organisation. Hierarchical structures with centralised decision organisations seem to be a direct result of the improved capacities for information processing that comes with computers and IT (cf., Postman, 1992, p. 142; Weizenbaum, 1976). This leads us to a first and fundamental point concerning how the use of IT influences the discharge of managerial responsibility. The entire societal configuration that produces management in the form that we know it is only possible in a mass culture under the condition of a high capacity to process data. Since this is a very fundamental issue, however, and since the individual manager cannot do much about it we will not dwell on the point.

In fact, the individual manager, even though his social role depends on IT, may not be interested in it at all. "Many managers are technologically inept or averse (McLeod & Jones, 1986), feel incapable of understanding — let alone managing — IT, and in a great many instances this is by choice: they run the business while the IT organisation provides them with IT solutions" (Ward & Peppard, 1996, p. 38f). On a macro level IT is a stabilising factor; on the meso level of the company and on the micro level of the individual it has been more of a revolutionising factor. While management uses IT for the solution of all kinds of problems concerning command, control, communication, or information, this same use of IT leads to new problems. With the advent of the Internet IT has even led to the development of completely new business models, which result in new problems and opportunities from the point of view of responsibility.

This brings us back to the core of the question concerning the relationship of managerial responsibility and information technology. The analysis of this relationship will start with the characteristics of responsibility and show how and where IT changes the way it can be assumed by managers. From there onwards we will concentrate on factors that affect managers and that managers as individuals and as representatives of their organisations have to pay attention to. It is not surprising that the increasing use of IT has advantages as well as disadvantages for the discharge of managerial responsibilities. Since we believe that the advantages are more obvious and the disadvantages pose the more serious problems for managers, we will continue with a discussion of the positive sides.

## Advantages of IT for Managerial Responsibilities

One of the most obvious and least controversial pros of IT for managerial responsibility is their structural similarity. Both are based on communication and can be understood to have as their aim the advancement of connections between people. Both, too, are means rather than ends. Neither IT nor responsibility nor management in general are ends in themselves. All of them need a certain kind of environment in order to be understandable and useful.

This leads us to the feature of openness. It is obvious that this characteristic is as important for IT as it is for responsibility. Information technology is in most cases designed to be open to as many different application as possible while limiting as few options as necessary. The distinction between hardware and software gives us a picture of how we can envisage openness of use for otherwise predetermined pieces of machinery. While the hardware does not change, the software makes an infinite number of uses possible. The property that links management and responsibility, the fact that they are by definition flexible and can change with the situation, is thus also true for information technology.

The proximity to action is another point in case that is as true for IT as for responsibility. IT can be seen as a tool that has no relevant theoretical side for most business users but is mostly needed for its practical applications.[3] The intrinsically practical nature of IT as well as management and responsibility leads to another feature that all of them share, to their consequentialism. Consequences are the basis for the attribution of responsibility. Information technology can help in this respect by making results clearer, by recording facts and by giving better prognosis of future results.

Summarily, for the positive points, it can be said that IT has several structural similarities to responsibility which make it seem likely that the two concepts can positively enhance one another. From the point of view of managerial responsibility one can state that it can greatly profit from the use of IT. Increased possibilities for communication, publication, discovery and establishment of facts can help the process of ascription or assumption of responsibility. This is true for classical problems of responsibility as well as for genuinely new problems as they are produced by the use of IT. In fact it is certainly not exaggerated to say that IT is by now an indispensable tool for the discharge of managerial responsibility.

## Threats to Managerial Responsibility Caused by IT

There is, however, another side to the relationship of responsibility and IT. Computers and information systems increasingly do work that humans used to do. The more sophisticated this work, the higher the level of computer involvement is and the greater the dangers for responsibility. When a computer makes a decision we have to ask who is responsible for this decision. There are examples of fatal decisions by computers and others can easily be imagined in the realms of air transportation, military but also everyday business. Is the producer of the software, the hardware or the user responsible? In many cases the potential object of responsibility seems to be the result of systemic action. That means that there is no discernible subject in the classical sense and the ascription of results to a person or another suitable entity appears impossible. This leads to the question of whether or not computers can be subjects of responsibility. For most applications relevant to businesses the answer is probably no, due to the fact that computers are not moral subjects. They have neither self-consciousness nor conscience nor emotions nor intelligence in the human sense. However, the ascription of responsibilities to computers could be a tool to achieve desirable societal ends. From this point of view it would not be a good idea to rule it out completely. If we accept responsibility by computers then this will lead to new responsibilities for those who produce and use them.

Even if circumstances arise under which we deem it appropriate to assign responsibility to computer systems, there will remain an important responsibility humans will need to bear. They will bear responsibility for preparing these systems to take responsibility. In this endeavor their responsibility will be comparable to that of parents and educators who must prepare those under theft tutelage to take responsibility. Hence, attributing responsibility to a computer will not relieve humans of all responsibility in using computers. (Bechtel, 1985, p. 297)

In this case management would face completely new responsibilities that result simply from the desire to facilitate responsibility.[4]

This leads us to the next problem, which is based on the sometimes difficult relationship between humans and computers. While information technology allows the increase in communication, which is to be judged positively from the point of view of responsibility, this communication is often lacking crucial components that are necessary for responsibility. Human communication is by its very definition ethically charged. As several branches of contemporary philosophy, especially the German discourse ethics (cf., Apel, 1988; Habermas, 1983; Habermas, 1991), have shown, all communication is based on presuppositions that can directly be translated into moral terms. If a human communicates, that means that he puts forward three claims of validity without which the communication is meaningless. The three claims are truth, normative rightness, and veracity. That means that every sentence we say is accompanied by the implication that the speaker holds it for true, for normatively right and that he is honest in saying it. These presuppositions are necessary regardless of the factual truth, rightness and veracity of the speaker. Even a lie only makes sense when we usually suppose that people speak the truth. Without going any deeper into the subject of discourse ethics, we want to state that these presuppositions run into problems as soon as we start to apply them to communication via IT. It is one of the problems of the Internet that we cannot judge the information by reference to its author. Here is also one root of problems of electronic communication which is caused by the lack of vital components of communication. Returning to the question of managerial responsibility we can state that computer communication cannot replace human communication. Especially in morally charged situations such as the ascription of responsibility it quickly runs into problems.

Additionally there are the many new objects of responsibility caused by the use of IT that management has to take into account and be constantly aware of. These are the legal and ethical challenges that arise from the use of IT. Here one can distinguish between three possible relationships between responsibility and IT. Management can be responsible for IT, because of IT, and through IT.

Being responsible for IT is something that is not qualitatively new to managers. It means that managers have to make sure that the social and technical subsystem of the organisation that we call IT works properly. In this way it is no different from any other part of managerial responsibilities with the possible difference that IT is relevant to most functional areas and levels of hierarchy. Some aspects of responsibility for IT such as defining rights of access or organisational matters come close to the second aspect, to responsibility because of IT. Here we find all the new objects of responsibility that are caused by the use of IT. The most frequently discussed among them are privacy/monitoring, intellectual property, quality of software, freedom of information, and legal issues such as fraud or other crimes. Managers who have responsibility because of IT may have to deal with some or all of these issues. The difficulty here is that technological developments change the issues and the relevant norms. The Internet, for example, gave a whole new meaning to property and its proper uses. Entire industries such as the music industry have to cope with new expectations and developments of their customers.

The last and maybe most complex aspect is that of managerial responsibility through IT. This stands for the use of IT as a medium or a tool for the discharge of responsibility. We have already mentioned that most managers nowadays use IT in some sort or another to realise their responsibility. Examples range from the use of a management information system to compile reports of sales data over the use of executive information systems for long-range planning to the use of email to inform an employee that he or she has been fired. Especially in this last aspect one can find some philosophical questions that are usually overlooked but that are in fact of high importance. We are talking about the metaphysical and anthropological implications of IT. Even without being able to go into greater detail it should be clear that IT on the one hand shapes what we perceive as real and on the other hand influences our view of the other, of humans in general and thus the way we communicate with them and we go about realising our responsibilities.[5]

# CONCLUSION

Drawing to a close, one can summarise the central thesis of this paper as follows: Managers have manifold responsibilities. These responsibilities, however, are often unclear, among other reasons, because of the ambiguities of the notion of responsibility. The clarification of this notion shows us that it is a social construction with the purpose of ascription characterised by openness, closeness to action and the emphasis on consequences. This concept is intrinsically close to management and at the same time has a great affinity to information technology. This then leads us to the topic of the book and we can state that information technology has several impacts on the manager's responsibility. In some respects the assumption or ascription of responsibility can be furthered by IT; in other respects it creates additional difficulties. Since it is imperative for a manager to live up to his or her responsibilities, it is important for him or her to think about the notion itself and its opportunities, but also about its limitations. This is all the more true for the genuinely new opportunities and problems that information technology and its use in business pose.

Managers who fail to realise this intellectual and practical challenge can easily be drawn into situations where this lack of responsible handling of responsibility can have serious personal and economic consequences. This article should be understood as one contribution to the process of building awareness of these complex problems. Essentially it is supposed to give managers a starting point from where to regard their own specific problems and applications of responsibility.

# ENDNOTES

1 This is not to say that responsibility cannot play a role in the functional view. One might even argue that the idea of responsibility can achieve more in an institutional setting. This article concentrates on the individual side firstly because it is less contentious and secondly because it is of more immediate relevance to most managers.

2 This comment is not meant to belittle the academic disciplines that research the theoretical side of IT. What we want to express is that for the average user of IT in business and especially for management these theories are of little immediate use.

3 For a more detailed discussion of the problem of computers as subjects of responsibility see Stahl (2001).

4 For more details on the anthropological implications of IT, see Stahl (2002).

# REFERENCES

Apel, K.-O. (1988). *Diskurs und Verantwortung: das Problem des Übergangs zur postkonventionellen Moral* (3rd ed.). 1997 Frankfurt a. M.: Suhrkamp.

Bayertz, K. (1995). Eine kurze Geschichte der Herkunft der Verantwortung. In K. Bayertz (Ed.), *Verantwortung: Prinzip oder Problem?* (pp. 3-71). Darmstadt: Wissenschaftliche Buchgesellschaft.

Bechtel, W. (1985). Attributing responsibility to computer systems. *Metaphilosophy*, *16*(4), 296-305.

De George, R. T. (1999). *Business Ethics* (5th ed.). Upper Saddle River, NJ: Prentice Hall.

Donaldson, T. & Preston, L. E. (1995). The stakeholder theory of the corporation: Concepts, evidence, and implications. *Academy of Management Review*, *20*(1), 65-91.

Etchegoyen, A. (1993). *Le Temps des Responsables*. Paris: Editions Julliard.

Ferguson, W. C. (1994). Building a social ethical foundation in business. In The Conference Board (Ed.), *Business Ethics: Generating Trust in the 1990s and Beyond* (pp. 9-10). New York: The Conference Board.

French, P. A. (1979). The corporation as a moral person. *American Philosophical Quarterly*, *16*(3), July, 207-215.

Galbraith, J. K. (1998). *The Affluent Society* (40th anniversary ed.). Boston: Mariner Books.

Gibson, K. (2000). The moral basis of stakeholder theory. *Journal of Business Ethics*, *26*, 245-257. Dordrecht: Kluwer.

Goodpaster, K. E. & Matthews, J. B., Jr. (1982). Can a corporation have a moral conscience? *Harvard Business Review*, Jan-Feb, 132-141.

Habermas, J. (1991). *Erläuterungen zur Diskursethik*. Frankfurt a. M.: Suhrkamp.

Habermas, J. (1983). *Moralbewußtsein und kommunikatives Handeln*. Frankfurt a. M.: Suhrkamp.

Hart, H. L. A. (1968). *Punishment and Responsibility–Essays in the Philosophy of Law*. Oxford, England: Clarendon Press.

Hendry, J. (2001). Economic contracts versus social relationships as a foundation for normative stakeholder theory. *Business Ethics: A European Review, 10*(3), 223-232. New York: Blackwell.

Höffe, O. (1995). *Moral als Preis der Moderne: ein Versuch über Wissenschaft, Technik und Umwelt* (3rd ed.). Frankfurt a. M.: Suhrkamp.

Johnson, D. G. (2001). *Computer Ethics* (3rd ed.). Upper Saddle River, NJ: Prentice Hall.

Kaufmann, F.-X. (1995). Risiko, Verantwortung und gesellschaftliche Komplexität. In K. Bayertz (Ed.), *Verantwortung: Prinzip oder Problem?* 72-97. Darmstadt: Wissenschaftliche Buchgesellschaft.

Korte, R. J. (1999). Ethische Positionen im Markt sozialer Hilfen. In P. Ulrich, A. Löhr and J. Wieland (Eds.), *Unternehmerische Freiheit, Selbstbindung und politische Mitverantwortung* (pp. 139-166). Munchen, Mering: Rainer Hampp Verlag.

Kujala, J. (2001). Analysing moral issues in stakeholder relations. *Business Ethics: A European Review, 10*(3), 233-247. New York: Blackwell.

Lenk, H. (1991). Komplexe Ebenen der Verantwortung. In M. Sänger (Ed.), *Arbeitstexte für den Unterricht: Verantwortung* (pp. 64-73). Stuttgart: Philipp Reclam jun.

Mason, R. O., Mason, F. and Culnan, M. J. (1995). *Ethics of Information Management*. Thousand Oaks, London, New Delhi: Sage.

Postman, N. (1992). *Technopoly–The Surrender of Culture to Technology*. New York: Vintage Books.

Rolf, A. (1998). *Grundlagen der Organisations- und Wirtschaftsinformatik*. Berlin et al: Springer Verlag.

Stahl, B. C. (2001). Constructing a brave new IT-world: Will the computer finally become a subject of responsibility? *Constructing IS Futures. Proceedings of the 11th BIT Conference*, October 30-31, Manchester, UK.

Stahl, B. C. (2002). Information technology, responsibility, and anthropology. *Proceedings of the Hawaii International Conference on System Sciences, HICSS-35*, January 7-10, Hawaii.

Ulrich, P. (1998). *Wofür sind Unternehmen verantwortlich?* St. Gallen: Institut für Wirtschaftsethik, Uni St. Gallen.

van Luijk, H. (1990). Les trois faces de la responsabilité. *Entreprise, la Vague éthique, Revue Projet*, (224), 40-48.

Wallace, R. J. (1996). *Responsibility and the Moral Sentiment*. Cambridge, MA: Harvard University Press.

Ward, J. and Peppard, J. (1996). Reconciling the IT/business relationship: A troubled marriage in need of guidance. *Journal of Strategic Information Systems*, (5), 37-65.

Weizenbaum, J. (1976). *Computer Power and Human Reason*. San Francisco: W. H. Freeman.

Zerdick, A. et al. (2001). *European Communication Councel Report: Die Internet-Ökonomie: Strategien für die digitale Wirtschaft* (3rd ed.). Berlin, Heidelberg: Springer.

Chapter VI

# IT-Based Project Knowledge Management

Michel J. Leseure
Al Akhawayn University, Morocco

Naomi J. Brookes
Loughborough University, UK

## ABSTRACT

*This chapter presents IT solutions supporting knowledge management initiatives within project organizations. The first section describes the background of the problem, that is the difficulty of managing knowledge in project-based organizations. The second section presents a model of knowledge management as the activity of managing compromises on a number of dimensions, and uses this model to present IT solutions for project knowledge management. The last section discusses future trends and key challenges and focuses on knowledge representation.*

## INTRODUCTION

This chapter primarily deals with project management and more especially the increasing tendency of modern organizations to use project organizations to carry out a range of vital operations or innovative activities. The use of project organizations is to be expected in industries for which this operating system is a necessity, e.g., the construction industry. The use of project management in these industries actually originated in the 1950s. However, the use of projects can now be observed across all industries, for new product development or for business performance improvement. This means that in today's economy the leverage of project performance on overall business performance keeps intensifying.

This chapter discusses project management from a knowledge management perspective. The concept of knowledge management, initially popularized by Nonaka (1991), has been quickly adopted by the business and communities at large; see Despres and Chauvel (1999) for a discussion of the rising popularity of the topic. This suggests that knowledge management is also a managerial approach which is here to stay.

The goal of this paper is to discuss IT applications, present and future, designed for *project knowledge management.* Capitalizing on existing knowledge for greater profitability is nothing novel: It has been implemented through management science since the dawn of the industrial revolution. This approach has only been possible in business sectors where operations can be highly routinized and can be improved in small steps. In the volatile and uncertain environment of project organizations, complexity has blocked such an effective management of knowledge.

# BACKGROUND

## Micro-Scale Knowledge Management

This chapter deals with the management of knowledge within and across project teams. The research approach used by the authors was to analyze the problem of project knowledge management at the operational level. In other words, this chapter does not discuss how to design a knowledge strategy and what kind of top commitment is necessary from top management. This is consistent with the school of micro knowledge management (µKM) as defined by Vergison (2000):

- *Micro-scale knowledge management* focuses on the capture, structuring and use of knowledge at a local level and does not necessarily require strong management support. It is not very sensitive to strategic plan variations.
- *Macro-scale knowledge management* is very sensitive to company strategic plans and it deals with knowledge flows within a large business entity. It definitely requires strong top management support and commitment.

As described by Vergison (2000) the micro-scale approach is based on the assumption that a top-down approach to knowledge management is rather ambitious and exposed to implementation problems. Thus, the goal of this chapter is to identify generic micro knowledge management problems faced by project teams and to describe what type of IT solutions have been or may be developed. This is not to say that any µKM problem can be solved with IT: In this chapter, many of the problems evoked can only be dealt with by using organizational design techniques. The goal of this paper is show how IT solutions can either solve some problems or facilitate the process of solving them.

## Job Context and Complexity of Managing Knowledge

Since its inception, knowledge management has already gone a long way and many models have been formulated. However most models, solutions, and techniques in knowledge management are either presented at the macro-scale level or in job contexts that are different from those encountered by project teams.

The typology of job design systems proposed by Leseure and Brookes (2000a) illustrates the criticality of the second point. Figure 1 indicates which job design theories are most appropriate when the context of knowledge usage is changing. The arrows indicate which job design practices are likely to be appropriate when one moves in a specific direction.

In this model, the technical interdependence of tasks and the environmental uncertainty of the task environment are combined to define the vertical contextual variable: the required frequency of knowledge interactions. Technical interdependency creates the background for knowledge interaction. Environmental uncertainty adds a time (frequency) dimension and controls how often these interactions need to take place.

Technical uncertainty is the second dimension of the context of micro-knowledge management. A low uncertainty describes a system that is primarily based on the reuse of routine knowledge. A high uncertainty occurs in systems where problems and products vary too broadly to be handled simply through reuse of knowledge. In high technical uncertainty environments, new knowledge needs to be created.

It is important to stress that the model in Figure 1 does not present four archetypes: Instead it presents a continuous space of systems. Hence, the horizontal axis origin reads as "0% innovation – 100% reuse" and its extreme point as "100% innovation – 0% reuse," and a system can be observed in any state within these two limits.

The point of focus in this chapter is the fourth quadrant, where the requirements of knowledge creation and collective work are merged together. The problem in this quadrant is to find how to smoothly combine the independence of the specialist and the requirement of frequent, extensive interaction.

Action theory is a relatively unknown school of job design which was originally developed by German researchers (Frese & Zapf, 1994). Work is defined as being action oriented, i.e., as being a collection of elementary activities. There are two important features of actions:

- An action encompasses a number of activities: defining a goal for the action, translating it into plans, executing these plans, and finally, receiving feedback from the action.
- Any action is subject to an individual cognitive regulation. Some actions become highly routinized (e.g., an assembly line worker's task) whilst some can never follow a rigid, identical structure (i.e., a commercial engineer's sales tactic).

The golden rule of action theory is that the active involvement of an employee is only possible if this employee is dealing with the entire action and not part of it. Second, action theory is probably less prescriptive than any other school in terms of practical recommendations. The tasks and context of executions of these tasks are

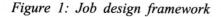
*Figure 1: Job design framework*

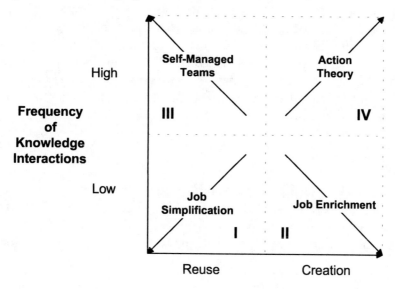

the determinant of the final job design to implement. For this reason, action theory has been coined as a *dynamic* form of job design (for more information on these schools of job design, see Leseure & Brookes, 2000a).

Newman (1999) reports that lean production (a concept that relies extensively on teamwork and that lies in Quadrant III) improves productivity at the cost of innovative capability. This confirms the opposite, diverging directions of job enrichment and self-managed teams, and the fact that the task of seeking the benefits of both types of job design systems is not trivial. This is why Quadrant IV is in management terms the most difficult of all regions. It is the environment where innovation needs to take place on a daily basis and in parallel with design reuse. Knowledge interactions need to be frequent and efficient. This chapter draws the specifications of an IT-based knowledge management system for organizations operating in Quadrant IV.

## Literature Review

A number of research studies, all from the UK, have recently targeted the improvement of project knowledge management. Gilbert and Holder (2000) take an organizational stance on the problem of project knowledge management and propose organizational consulting services to address these problems. Braiden and Hicks (2000) study the management of knowledge in the engineered-to-order industry and adopt primarily a process-oriented approach to managing project knowledge. The IKON project studies the management of knowledge in conjunction with innovation processes (Hislop, Newell, Scarbourgh & Swan, 2000). In the IKON project, the term innovation is used in its broadest possible meaning—change of practices—and the objectives are to formulate best practices in knowledge management terms when a company is innovating. Finally, the B-Hive project formulated a Cross Organizational Learning Approach system, labeled COLA. COLA consists of innovative processes supported by information systems for the review, evaluation, feedback and organizational learning linked to project work (Orange, Cushman & Burke, 1999). The COLA system will be mentioned later in this chapter as an example of an IT solution.

## Data Sources

The research and model presented in this paper are the outcomes of a multi-disciplinary research project at the University of Loughborough (UK). The data was collected through semi-structured interviews focusing on knowledge management problems and practices. Table 1 displays some general information about the interviews.

*Table 1: Data sources*

| Company | Industry | Interviewees | Size of Organizational Unit Being Discussed | Project Strategy |
|---------|----------|--------------|----------------------------------------------|------------------|
| 1 | Aerospace | Project Manager | More than 1000 | One-off |
| 2 | Aerospace | Business Development Manager | Less than 100 | Focused Innovation |
| 3 | Aerospace | Program Manager | Less than 100 | Focused Innovation |
| 4 | Aerospace | Engineering Manager | Less than 100 | Focused Innovation |
| 5 | Aerospace | Program Manager | Between 100 and 500 | One-off |
| 6 | Utilities | Project Manager | More than 1000 | One-off |
| 7 | Capital Goods | Vice President | More than 1000 | Both |
| 8 | Utilities | Director | More than 1000 | Both |
| 9 | Capital Goods | Director Chief Engineer | Less than 100 | One-off |
| 10 | Capital Goods | Director | Less than 100 | Focused Innovation |
| 11 | Construction | Division Director Foreman Project Manager Construction Planner Estimator | Between 100 and 500 | One-off |
| 12 | Service | Division Director | More than 1000 | One-off |
| 13 | R&D, Engineering | Division Director | More than 1000 | One-off |
| 14 | R&D, Engineering | Project Manager | More than 1000 | One-off |

# PROJECT KNOWLEDGE MANAGEMENT
## Knowledge Management as Managing Compromises in System Configuration

Since the goal of this paper is to present which IT solutions have been or should be developed to support project knowledge management, it is necessary to benchmark the various problems observed in the companies surveyed against a generic model of an effective knowledge management system.

The model of knowledge management as compromise management of Leseure and Brookes (2000b) will be used to this end. This model is based on the premise that what is being questioned through the recent focus on knowledge management is the notion that work groups, teams, and organizations are systematically effective at managing collective knowledge. A more realistic model of collective work is to acknowledge that there are a number of dimensions which constrain, limit, or block an effective and timely exchange of knowledge between the different members of a project team.

The following list of compromise dimensions is used:

- *Reuse/Innovation*: Is a work unit achieving a productive compromise between the reuse of knowledge and innovation? Or does it have a tendency to reinvent the wheel? Or does it have a tendency to be a poor innovator?
- *Collaboration/Competition*: Is a work unit achieving a productive compromise between collaboration and competition (1) in its internal, interpersonal and intergroup interactions and (2) in its interaction with external parties?
- *Tacit/Explicit*: Is an organization achieving a compromise between the tacit and explicit forms of knowledge that it is manipulating in the course of operations? Or does is suffer from the predominance of tacit forms of knowledge? Or a predominance of explicit forms of knowledge?
- *Informality/Formality*: Does an organization achieve a productive compromise between informality and formality? Or does procedural compliance block spontaneity in the workplace? Or does spontaneity and informality lead to chaos and anarchy?
- *Internal/External*: Does a work unit manage effectively its compromise of internal and external knowledge? Or does it tend to take unnecessary risk by reinventing or taking the responsibility for elements of knowledge that should be brought in by third parties? Or has a work unit lost its core competencies?
- *Individual/Group*: Does an organization distribute roles and responsibilities to individuals and group in a productive manner? Or does it suffer from knowledge bottlenecks attached to individuals? Or does it suffer from groups being unable to manage knowledge efficiently?
- *Private/Public*: Does an organization manage effectively the commercial sensitivity attached to knowledge? Does it suffer from an overly secretive corporate culture? Or does it suffer from diffusing its knowledge too broadly?

According to this model, a knowledge management problem can be explained by one (or several) imbalance along these dimensions.

## Reuse vs. Innovation

### Common Problems

In the course of the research interviews, most interviewees stressed that they had difficulty with reusing knowledge. To be more precise, they indicated that they had problems re-creating previously used knowledge without making new mistakes and in many cases, without making exactly the same mistakes that they did in the past. This can be analyzed as an indication of a double problem:

1.  Knowledge reuse capabilities are poor in project teams. This is not surprising if one considers that project organizations are structured for knowledge creation, i.e., to formulate solutions to new problems. As the organization of a project team targets knowledge creation capabilities, a side effect could be to naturally create a tendency to "reinvent" the wheel.

2.  Despite the advantages of being organized as a project team, knowledge creation and innovation remain delicate tasks, and without clear guidelines, project teams are likely to reproduce past mistakes.

Some of the interviewed companies declared having solved these problems by adopting a focused innovation strategy as defined by Sivaloganthan and Shahin (1999): A company merges an existing design with other independent designs to develop a common core design, which can then be built in a variety of products. With this strategy, knowledge reuse is linked to the core design and easily managed and controlled. Innovation is limited to product variations and therefore is also easier to manage. However, it should be clear that this focused innovation strategy consists in moving away from Quadrant IV, as reuse increases and innovation diminishes. By generalizing this idea, one is at risk of transforming the upper right-hand corner of Quadrant IV into a "no-man's-land" where activity is deemed impossible. Many companies, those selling engineered-to-order products and services ("one-off" projects), operate in this zone of Quadrant IV and are in crucial need of better knowledge management: Their problem is to improve innovative capabilities whilst reusing any relevant knowledge. This is illustrated in Figure 2, where a distinction is introduced between generic project knowledge and project-specific knowledge.

This section addresses how all the companies displayed in Figure 2 can improve their knowledge reuse capabilities. The issue of dealing with dealing with knowledge appropriation (a problem faced especially by Companies 2 and 4) is discussed in the *Internal vs. External* subsection.

### Improving Knowledge Reuse

Matta, Ribière, Corby, Lewkowicz and Zaclad (2000) define project memory as "lessons and experiences from given projects" or as "project definition, activities, history and results." Although the model proposed by Matta and his colleagues deals exclusively with design projects, it can be generalized to other projects. Project memory is structured in two components:

*   *Project characteristic memory*: This part of the memory includes all the information about the context, the organization and the results of the project.

*Figure 2: Relative importance of reuse and creation in Quadrant IV*

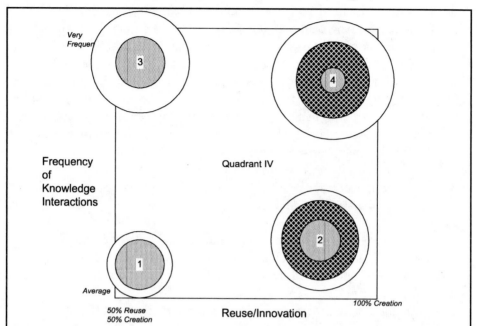

*In this graph, dealing with project-specific knowledge (outer white circles) is a knowledge appropriation task which is different than knowledge creation. At the origin of the quadrant, Company 1 deals with a limited knowledge stock composed of a reusable core (dotted inner circle) and of some project-specific knowledge which requires integration. Company 2 deals with a limited amount of project-specific knowledge but has to create of lot of knowledge linked to its technical core (black circle). Company 1 primarily reuses knowledge in its technical core whereas Company 2's technical core is about innovation. Company 3 requires a lot more project-specific knowledge than creating new core knowledge: It is a problem of appropriation rather than creation. Company 4 combines the challenges faced by Companies 2 and 3.*

For instance, one may recall what the objectives of the project were, specific instructions received, the environment in which the project took place, who was part of the project team, what was each participant's respective responsibilities, etc.

• *Project rationale memory*: Project rationale memory covers the problem solving stage, that is, a description of which methodology was used and why, a list of the actors and their roles and views about solving the problem. This may include the memory of dissenting views within the project team. This may also include the memory of alternative solutions considered but rejected and of the rationale for doing so. Finally, project rationale memory includes all decisions made, from arguments about the decision to the analysis of each pro and con about the decision.

During the research interviews, most interviewees were aware of the possibility of using knowledge intranets to "memorize" knowledge. One of the interviewed companies in particular had developed internally a state-of-the-art knowledge intranet system including a bought-in search engine. However, after a review of what this intranet system could do, it became clear that it only dealt with project characteristic memory. At best, the system could memorize a problem with simple specifications (i.e., reasons for interrupting work on a site) and who solved that problem in the past in the company. This is consistent with the technical assessment of Matta et al. (2000), who report that as project characteristics are usually described in textual documents, tools that index textual documents such as LEXTER and FX-Nomino combined with database management tools are sufficient to implement a system for project characteristic memory.

Thus, the real challenge in terms of improving reuse of knowledge is to find a tool to memorize project rationales. This is a difficult issue given the evasive and fuzzy form of project rationale knowledge. Matta et al. present a review of existing models (2000):

- The tool IBIS is a process-oriented approach to support complex problem solving by structuring a problem as "issue, positions and arguments."
- QOC is a decision-oriented approach which structures rationales as "questions, options and criteria."
- The Drama system uses goals, options, criteria and choices to build a decision table representative of a decision made.
- DCRS is a system based on three sub-models. An intent model describes the problem at stake and its context. A version model represents the different options in terms of solutions, and the argumentation model describes how the decision is made.
- DIPA is a model attempting to model cognitive processes in terms of design rationales. It structures a rationale formulation situation as a problem, facts, interpretations, abstract and actual constraints, proposition and arguments. An interesting feature of DIPA is the capability of differentiating the processes of analysis and synthesis and memorizing both.

During the research interviews, many project managers or senior managers agreed that their organization would benefit from more knowledge reuse. Although they did not have an IT system which would capture project memory, it was clear that they themselves had memorized projects' characteristics *and* rationales. Despite this fact, they were still unable to generalize knowledge reuse within their company. This means that project memory is a necessary but not a sufficient condition for knowledge reuse. The other component that is needed is a reuse management system that provides a systematic method to specify when to store, retrieve, and update project memory. Shahin, Sivaloganathan, and Gilliver (1997) provide an example of such a reuse system in the case of a design project.

Figure 3 displays the full structure of a knowledge reuse system as discussed in this section. As shown in Figure 3, one should bear in mind that a project memory model relies on two other systems: one representing the product (or service) and the second representing processes.

*Figure 3: Project knowledge reuse system*

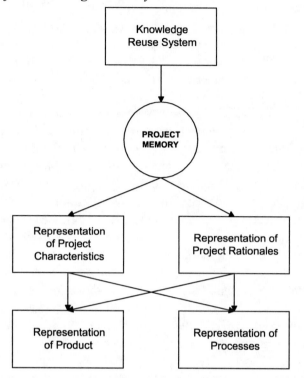

## Collaboration vs. Competition

The collaboration/competition compromise dimension is concerned with the environment of a project task. Whereas a competitive spirit can be a powerful driver of productivity, too much competition can be unproductive. The actual balance between competition and collaboration is a function of the context of the project. In the research interviews, managers all agreed that their organizations could benefit for more collaboration at several levels:

- *Across ongoing projects*: Project managers' performance is assessed on their ability to complete a project on time, within budget, and according to specifications. Project managers consider (legitimately) that time spent visiting another site to help a peer and sending another team member to another site would only endanger their own performance. This blocks any type of cross-project collaboration, and hence blocks knowledge sharing.

- *Across hierarchical levels or fields of specialization*: During the interviews, a lot of problems were identified with people refusing to collaborate because "it was not their job." In these cases, individuals had job descriptions and although they had the knowledge to solve a problem, they would not do so because they felt this violated the instructions that they had received. This is clearly a confusion of Quadrant I and Quadrant IV. This observation is confirmed by experts in work design, who report that the job simplification school tends to often be a "default model" (Parker & Wall, 1998).

- *Along the supply chain*: Subcontractors often perceive their relationship with their customer as adversarial. Their customer will require tasks not laid out in the contract whilst the supplier will try to provide less. This leads to a form of relationship management based on strict contract management and leaves little room and incentive for knowledge sharing along the supply chain.

It is necessary to distinguish the two reasons explaining why collaborative behavior is difficult in project teams. The first reason is cultural: Through involvement in projects, individuals have developed a certain distrust of suppliers and dislike the project schedule not being respected. The lessons learned are reinforced by senior managers' stance on these problems and by the guidelines they issue. These are internalized and become a way of thinking. When cultural habits turn out to be unproductive, they need to be changed. This task is addressed by the management and organization design disciplines and is beyond the scope of this chapter.

The second reason is infrastructural: Individuals do not collaborate because they feel that doing so would violate a written procedure and would go against orders; they cannot collaborate because they do not know who to collaborate with, or if they know, they are not able to collaborate because their counterpart is located elsewhere.

The IT solutions discussed in this section attempt to overcome infrastructural barriers. Although cultural barriers are not discussed here, they should not be overlooked. As stated by Davies (2000), using IT to facilitate knowledge sharing gives an opportunity to discover cultural resistance and to overcome it. In other words, IT can be used in this case as a technology driver to improve collaboration.

Know-who databases are the simplest IT tools that address the problems described above. Simply put, they allow a user to know who to contact to find the answer to a specific problem. It is noteworthy that a know-who database is a subsystem of the project memory system described in an earlier section.

Walström and Lindgren (2000) discuss the problems observed with five stand-alone know-who databases systems in seven companies through 24 semi-structured interviews. They identified five problems areas:

- *Knowledge mapping*: There is an ambiguity regarding what competencies are and how to provide an organizational structure for them.
- *Knowledge evolution*: Know-who knowledge is a volatile entity as both competencies and people change with time. This issue is complicated by the fact that individuals may also voluntarily omit some information when they fill in forms or prepare CVs.
- *Knowledge isolation*: The system may point to the individual who holds the knowledge sought, but hierarchy and/or procedures may prevent actual access to this individual or to the knowledge held.
- *Knowledge interaction*: Once a contact person is identified, there are often no corporate mechanisms to initiate the dialogue and for knowledge sharing to take place.

- *Operative knowledge management*: Know-who databases are unable to handle the logistical aspect of knowledge sharing. For instance, the system cannot express if an individual is free to collaborate when queried.

The conclusion of Walström and Lindgren (2000) is that know-who database systems often do not differ significantly from traditional personnel files as they only name individuals.

As stated in the section on the reuse/innovation compromise dimension, the concept of project memory needs, in order to be implemented on an IT system, an effective representation scheme of both product and process. Therefore, the concept of project memory as defined previously provides a solution to the knowledge mapping problem mentioned by Walström and Lindgren.

The issues of knowledge evolution, isolation and interaction are addressed by virtual communities of practice. A community of practice is a group of people who have similar functions or duties in a corporation, without necessarily knowing each other. There is nothing formal about communities of practice: They are an informal network of individuals connected by mutual interest and they get involved in the community on their own accord. Their corporation provides for them the platform and the infrastructure for knowledge sharing. An example of such a system is BT's Jasper system, which is a WWW-based designed for knowledge sharing within BT. Jasper holds a list of registered users details and uses intelligent software agents to organize news, users' interests and users' documents (Davies, 2000). Although it is clear how such systems address the issues of knowledge evolution (as they are designed to evolve as users and their interests change) and knowledge isolation (as content is available from the system), it does not address the operative issue.

The operative component is a challenge left for IT solutions developers. The challenge is to go beyond connecting the people and helping them to actually collaborate. For example, BT has begun to develop interesting job trading systems where BT maintenance fleet employees can trade jobs whilst on the road. The objective is to optimize the productivity of the maintenance fleet by constantly revising its schedule according to the problems faced earlier in the day. This idea can be generalized to a "project trading system." The scope of such a system would be to support information sharing (or information trading), job trading (exchanging two workers between two project teams), and job sharing (temporarily sending a team member to another team). The difficulty in implementing such a system is to integrate it fully with the corporate planning system and to verify that trading/sharing activities do result in increased productivity.

## Tacit vs. Explicit

During the research interviews, the following common problems were identified:

- Many companies suffered from knowledge being held in a tacit form. This, however, was not a universal problem. Some companies held tacit knowledge and had no problems working with it, whilst others need to go through the internalization process suggested by Nonaka (1991), that is, to transform tacit knowledge into explicit knowledge.

- In some cases, some companies indicated that although they may have an explicit source of knowledge, for instance, documents about a past project characteristic, they did not feel confident applying this knowledge, as they were unsure about the rationale aspect of this explicit knowledge.

In this section, we discussed IT issues in three cases:

1.    The case of a company which has problems transferring tacit knowledge but which believes that the tacit/explicit balance is respected. In other words, it does not want to internalize knowledge, just to transfer it in a tacit form.

2.    The case of a company which has concluded that it suffers from the tacit character of its knowledge and which has decided to internalize it. In others words, this company wants to use IT to reposition itself on the tacit/explicit dimension.

3.    The case of a company which is satisfied with its tacit/explicit balance but its explicit knowledge base lacks scope and quality.

In the first case, the problem is to facilitate the transfer of tacit knowledge between different parties. The problem here is not the tacit nature of knowledge but the difficulty of transferring it. Nonaka (1991) describes this transfer as being based on a socialization process, for instance, between a master and an apprentice. This is a knowledge sharing problem and can be addressed by virtual communities of practice or project trading systems, as discussed in the collaboration/competition section.

In the second case, knowledge engineering and knowledge-based systems (KBS) provide the solution to internalization of tacit knowledge. KBS are IT systems specialized in problem solving and decision making from the application of a substantial body of knowledge. With knowledge engineering, the knowledge of experts is analyzed, modeled and documented (i.e., made explicit). Once implemented in a knowledge-based system, the application of knowledge is automated. As there is an extensive literature available about KBS, the characteristics of these systems are not discussed further in this chapter.

In the third case, it is necessary to consider two different scenarios:

1.    The poor quality of explicit knowledge is linked to the internalization process. For example, Carter (2000) gives the example of a utility company where a large body of engineers was replaced by a rule-based engineering system. When asked to comment about the knowledge engineering process, one of the engineers declared that since the rule-based engineering program was not a viable idea, he was purposefully giving wrong information to the knowledge engineers. In this scenario the problem is linked to the solution and not to knowledge itself. This is often an issue as verification and validation of KBS are issues that tend to be overlooked (Preece, 2000). Verification means checking that the specifications are matched (building the system right) whereas validation means checking that the system actually works (building the right system). The development of effective verification and validation procedures is a challenge for IT.

2.  The second scenario takes place when the company has internalized some knowledge, but the nature of the knowledge itself is such that there is an unavoidable loss of content when converting it from a tacit form to an explicit form. The integration of a KBS with a project memory system addresses this problem as the project memory concept includes object attributes such as options, perspectives, opinions, etc. However, it is more realistic to acknowledge that there are limits to what explicit knowledge can convey. In this case, as stated by one of the interviewees, what needs to be in place is a system of "holding hands," i.e., a system where an individual can validate his or her assimilation of explicit knowledge by comparing it to the tacit knowledge of another individual. Communities of practice provide a platform for this.

## Informal vs. Formal

It is more difficult to identify generic problems along this compromise dimension as the interviewed companies exhibited several types of problems:

- In some companies, knowledge was not accessed by some parties because of problems of compatibility between software, versions and formats. This is a case of lack of formality in the structure of information.
- In other companies, the opposite problem was observed. The structuring of information would be so formal that it would actually constrain the content of the message. For example, one interviewee reported that a memo from a project manager to a senior manager could only be written in a specific style and tone. Likewise, the answer from the senior manager would follow specific guidelines. Such a "bureaucracy of knowledge" prevents certain concepts (emotions, opinions, etc.) to be carried in a message. This level of formalism was seen as unproductive.
- Some companies relied heavily on procedures and a mechanistic organization of operations. This formalism can block knowledge sharing, collaboration, innovation and any other activities based on informal relationships.
- In stark contrast, other companies preferred a more organic organizational approach and did not stress formalism and strict compliance to written operating procedures. These companies suffered from too much anarchy in operations.

As in the case of the collaboration/competition dimension, most of the problems faced in informal/formal dimension are either cultural or infrastructural. This section discusses how to address the latter and how to use IT as a technological driver to tackle the former.

First is the case of the company aware of the fact that it suffers from the fact that it is too formal. In this case virtual communities of practice provide the platform for informal exchanges as they are precisely designed as communities escaping the rules and structure of the formal organization.

In the second case, a company may be aware that it faces problems along the informal/formal dimension and may decide to improve its knowledge management capabilities by repositioning itself on this spectrum. This calls for a critical analysis of the relationship between project knowledge and project processes to identify when and why knowledge is not passed on, is lost, or is wrongly applied. What is needed in this case is a tool targeting the improvement of project knowledge management through process modeling. Modeling workshops are computerized integrated systems designed with this task in mind. Modeling workshops permit simulation of working practices under different scenarios of activity/role matrices within a working group and can help diagnose where knowledge management is inefficient. For an overview of MAMOSACO as an example of a Modeling workshop, see Vergison (2000). Another example is the COLA review process (Orange et al., 1999). Whereas MAMOSACO provides an example of a system that can be used for simulation (and improvement) purposes, the COLA review process is an example of a system able to trigger reflection and the formulation of lessons learned. COLA was developed in the construction industry to address the problem stated by Fisher (1998): "The construction industry struggles with its ability to capture the lessons learned from its projects and activities for the benefit of future, similar work." According to the designers of COLA, what lacks in the construction industry is reflective practice. Thus, COLA was designed to provide a review process forum for the social construction of knowledge.

## Internal vs. External

In the case of project knowledge management, reaching a balance along this dimension means that all forms of generic project knowledge are internal to the company and are passed on to the different generations of project teams. It also means that project teams are able to assimilate project-specific knowledge without developing a full expertise about this external knowledge.

Common problems along these dimensions quoted by the interviewees were:

- A project team has to solve a very specific problem. Although there are sources both within and outside the company that could contribute to the supply of knowledge relevant to this problem, these sources are too dispersed (in space, time, objectives and values) for the project team to assimilate and aggregate their inputs. Instead, they prefer to engage in the risky and costly exercise of creating the missing knowledge themselves with limited resources. This often results in wrong decisions.
- A company has lost its internal competencies as people have moved on. In this case, internal knowledge has become external.

In the second case, project memorization and KBS are two IT solutions that provide the benefits of making sure that core knowledge remains within the company, as it has been internalized and embedded in IT systems. One of the interviewees gave the example of a key competency related to product testing. His company had a significant competitive advantage in terms of verifying that a product would match their industry regulations. Although this knowledge could have easily been applied from a manual, the company preferred to use a computerized system. Any modifications of the system are subject to extensive documentation requirements so that the company can trace (and revert when necessary) the evolution of the system. The interviewee stressed that the advantage of this procedure was to provide full management control about key internal knowledge.

A second interviewee provided the IT solution to the problem of assimilating quickly and in a cost effective manner external knowledge. One of his project teams had to work on a construction project where local conditions (weather, topology, nature of soil) were such that it was not clear how to apply regulations. In more standard projects, how to interpret and apply regulations was part of the experience of the company. In this specific project, conditions were such that the project team had to consider constraints and issues not dealt with previously in the company. However, there were a number of individuals from the project team, the company, and outside the company that had some ideas and experiences in some aspects of the problem faced by the interviewee. The problem was to find a tool that allowed the interviewee to tap into this dispersed source of knowledge and to aggregate the collected information into a whole. The interviewee decided to use a groupware system (in this case, Lotus Notes) to facilitate this acquisition and assimilation process. In his opinion, the project was a success thanks to the use of the groupware system.

In addition to groupware systems, knowledge intranets are useful in the acquisition and assimilation of external knowledge, provided that they are enriched with knowledge discovery and data mining capabilities. This constitutes an automation of the processes supported by groupware systems, but it is doubtful that the complex problems handled by project teams can all be solved by knowledge discovery applications, at least at the time of writing this chapter.

## Individual vs. Group

The interviewed companies mentioned the following problems along this dimension:

- *Knowledge retention, extinction and dominance*: In an organizational process, an individual becomes a knowledge bottleneck when he or she retains some knowledge useful at the group level. A first major risk associated with knowledge retention is that of knowledge extinction when the individual or group at stake leaves the company. A typical example of knowledge extinction is the retirement problem: When an individual retires he or she takes with him or her product and process knowledge. The company often has to find a last-minute "quick-fix" solution to cope with this event. Downsizing operations were also blamed by interviewees as a factor weakening a group's knowledge stock. A second risk of knowledge retention is to use individually held knowledge to build authority and/or bargaining power. In this case, dysfunctional processes leading to delays, low innovation and poor performance can be observed.
- *Knowledge dispersion*: Knowledge is dispersed in and outside the organization but its application can only take place at the group/team level. This is a

problem commonly encountered by project managers installing IT systems or change programs. Knowledge exists dispersed in individuals but it is difficult to create group awareness.

- *Knowledge factions*: Knowledge may exist in different (conflicting) versions in different individuals or groups within the company. When different knowledge factions meet in a project team, a number of disputes and political issues arise. In the worst-case scenario, several people work in a project team with different objectives and specifications, as they refuse to exchange their information and experiences.

The basic challenge behind the individual/group compromise dimension is the management of ownership rights. In other words, it is to decide who has precedence and ownership of different classes of knowledge.

Knowledge retention is a problem solved by knowledge engineering as they force the expertise of an individual into a project memorization system. Another approach is to detect when knowledge retention is unproductive with a modeling workshop system. This would allow the company to reposition itself on the individual/group scale after it has decided if a specific class of knowledge is better owned by a single individual or by a group of individuals.

The knowledge faction problem is addressed by intranets and communities of practice. The knowledge dispersion problem is addressed by groupware systems.

All these modules (project memorization, modeling workshops, knowledge intranets, communities of practice and groupware systems) may all include their internal ownership rights specifications. However, as they all share the same needs, an optimal knowledge project management system should include a unique ownership rights module.

## Private vs. Public

Whereas the individual/group dimension addressed who should own an element of knowledge, i.e., has the right to create and modify it, the private/public dimension defines who has the right to access and apply this knowledge.

The research interviews revealed the following generic problems:

- Too much corporate secrecy results in individuals needing some knowledge not being granted access to it. Such a corporate policy is motivated (1) by the fear that if too public, knowledge could get to the competitors and (2) by the fear that individuals may not be able to apply the knowledge properly.
- Too much leniency in protecting information does result in the problems quoted above and can also create anarchy and unproductive speculation about strategy, product and processes, as individuals feel free to voice their different perspectives, be they aligned or not with corporate objectives. For example, there is nothing more unproductive than the analysis of a quality problem about a cutting tool degenerating into a debate about the roles of project managers. Although the debate about project management may be relevant (by the parties allowed to do so), the debate about cutting tool quality should be addressed with the relevant actors focused on relevant knowledge.

The management of access rights to information is in fact easier to manage through IT than human systems. In the example of the product testing computerized system quoted above, the interviewee stressed that only accredited individuals were allowed to access the content of the software along specific rules. For normal team members, they interacted with the system through queries and answers.

# FUTURE TRENDS

This section is divided in two parts. Throughout this chapter it is clear that knowledge representation is a fundamental issue in project knowledge management, especially with the concept of project memory. Project memory and representations about product and process are the link between each of the IT systems discussed in this chapter. Therefore, a unique and universal knowledge representation scheme is a *sine qua non* condition of an integrated project knowledge management system.

## Challenges in Knowledge Representation

The key challenge in terms of knowledge representation is to develop a scheme which is universal enough to be queried and updated by all the other components of a project knowledge management system. To illustrate this challenge, consider the case of one of the interviewed companies which tried to design an expert system for the pricing of its project. The product is engineered to order production machines. The pricing is done by top management of the company (only three senior managers know how to formulate a price quote). Needless to say, this pricing knowledge is entirely tacit and unstructured. After a few knowledge engineering sessions it appears that the experts used three key pricing schemes:

- *Technical pricing*: The experts decompose a component of the machine in material, component and working hours. Then, they add all of the elements up and take into account margins and overhead expenses.
- *Case-based reasoning*: The experts see that a subset of the machine is similar to a subset previously designed on another machine. As they have some first-hand experience on what this previous subset cost, they can formulate a price estimate directly. It is noteworthy that the accounting department did not have any cost accounting capability and did not formulate what the costs of subsets were; in fact as far as accounting was concerned there were no subsets. The price estimate of the experts was based on the initial quote corrected for the problems encountered when the subset was designed and built.
- *Function pricing*: Experts have also devised rules of thumbs that are based on classification of functions. For instance, experts were able to give a price for the "grasping" function provided that they were specified the weight of the element to grasp, the speed of the machine, the dimension of the object, and the degree of precision required when grasping.

The problem is that when pricing, experts use these three approaches *simultaneously*. Although this may be perceived as a methodological flaw, this price assessment flexibility is what allows experts to give the price of a machine before it is designed solely from its specifications.

The accounting department of this company was particularly interested in this pricing project and wanted to develop a cost accounting system that would provide direct feedback on the original project. The problem was that although a pricing expert system was developed, it added apples and oranges, as it used the three approaches. It was a question-driven system, rather difficult to use, which did not integrate a concept of "machine" that could be tested for consistency and complete-ness. The accounting department implemented a cost accounting system based on subsets, but there was never any integration between the two systems.

This example illustrates the challenge faced by IT in terms of knowledge representation. It is easy to develop a knowledge representation or a set of representation schemes for one application but much more difficult to have a universal and flexible representation scheme for a variety of applications.

## Other Key Challenges in Project Knowledge Management

The other key challenges are the development of modeling workshop systems and project trading systems. Modeling workshops are critical to project knowledge management as they address the performance assessment of how knowledge is managed within projects as well as how projects are organized in relation to the use of knowledge. It is through the modeling workshops that improvement in methods and practice for knowledge management comes from. Project trading systems can also contribute to a new generation of project management techniques as they allow project teams to move away from planning and scheduling rigidity toward a more flexible and dynamic approach to organizing projects.

# CONCLUSION

In this chapter, a number of IT systems were presented to address project knowledge management issues. Amongst the most important are project memoriza-tion systems, knowledge intranets, know-who databases, communities of practices, knowledge-based systems, modeling workshops, etc. As stressed in the first part of this chapter, each of these systems can be easily developed at an operational level. It is possible to envision a large, integrated computer system including all the different systems discussed in this chapter. However, one should realize that such a system would definitely escape the micro-scale knowledge management approach used here: Such an integrated system would require considerable resources and top management support. Moreover, as stressed in the section discussing the issue of knowledge representation, a large integrated system could require such a level of formality in its specification that it could fail to capture the flexible methods through which knowledge can effectively be transferred between project teams. Although there is a cost to develop non-interfaced, isolated IT applications within a company, the research interviews showed that companies and project teams seldom have a crucial need in all these systems at once. For instance, "one-off" project organizations had a need for knowledge reuse and reflection process, IT project implementation teams had a more crucial need for communities of practice, large R&D department for knowledge intranets, and large project sites for groupware systems. These companies confirmed that once identified, simple and cost-effective IT tools could be built and adopted.

# REFERENCES

Beer, M., Eisenstat, R. & Spector, B. (1990). Why change programs don't produce change. *Harvard Business Review*, November-December, pp.158-166.

Braiden, P. & Hicks, C. (2000). Assessing knowledge management activities in the design and manufacture of engineered to order capital goods. *Proceeding of the BPRC Knowledge Management: Concepts and Controversies Conference*, 103. Warwick, UK.

Carter, C. (2000). *The strange death of the professional engineer: A sojourn into the management of knowledge*. Unpublished Working Paper, University of Leicester Management Centre.

Davies, J. (2000). Supporting virtual communities of practice. In R. Rajkumar (Ed.), *Industrial Knowledge Management: A Micro Level Approach* (pp.199-212). London: Springer-Verlag.

Despres, C. & Chauvel, D. (1999). Knowledge management(s). *Journal of Knowledge Management*, 3(2), 110-120.

Frese, M. & Zapf, D. (1994). Action of the core of work psychology: A german approach. In H. Triandis, M. Dunette and J. Hough (Eds.), *Handbook of Industrial and Organisational Psychology* (4th ed.), 4, pp.271-340. Palo Alto, CA: Consulting Psychologists.

Gilbert, M. & Holder, N. (2000). An approach to project knowledge management. *Proceeding of the BPRC Knowledge Management: Concepts and Controversies Conference*, 193. Warwick, UK.

Hislop, D., Newell, S., Scarbrough, H. & Swan, J. (2000). Innovation processes and the management of knowledge. *Proceeding of the BPRC Knowledge Management: Concepts and Controversies Conference*, Warwick, UK.

Leseure, M. & Brookes, N. (2000a). Micro knowledge management: A job design framework. In R. Rajkumar (Ed.), *Industrial Knowledge Management: A Micro Level Approach* (pp.163-178). London: Springer-Verlag.

Leseure, M. & Brookes, N. (2000b). A support tool for knowledge management activities. *Proceedings of the 2000 IEEE International Conference on Management of Innovation and Technology* (pp.696-701), Singapore.

Matta, N., Ribière, M., Corby, O., Lewkowicz, M. & Zaclad, M. (2000). Project memory in design. In R. Rajkumar (Ed.), *Industrial Knowledge Management: A Micro Level Approach* (pp.147-162). London: Springer-Verlag.

Newman, V. (1999). *The limitations of knowledge management*. Unpublished presentation at the BPRC Seminar on Knowledge Management in Manufacturing, November 29, BPRC, University of Warwick, UK.

Nonaka, I. (1991). The knowledge-creating company. *Harvard Business Review*, November-December, 96-104.

Orange, G., Cushman, M. & Burke, A. (1999). *COLA: A cross organisational learning approach within UK industry*. Paper presented to 4th International Conference on Networking Entities (Neties '99), Donau-Universität, Krems, Austria, 18-19 March.

Parker, S. & Wall, T. (1998). *Job and Work Design*. London: Sage.

Preece, A. (2000). Evaluating verification and validation methods in knowledge engineering. In R. Rajkumar (Ed.), *Industrial Knowledge Management: A Micro Level Approach* (pp.91-104). London: Springer-Verlag.

Shahin T., Sivaloganathan, S. & Gilliver, R. (1997). Automation of feature-based modelling and finite element analysis for optimal design. *Proceedings of ICED97*, Tempere, Finland, August.

Sivaloganthan, S. & Shahin, T. (1999). Design reuse: An overview. *Proceedings of the Institute of Mechanical Engineers*, Part B, *213*, 641-654.

Vergison, E. (2000). Micro-scale knowledge management: A necessary condition for getting corporate knowledge properly implemented. In R. Rajkumar (Ed.), *Industrial Knowledge Management: A Micro Level Approach*, 3-16. London: Springer-Verlag.

Wallström, C. & Lindgren, R. (2000). A close look at knowledge management systems. *Proceeding of the BPRC Knowledge Management: Concepts and Controversies Conference*, 37. Warwick, UK.

## Chapter VII

# A Case Study of How Technology and Trust Enable the Projectized Team-Based Organization

Marjorie A. Jerrard and Ting Yee Chang
Monash University, Australia

## ABSTRACT

*The phenomenon of projectized teams operating via teleworking and moving towards the virtual mode of operation is explored. The major developments in the relevant HRM and trust literature are covered prior to the consideration of how IT can enable the development of unconditional trust as part of the formation of projectized teams. The case study company is a small but rapidly growing enterprise in the technology and software industry. A model of its new organizational structure is developed and recommended steps for moving from a flexible work-based organization to a virtual organization are provided based on the case study and the literature. Finally, future challenges and recommendations for organizations using IT-enabled projectized teams are considered.*

## INTRODUCTION

Organizations today are often searching for new ways in which to promote cooperation between people and teams and to enhance the value created (Mayer, Davis & Schoorman, 1995; Jones & George, 1998) through the use of technology (Hunsaker & Lixfield, 1999; Townsend, DeMarie & Hendrickson, 1998). Many organizations seek to use technology strategically to assist in the reengineering of their structures into flatter, more team-based forms (Jones & George), with no middle management level, a chief executive officer (CEO) responsible for "managing the company," and employees responsible for managing themselves (Lipnack & Stamps, 1997, 1999). This is particularly so in medium and small enterprises in the technology and software industry where knowledge workers and professionals predominate and the use of teams is further complicated by the "virtual" component (Jarvenpaa, Knoll & Leidner, 1998). For example, teams of teleworkers come together to work on a project in a task force team (Eom & Lee, 1999), a parallel team (Duarte & Snyder, 1999), or project team (Kharbanda & Stallworthy, 1990; Porter & Lilly, 1996) that is cross-functional (Bishop, 1999; Jassawalla & Sashittal, 1999; Pinto, Pinto & Prescott, 1993) and will disband on project completion. A company operating with a projectized team structure or a networked structure based largely on virtual teams (Kharbanda & Stallworthy; Lipnack & Stamps, 1999), must have an organizational culture of trust that in turn promotes unconditional trust amongst individual team members (Barney & Hansen, 1994; Cascio, 2000; Fiol, 1991; Handy, 1995; Jones & George) so that team effectiveness and intellectual capital can be maximized. There is a range of demands placed upon managers in these organizations, requiring foci and skills other than those expected from traditional managers (Cascio; Duarte & Snyder; Gainey, Kelley & Hill, 1999; Lepak & Snell, 1998; Nilles, 1998). This also applies to employees working within the projectized teams and who are themselves teleworkers or virtual office employees and likely to experience problems such as isolation (Gainey et al.) and distrust of unseen and "unknown" team members (Jarvenpaa et al.) and managers.

This chapter investigates the manner in which the management of technology, particularly the use of Internet, online project rooms, and peer to peer (hereafter referred to as P2P) systems allowing real-time emails (e.g., ICQ) and collaboration between users involved in computer-supported cooperative work (Mills, 1999) can be used to build trust within an organization—enabling it to move from the physical office to the virtual office—and in doing so, establish regional, national, and international alliances. This technology promotes projectized virtual teams as the new organizational structure and enables these teams to operate with maximum flexibility and creativity and to successfully produce optimizing products to meet their clients' individual needs (Porter & Lilly, 1996). Technology used as a strategic tool enables parallel or concurrent team membership and completion of synchronous (Duarte & Snyder, 1999) and asynchronous tasks (Duarte & Snyder; Jackson & Grossman, 1999; Morris, Neuwirth, Regli, Chandhok & Wenger, 1999). The organizational structure is flattened because self-managing, temporary projectized teams replace middle management. Further, electronically available procedural guidelines and policies eliminate many of the repetitive administrative tasks that previously accompanied teams. The CEO is to manage the organization's culture and resources and facilitate the functioning of the projectized teams.

For this chapter, we combine three frameworks by two groups of researchers and a consultant to provide the theoretical and conceptual background. Jones and

George (1998) established the implications of trust from a psychological perspective; Jarvenpaa et al. (1998) tested trust antecedents in global virtual teams; and Owen (1996a, 1996b), via consulting work, developed the theory of the dual synergy chain process of team formation. An Australian case study based on Acumen Multimedia,[1] a small enterprise producing interactive multimedia, software, and corporate Web sites, is used to demonstrate that projectized teams of teleworkers operate most effectively when there are high levels of trust, particularly unconditional trust, within teams and the organization and where technology is used to promote trust and efficiency. This chapter therefore covers a range of topics encompassing the new mandate for management that is being created by IT: projectized organizational structure enabled by IT, the team management of projects using IT, and some specific challenges imposed by IT on people management with regard to establishing trust relationships between geographically dispersed employees working in projectized teams.

# TEAMS, TELEWORKERS, TRUST, AND THE VIRTUAL ORGANIZATION: TERMINOLOGY DEFINED

A team "is an officially sanctioned collection of individuals who have been charged with completing a mission by the organization and who must depend upon one another for successful completion of that work" (Alderfer, 1987, p. 211; quoted by Al-Kazemi, 1998, p. 71). Al-Kazemi identified four criteria that must be met in order for a team to formed: There must be clear objectives, the members of the team are identifiable as such and are dependent upon each other, and collaboration between members is expressed as help and support for one another.

The term "projectized team" combines the functions and operation of a project team with those of a task force team and with some of the elements of a self-directed or self-managed team. That is, the projectized team is a small group of individuals working outside of traditional hierarchical lines of authority (Porter & Lilly, 1996) and outside of traditional organization structures, similar to a project team. It is also possible for projectized teams to replace the traditional bureaucratic and hierarchical organization structure (Lipnack & Stamps, 1999) so that it is more flexible and akin to a networked structure as the teams disband and re-form across members or as members work concurrently in multiple teams across projects (Cascio, 2000). The team members can therefore be simultaneously engaged on asynchronous tasks (Duarte & Snyder, 1999; Jackson & Grossman, 1999; Morris et al., 1999) and synchronous tasks (Duarte & Snyder). The independent projectized team is akin to the supervisor-less workgroup identified by the TORI (trust, openness, self actualisation/realisation, interdependence) theorists (Al-Kazemi, 1998; Dimock, 1987) because the members assume responsibilities traditionally reserved for higher-level managers: Typically they manage themselves, assign jobs, plan and schedule work, make production- or service-oriented decisions, and solve problems (Kirkman, Jones & Shapiro, 2000; relying on Wellins et al., 1990). A project leader may on occasion be appointed externally from the group to ensure overall completion within the requisite time frame (Kharbanda & Stallworthy, 1990). Each projectized team's life span is temporary (Eom & Lee, 1999; Kharbanda & Stallworthy; Porter & Lilly), and the team works towards the solution for a specific problem or a new product for a client, again similar to a project team or a even a task force team (Eom & Lee). However, the team members do not belong permanently to a department or section to which they return on project completion; instead they move onto another project, as shown in Figure 2. Therefore the projectized team is not simply a form of horizontal contact across multiple departments or sections with representatives from each (Cleland, 1996; Eom & Lee; Galbraith, 1971; Pinto et al., 1993), but operates vertically as well. Projectized teams should fulfil the "promise to be a cornerstone of progressive management for the foreseeable future," a claim made by Kreitner and Kinicki (1992, p. 394; cited by Al-Kazemi, 1998, p. 70) of teams in general. However, a number of the problems and limitations of task force teams and regular project teams may also affect the projectized team and must be overcome. A major disadvantage of a projectized team structure is the expense and time associated with the repetition of administrative tasks for each team, rather than having a separate and permanent department for the administration of all concurrent projects. This can now be overcome using file sharing systems and P2P technology.

The type of project on which the team works is a significant determinant of the success of the projectized team (Hackman & Morris, 1975; Porter & Lilly, 1996). The type of product often determines this. For example, new product development or products that are tailored to suit individual clients' needs will be more complex, will require a higher level of information sharing, and will have multiple stages prior to completion (Porter & Lilly). Projects requiring high degrees of creativity and uniqueness, such as those in IT and multimedia, and which are assessed on how well the product meets an ideal are said to be optimizing rather than maximizing because success is not simply determined by speed of completion or amount produced (Porter & Lilly; Steiner, 1972). These projects also require high levels of shared communication and therefore trust to boost performance, particularly when being completed by virtual teams (Jarvenpaa et al., 1998).

A virtual team, or a virtual projectized team, is one that "is without a place as its home" (Jarvenpaa & Ives, 1994, p. 44; quoted by Jarvenpaa et al., 1998, p. 29) and which uses technology as the means of communication and to improve team effectiveness for project completion (Duarte & Snyder, 1999; Eom & Lee, 1999; Hunsaker & Lixfield, 1999; Mills, 1999; Townsend et al., 1998). A projectized virtual team may be made up of teleworkers who work off-site from the office base, but not necessarily at home, and who use generic and specific computer tools as the primary means of communicating with other team members (Cascio, 2000; Duarte & Snyder; Townsend et al.). The team may include teleworkers from global, national, and regional alliance partners as part of the organization's strategy. The use of alliance partnerships and external collaboration moves beyond the former practice of outsourcing a range of functions for flexibility and cost-saving and also goes beyond the associated current short-term measure of international labour arbitrage whereby skills are purchased in the international labour market either via traditional outsourcing to technology firms overseas or else skills are brought into a corporation for a specified period from outside its geographical base.

For the purpose of this chapter, a teleworker is classified as a full-time employee of the organization who works remotely as a part-time or full-time teleworker with the aid of IT and communications equipment (Gainey et al., 1999; Nilles, 1998). There need not be a formal teleworking agreement as part of an employment contract. Employees from other organizations working in joint alliances are included. Like telework, the concept of the virtual organization or office is difficult to comprehensively define (Harris, 1998). A virtual organization exists where IT enables the dispersion of employees across both time and space (Davidow & Malone, 1992; Handy, 1995). Technology enables organizational redesign to efficiently meet client and market demands while offering employees and managers flexibility and control denied to regular office workers. However, virtuality can be used to tighten or even remove autonomy and control from employees and lower level managers in some companies as the technology is used directly as a restraint and surveillance strategy (Brey, 1999; Fairweather, 1999). This approach to IT usage is not advised for use in a projectized team-based organization because it directly negates trust.

For any type of virtual team within a virtual organization to be successful, there needs to be high levels of trust (Handy, 1995; Harris, 1998). While the direct contribution of trust to performance can be debated (Porter & Lilly, 1996), the literature makes universal acknowledgment that trust is a significant factor in building communication, sharing of knowledge, and cooperation across teams (see Jones & George, 1998, for a review of this body of literature). Researchers (e.g. Axelrod, 1984; Bateson, 1988; Mayer et al., 1995) have commonly viewed trust as "an expression of confidence between parties in an exchange of some kind—confidence that they will not be harmed or put at risk by the actions of the other party" (Jones & George, 1998, p. 532), particularly when the trustee has no control or ability to monitor the actions of the trustor (Mayer et al.); or "confidence that no party to the exchange will exploit the other's vulnerability" (Jones & George, 1998, p. 532; referring to Sabel, 1993). There is overall consensus that trust is a complex multi-dimensional construct (e.g., Barber, 1983; Butler, 1991; Driscoll, 1978; Jones & George; Scott, 1980) but it is also built upon a psychological construct that is the outcome of people's values, attitudes, moods, and emotions (Jones & George). The ideal form of trust is unconditional as opposed to conditional (Jones & George) and in the case of virtual teams, it should be "swift" trust (Jarvenpaa, et al., 1998) that promotes high levels of trust from the outset of the team formation. Swift trust enables team members to move over the first three stages of developing the working relationship—orientation or initial "sizing up"; exploration or learning about each other's goals, roles, and priorities; and testing, which involves working through unresolved differences to begin developing trust—to arrive at the stabilization stage of maintaining the relationship through having developed trust (Gabarro, 1990;

Reinsch, 1997). A new form of psychological contract based on employee choice as to type of working arrangements, degree of involvement in the workplace and team, and connected relationships between other employees and clients (Seiling, 1999) can hasten the process of trust building. Also, situational factors can serve as impersonal substitutes for trust (Mayer et al., 1995), such as the obtaining and disseminating of information on performance and the aligning of individual goals, team goals, and organizational goals through reward systems (Spreitzer & Mishra, 1999). These HRM-derived substitutes are used to reduce risks in the employment relationship by maximizing self-interested behaviour that can achieve personal and common goals (Spreitzer & Mishra) but not at the cost of the overall organizational objective. Trust substitutes can also be combined with actual trust to give rise to an organizational culture capable of developing from distrust to conditional trust and finally to unconditional trust (Jones & George).

# THE LITERATURE AND BACKGROUND: TRUST, TECHNOLOGY, AND THE PROJECTIZED TEAM

Members of any type of virtual team need to be certain that the other team members will fulfil their obligations to the required performance standard and will behave in a consistent and appropriate manner (Cascio, 2000). This certainty building, firstly, upon conditional trust and, secondly, unconditional trust, leads to a set of behavioural expectations that allows the team members to manage risk or uncertainty and to jointly maximize the gains that will result from their cooperative behaviour (Jones & George, 1998). The interactionist model developed by Jones and George (1998, pp. 532-539) proposes three distinct states of the trust experience: (1) distrust, (2) conditional trust, and (3) unconditional trust which evolves as a result of people's values, attitudes, moods (George & Jones, 1997), and emotions. The findings of Owen (1996a, 1996b) that self-awareness is the basis of the evolution of the trust experience also fit within the interactionist model because self-awareness underlies values, attitudes, moods, and emotions. Conditional trust exists when parties cooperate for the present but without entailing personal costs or increasing personal risks and without developing shared values that enable forward-looking behaviour. Jones and George emphasise unconditional trust as the preferred state of experience for team members because it directly promotes interpersonal cooperation and teamwork and also seven other kinds of social processes that can lead to superior team and organizational performance. These include: (1) broad role definitions that include actions to improve or contribute to the common good and hence (2) improved communal relationships characterized by helpfulness and trust; (3) high confidence in others because each person is assured of the others' intentions and goals with regard to the team; (4) help-seeking behaviour which arises as a positive force promoting interdependence, cooperation and (5) free exchange of knowledge and information to be used for the common good; which in turn encourages (6) subjugation of personal needs and ego for the common good; and (7) high involvement; all of which promote synergistic team relationships. The interactionist model of unconditional trust is the ideal model for projectized virtual teams to follow, particularly if there is an emphasis on individual self-awareness (Owen, 1996a, 1996b) and on the presence of "swift" trust (Jarvenpaa et al., 1998), because it will assist in overcoming problems experienced by traditional and also virtual teams.

The use of technology such as P2P systems can positively contribute to the seven social processes needed to develop unconditional trust. P2P collaboration systems that are currently being developed by American companies such as Groove Networks, Endeavours Technology, and Ikimbo combine file-sharing abilities with instant-messaging capabilities in a secure environment. Such systems will boost the level of communication and information sharing between team members, specifically allowing colleagues to connect with each other in virtual environments to pursue a range of computer-supported cooperative work (Mills, 1999), from brainstorming and discussion, to specific problem solving, file and document sharing, and even Internet searching for everything from information and databases through to seeking new clients and customers. Easy and secure communication and transference of work materials will contribute to quicker and higher development of trust levels between projectized team members working in virtual environments and will promote security of exchange between alliance partners, particularly those operating across national borders. The software interaction technology of P2P enables those team members involved in alliance-based projects to link large numbers of computers across countries into one giant database, which will allow the creator or original producer of the data or information to retain ownership and copyright while permitting secure access by alliance partner employees, contractors, and project clients. This technology eliminates lag time in updating data because the creator is responsible for the updating and maintenance of their section of the database. The technology can be used on a smaller scale to enable more efficient project completion simply by applying the same principles of ownership and responsibility to each section of the project. A large project can be completed in a series of smaller stages and a complex problem broken into smaller, more manageable components. P2P technology boosts the ability of projectized team members to work on concurrent projects and synchronous and asynchronous tasks by promoting direct and easy electronic communication and information sharing, which benefits the members of projectized virtual teams at all stages of team development. Thus, technology becomes a trust-building tool, enabling the operation of projectized teams and allowing the organization to restructure.

Owen's (1996a, 1996b) synergy chain process theory identifies two chains, one symbolising the objectives of the whole team and the other the individual's personal goals. Owen proposes that links in each chain are connected with other links, both in the same and in the other chain; and this demonstrates how work or action on any one link will affect others, hence the label "synergy chain process." When teams include personal goals, individual motivation and commitment are subsequently higher; therefore, performance increases and organizational goals are also met. Linking individual, team, and organizational goals creates a triple synergy chain. Our new triple synergy chain process (Figure 1), if included as part of the team-building strategies and setting of team performance objectives and task and role allocation, will make a significant contribution to the overall team performance. The setting and inclusion of personal goals are not used as means of promoting personal good and ego over that of the common good, which would be counter to the state of unconditional trust proposed by Jones and George (1998), but is a means of ensuring early or swift development of the sense of "belonging" to the team and of actively wanting to cooperate with other team members to achieve the common objectives to which the individual ones are linked.

Jarvenpaa et al. (1998) found that teams that reached the state of unconditional trust identified by Jones and George (1998) were those utilising the strategies shown to be most effective in building "swift" trust and in achieving high levels of trust. The effective strategies identified by Jarvenpaa et al. match closely with the seven social processes of Jones and George to give rise to our current hypothesis that strategies promoting high trust levels in projectized teleworking teams are drawn from those seven social processes which are the basis of unconditional trust and that advances in IT can actively promote the development of trust within these teams. Further, there is a significant contribution that can be made to the theory and conceptualisation of unconditional trust if the synergy chain process of Owen (1996a, 1996b) is included as an antecedent of the development of unconditional trust in projectized teams operating without country, or even company, boundaries.

*Figure 1: Interactionism and the triple synergy chain*

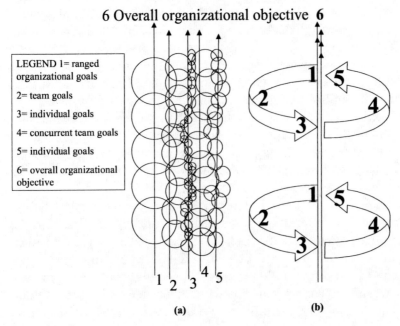

# THE CASE STUDY: USING IT FOR DEVELOPING TRUST AND PROMOTING A PROJECTIZED TEAM STRUCTURE

## Company Background

Acumen Multimedia is an Australian leading producer of interactive multimedia, software, and corporate Web sites, with its office located in Melbourne. It has been operating for 16 years and produces unique multimedia applications, Internet Web sites, and other software solutions for communication problems and access dilemmas for many leading local and international organizations including the public sector, the tertiary education sector, publicly listed companies such as Telstra, the ANZ Bank, Mayne Health, and Hewlett-Packard, and other organizations such as the Australian Ballet. The three areas of business are categorized into online government, business-to-business e-commerce (corporate), and training and education. In order to successfully meet the expectations of clients while reducing its risks, Acumen Multimedia established strategic alliances with multiple national and global companies to develop a network of support to provide a competitive advantage in supplying increasingly sophisticated online applications for clients within and outside of Australia. IT enables these alliances to be effective and offers the potential to expand the projectized teleworking teams that are the basis of the company's structure into global virtual projectized teams delivering successful outcomes for all stakeholders. Acumen Multimedia recognizes that to achieve its corporate goals of continuing to deliver high performance, reliable solutions and Web sites for clients, the attraction, retaining, and maintaining of the brightest and best people are essential. This emphasis on retaining employees for the long term is unusual in the IT and multi-media industries where, irrespective of the country of operation, employee turnover is relatively high (Ibaria & Greenhaus, 1992; Teo, Lim & Har, 1999). In contrast, Acumen Multimedia, while growing at over 800% in the last 4 years, experienced only a 2 to 3% turnover, with most of these employees leaving for personal reasons but seeking to return to the company at a future date.

## Pillars of the Company Culture: Trust, Teleworking, Technology

The culture of Acumen Multimedia is based upon openness, trust, and employee empowerment and responsibility. The procedural guidelines for establishing teleworking bases are developed consensually, with all employees contributing from their own knowledge and experiences. Other procedures are constantly modified in this way and issues related to the projects are updated via the online project room, to which all employees have access and can add ideas that may then be formally included in the company policy by the CEO or in project procedures by the project manager. Acumen Multimedia advocates continuous improvement by adopting elements of Toyota's ANDON system of worker control of quality, where anyone can stop production, or in this case a project, if they find something wrong or that can be improved.

Acumen Multimedia, through its CEO, describes itself as "a very human company." After winning the Top 10 Employers to Work for in Australia award, the company wrote on its Web site in September 2000, "[we] recognized three years ago that to achieve our goals, we needed to attract the very brightest and best people to work for us. This means Flexibility." The CEO believes that "everybody can [tele]work at home if they want. However, [it] is not something we measure. I don't want to ask people." Teleworking is about trust and employees should be measured based on their output rather than the number of hours they spend in an actual office or even sitting in front of a computer. Technology is not a means of controlling the members of the virtual team but of granting them independence and autonomy and enhancing their performance. Consequently, Acumen Multimedia developed its own interactive online project rooms where team members and clients can communicate and see the current progress of the projects. Clients can easily use their secure password to access project team members for feedback, to add to the original brief or to provide additional information and requirements necessary to complete the project, and to view the project to its current stage of completion.

## Project Tendering and Management

Projects are usually tendered for by the CEO or because a client has contacted the company. However, employees may also attract projects. Usually, the CEO undertakes client negotiations, but a team-appointed project leader may carry out negotiations. In teams where a project leader is appointed externally from the team (i.e., by the CEO), this person is a design team leader with overall responsibility for ensuring that each stage of the project is completed successfully within the deadline and that problems are prevented or solved within the team. All projectized teams, including those with an externally appointed leader, operate on the basis of "pass the baton," which enables employees to share responsibility and set personal goals in terms of individual development. This assists in aligning individual goals with team and organizational goals (Figure 1). Employees may be concurrently involved in up to eight projectized teams of varying size, emphasizing the need to be able to personally and technologically work on synchronous and asynchronous tasks (Duarte & Snyder, 1999; Jackson & Grossman, 1999; Morris et al., 1999) and to be able to take on parallel responsibilities across teams (Figure 2).

Initially, roles are defined, individual project stage responsibility allocated, running style decided upon, and procedures clarified. From the project inception, the use of the project room, ICQ, and other P2P technology allows trust to develop more quickly as both group and individual interaction between employees is possible. The technological advancements and the success of the teleworking program enabled

*Figure 2: Adaptive projectized team structure*

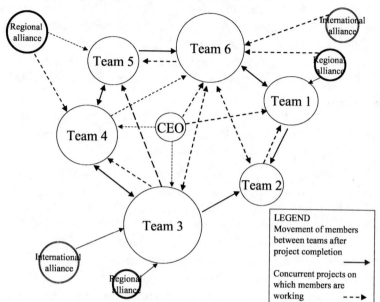

*Figure 3: Relationship of virtual organizational components (internal and external)*

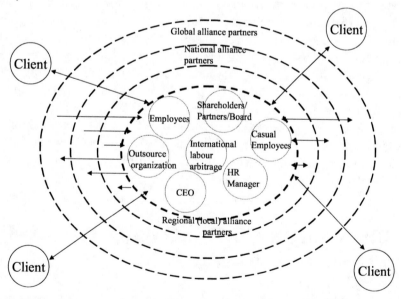

Acumen Multimedia to set up global alliances and to expand its client base offshore. The skill set required for a project is broad so that team members have to be able to rely on each other for help and information in order to achieve both personal goals and team goals. In this way, interdependence, cooperation, and high levels of individual involvement are promoted (Jones & George, 1998). This is particularly apparent in projects with teams of 8 to 12 people. The projectized teams may consist of people not only from Acumen Multimedia but also from other regional, national, or international companies (Figure 3), highlighting the importance of P2P and other communications technology as trust-building tools to promote team efficiency and performance across distances and cultures.

## Technology, Teams, and Trust

The online project room and P2P technology encourage the development of swift trust between members (Jarvenpaa et al., 1998) because they promote the free exchange of information and ideas from the initial planning stages of the project through to completion and follow-up. Less experienced employees also have mentors and the more experienced team members to rely upon for additional support and advice. A team member can raise any issue on the project via the online project room and leave it there for open discussion with team members and the project leader before the project leader assumes ultimate responsibility for including the suggestion or a modified version arrived at by the team's electronic discussion or perhaps rejecting it altogether. Team members are able to actively seek assistance and advice on their stage of the project and if a problem arises, to raise this with their team or with individual team members. This type of behaviour is rewarded within the projectized team and the company through its performance management and the remuneration systems because it contributes to the development of company and team procedures. It also adds to overall performance by preventing a recurrence of the problem in that team or other teams and reducing the costs of repetitive administration usually associated with projectized team structures. Help-seeking behaviour, one of the seven social processes identified by Jones and George (1998), arises out of improved communal or team relationships and a high confidence in other team members' ability (Jones & George). Acumen Multimedia's employees exhibit high confidence levels in their team members' skills and abilities and hold a high level of professional respect for one another.

# DISCUSSION AND RECOMMENDATIONS

## Future Challenges and Trends

### Case Study Company

The challenge for Acumen Multimedia is to continue growing while maintaining a high trust culture that is based on unconditional trust, not conditional trust, and which continues to allow the triple chain process to operate. The management of culture requires adequate resourcing and support to actualize employee self-management as a reality, particularly in a projectized team structure that is also dependent upon teleworkers operating from a number of companies and countries within an alliance.

Suggested steps for a small to medium-sized organization seeking to move from flexibility of work to telework to the virtual office include flexibility of work to telework to the virtual office are shown in Table 1.

It is important to note that the management of culture, rather than of people, will necessitate strategic and operational human resource policies that allow employees to manage themselves and be rewarded for doing this. IT remains a tool to be used by the employees for the triple achievement of individual, team, and organizational objectives as shown in Figures 1 and 2.

### Other Organizations

The steps suggested in Table 1 can be adapted to suit other organizations' needs and are not intended to provide a model of best practice or a blueprint. Further, some steps may be limited or inappropriate in application for larger organizations, having been designed for small and medium-sized enterprises and deriving from a study of one small enterprise only. Other organizations, particularly those not specifically in the IT and multimedia industries, may include additional or alternative steps: for example, a focus on the management of human resources throughout each development stage; or involving international labour arbitrage and using particular IT specialists on a contract basis for small parts of a project to save on labour costs or importing IT specialists into a company from another country for a specified period.

IT-enabled projectized teams, as shown in Figure 2, are recommended as a strategy for organizations to move from a teleworking organization to a virtual

*Table 1: Steps to move towards the virtual organization*

| | |
|---|---|
| 1. | CEO to promote trust as the basis of organizational culture. CEO/HR Manager to ensure HR policy and practices function strategically and operationally |
| 2. | Introduce non-IT-dependent forms of flexible work |
| 3. | Improve existing technology to assist with traditional project management |
| 4. | Develop and trial teleworking program across organization |
| 5. | Establish telework as a preferred method of work |
| 6. | Outsource non-core, non-IT development functions, e.g., accounting, legal, maintenance, some HRM functions |
| 7. | Move to performance assessment based on outputs, not inputs, and develop all HRM policies accordingly |
| 8. | Update and develop technology via use of P2P, etc. |
| 9. | Establish projectized teams as the organizational structure |
| 10. | Establish initial regional alliances, then national, then global as needed |
| 11. | Maintain the virtual organization using trust, innovative management practices, and IT |
| 12. | Retain and develop the "human focus" on employees, alliance partners, and clients |

organization and to effectively maximize outcomes from alliances. However, as Acumen Multimedia's CEO advocates, this move does not necessitate surrendering central office premises in a prime location that may be used as vantage point for directly advertising the organization's business to the general public and potential clients via the building itself. Retaining physical office space can also provide a central meeting point if managers, employees, and clients wish to use it. Managing the resulting virtual organization and its alliances, as depicted in Figure 3, poses challenges for all levels of management as organizational structure, culture, client, and employee contact regularly changes.

## CEOs and Senior Management

The use of IT as a trust-building tool rather than as a managerial control or surveillance strategy must remain an essential part of virtual projectized teams, irrespective of organization size, location, and industry type. This may pose specific cultural challenges for some managers and is highlighted in the research of Khan, Tung and Turban (1997) on Singapore teleworkers but is equally applicable to other southeast Asian countries, as well as Australia, where an autocratic management style may be reflective of a more paternalistic culture or at least of a high emphasis upon direct supervision or control of employees. National culture and controls, rather than organizational culture and controls, may pose the greatest challenge to management seeking to reengineer or restructure their organization and the way in which work is done. Consequently, CEOs and other members of the senior management team may need to adopt high community profiles outside their companies. Community leadership roles and political, social, and even religious lobbying may therefore become part of their portfolios to achieve change within their organizations. For example, managers in Singapore may be able to begin a change in societal attitudes towards married women returning to work after having a baby; managers in Australia may be able to encourage local government authorities to loosen zoning restrictions in some suburbs, thereby allowing more use of home offices to promote teleworking as a step towards the virtual organization; and in the USA, managers may be able to lobby government to change taxation policy and law to promote various types of telework and to take steps towards promoting the virtual organization. CEOs and senior management must take responsibility for creating an organizational culture of trust, for resourcing projectized teams appropriately, and for focusing on outputs rather than inputs from employees. This latter point is also important for human resource managers to heed.

## Human Resource Managers

From the case study based on Acumen Multimedia and literature analysis, the strategic and operational importance of human resource functions such as recruitment, selection, induction and mentoring, performance management, rewards, and remuneration become apparent. For large organizations, the sheer size of the task of managing all aspects of their human resources makes outsourcing or consultants particularly attractive, just as small organizations find the cost savings of outsourcing attractive. However, as Acumen Multimedia's CEO states: "People [remain] the competitive advantage," which is a major consideration when outsourcing any aspect of HRM.

## Research

There remains a need for further empirical and case study research of actual companies in order for the findings in this chapter to be tested and broader inferences and applications made. This is consistent with recent recommendations in the teleworking literature because practitioners and consultants have largely driven research on teleworking during the first half of the 1990s, which has given rise to a paucity of critical empirical evidence. The teleworking and virtual organization literature has also been of an optimistic nature with predictions that may not necessarily reflect reality. Longitudinal studies of the impact and use of P2P and other such technology are also recommended. Further research on the use of trust as a performance enhancer within virtual organizations and also within projectized teams is recommended to ascertain whether our triple synergy chain (Figure 1) is an effective technique in boosting swift trust development and organizational performance in organizations across a range of industries. This is essential given the findings in the case study and the existing literature, particularly as the move towards virtual organizations increases with IT advances.

# CONCLUSIONS

The current chapter has explored the phenomenon of projectized teams operating via teleworking and moving towards the virtual mode in a small enterprise in the technology and software industry. It considered the value of IT to promote the development of swift trust within projectized teams via P2P systems encouraging file sharing and user collaboration as well as online project rooms and emails. The findings from the case study fit with the theoretical findings in the literature and demonstrate that swift trust (Jarvenpaa et al., 1998) can be developed across projectized virtual teams using technology-based communication and that the ideal of unconditional trust can be achieved in an organization that actively promotes teamwork, open communication, employee autonomy, and self-management to promote the social processes necessary for unconditional trust to develop (Jones & George, 1998). The alignment of personal goals with team goals and company goals gives rise to the preferred triple chain synergy process of interactionist trust building (Figure 1) as opposed to the double chain identified by Owen (1996a, 1996b). Further, the advances made in P2P technology will certainly contribute to trust development within projectized teams if surveillance is not regarded by management as a major tool of employee and contractor control.

The case study demonstrates that the triple chain synergy process, IT-based strategies for swift trust development, and the social processes used for building unconditional trust can be combined to provide the ideal team and organizational environment for projectized virtual teams. An organizational culture of unconditional trust can be achieved if the CEO and other senior management can distinguish between managing people and managing culture and if technology is used as a strategic tool rather than as a driver of the organization's strategy. Finally, the lessons learned from this Australian case study have relevance for management operating in other countries and can be adapted to suit their social, political, legal, and technological cultures to arrive at their own "best practice model" of IT and organizational culture management.

## ENDNOTE

1 The authors express their gratitude to Acumen Multimedia CEO Russell Yardley and to all the staff at Acumen Multimedia who kindly assisted in this research. The research was carried out in September-October 2000 as part of a broader qualitative project on teleworkers and teams using in-depth semi-structured and structured face-to-face, ICQ, and telephone interviews. Data themes were analysed using NUD*IST software and also manually coded for cross-checking.

## REFERENCES

Alderfer, C. P. (1987). An intergroup perspective on group dynamics. In J. Lornsch (Ed.), *Handbook of Organizational Behaviour* (pp.191-222). Englewood Cliffs, NJ: Prentice Hall.

Al-Kazemi, A. (1998). The self-managed team and tori theory. *International Journal of Commerce and Management, 8*(1), 70-87.

Axelrod, R. (1984). *The Evolution of Co-operation.* New York: Basic Books.

Barber, B. (1983). *The Logic and Limits of Trust.* New Brunswick, NJ: Rutgers University Press.

Barney, J. B. & Hansen, M. H. (1994). Trustworthiness as a source of competitive advantage. *Strategic Management Journal, 15,* 175-190.

Bateson, P. (1988). The biological evolution of cooperation and trust. In D. Gambetta (Ed.), *Trust: Making and Breaking Cooperative Relations* (pp.14-30). New York: Basil Blackwell.

Bishop, S. K. (1999). Cross-functional project teams in functionally aligned organizations. *Project Management Journal, 30*(3), 6-12.

Brey, P. (1999). Worker autonomy and the drama of digital networks in organizations. *Journal of Business Ethics, 22*(1), 15-25.

Butler, J. K. (1991). Toward understanding and measuring conditions of trust: Evolution of a trust inventory. *Journal of Management, 17,* 643-663.

Cascio, W. (2000). Managing a virtual workplace. *The Academy of Management Executive, 14*(3), 82-90.

Cleland, D. I. (1996). *Strategic Management of Teams.* New York: John Wiley & Sons.

Davidow, W. H. & Malone, M. S. (1992). *The Virtual Corporation.* London: Harper Business.

Dimock, H. G. (1987). *Groups: Leadership and Team Development.* San Diego, CA: University Associates.

Driscoll, I. W. (1978). Trust and participation in organization decision making as predictors of satisfaction. *Academy of Management Journal, 21,* 44-56.

Duarte, D. L. & Snyder, N. T. (1999). *Mastering Virtual Teams.* San Francisco: Jossey-Bass.

Eom, S. B. & Lee, C. K. (1999). Virtual teams: An information age opportunity of mobilizing hidden manpower. *S.A.M. Advanced Management Journal, 64*(2), 12-16.

Fairweather, N. B. (1999). Surveillance in employment: The case of teleworking. *Journal of Business Ethics, 22*(1), 39-49.

Gabarro, J. J. (1990). The development of working relationships. In J. Galegher, R. E. Kraut, and C. Egido (Eds.), *Intellectual Teamwork: Social and Technological Foundations of Cooperative Work* (pp.79-110). Hillsdale, NJ: Lawrence Erlbaum Associates.

Gainey, T. W., Kelley, D. E. & Hill, J. A. (1999). Telecommuting's impact on corporate culture and individual workers. *S.A.M. Advanced Management Journal, 64*(4), 4-10.

Galbraith, J. R. (1971). Matrix organization and designs: How to combine functional and project forms. *Business Horizons, 14,* 29-40.

George, J. M. & Jones, G. R. (1997). Experiencing work: Values, attitudes, and moods. *Human Relations, 30,* 393-416.

Hackman, R. J. & Morris, C. G. (1975). Group tasks, group interaction process, and group performance effectiveness: A review and proposed integration. In L. Berkowitz (Ed.), *Advances in Experimental Psychology* (8th ed., pp.45-99). New York: Academic Press.

Handy, C. (1995). Trust and the virtual organization. *Harvard Business Review,* May-June, 40-50.

Harris, M. (1998). Rethinking the virtual organization. In P. J. Jackson and J. M. Van Der Wielen (Eds.), *Teleworking: International Perspectives–From Telecommuting to the Virtual Organization* (pp.74-92). London: Routledge.

Hunsaker, J. R. & Lixfield, G. E. (1999). How technology improves team effectiveness. *The Journal for Quality and Participation, 22*(3), 30-38.

Igbaria, M. & Greenhaus, J. H. (1992). Determinants of MIS employees' turnover intentions: A structural equation model. *Communications of the ACM, 35,* 35-49.

Jackson, L. & Grossman, E. (1999). Integration of synchronous and asynchronous collaboration activities. *ACM Computing Surveys, 31*(2es). Retrieved January 15, 2001, from http://www.informatik.uni-trier.de/~ley/db/journals/ csur/ csur3. html.

Jarvenpaa, S. L. & Ives, B. (1994). The global network organization of the future: Information management opportunities and challenges. *Journal of Management Information Systems, 10*(4), 25-57.

Jarvenpaa, S. L., Knoll, K. & Leidner, D. E. (1998). Is anybody out there? The antecedents of trust in global virtual teams. *Journal of Management Information Systems, 14*(4), 29-64.

Jassawalla, A. R. & Sashittal, H. C. (1999). Building collaborative cross-functional new product teams. *The Academy of Management Executive, 13*(3), 50-63.

Jones, G. R. & George, J. M. (1998). The experience and evolution of trust: Implications for cooperation and teamwork. *Academy of Management Review, 23*(3), 531-546.

Khan, M. B., Tung, L. L. & Turban, E. (1997). Telecommunicating: Comparing Singapore to Southern California. *Human Systems Management, 16*(2), 91-98.

Kharbanda, O. & Stallworthy, E. (1990). *Project Teams: The Human Factor.* London: NCC Blackwell.

Kirkman, B. L., Jones, R. G. & Shapiro, D. L. (2000). Why do employees resist teams? Examining the "resistance barrier" to work team effectiveness. *International Journal of Conflict Management, 11*(1), 74-92.

Kreitner, R. & Kinicki, A. (1992). *Organizational Behavior.* Homewood, IL: Irwin.

Lepak, D. P. & Snell, S. A. (1998). Virtual HR: Strategic human resource management in the 21st century. *Human Resource Management Review, 8*(3), 215-234.

Lipnack, J. & Stamps, J. (1997). *Virtual Teams: Reaching Across Space, Time, and Organizations with Technology.* New York: John Wiley & Sons.

Lipnack, J. & Stamps, J. (1999). Virtual teams: The new way to work. *Strategy & Leadership, 27*(1), 14-19.

Mayer, R. C., Davis, J. H. & Schoorman, F. D. (1995). An integrative model of organizational trust. *Academy of Management Review, 20*(3), 709-734.

Mills, K. L. (1999). Introduction to the electronic symposium on computer-supported cooperative work. *ACM Computing Surveys, 31*(2), 105-116.

Morris, J. H., Neuwirth, C., Regli, S. H., Chandhok, R. & Wenger, G.C. (1999). Interface issues in computer support for asynchronous communication. *ACM Computing Surveys, 31*(2es). Retrieved January 15, 2001, from http:// www.informatik.uni-trier.de/~ley/db/journals/ csur/ csur3. html.

Nilles, J. M. (1998). *Managing Telework: Strategies for Managing the Virtual Workforce.* New York: John Wiley & Sons.

Owen, H. (1996a). Building teams on a display of trust. *People Management, 2*, 34-37.

Owen, H. (1996b). *Creating Top Flight Teams.* London: Kogan Page.

Pinto, M. B., Pinto, J. K. & Prescott, J. E. (1993). Antecedents and consequences of project team cross-functional cooperation. *Management Science, 39*, 1281-1297.

Porter, T. W. & Lilly, B. S. (1996). The effects of conflict, trust, and task commitment on project team performance. *International Journal of Conflict Management, 7*(4), 361-376.

Reinsch, N. L., Jr. (1997). Relationships between telecommuting workers and their managers: An exploratory study. *Journal of Business Communication, 34*(4), 343-369.

Sabel, C. F. (1993). Studied trust: Building new forms of cooperation in a volatile economy. *Human Relations, 46*, 1133-1170.

Scott, C. L., III (1980). Interpersonal trust: A comparison of attitudinal and situational factors. *Human Relations, 33*, 805-812.

Seiling, J. G. (1999). Reaping the rewards of rewarding work. *Journal for Quality and Participation, 22*(2), 16-20.

Spreitzer, G. M. & Mishra, A. K. (1999). Giving up control without losing control: Trust and its substitutes' effects on managers' involving employees in decision making. *Group & Organization Management, 24*(2), 155-187.

Steiner, I. D. (1972). *Group Processes and Productivity*. New York: Academic Press.

Teo, T. S. H., Lim, V. K. G. & Har, W. S. (1999). Assessing attitudes towards teleworking among information technology (IT) personnel. *Singapore Management Review, 21*(1), 33. Retrieved January 12, 2001, from http://global.umi.com/pqdweb?TS=97927090.

Townsend, A. M., DeMarie, S. M. & Hendrickson, A. R. (1998). Virtual teams: Technology and the workplace of the future. *The Academy of Management Executive, 12*(3), 17-29.

Wellins, R. S., Wilson, R., Katz, A. J., Laughlin, P., Day, C. R., Jr., & Price, D. (1990). *Self-Directed Work Teams: A Study of Current Practice*. Pittsburgh, PA: DDI.

**Chapter VIII**

# What Can We Do For Corporate Nomads? IT and Facilities Management

James McCalman
Ashridge Management College, UK

## ABSTRACT

*This chapter examines the impact of technology on facilities management. By focusing attention on the needs of the "corporate nomad," individuals who take advantage of technology and new forms of work organization to break out of the 9-5 mentality of corporate life, it suggests that even the virtual office requires a degree of facilities management. It argues that organizations will become increasingly aware of the need to better utilise expensive real estate in real time to ensure a synergy between organizational and individual needs.*

## INTRODUCTION

Does the establishment of electronic business (eBusiness) mark the beginning of a revolution? Tapscott (1995, p.1) describes its growth as part of the burgeoning of a digital economy where,

We are witnessing the early, turbulent days of a revolution as significant as any other in human history. A new medium of human communications is emerging, one that may prove to surpass all previous revolutions ... in its impact on our economic and social life. The computer is expanding from a tool for information management to a tool for communications ... In this digital economy, individuals and enterprises create wealth by applying knowledge, networked human intelligence, and effort to manufacturing, agriculture, and services. In the digital frontier of this economy, the players, dynamics, rules, and requirements for survival and success are changing.

The impact of information technology (IT) on workplace design can also be viewed as a management fad which goes in and out of favour as tastes change. Like management trends in general, the newest incarnation of IT, eBusiness, has just about reached the stage of popular critique and many would argue that it is only a matter of time before it is seen as a populist notion or fad more associated with youth culture than organizational logic. However, the concept of workplace design has a much deeper history and has been a popular practice that has survived intact for over 50 years.

This chapter sets out to analyze the social and psychological impact of technology enhancements and organizational change on the nature of work and employment. It takes as its focus how workplace design can be used to combine the physical work environment, technology and the flexible workforce in a more employee-centred manner. It therefore raises issues associated with facilities management.

Although globalism and the e-explosion have placed significant attention on the concept of the nonphysical workplace, there has been little by way of research on the impact on facilities design for organizations. Systems of work which stress the significance of the Internet and the growing role of flexibility of work remain ill-defined and tend to focus attention on technology, knowledge management, and the need for "rethinking" the organization of the future. A focus on human-computer interaction which places emphasis on the link between person and machine without considering the physical workplace is futuristic at best and naïve in its conceptualization of the brave new world. Organizations going through the change process of the "e-age" will have to think radically about organizational form. However, a crucial mistake would be to deny the significance of the physical form through assertions of Internet supremacy. The management of IT needs to analyze the impact between organizational structures, teamwork, and inter/intra-organizational collaborations. People need places to work, and eBusiness, if it does anything, provides us with an opportunity to examine how workplace design can be used to reinvigorate the corporation, providing us with new models of doing business and enjoying work.

In this chapter a case study of workplace design with an eBusiness emphasis is used to explore the key issues in developing work organizations capable of managing flexible workforces. The emphasis is on what is termed the "corporate nomad," a form of flexible worker whose needs are to combine technology advancement, temporal distortions, and team working. This chapter therefore focuses on the key issues organizations will need to take into account during the introduction of more flexible forms of work driven by technological and eBusiness concerns.

# WORKPLACE DESIGN

The boundaries of what management once considered acceptable work redesign have been expanded by information technology combined with continuous competitive pressures.  The approaches now being developed give employees considerably enhanced discretion and opportunities for skills development, lifestyle change and improved performance. However, are such assertions necessarily new? In the 1980s, Reich argued that rapid changes in the technology of products and production demanded the development of "flexible systems" (1983). Market segmentation, increasingly informed and demanding consumers, complex and sophisticated product and process technologies, and changes in tastes and fashions meant that speed and flexibility of response were going to be essential organizational characteristics. Hirschhorn (1984) argued that while modern organizational systems involved little manual work, the need for employee autonomy and problem solving skills needed to be enhanced, and work reorganization based on the socio-technical systems design approach would prove more effective. There may be a sense in which the concept of "new wine in old bottles" appears appropriate for discussions of the impact of IT on workplace design.

If we define eBusiness as a combination of technologies, applications, processes, business strategies and practices necessary to do business electronically (Taylor & Berg, 1995), then how does this affect the nature of the relationships between buyers and suppliers and between organizations and their customers? eBusiness technologies such as the Internet have had a significant effect on business-to-consumer trading over the last 5 years.  However, there appears to be an even greater potential associated with business-to-business transactions (Kehoe & Boughton, 1998). Benjamin, Malone and Yates (1986) argue that electronic commerce can reduce the costs of integrating customers and their suppliers, and through electronic networks companies can achieve integration by tightly coupling processes at the interfaces between each stage of the value chain. The effective implementation of eBusiness to support supplier relationships and to optimize the supply chain requires that eBusiness is fully integrated into both business architecture and technology infrastructure of both the supplier and the customer. eBusiness technologies are eliminating activities normally carried out in customer and supplier organizations. Such changes pose an immense challenge to the role of the functions in managing the interorganizational interactions. eBusiness is also having the effect of "blurring" the traditional boundaries in the value chain between suppliers, manufacturers and end customers  (McIvor, Humphreys & Huang, 2000). On a related theme, MIT's "Management in the 1990s" research project differentiated business process reengineering from business network redesign (BNR).  While the former focused attention on the redesign of internal organizational processes, the latter concerned itself with the wider business network (Peppard, 1996).

So what is new about the impact of eBusiness and design? Bradley and Woodling (2000, p.162) suggest that eBusiness, through the effective use of information and communications technologies (ICT), is having an impact on the way in which business space is managed: "Most organizations are seeking to minimize fixed costs of business space and ICT infrastructure. However, they often need to rapidly accommodate fluctuations in number and locations of personnel (often project-based) for a restricted duration and ideally without incremental increase in support costs." Similarly, Sparrow (2000, p.215) suggests that, "key organizational behaviours came to the fore in this teleworking environment. Companies began to shift their internal and external resourcing systems towards the assessment of important competencies such as information search, flexibility and problem genera-tion skills." eBusiness brings with it certain design necessities for management which include:

- how to manage knowledge and labour;
- how to manage the interaction between people in numerous workplaces in synchronous and asynchronous patterns;
- how to control organizations in nontraditional manners;
- how to manage closer relationships between the supplier, producer and consumer (both on a business-to-consumer and business-to-business basis);
- how to manage the integration between the information networks of customers and suppliers.

The challenge, as Bradley and Woodling (2000, p.162) suggest, is, "How can alternative workplaces maintain the corporate values of identity, service and environmental quality as well as enabling rapidly assembled teams to form and perform effectively from the outset?" The management of facilities design brings with it a growing, unsatisfied demand for faster response, limited duration business space and infrastructure.

Paralleling the change in the demand for business space usage is an eBusiness technology revolution which offers the advantages of:

- moving the concept and purpose of work towards the use and management of knowledge;
- temporal space reduction enabling multiple projects/people/places interaction;
- loosening traditional management controls and hierarchies in favour of collabo-rative information sharing project processes;
- closer relationships between buyers/suppliers/customers;
- integration of information networks between customers and suppliers;
- focusing on core business and outsourcing the rest (Bradley & Woodling, 2000, p.163).

eBusiness thus allows us to reformulate what we mean by the organization and the workplace. The reformulation has two crucial aspects to it:

1. For the individual charged with the challenge of working within an eBusiness environment, the concept of space and time are different. We can visualize this individual as being capable of working independently of location and time. What these individuals need is access to their organization as a "club" to meet with other highly autonomous eBusiness collaborators (Worthington, 1997).

2. The workplace itself also needs to be reconstituted. Organizations need to "rent access to facilities and resources wherever they may be, whenever

needed. The ability to gain access 'anytime, anywhere,' is a fundamental aspect of new ways of working, and a major attribute of the quality of place (the *genus loci*) in the new economy, in which speed of access will be the major provider of comparative advantage." (Bradley & Woodling, 2000).

We can therefore envision the eBusiness as an organization utilizing a multimedia environment through computer-supported collaborative work (CSCW) in project-based teams (*thus creating oases for corporate nomads*).

# THE IMPACT OF E-BUSINESS ON FACILITIES MANAGEMENT

It would be true to say that concern over the ability to provide organizations with infrastructure services management have generally been considered to be secondary to the delivery of an organization's core business activities. However, as business has become ever more competitive there has been a focus on the need to drive down the costs of doing business and a growing need to move beyond simple "least cost" and "non-core" evaluations of facilities management (FM) delivery. The design of space in the organization has become relevant to business success in ways that many do not fully understand. The design of the working environment has for a long time been considered a marginal and technical matter, best left to experts to sort out. With the onset of eBusiness, changes in the ways in which organizations operate are dependent upon attracting, retaining and stimulating people. This has led to a growing awareness that FM needs to develop in response to organizational change (Becker, 1990; Grimshaw, 1999; Cairns & Beech, 1999; Nutt, 1999). Modern eBusinesses will need to strive to be more attractive to ordinary people. One crucial aspect of this attractiveness is the accessibility and functioning of office space. In general, the design of buildings has stayed physically more or less exactly where office design began at the beginning of the 20th century. Facilities managers are inherently conservative even though the concept of facilities management developed largely because of a growing realization that the physical environment of the office was not enough to solve rapidly developing business requirements. Duffy (2000, p.2) argues that facilities management is a static profession because of a set of fundamental beliefs concerning how people and buildings interact. These place a focus on a set of criteria:

- an idle underclass has to be constantly supervised (the open plan);
- each step in career advancement within stable organizational hierarchies must always be marked (elaboration of grade and status);
- everyone needs to be constantly reminded who is on top (sharply differentiated space allocation);
- departments, functions and individuals should be kept apart (strict boundary maintenance);
- quasi-monopolies must control information flow (yet more boundary maintenance);

- presenteeism (as opposed to absenteeism) is always a good thing (a fixed desk for everyone all the time);
- home and work are two different and irreconcilable worlds (commuting is the natural state of mankind).

We have seen throughout the e-business revolution trends towards greater organizational flexibility coinciding with more intensive use of information technology. In the early 1990s a study involving 22 in-depth case studies in eight European countries entitled "The Intelligent Building in Europe," suggested that whilst the impact of information technology on organizations and buildings has been enormous over the last 20 years, it would be regarded as a liberating rather than a constraining force during the next decade. "It will allow greater flexibility of building usage and encourage new ways of working" (DEGW, 1992).

Just as the effective application of information technology is recognized as an essential resource for business, the DEGW study recognized the need for intelligent buildings that provide a responsive, effective and supportive environment within which the organization could achieve its business objectives: "Building, space and business technologies are the tools that help this happen" (DEGW, 1992). This concept of "building intelligence" was regarded as, "a collection of technologies able to respond to organizational change over time" (DEGW, 1992).

Buildings as physical entities have, of course, no innate intelligence; however, effectively designed, equipped and managed environments can foster the conditions where the collective actions of individuals can more effectively generate, manipulate and distribute knowledge throughout the organization and externally to customers and suppliers.

The blurring of the boundaries between social life and work life provide both opportunity and different types of stress on the individual. Organizations are, at their simplest level, collections of people who through their combined efforts can achieve extraordinary results. Man is essentially a social animal whose psychological needs include those for social interaction, a sense of purpose and a sense of belonging. Offices are social spaces. The whole reason for their existence is as a place for people to meet and work together.

Whilst for a proportion of people, ICT allows them to work remotely and on the move; for the vast majority, the notion of a single workplace will remain. As our ability to generate and process information anytime, anyplace increases, organizational development will see more team-based working, flattening hierarchies, empowerment and customer interactions. The fact is that work has changed dramatically over the last 10 years, yet changes in workplace design have been slow to respond. Traditional office environments are already outdated and future work settings are likely to challenge our paradigms further.

What then might the future workplace look like? What we do know is that traditional office design is socio-fugal. It drives people into cellular offices at the expense of interaction. In the knowledge-based organization people need to be able to come together and interact in teams. With less hierarchy and more open access to knowledge, the workplace becomes a catalyst for creativity.

Traditionally offices have been used to confer the status of individuals and to demonstrate the distribution of power within the organization (Barnard, 1946; Katz & Khan, 1978; Konar, Sundstrom, Brady, Mandel & Rice,1982). We also know that the highest quality and amount of space is usually reserved for the most senior staff, who conversely spend the least amount of time there. In the future knowledge workers will place increased demands for a more equitable allocation and distribution of space and resources. Traditional signs of status have included location (Steele, 1973), accessibility (Langdon, 1976), floor space (Fetridge & Minor, 1975), furnishings (Duffy, 1969), and personalization (Sundstrom, 1986). In the knowledge-based organization, where people are constantly changing their team-based structures, new ways will have to be found to confer rank or status where important.

We also know that space use over time varies dramatically over the course of a typical day. At some times there are very low levels of occupancy in some locations and high intensity demand on others such as meeting rooms. As companies move towards a more flexible cost base, contingency workers have become more common, and organizational restructuring has seen a migration towards more contract-based staff to meet short-term changes in demand to tailor services to meet customer requirements. The office of the future therefore must be flexible and adaptable to sudden changes in organizational demand.

Office design has latterly seen migration towards a range of alternative workplace strategies including universal footprints, multiple activity settings, non-territorial offices, shared assigned spaces, touchdown areas and hotelling. In addition workplace strategies often encompass a wider range of off-site options such as home working, telecommuting, virtual offices, satellite offices and the use of serviced office space.

Gordon (2000) highlights that telecommuting is on a steady growth curve. Many employers are starting to divide work done in the traditional office versus work done elsewhere. The increasing army of "corporate nomads," who spend time between offices, working from home or traveling, also requires an oasis, a place to replenish supplies, gain access to resources, socially interact and share knowledge. However, many authors agree that the growth of teleworking has so far failed to live up to the expectation that it would become the new way to work. Tate (2000) highlights the fact that many people still continue commuting to the office. Charlton (1996) claims that teleworking will have continued low growth and that it will be restricted to niche markets.

In the age of the Internet, at the dawn of the knowledge-based society, it is strange that we tolerate buildings—and building environment systems—that assume that everyone comes in at 9 and leaves at 5 and sits solidly at a desk for 5 days a week. The model, of course, is still the factory where foremen had to put enormous emphasis on synchrony to force a barely literate proletariat to work at the loom and the lathe. When the bell rings the work begins. When the siren blows it is over—for the day.

The reality of eBusiness working life is far more complex. There are aspects associated with managing knowledge and time that create greater degrees of individual independence, yet place a higher focus on inter- and intra-organizational teamwork. This suggests that, "ubiquitous networks mean that the office is wherever we want it to be" (Duffy, 2000, p.3).

The following case study demonstrates the integration of strategic real estate management with business planning and the design of the working environment. Office design can play a pivotal role in supporting new ways of working. The case recognizes that after people and knowledge, space is a major organizational resource that must be managed efficiently and imaginatively if it is to be used to maximum advantage.

## MANAGING THE CORPORATE NOMAD

Opportunities to rethink the way in which the working environment supports an organization arise in response to either business or real estate triggers. The two however should not be seen as mutually exclusive, rather as interrelated dimensions that collectively impact upon organizational performance.

Real estate triggers such as lease breaks focus attention on considerations such as space- and image-related requirements, technological requirements, and the need for real estate flexibility in line with dynamic business needs. Each of these has a bottom line impact through the costs of facilities to be provided.

Business triggers might include changes in staff size or structure, company mergers and acquisitions, changes in customer expectations, new product offerings, and investments in new technologies. Each of these may require specific real estate requirements.

Despite the fact that offices are available 365 days per year, by the time the working pattern has been reduced to a 5-day week, an 8-hour day and staff have gone on holiday, had lunch, been ill and visited clients, buildings are used for less than 10% of their full potential. The pressure to maximize the potential of space by increasing staff density is understandable.

The potential exists to reduce costs by reviewing and changing working patterns and by designing working environments that reflect these.

ABC was one of the world's largest media services groups employing more than 30,000 staff in over 50 countries. In 1996 the group introduced a new workplace programme which provided guidance to all group companies on best practice in real estate management and space planning. The programme was developed in response to a realization that after people the group invested more money worldwide in real estate than anything else.

An internal team of specialist workplace consultants and designers was set up to administer and implement the workplace programme worldwide. Three teams had geographic responsibility for the Americas, Europe, and Asia Pacific, and each team was responsible for providing strategic advice to individual companies on areas ranging from real estate acquisitions or disposals to workplace relocation and reconfiguration.

Each team was required to be highly flexible in order to respond to the needs of individual business units who themselves operated in a particularly dynamic industry; none more so than in the Asia Pacific region, operating across significantly different time zones. The teams made use of videoconferencing for design team meetings and would transfer data and drawings electronically to the European office for ongoing development at the end of the Asian working day. Collectively, the teams had the capacity for 24-hour working on time-critical projects. The teams were highly mobile and autonomous and spent little time in a single location. As such the workplace consultancy teams were virtual operations in every sense of the word. They were in fact a microcosm of many elements of the operational structure of the larger group companies.

Whilst the drivers for organizational change vary for any company, a number of factors characterized the Asia Pacific business of the group:

- Real estate cycles tended to be significantly shorter than those in Europe are; typically office leases were only for 3 years.
- Most office developments were speculator designed. In rapidly developing economies investment in speculative office developments could quickly lead to an oversupply situation, increasing tenant choice and driving down rental costs. Often rental savings between locations could offset the costs of moving to new offices including fitting out.

In cities such as Hong Kong, Shanghai, Auckland, Sydney, Mumbai and New Delhi, up to 10 companies from the group operated from independent locations. Opportunities existed therefore to colocate companies, pooling the overall space requirement and deriving both financial benefits from economies of scale, but also organizational and operational synergies from being together.

A pervasive characteristic of office use in all locations analyzed by the workplace consultancy was that increasingly staff spent less time in the office and more time traveling or in alternative office arrangements. Hong Kong, in addition to servicing a significant market in its own right, acted as the Asia Pacific regional headquarters for each of the group companies. A high proportion of staff spent a significant amount of their time traveling and working from other locations. A further characteristic of the nature of businesses such as advertising, marketing, and public relations was that they were primarily concerned with the communication of information or ideas to allow people to be able to make choices about what to buy, about lifestyle choices, about health or how to vote, etc.

The development of communications products relied heavily upon teamwork to allow the exchange of ideas and information from a variety of sources and to transform these ideas into a communications strategy. The client and the consumer were also integral parts of the production process.

Whilst ICT enabled new ways of communicating and working, in itself it was not the main reason for organizational change and workplace redesign—customers, competition and change were the primary change drivers. Getting closer to customers and involving them in the supply chain, maintaining competitive advantage, and being flexible, adaptable and responsive could be achieved through the creation of an enabling business infrastructure.

The Hong Kong colocation project provided an opportunity for the group to optimize returns from real estate as a factor of production. Within a period of 12 months, 10 group companies would reach lease expiry points at a time when the Hong Kong office market was in a substantial oversupply situation. The Asian economies had recently slowed and a number of companies were experiencing a period of consolidation or negative growth. The group also wanted to use the workplace reconfiguration exercise as a means of introducing and implementing a wider programme of new work practices, in particular to improve organizational communications and facilitate teamwork, and to gain synergies from merging back-office operations.

The workplace consultants wanted to create environments that provided more flexible and effective use of space that could accommodate changes in organizational demand over the medium term. In addition the environment needed to be branded to reflect the culture of each company to visitors and employees.

In every case the organizational analysis was an organizational intervention aimed at exploring the art of the possible in terms of existing working practices and how they could be improved upon. To this end the intervention focused on the interrelationship between people, process and place over time.

Employee education and communications were seen as a fundamental output of the exercise. It was insufficient to merely undertake organizational and building research and subsequently implement a design solution. The resultant design solutions would have to have a high degree of employee ownership following significant input and "education" into new ways of working. As such the exercise could be regarded as an opportunity for organizational learning.

Office environments were reconfigured as multiple activity settings that better reflected the way in which the workplace provided support to the individual and the team. The reconfigurations allocated space by task and function rather than rank or status. Areas were provided for formal and informal meetings, stimulating brainstorming tanks, and visibility and circulation routes were redesigned to provide greater opportunities for chance encounters. Social spaces such as cyber cafes, libraries and staff clubs were created to enhance the sense of cohesion and teamwork within the office. Settings were designed to meet work requirements ranging from quiet concentration to noisy and humorous brainstorming. The workspaces included opportunities for hotdesking, touchdown areas, hotelling and bookable and nonbookable meeting areas.

Whilst the consultancy and design teams encountered inevitable cultural barriers, in general the opportunity to implement alternative workplace strategies was welcomed and embraced. The success in introducing workplace change was not down to the development of e-business and ICT. It was about developing an appreciation of the way in which the workplace supported the organization and the individual. The new workplace configurations had to be seen to be equitable. As Becker (1981) has suggested, the concept of equity, one of the basic principles of space standards, may be enhanced through variety, which provides individuals who differ in work style or level of competence with a range of environmental supports to suit the diversity of individual needs. Equity from the employee perspective was not defined in terms of having the same amount of something. Equity became defined as the provision of appropriate environmental supports for a given level of activity and knowledge. All design processes involved a series of trade-offs. The accommodation of diversity created environments that were both flexible and resilient; however, end user involvement in workplace design was a fundamental component in design solution acceptability.

# CONCLUSION

If knowledge is the fundamental currency of the modern business, then the ability to share and manipulate it cannot be realized solely through investment in ICT alone.

The new workplace must accommodate a much wider variety of settings than those provided by traditional design solutions. Not all work happens at a desk. Not all meetings take place in meeting rooms. Knowledge workers need a variety of different settings to suit their different needs at different times of the day. They need places for individuals to think and work quietly, places for groups to gather and exchange ideas, places for people to meet—which may be formal or informal, scheduled or impromptu, electronically or face-to-face—places for teams to set up long-term projects, and places for those just dropping in.

The success of alternative workplace strategies is ultimately measured by their impact in contributing towards increased organizational effectiveness, often measured in terms of the organization bottom line. But organizational effectiveness might also be measured in terms of an organization's general state of health: the ability to achieve goals, the presence or absence of organizational stress, the quality of life of staff, the capacity to be flexible, adaptable and resilient to change.

Enabling technologies often play a key role in harnessing the potential of truly flexible working, providing access to information regardless of location. Workplace flexibility in the case study above was achieved not through investment in enabling technologies but through an in-depth analysis and understanding of the functioning of the business and the way in which the physical environment supports it.

Many of the most fundamental tasks in a knowledge-based organization are in fact "low-tech"—such as thinking, social interaction and generating ideas, the act of being creative.

Increasingly facilities are being seen as a factor of production and business resource rather than a corporate overhead. As any factor of production they must work for the business and allow companies to release the potential of the workforce. Whilst organization's needs are inherently dynamic, physical facilities are by contrast relatively static and have often been regarded as slow to respond to the needs of business.

The notion of the virtual workplace—anytime, anyplace—pervades the language surrounding e-business. The stark reality however is that the office provides us with a physical touchstone amidst the virtual reality of modern business. The workplace provides us with a sense of place, a sense of belonging, an oasis, and in some cases the office might be construed as a metaphor for the corporate entity itself—purposeful, collegiate, social, resilient and flexible.

Nobody knows what a better workplace might look like. The responsibility of designers and managers should therefore be to help organizations manage their workplace experiments more intelligently. Albert Einstein once said, "Imagination is more powerful than knowledge." Despite all the knowledge we might have of business and human needs, unless we can imagine a better workplace, how can we design one?

# REFERENCES

Barnard, C. (1954). Functional pathology of status systems in formal organizations. In W. Whyte (Ed.), *Industry and Society*. Chicago: McGraw-Hill.

Becker, F. (1981). *Workspace: Creating Environments in Organizations*. New York: Praeger.

Becker, F. D. (1990). *The Total Workplace: Facilities Management and the Elastic Organization*. New York: Van Nostrand Reinhold.

Benjamin, R. I., Malone, W. T. & Yates, J. (1986). *Electronic markets and electronic hierarchies* (CISR Working Paper No. 137). Centre for Information Systems Research, Boston: Massachusetts Institute of Technology, Sloan School of Management.

Bradley, S. & Woodling, G. (2000). Accommodating future business intelligence: New work-space and work-time challenges for management and design. *Facilities*, *18*(3/4).

Cairns, G. & Beech, N. (1999). Flexible working: Organizational liberation or individual straitjacket. *Facilities*, *17*(1/2).

Charlton, J. (1996). Home or away. *Computer Weekly*, May.

DEGW & Teknibank. (1992). *The Intelligent Building In Europe; Study Report*, May.

Duffy, F. (1969). Role and status in the office. *Architectural Association Quarterly*, 1.

Duffy, F. (2000). Design and facilities management in a time of change. *Facilities*, *18*(10/11/12).

Fetridge, C. & Minor, R. (Eds.) (1975). *Office Administration Handbook*. Chicago: Dartnell Press.

Gordon, G. (2000). *Administration and General Information FAQ*. Internet–Telecommuting Tools.

Grimshaw, R. W. (1999). The wider implications of managing change. *Facilities*, *17*(1/2).

Katz, D. & Khan, R. (1978). *The Social Psychology of Organizations*. New York: John Wiley & Sons.

Kehoe, D. F. & Boughton, N. J. (1998). DOMAIN: Dynamic operations management across the Internet. In *Strategic Management of the Value Chain*, sponsored by the International Federation for Information Processing, University of Strathclyde.

Konar, E., Sundstrom, E., Brady, C., Mandel, D. & Rice, R. (1982). Status markers in the office. *Environment and Behaviour*, *14*, 3.

Langdon, F. (1966). Modern offices: A user survey. *National Building studies Research paper*. London: HMSO.

McIvor, R., Humphreys, P. & Huang, G. (2000). Electronic commerce: Re-engineering the buyer-supplier interface. *Business Process Management Journal*, *6*(2).

McLoughlin, I. & Clark, J. (1984). *Technological Change at Work*. Milton Keynes: Open University Press.

Nutt, B. (1999). Linking FM practice and research. *Facilities*, *17*(1/2).

Peppard, J. (1996). Broadening visions of business process reengineering. *Omega*, *24*(3).

Sparrow, P. R. (2000). New employee behaviours, work design and forms of work organization: What is in store for the future of work? *Journal of Managerial Psychology*, *15*(3).

Steele, F. (1973). *Physical Settings and Organizational Development*. Reading, MA: Addison-Wesley.

Sundstrom, E. (1986). *Work Places: The Psychology of the Physical Environment in Offices and Factories*. Cambridge, MA: Cambridge University Press.

Tapscott, D. (1995). *The Digital Economy: Promise and Peril in the Age Networked Intelligence*. London: McGraw-Hill.

Tate, R. (2000). The real virtual office. *BA Business Life*. London: Premier Media Partner Ltd.

Taylor, D. & Berg, T. (1995). The business value of electronic commerce. *Strategic Analysis Report*. Stanford, CT: Gartner Group.

Worthington, J. (Ed.). (1997). *Reinventing the Workplace*. Oxford, England: Butterworth-Heinemann.

## Chapter IX

# Managing the Virtual Corporation Using IT

Reuven R. Levary and Fred Niederman
Saint Louis University, USA

## ABSTRACT

*Virtual organizations are characterized and various types of virtual organizations are described. Factors contributing to the success of virtual organizations are identified. Various technologies for intra-organizational coordination are described and concerns regarding the reliance on technology in virtual organizations are elaborated upon. Issues regarding multilingual Web pages are identified. Finally, the role of the semantic Web in the future of virtual organizations is described.*

## CHARACTERISTICS OF A VIRTUAL ORGANIZATION

A virtual organization is a temporary network or loose coalition of manufacturing and/or services that comes together for a specific business purpose and then disassembles when the purpose has been met (Christie & Levary, 1998). The life cycle of a virtual organization depends upon factors such as the intended objective(s) of the alliance, the type of products manufactured, or the services rendered. Virtual organizations can be ad hoc or can last over a longer time period. Frequently, firms team up in a virtual organization to exploit an opportunity in the market before it evaporates. Once an intended objective is met, the alliance is disbanded. These ad hoc alliances are short lived, extremely focused, goal driven, and powered by time-based competition. They are both created and dissolved quickly. Organizations that are partners in one instance can be rivals and competitors in the next. Longer-term virtual organizations are generally continuously evolving networks of independent companies linked together to share skills, costs, and access to one another's markets and data (Christie & Levary, 1998). Frequently the persistence over time of these links provides ongoing benefits for the participating companies, stability and growth in their relationships, and a sense of predictability for customers and other stakeholders.

We see the virtual organization as a subset of all organizations. Those that are "virtual" are distinguished by two essential characteristics—first they are comprised of two or more independent organizational units and second they are supported at least to a significant degree and in some cases extensively by electronically mediated communication. These two characteristics address two aspects of "virtualness." When discussing an organization consisting of only one unit, then you have a traditional corporation that uses technology. Where you have two or more independent units, then you have some degree to which the management of the linkage between the two has become "virtual." There are examples of this that are completely handled by traditional face-to-face communication, such as building sites using a variety of subcontractors. While this is organizationally "virtual," this sort of arrangement doesn't capture the second aspect of "virtualness," being electronically mediated. An example of such a virtual organization is the alliance among various airlines for purposes of streamlined routing and consolidation of frequent flier arrangements. Additional examples of virtual organizations based on this definition will be presented throughout this chapter.

Such virtual organizations can engage in either business-to-business or business-to-consumer commercial activities. For purposes of focusing within a reasonable scope, in this chapter we wish to focus on the "business-to-business" type of virtual organization. The subset of virtual organizations discussed in this chapter is illustrated in Figure 1.

*Figure 1: Virtual organization definition*

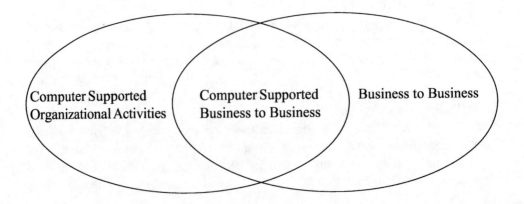

# DISTINCTIONS AMONG DIFFERENT TYPES OF VIRTUAL ORGANIZATIONS

## Dimensions of Virtual Organizations

Although virtual organizations share some commonalities, such as use of information technology for coordinating activities and the relatively loose coupling of multiple organizations, there remain various ways that such virtual organizations can be manifest. Table 1 shows several different kinds of virtual organizations, presents examples of each, and discusses three dimensions on which they vary: control issues, value added, and time span/frequency of interaction.

Given that the virtual organization represents a collaborative effort among independent entities, some attention must be given to the coordination of activities and the ultimate authority for decision making and action taking. There are a number of approaches to addressing control issues that can be taken by firms. These range from setting up shared policies followed by adherence of individual players to those policies, as we see in the case of "alliance" type virtual organizations, to more formal contractual arrangements. Generally, companies that have a name-brand product or service that is widely recognized insist on control of each virtual organization to which they belong (e.g., Wal-Mart, Boeing, GM, etc.).

Since the virtual organization represents a new approach, the organizations engaged in it require some kind of motivation. In general, this will take the form of an added value for the participants or for the customer. An example of added value for the customer would derive from bundling of services to provide a common interface. This would allow, for example, the customer to reserve airline tickets and hotel reservations in a single transaction. Added value for the virtual organization participants would include lower transaction costs in an electronic supply chain arrangement and the application of larger volumes of intellectual capital to given problems in the open systems category of virtual organization. Some firms involved in producing a product or a service (e.g., Dell Computers) allow customers to track the status of their order via the Internet. This ability, an added value to the customer, results from Internet technology that is used to support communication and data transfer among the various firms comprising a virtual organization (e.g., suppliers, manufacturers, transportation companies).

An additional distinction among virtual organizations derives from timing issues. This can involve both the length of time they are expected to last and the frequency with which they are used. Some virtual organizations will last for the duration of a single project, such as the deployment of information technology during an Olympics or World Cup activity. In such a virtual organization, a variety of firms will contribute from their particular expertise — IBM in computers, AT&T in communications, for example — to provide a seamless set of information services in support of a particular project. Other organizations may fill these roles in future projects, for example, Microsoft in computers, and Southwest Bell in communications. In contrast, other virtual organizations will benefit from longer-term relationships. Alliances between various airlines serving different regions in the world will benefit from long-term

*Table 1: Categories and examples by dimensions*

| Category | Examples | Control Issues | Value Added | Time span/ frequency |
|---|---|---|---|---|
| Alliance | Airline alliance<br><br>Star Alliance including: United, SAS, Lufthansa, Varig, Air Canada, Singapore Airlines | Shared control through policies<br><br>Balance between actors | Common Interface for customer<br><br>Lower costs to customer/increase size of purchase<br><br>One-stop shop for customer | Among partners: Long term for best results<br><br>Customers long term for redemptions, may have multiple relationships |
| Supply chain | Wal Mart & suppliers<br><br>Land's End & UPS | Asymmetrical partners -- Imposition from buyer at each stage<br><br>Contractual | Lower transaction costs distributed through network | Long term for best results<br><br>Transactions may be long or short |
| Project contractor | World Cup<br><br>Boeing engineers<br><br>Construction project | Contractor hierarchy<br><br>Contractual of varying formality | Common interface for customer<br><br>Modular accumulation of specialized skills | Generally short term, may vary with project size |
| Tele-immigration<br><br>Tele-work | India service centers<br><br>Labor auctions | Contractor<br><br>Rare-skill bargaining power | Advantages of lower cost economies | Generally short term |
| Auction<br><br>Reverse auction | Manheim Online | Middleman sets terms and arrangements | Clear market at optimal costs<br><br>Generate additional transactions | Short term<br><br>May build pattern of repeated use |
| Information and referral | Web MD<br><br>Yahoo | Middleman | Multiple uses for same information<br><br>Can provide advantage for high quality/ eliminate low quality suppliers | Short term, may build pattern of repeated use |
| Finance | Group Health Insurance | Middleman | Save steps<br><br>Transaction is the product<br><br>Integrate multiple products<br><br>Provide expertise in portfolio | Long term for best results (customer-broker; broker-service provider)<br><br>Short term for transactions |
| Open system | Linux | Community peer pressure and testing | Fast contributions in short time period<br><br>Collective and persistent knowledge base | Long term advantages<br><br>Short term for individual contributions |

relationships in developing user awareness and avoiding costs associated with frequent revision of schedules and flight connections. Many manufacturers (e.g., Ford, GM, Toyota, Boeing) have established long-term relationships with some of their suppliers. These suppliers depend on the business volume from those manufacturers and a long-term relationship is beneficial to both parties.

## Types of Virtual Organizations

The authors have identified eight distinct types of virtual organizations (see Table 1). These are: alliance, supply chain, project contractor, tele-immigration/ telework, auction and reverse auction, information and referral, financial, and open systems. These types of virtual organizations differ in terms of controls, value added, and timing of their activities.

The alliance is typified by independent companies that work independently but provide coordinated services. Various airlines will develop alliances to provide relatively seamless global service to customers by coordinating schedules, reservation methods, and frequent flier miles. From the customer perspective, a unified itinerary is provided for global travel even as each independent corporate entity provides a particular segment of the flight. The Star Alliance including United Airlines, SAS, Lufthansa, Varig, Air Canada and Singapore Airlines, is an alliance of independent airlines that provides customers a coordinated travel service worldwide.

The supply chain combines efforts by independent firms to provide transformation of goods or services from raw material to end product. This may involve a single structured sequence of firms from raw material extractors through transporters to retail merchants or may involve a broader network of providers at each stage. It is advantageous to the many companies within a supply chain to effectively coordinate activities. Information technology makes implementing firm-to-firm coordination of activities feasible. This coordination of activities is the core of supply chain management (Levary, 2000). A special business relationship must be established among the companies along a supply chain if the coordination of activities is to be optimized. This relationship promotes the combination of several independent firms into a "virtual organization." The short lead-time between the order of a Dell Computer and the delivery of the computer to the customer is the result of effective coordination of activities within Dell's supply chain.

The project contractor model builds around a central organizing agent who assembles various project participants based on the needs of the particular project. For example, installing a computer system for a particular department of a multinational firm may involve coordination of efforts among computer hardware, software, and telecommunication vendors as well as units for installation, maintenance, training, and ongoing troubleshooting. This sort of project contractor model tends to be ad hoc, though configurations and patterns may develop for repetitive projects. In the field of telecommunications, for example, a mobile virtual corporation was created by EDS, Sprint, and Sun Microsystems to manage the security, press, administration, and public information systems for the World Cup. In the manufacturing industry, the Boeing 777 was created by a virtual network of partners.

The tele-immigration/telework category is typified by the firm that outsources computer programming or other information technology work particular to overseas providers. Such work is typically ad hoc or project by project and may involve segmenting larger projects and outsourcing them as smaller chunks to be assembled by the contracting firm. This may be a special case of the project contractor model for software and other IT projects. It is, however, characterized by especially high levels of reliance on computer technology for communication among participating organizations. Several manufacturers and software development companies often characterize the specifications of specific parts that need to be designed or software models that need to be developed. Those characteristics together with schedules and proposed compensation are transmitted via the Internet to freelance engineers and software developers in countries such as India and Russia. Interested parties submit their credentials via e-mail and the manufacturer or software development company chooses the tele-immigrant to work on the project. The tele-immigrant is paid only after his design was submitted and approved by the originating firm.

The auction and reverse auction represent something of an intermediate category between supply chain and project contractor. In essence, the auction/ reverse auction approach creates a marketplace for the exchange of partial goods. In contrast to supply chain, it does not necessarily imply long-term interconnections for transacting business, but does address the same transfer of partially completed products. Examples are provided below in the section entitled "Software Used as a Platform for Online Business-To-Business."

Information and referral pertains to the sort of virtual organization that acts as a switching and guiding station for connecting clients with mutual interests. In the medical realm, such a virtual organization might compile information regarding insurance plans and benefits as well as medical needs to build bridges for practitioners. Web-MD is useful to both patients and health care providers, such as physicians, hospitals, HMOs, pharmacists, and medical laboratories, and to insurance companies. Various health care providers use Web-MD to search and obtain needed, current medical information via the Internet. This is both a time and cost efficient process.

Financial refers to institutions that facilitate monetary transactions. This can resemble the project contractor model in bringing together teams of insurance, banking, legal, and investment specialists to build comprehensive programs for particular clients. It can also work in terms of electronic funds transfer for the coordination of financial aspects of electronic data interchange type transactions following the supply chain model. For example, Group Health Insurance offers electronic fund transfer opportunities for health care providers to receive payment for claims efficiently (GHI, 2001).

Open systems approaches represent a unique type of virtual organization. In essence, a wide range of people and organizations with a common interest will contribute to some kind of creation — most notably software systems as in the Linux case — for the common good. Even without contributing, anyone can access the products of these collaborations. However, contributors are recognized for their work and others may profit from selling related services such as training or customization for a particular installation.

As can be seen, these virtual organizations can take a variety of forms. That diversity implies that the technology base for operating these will vary. However, given the reliance on telecommunication and group technologies as well as the aspect of collaboration among independent entities, there are some key commonalities that must be addressed by virtual organizations in general.

# FACTORS CONTRIBUTING TO THE SUCCESS OF VIRTUAL ORGANIZATIONS

Analysis of successful and unsuccessful virtual organizations has resulted in the identification of nine factors that may contribute significantly to the success of virtual organizations (Christie & Levary, 1998). They are outlined below.

## Focus on Customer Needs

By definition, a virtual organization is a network of organizations coming together for the specific purpose of meeting customer needs. The virtual organization should be highly focused on the customer. It should arise from a response to customer need and it should disintegrate with the fulfillment of that need for ad hoc varieties. In successful virtual organizations, the "pull" strategy, which draws from the market customers, replaces the "push" strategy. In today's fast-paced economy, organizations that intelligently forecast or discern customer needs and meet them in a timely fashion reap success.

## Choice of Right Partners With Right Core Competencies

The structure of virtual organizations is predicated on competency needs rather than on convenience of location, cost, etc. Core competencies form the fundamental nucleus of virtual organizations and represent the most important factor in success or failure. Virtual organizations should focus only on those core competencies that create value and give competitive advantage. Ideally, core competencies should be "those things that are difficult for the competitors to replicate," according to Ogilvie (1994). Each core competency brought into the alliance should complement other competencies in the virtual organization. A synergy should develop that helps the alliance reach its goal quickly, efficiently, and effectively. Partners who are trustworthy, open, and cooperative and who enjoy certain competitive advantages in the marketplace are vital to the success of virtual organizations. It demands effort and scrutiny to find honest organizations that have the necessary core competencies and that are reliable.

## Win-Win Outcome for All Participating Organizations

The goal of the virtual organization must merge the interests of all partners, as the success of a virtual organization depends on the degree of collaboration and cooperation between each of the allied partners. All participating companies rely on the competencies and support of everyone to achieve the goal. Exploitation or bullying will derail the alliance. The role and function of each participating company should be clarified. A balance of power among all involved must be established for the success of virtual organizations.

## Protection of Companies' Proprietary Information

In many categories of virtual organization, particularly alliances, companies must share information regarding their customers, suppliers, and technology. Total restriction of access to information would defeat the purpose of virtual organizations. Companies may even find it valuable at times to establish alliances with companies simultaneously in order to meet different market requirements. Companies should be able to quickly establish information technology with one another and just as quickly disconnect when the alliance is disbanded so that proprietary information is not jeopardized. Two things become essential. First, it becomes the responsibility of each company to make available all information relevant to successful completion of the task of the virtual organization, while segregating that information from what it wishes to retain privately. Second, when some private information is needed for successful completion of the project, the firm must seek means to allow the information to be known but not usable by its partner/competitors.

If a company's sensitive information, trade secrets, and intellectual properties that are vital to its success are not securely protected against duplication, the company may not survive. Given the crucial nature of this challenge, participating companies must establish strategies to protect proprietary information; MCI, for example, focused on nondisclosure agreements with outside companies as well as on education programs for employees. It also hired an outside agency to develop information protection policies.

## A New Kind of Organization Structure

Virtual organizations should be lean and flexible so that they can be responsive to the needs of customers. A virtual organization is conceptually leaner and flatter because of a reliance on information technology. The middle management that is usually an information conduit in traditional structures is replaced by information technology. In this flattened organization, managers have a broader span of control and must have expertise in communicating via electronic media.

Virtual organizations have the essence of a traditional organization without the structure and boundaries. Boundaries between organizations become hazy as corporations strike deals to establish more and more virtual organizations. Management must be open to a completely new type of practice in which managers may not have complete control of the situation.

A broad change in the organization's culture is marked by a shift from traditional structure and "strategic marketing" to virtual structure and "value marketing." This shift necessitates changes in the attitudes for managers and employees, types of control and monitoring systems, reward systems, and loyalty to the organization. The organization that cannot cope with constant change will not survive in today's context. Virtual organizations must build internal mechanisms for coping with such change.

## Trust

As the virtual organization moves beyond the traditional boundaries of the office or manufacturing plant, trust becomes essential. A virtual organization is built on core competencies but it is cemented with trust. Participating organizations must have total trust in each other's ability to contribute successfully to the virtual organization. While component companies may be competitors or archrivals in other areas of business, there must be collaboration within the venture. The cooperative relationship is strengthened by constant and open two-way communication.

There is a need for trust at all levels—trust between management and employees, management and managers, employers and employees, and customers and organization. Trust requires a new breed of leaders who can trust employees and a new breed of employees who can be trusted and who are trustworthy. In virtual organizations, one often needs to manage people who cannot be seen. In these cases, we manage on results and expected results rather than on observable activity. The decision regarding with whom to partner becomes even more critical since there may be no recourse if a trusted partner fails to fulfill contracted agreements. This is an obvious challenge to management systems that have often been based on mistrust and control.

## Communication and Power of Information

Communication is elevated to an essential ingredient. It binds all those involved in achieving the goals of the virtual organizations even if they are scattered throughout the globe. For this reason, according to Davidow and Malone (1993), the company needs to have "a sophisticated information network that gathers data on markets and customer needs, combining it with the newest design methods and computer-integrated production processes, and then operating this system with an integrated network that includes not only highly skilled employees of the system but also suppliers, distributors, retailers, and even customers." The success of a virtual organization depends on its ability to handle a massive flow of information. Davidow and Malone also claim these abilities to "acquire, distribute, store, analyze, and invoke actions based on information will determine the winners and losers in the battle for customers."

Technology is the cornerstone of virtual organizations. Modern real-time communication technologies such as electronic mail, EDI, videoconferencing, and network of CAD/CAM systems will enhance the power of information of virtual organizations. While these technologies convey and store immense amounts of data, the quality of inputs and the correct interpretation of outputs must also be of high quality to achieve the highest level of success.

## Need for a New Breed of Leader

According to Peters (1996), "Leadership is a sine qua non for standout performance" in any organization and more so in a virtual organization. A company's success is not just related to the powerful information technology it has installed, the highly skilled workers it has recruited, or the core competencies it may possess. According to Peters, the only constant that correlates with success is top leadership. Such leadership must have passion for the product being produced.

The manager's role becomes one of facilitating and supporting rather than one of dictating orders. Managers function as communication nodes among employees, work teams, departments, and partnering companies. They also need expanded management skills for persuading, delegating, and monitoring activities of employees within and outside of their own organization. Decentralization and empowerment are important success sustainers in a virtual organization. Virtual organizations need to decentralize and give adequate autonomy to different units and teams. When employees are empowered, they can make quick decisions on the floor that are essential in any virtual organization. Such highly decentralized and empowered organizations also require a new breed of employees.

## A New Breed of Worker

Since the focus of virtual organizations is a "marriage of core competencies," there is a need for highly motivated, self-directed, educated, highly skilled, reliable employees who can make significant contributions to the alliance. Since there is a greater reliance on information technology, employees should also be computer literate.

Openness to learning is also a highly desired quality in employees since virtual products and services necessitate perpetual mixing and matching of teams. As employees from one company interact with employees from another company, there is ample opportunity for employees to fine-tune skills and expertise. Continuous learning will differentiate those who survive and those who do not. Since workers will have great decision-making powers, they should be able to make fast and informed decisions on the floor based on the available information.

A virtual organization thrives only in the environment of teamwork. Regardless of how skilled and educated employees are, if they are incapable of working on teams, there is no place for them in the virtual organization. Since virtual organizations require continual recasting of work groups (based on the changing needs of organizations), there is a need for workers with a high sense of autonomy and little need for company affiliation. Workers should require minimal supervision and direction since they are likely to be geographically dispersed.

Over time, it is likely that a core of "free-agent" workers will develop where each worker is only loosely affiliated with any particular organization (Pink, 2001). Such free-agents may be positioned to act quickly and effectively to achieve stated results without necessarily following the corporate dictates of any one organization.[1]

# TECHNOLOGIES FOR INTRA-ORGANIZATIONAL COORDINATION

Software designed for intra-organizational coordination can significantly enhance the effectiveness of virtual organizations. Three categories of software are described below.

## Supply Chain Planner (SCP)

This category of software is designed to coordinate, plan and optimize intra- and interorganizational activities related to manufacturing, demand, supply and transportation of products and materials along supply chains. Examples of such software include i2 Technologies' RHYTHM and SAP's Supply Chain Management. The Web-based applications of these two kinds of software makes them attractive to many companies around the world.

To optimize the effectiveness of integrating and coordinating interorganizational activities along supply chains, companies should first integrate their intra-organizational activities (Levary, 2000). Enterprise resource planning (ERP) software systems are designed to link and integrate the various business activities of enterprises and can significantly improve the coordination of business activities. ERP software systems are composed of several modules. Each module is designed to support a functional area (e.g., financial accounting, manufacturing, logistics, sales and distribution, or human resources). All modules use the same comprehensive database and are linked to one another. When an activity is performed in one functional area, all the other functional areas are instantly updated as to the consequences of that activity in every other area. The software companies that design, sell, and maintain ERP systems continuously improve their product by adding capabilities such as optimization of logistics activities. Implementation of these software systems, however, requires significant resources as well as a change in companies' procedures (Levary, 2000).

## Internet-Based Electronic Data Interchange (EDI)

EDI software is designed to automate interorganizational communication and thus improve the effectiveness of virtual organizations. EDI is the computer-to-computer interorganizational communication of business transactions in a standard format. With EDI, order information placed by a company along a supply chain is transmitted directly from the company's computer to its suppliers' computers. Suppliers' billing information is transmitted directly from the supplier computers to the ordering company's computer. EDI technology is helpful in concurrent engineering by allowing instant transfer of graphic files among computer-aided design (CAD) systems of manufacturers and their subcontractors.

The transmitted data must be set in a standardized format that has been agreed upon by all companies involved so that data files from the computers of different organizations can flow smoothly. Furthermore, all the application software that is involved in generating the required data must be compatible. This requires a high degree of cooperation and coordination among the companies involved. The greater the number of companies composing a virtual organization, the greater the complexity of the coordination needed.

The advantages of EDI include:

- Real time exchange of data
- Reduction in paper handling that results in savings of both time and money
- Greater coordination of activities between partners of virtual organizations because of better data sharing
- Fewer errors resulting from data that is keyed in only once
- Quicker transfer of money, making it possible for more immediate receipt of payment

Until recently, most EDI traffic was handled by privately owned value-added networks (VANs). The use of such networks was very expensive and could only be afforded by large corporations. Today, however, Internet-based EDI is able to provide EDI capability at low cost. Corporations can use Internet EDI software. This is becoming increasingly popular both because of the lower cost and because Internet-based EDI has the advantage of being global. Additionally, the multimedia capability of the Internet can broaden the type of EDI applications and thus further increase EDI contributions to the effectiveness of virtual organizations. It must be noted, however, that Internet-based EDI has a lower reliability than VAN-based EDI.

## Software Used as a Platform for Online Business-to-Business (B2B)

Several software systems were developed to enhance various aspects of online B2B transactions. Companies such as Ariba and Commerce One developed enabler software to help other companies create marketplaces on the Internet. Their software systems are, in essence, platforms for e-commerce. Each platform has a different objective. Ariba's platform, for example, emphasizes how suppliers can best display their products. Commerce One's platform, to the contrary, emphasizes procurement activities.

Some software platforms focus on standardizing online transactions in a specific industrial sector. Covisint, for example, provides such a platform for the automotive industry. Similar platforms have been developed for other industries. Several software systems were developed to become an auction platform for online B2B. Manheim Online, for example, is an online auction platform for companies and dealerships that want to resell used cars. Each of the software platforms for online B2B is capable of enhancing the effectiveness of virtual organizations in one way or another.

Multilingual capabilities of SCP, EDI, and platforms for online B2B can increase the effectiveness of global use of these software systems. Such capabilities also facilitate the establishment of multinational virtual corporations and enhance their effectiveness.

## MultiLingual Web Pages

In today's global marketplace, virtual organizations have been created by firms from various countries. To enhance the likelihood that a company will be invited to become part of a multinational virtual organization, it should design its Web page to provide multilingual capabilities. This is especially important for companies located in countries where the local language is not English. Since English is considered the international language of business, it is beneficial for all companies to design Web pages with English capability. Only with this capability can companies expect to attract business from companies located in countries speaking a language other than their own. A multilingual Web page makes it possible for managers of potential business partners around the world to familiarize themselves with the characteristics of the product or service that a company can provide. This increases the likelihood of being invited to become part of a multinational virtual organization.

## Peer-to-Peer Architecture

In spite of the recent legal difficulties of Napster, the concept of peer-to-peer computing has been growing in popularity, and applications within the corporate setting are likely to continue growing. The peer-to-peer architecture changes the concept of computer networking from a centralized server providing value to decentralized clients to one of equivalent distributed clients that can exchange information freely among each other. Though the authors are not currently familiar with cases where this technology is deployed to support virtual organizations, this approach to computing would seem particularly congruent with the philosophy of virtual organizations.

# CONCERNS REGARDING THE RELIANCE ON TECHNOLOGY IN VIRTUAL ORGANIZATIONS

The concerns regarding reliance on technology in virtual organizations can be separated into two categories: information security and reliability.

## Information Security

Every organization that uses the Internet for some business activity faces four types of security threats to the flow of information:
- Interruption
- Interception
- Modification
- Fabrication

Interruption of information flow is generally caused by hackers for the purpose of showing their technological skills to themselves and, perhaps, their friends. There is typically no business motivation underlying this type of information vandalism. Denial of Web service is one form of interruption. In this case, hackers overload the target company's Web site and thereby deny access to legitimate business. It is possible, of course, that the hacker incapacitates the Web site in the hopes of profiting from the potential drop in share price of the target company due to loss of business.

Interception of information flow is generally motivated by industrial or business espionage. Competitors may attempt to obtain unauthorized access to confidential information of a target company by intercepting the flow of information of the target company. The interceptors want the competitor's propriety information in order to obtain a competitive advantage. Unauthorized access to a target company's database is another type of interception of information flow. Companies that form a virtual organization are most susceptible to this type of security threat because of the computer network links used for business communication and transactions as well as a shared database. Partners of a virtual organization have easier access, authorized or not, to confidential information of their partners in the virtual corporation. Such information can be used to achieve competitive advantage. To prevent interception of information flow, companies have been installing a variety of firewalls with varying levels of success.

Modification of information flow is when a hacker tampers with information flow among business partners or with the databases of a business. The motivation of such an act is strictly malicious and is unlikely to be originated by legitimate businesses.

Fabrication of information flow is when a hacker obtains unauthorized access to the computer intra-network of a company and fabricates data. The motivation of such an act is also strictly malicious and is unlikely to be originated by legitimate businesses.

## Reliability

As mentioned in an earlier section, while Internet-transported EDI is less costly than VAN-transported EDI, it can also be less reliable. There are both technical and content communication aspects to the reliability issue. Technically, the VAN network is more fully under a single control structure. Whatever company providing the service can take steps to ensure complete, uninterrupted, and secure transmission of data. VANs often provide additional services such as backup, redundancy, post-box, and translation software. The Internet, being a public and relatively ad hoc collection of networks, is generally quite reliable, but has been prone to overloads and some periodic delays, security lapses, and some general unpredictability. For most applications where activities are measured in days and hours (rather than milliseconds), particularly where encryption is used, the security issues with the Internet are generally outweighed by cost considerations. From a content communication perspective, the Internet creates a scenario where firms are freer to create whatever type of communication they wish and are not limited to EDIFACT or similar standard protocols. This facilitates ad hoc communications and quick reaction to unexpected situations. However, organizations that create ad hoc communications must recall the original reason for the strict standardization of EDI systems—the need to eliminate ambiguity and potential misunderstanding from messages. Communications between two firms with much trading history may trigger investigation with unusual messages. Communications among thousands of firms in near real-time settings could trigger disasters, if ambiguous interpretations of nonstandard messages occur.

In addition to concern for reliability of the network and transmission of data, organizations involved in electronic commerce need to be concerned about the reliability of transaction processing and data storage. In many respects this will involve the same issues that are faced by organizations that are not "virtual" in the way we have been using the term. However, it is worth noting that whenever organizations become dependent on real-time interactions with customers or trading partners, they must develop strategies to continue operations when computer hardware or software are temporarily unavailable. An expensive, but effective strategy involves duplication of data processing at multiple sites. Such a move doubles some costs, such as for hardware—unless the purchaser can negotiate a multiple purchase discount—adds communication costs; and adds costs for software to insure the completely parallel collection and storage of data. Other firms will purchase computer hardware with multiple processors, leaving at least one processor as a backup such that processing can be shifted to it when the others are down (Treese & Stewart, 1998).

Although successful backup of existing data may have less impact on immediate transaction processing than failure of computer hardware or software, such data can be crucial for accounting/auditability, decision making, and other purposes. It is important that members of virtual organizations understand what data is collected, by whom, and where it will be stored for longer-term usage.

## Technology Trade-offs

It is always tempting to wish to provide the latest and most sophisticated technology available. This is particularly tempting in business-to-consumer e-commerce, where consumers can be impressed by flashy appearances. Even in business-to-business e-commerce there can be significant marketing and transaction-by-transaction decision making (particularly in areas such as auctions/reverse auctions or information referral). However, the use of more sophisticated multimedia requires that the client have equally sophisticated software for receipt of these complex messages. Where virtual organizations work on longer term and less ad hoc basis and where cost cutting rather than attracting new clients is more prevalent, selecting standard and thoroughly diffused technologies will tend to be more cost-effective than providing the latest and greatest (Treese & Stewart, 1998).

For those e-commerce applications that involve the creation and delivery of physical goods, some interface between the electronic and the physical must exist and be treated seriously. Virtual organizations need to recognize the need for policies regarding shipments, returns, stock-outs, and the many inventory-related issues that traditional, non-computer-mediated firms also deal with. The degree to which these tangible activities can be supported with organized and available data and support processing will aid in creating added value for customers. When a variety of organizations are collaborating in the generation and delivery of these products, there can be added complexity in the storage, transmission, and accessing of all relevant data to support these "non-virtual" but critical activities.

## The Role of the Semantic Web in the Future of Virtual Organizations

The semantic Web, currently under development, is an extension of the existing Web (Berners-Lee, Hendler & Lassila, 2001) that will add significant new capabilities to computers searching the Web. Computers will be able to "understand" data and then act based on this understanding. Since today's computers simply display data in the form of Web pages, this "understanding" of data will mark a significant improvement. The semantic Web will enable software agents to automatically execute complicated tasks for the user by roaming among pages without the user's intervention. The automatic search process creates a value chain of information as the search progresses from one page to another based on newly added information. The increased capabilities at the semantic Web will encourage firms to broaden the amount of information provided on the Web pages. This will further enhance the capabilities and effectiveness of the Web.

The enhanced capabilities of the semantic Web will increase the effectiveness of creating virtual organizations. A manufacturer that is looking for a supplier to supply a given quantity of a needed part during a specific time window and having certain degree of quality, for example, currently needs to search the Web pages of several potential suppliers to find the needed part. It is very likely that the manufacturer will not be able to find all the needed information on the potential suppliers' Web pages and may have to resort to the phone. Such a search process is time-consuming and ineffective. The new semantic Web, however, will make it possible for a manufacturer to key in the characteristics of the needed part and automatically search the Web pages of suppliers to find the one who can supply the needed quantity of the required part during the specified time window. Once the required supplier is found, a new virtual organization is established.

# CONCLUSION

Clearly, virtual organizations come in many flavors and, therefore, have a diverse set of requirements both managerially and technically. Nevertheless, there are also some similarities among virtual organizations, beginning with the relationships among various partners and the potential benefits and shifting challenges in achieving them. This chapter has presented an overview of the topic and introduction to the many aspects of planning and executing virtual organizations that should lead to higher levels of success.

# REFERENCES

Berners-Lee, T., Hendler, J. & Lassila, O. (2001). The semantic Web. *Scientific American*, May, 1-9.

Christie, P. & Levary, R. (1998). Virtual corporations: Recipe for success. *Industrial Management*, July-August, 7-11.

Davidow, W. H. & Malone, M. S. (1993). *The Virtual Corporation: Structuring and Revitalizing the Corporation for the 21st Century*. HarperBusiness.

GHI. (2001). *Group Health Insurance website outlining electronic funds transfer business-to-business program.* Accessed August 14, 2001. http://www.ghi.com/provider/medical/medeft.htm.

Levary, R. R. (2000). Better supply chains through information technology. *Industrial Management*, May-June, 24-30.

Ogilvie, H. (1994). At the core, it's the virtual organization. *Journal of Business Strategy*, September-October.

Peters, T. (1996). Brave leadership. *Executive Excellence*, January.

Pink, D. H. (2001). *Free Agent Nation: How America's New Independent Workers Are Transforming the Way We Live*. New York: Warner Books.

Treese, G. W. & Stewart, L.C. (1998). *Designing Systems for Internet Commerce*. Reading, MA: Addison-Wesley.

Chapter X

# An IT-Based Heuristic Model
# for Enterprise Engineering

Luiz Antonio Joia
Brazilian School of Public and Business Administration,
Getulio Vargas Foundation and Rio de Janeiro State University, Brazil

## ABSTRACT

*Around the world complex enterprises are being undertaken in distributed and even virtual environments. Processes, services, infrastructure and so forth must be developed to address these major projects. This article presents an information-technology-based heuristic model to help the enterprises' integrators in their new responsibilities and duties. This IT-based model conveys to a taxonomy to manage the coordination and transaction among all the partners of a major project, addressing a new discipline named enterprise engineering. This is an issue challenging most companies in the world, as new ways of operating these complex enterprises are being undertaken worldwide by most integrators. The search for a new model is therefore demanded by most of the international companies. Hence, this article intends to present an heuristic model that is able to integrate productive processes, services and information technologies among the players through a huge network of coordination. Conclusions are presented at the end of this article.*

## INTRODUCTION

Enterprise engineering deals with the implementation and operation of an enterprise (Liles, Johnson, Meade & Underdown, 1995). In a continually changing and unpredictable competitive environment, enterprise engineering needs new tools to analyze, design and deploy an enterprise. It addresses how to design and improve all elements associated with the total enterprise through the use of integrated systems, processes, information and organizational design.

A new enterprise workflow is being asked for, to overcome the barriers of this distributed and virtual environment where coordination is absolutely fundamental (Lefler,1994).

Three worldview assumptions reflect the depth of enterprise engineering (Liles et al., 1995):

- the enterprise is a complex adaptative system (Sherman & Schultz, 1998; Brown & Einsenhardt, 1998);
- the enterprise is a system of processes that can be engineered (or reengineered) both individually and holistically (Brown & Einsenhardt, 1998);
- coordination science is paramount to better implement an enterprise (Malone & Crownston, 1993)

There are nowadays different types of hiring an enterprise from an integrator— the one in charge of the enterprise through the coordination of all the players involved. To better understand this article, a brief description of these ways of contracting are presented:

## Turn-Key

This encompasses all the stages of an enterprise. The data have shown that profits reach at most 2% of the total operational revenue. Nevertheless, there is a great possibility of losses, not only at the end of the enterprise, but also due to severe cash-flow variations. This is, obviously, a type of contract whose risks should be forecast before the beginning, as the price is determined previously for a well-defined scope. Naturally, it is impossible to foresee formerly all the involved risks.

In this kind of contract, all the risks are taken for granted by the contractor, not by the owner of the enterprise. Risk analysis is therefore imperative. According to Macomber (1982), this is the ideal contract for an integrator with large experience in similar enterprises.

## BOOT  (Build-Own-Operate-Transfer)

As it was said there is a global trend for privatizations, due mainly to the:

- lack of investments from the third-world governments;
- reduction in the amount of investment transferred from the developed countries to the emergent economies;
- awareness that the state is a quite inefficient manager to resource allocation;
- visible perceptions of privatization's benefits to the countries.

In the BOOT contract, the integrator gets a concession from the state to build and operate, for a certain time, an enterprise. The firm must get its return on investment from the time it is the enterprise's operator. Thereafter, the state may either reassign or cancel the concession to the firm, according to its performance.

There are a lot of examples of BOOT implementations worldwide (Mathews,1986), such as the Dartford Express Highway (Thames River, London), Eastern Harbour Crossing (Hong Kong), some enterprises in Malaysia and Turkey (energy, highways) and finally the Channel Tunnel linking France and England.

Financial engineering is absolutely essential in BOOT projects, which involves investment banks as partners in this kind of enterprise.

# THEORETICAL FRAMEWORK

## Organizational Design

There are so many companies involved in a major enterprise that an IT coordination model must be developed and applied. To be more specific, Coase's theory is used (Coase, 1993) to determine what the firm must handle internally (coordination) and what must be outsourced (transaction). Information technology is now much more about coordination and transaction than about information. Hence, it is very important to have a coordination-transaction model that lowers the costs of managing the major project, the players and their dependencies, interfaces and constraints.

Linking, like grouping, involves several sets of consideration. The right set of linking mechanisms must be selected to deal with (Nadler & Tushman, 1997):

(1)   workflows between distinct yet interdependent units;
(2)   the need for disciplinary or staff-based professionals to have contact across the enterprise;
(3)   workflows associated with emergencies or temporary, short-term goals.

Up to this point, one has discussed linking mechanisms largely in terms of the formal roles and structures that constitute the hierarchy of any enterprise. But designers of organizations (see, for example, Galbraith, 1973; Nadler & Tushman, 1997; just to name a few) have become increasingly aware in recent years that processes and systems also play a vital role in coordinating activity and in enabling people to link their efforts into productive work.

According to Nadler & Tushman (1997, p.104):

In this context, the term "process" is used to describe sequences of collaborative efforts by groups and individuals, at various organizational levels and frequently across structural boundaries, performed in the pursuit of a common objective. The term "systems" refers to mechanisms that use human or physical technology to enable people and groups to perform the work required by a particular process. Although process and systems seem somewhat nebulous in contrast with formal hierarchical structures, they are gaining growing attention as potentially powerful sources of linking in coordination.

Confirming the former statement, some experiences have been made so as to develop and implement a process-based organizational structure. Successful examples coming up from IBM, Texas Instruments, Owens Corning and Duke Power are today well-documented (Hammer & Stanton, 1999).

Based on the experiences undertook by these former companies, a process-based organizational design can be proposed for the business ecosystem (Moore, 1997) created within a major enterprise. This organizational design can be also called a metabusiness, i.e., a quasi-firm created and sustained by digital links among their players (Keen, 1991).

Hence, a process-centered organizational structure addressing the enterprise can be presented below, always bearing in mind that the transactions with the other partners must be digital-based, as the relationships among the internal processes within the integrator. The process map in Figure 1 draws heavily on the one presented by Texas Instruments (Hammer & Champy, 1993) and depicts the integrator's macro-processes and their interfaces with their partners within an enterprise.

As can be realized there was no constraint on splitting the company's structure in processes far different from the ones already established, such as strategic development or market research. These and other more traditional processes are, for instance, embedded in the diagram presented within new products and services development process.

# METHODOLOGY

An explanatory methodology is used in this research, drawn on Winter's (1987) concepts associated to explanatory frameworks. The *heuristic frame* concept developed by him in his article "Knowledge and Competence as Strategic Assets" is heavily used, being the model proposed later in this research classified as a heuristic frame. As Winter says:

*Figure 1: Process map*

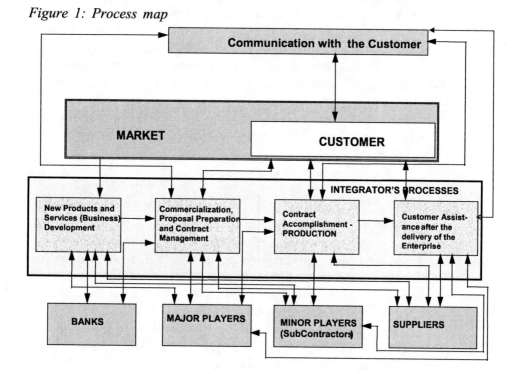

A heuristic frame corresponds to a degree of problem definition that occupies an intermediate position on the continuum between a long and indiscriminate list of things that might matter at one end and a fully formulated control-theoretic model of the problem at the other. Within a heuristic frame, there is room for a wide range of more specific formulations of the problem—but there is also enough structure provided by the frame itself to guide and focus discussion. On the other hand, a rich variety of different heuristic frames may represent plausible approaches to a given problem. (Winter, 1987, pp.172-3)

Based on this assumption, the model presented is one among many that can still be used in the very near future and represents an effort to overcome the *paralysis by analysis effect* (Ansoff, 1984) too common when dealing with intangible things, leading to everlasting discussions rather than practical results. A model is good not on account of the excess of rigour it applies itself, measured by the number of variables taken into consideration, but rather if it adequately models and expresses the reality we are facing. Hence, complexity is not necessarily synonymous with good results, and some flexibility is required when dealing with topics for which a great amount of critical sense is needed.

Hence, an IT-based heuristic model is developed so as to integrate systemically both information and communication technology and enterprise management.

# THE IT-BASED HEURISTIC MODEL

For more than one decade, people have begun to use computers for the first time. However, most of them are using computers just for individual tasks, such as to create and/or revise a text or a spreadsheet. Currently, the networking boom, mainly based on Internet, intranet and extranet potentialities, has changed the computer from a calculation machine to a communication device. This allows people to work together in a collaborative and integrated environment. As an example, several softwares have been developed to:

- allow different persons working at the same time on the same document;
- allow the intelligent tracking of messages and documents within a productive process;
- help the employees together to view and manipulate information in a more efficient way.

CSCW (computer supported collaborative work) is now a reality and can be used in complex enterprises. The model herein presented fits in this environment.

People are acquainted with the functional charts of companies and try to find in them a process-based organizational structure, most of the time without success. The Taylorist vision conveys some difficulties in understanding companies decomposed in processes linked among themselves, either inside the company (coordination) or with the other partners (transaction).

In order to integrate information technology and the management macro-processes, a taxonomy is developed based on Joia (1995). This taxonomy links systemically all the facets within an enterprise.

*Figure 2: Model tapping the enterprise*

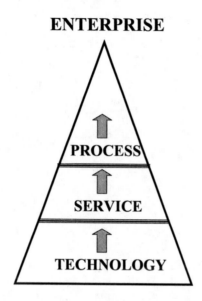

The model lays on the information technologies. The information technologies support the services[1] available in the enterprise, and the services themselves are in charge of the macro-processes developed in the business ecosystem.

This model taps the enterprise through the structure shown in Figure 2, to be detailed later in this article.

The main target of the model is to allow the easy understanding of the processes, the necessary services and the required information technologies. This taxonomy can be used to quickly understand the interrelationship among all the players within an enterprise, allowing enterprise engineering to be implemented.

The enterprise can be divided into macro-processes, allowing a deeper analysis. This decomposition is presented in Figure 3 based on the decomposition theory (Malone, Crowston, Lee & Pentland, 1993). Some enterprises do not have all these macro-processes, although the global dimension is presented.

## Processes

A brief description of each process shown in Figure 3 is necessary for a better understanding of the proposed taxonomy.

**a)   Business Development**

This is the enterprise conception. It is without doubt the most important phase of the enterprise. The players are chosen by the integrator and the basic design of the enterprise is formalized. In this stage, the later a mistake is picked up, the more financial losses and delays there are in the project. So, it is paramount to have the players working together, using IT as an enabler, and taking advantage of the concurrent engineering systems described later in this paper (Zangwill, 1992).

*Figure 3: Processes decomposition in an enterprise*

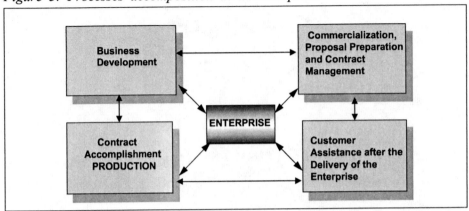

**b)    Commercialization, Proposal Preparation and Contract Management**

This process aims to make reality the enterprise conception developed in the former one. It receives, therefore, as input, data and information coming up from the business development process. Coordination is now paramount so as to manage the full contract effectively. Coordination science must be used in this stage that lasts along all the enterprise's life cycle. As said by Malone and Crowston (1993), coordination science is the adequate management of restrains and dependencies within an enterprise, involving all the ecosystem and the players within it.

Hence, this workflow analyzes the coordination among the entities in charge of the productive processes presented at Figure 3. This is where enterprise engineering integrates all the former stages into just one—the enterprise workflow. Usually, PERT/CPM networks and Gantt charts are used. All the information of the enterprise should pass through the integrator, the one in charge of all this complex workflow. The integrator, without doubt, can be considered as an information factory (Joia, 1999).

**c)    Contract Accomplishment and Production**

The work now is much more repetitive, not always presenting an actual added-value. Most of the detailing is done by subcontractors (small players) coordinated and managed by the integrator that is in charge of the quality assurance of the work done.

In this stage the builder and the assembler who have taken part in the basic design play their role. Once again all the work must be coordinated by the integrator that manages the dependencies and constraints.

The equipment (if needed) is then delivered by other companies, according to the specifications of the integrator, who is in charge of auditing them before they go to the site. They must arrive just in time for the builder and assembler to locate them in the field according to the schedules, which shows, once again, a complex chain of dependencies and restrictions that must be managed by the integrator, using information technology and the necessary services.

**d)   Customer Assistance after the Delivery of the Enterprise**

This is a paramount process today, when customers have so much power in the business realm. All the activities of this workflow aim to keep the customer satisfied after the delivery of the enterprise. This takes into account being responsive, choosing the right person(s) to take charge of the demands, and so forth. Several systems and technologies explained further in this article are today available so as to allow the contractor to achieve the former purpose.

## Services

The main services needed in enterprise engineering so as to support the processes presented are:

**a)   Services of Personal Productivity**

This service allows the employees to generate their documents, spreadsheets, presentations, memos, faxes and so forth through the use of specific software (personal productivity software) and adequate computational infrastructure.

**b)   Services of Interpersonal and Organizational Communication**

The use of electronic mail allows the flow of structured messages and attached files within the Integrator and between it and its partners. Internet, intranet and extranet are all equally important for this kind of transaction, as well as workgroup software. Traditional EDI (electronic data interchange) can also be used to speed documents' production, data and information flow, transactions among the integrator and its partners and so forth, as well as Internet-based EDI—cheaper, more user-friendly and without compatibility problems typical of traditional EDI (Turban, Lee, King & Chung, 1999). Extranet systems can also be used to link the partners, either based on data communication private lines or VPN (virtual private networks; Loshin, 1997).

**c)   Services of Knowledge Management**

Through the use of intranet systems, authoring systems based on hypertext and/or intranet-based databases, the integrator can collect all codes, best practices and procedures to be used over the enterprise, to be shared by all the players through systems of organizational communication. So a specific code can be consulted by a supplier or another player, for instance.

These services deal with explicit knowledge, the one that can be structured and codified (Nonaka & Takeuchi, 1995). The tacit dimension of the knowledge can not be addressed by these services, but through socialization and conversation management (Polanyi, 1958; von Krogh & Roos, 1995).

**d)   Services of Concurrent Engineering**

The business development and proposal preparation processes of the forthcoming enterprise must be developed with the involvement of all the companies, as they can forecast any kind of problem that would turn up just long after the beginning of the enterprise. By the same token, the production process must also be developed with the support of these systems. This way, all the players can work simultaneously in their tasks, notifying the possible mistakes, just in time, for the others. The sequential workflow is disregarded, as it is more expensive and longer than the concurrent one (Zangwill, 1992). Of course, concurrent engineering depends deeply on hardware and software tools, not to say on people training.

**e)   Services of Documentation and Workflow Control**

In a major enterprise, documents are produced as in a factory and must be managed; otherwise, problems such as the use of outdated revisions or the loss of relevant information, can happen, just to name a few (Joia, 1998). The tracking of documents is done through workflow systems, normally embedded in EDMS systems (electronic document management systems). Both administrative and production workflows, according to Korzeniowski's (1993) taxonomy, deal with documents. Only the *adhocs* workflows are unstructured. Hence, as most processes deal with documents, they play a primal role in an enterprise.

## Information Technologies

Most of the services presented earlier in this article depend, as already said, on the implementation of adequate computational infrastructure.

As this is not the purpose of this article, just a brief quotation of the main necessary technologies is presented: client-server architecture, with corporate database and network; workgroup and personal productivity software; communication networks (LAN, WAN, Internet/intranet/extranet, satellite, etc.); expert systems and authoring tools software; visualization tools (solid modelling, CAD/CAE/CAM/CIM); EDMS (electronic document management systems and workflow software); ERP (enterprise resource planning); CRM (customer relationship management); call centers; supply chain management; data mining and data warehouse.

# TAXONOMY OF THE IT MODEL

The IT model's taxonomy is based on Figure 2, as it aims to link the enterprise workflow with its minor subprocesses (Figure 3), these subprocesses with the services supplied by the technological innovation, and these services with the information technologies.

This is an original approach (Joia, 1995) as most of time processes are decomposed into smaller ones (Malone et al., 1993) without a clear relationship network between them, the needed services and the involved technologies.

Through this model, one can know which technologies are necessary for having certain services that in turn are imperatives for certain productive processes. The readers can navigate easily in the taxonomy model shown in Figure 4 (Joia, 1995). For instance, given a certain process, one can realize which services support it and also which technologies are needed for it to be implemented in the enterprise.

Although the main target of this article is a logical approach for coordination among the participants of an enterprise, it can be presented as one among many possible network physical infrastructures to be deployed by the enterprise's integra-

*Figure 4: Taxonomy model*

| PROCESS | Business Development | Commercialization, Proposal Preparation and Contract Management | Contract Accomplishment and Production | Customer Assistance after the Delivery of the Enterprise |
|---|---|---|---|---|
| SERVICE | Personal Productivity; Interpersonal and Organizational Communication; Concurrent Engineering; Documentation and Workflow Control | Personal Productivity; Interpersonal and Organizational Communication; Concurrent Engineering; Documentation and Workflow Control | Personal Productivity; Interpersonal and Organizational Communication; Knowledge Management; Concurrent Engineering; Documentation and Workflow Control | Personal Productivity; Interpersonal and Organizational Communication; Knowledge Management; Documentation and Workflow Control |
| INFORMATION TECHNOLOGY | BASIC INFRA-STRUCTURE (*); EDMS (Electronic Document Management Systems and Workflow Software) | BASIC INFRA-STRUCTURE (*); EDMS (Electronic Document Management Systems and Workflow Software); ERP (Enterprise Resource Planning) | BASIC INFRA-STRUCTURE (*); Visualization Tools (Solid Modelling, CAD/CAE/CAM/CIM); EDMS (Electronic Document Management Systems and Workflow Software); ERP (Enterprise Resource Planning); Supply Chain Management | BASIC INFRA-STRUCTURE (*); Expert Systems and Authoring Tools Software; EDMS (Electronic Document Management Systems and Workflow Software); CRM (Customer Relationship Management); Call Centers; Data Mining and Data Warehouse |

**(*) BASIC INFRASTRUCTURE** = *Client-Server Architecture, with Corporate Database and Network; Workgroup and Personal Productivity Software; Communication Networks (LAN, WAN, Internet/ Intranet/Extranet, Satellite, etc.).*

tor (Figure 5). So, the reader will feel the tangibility of the proposed model analyzing one possible computational infrastructure.

# IT MODEL - THE ENTERPRISE WORKFLOW

The whole enterprise workflow associated to the IT model can also be analyzed through the coordination among the processes in charge of it, as presented in Figure 3.

*Figure 5: Enterprise's integrator (adapted from Joia, 1999)*

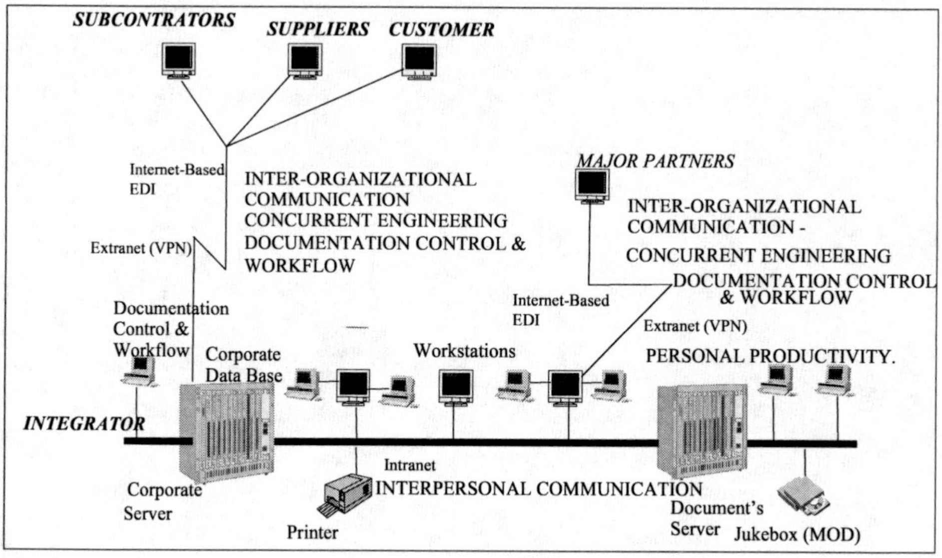

It can be said that (Joia,1995):

$$EW = f(E,P,S,IT,O,t)$$

where:

EW= enterprise workflow;

f= function;

E= entities (players involved within the enterprise);

P= processes;

S= services (also named systems);

IT= information technologies;

O= information objects;

t= time.

One concept remains to be analyzed: the information objects. They are the ones that go from one entity to another (e.g., from integrator to subcontractors), digitally. They can be classified, in a general sense, into drawings, structured messages, text documents, and database transactions.

## Drawings

They can be either vector or raster drawings. The vector drawings are conveying to the STEP (Standard for the Exchange of Product Model Data) communication standard (Liu & Fischer,1993). Although, the *defacto* standard is the DWG format from Autocad™.

For the raster drawings there are no standards. Firstly BMP, PCX, CCITT groups 3 and 4, and TIFF were largely used. Due to the Internet phenomenon, two more compression standards of communication have also been largely used:

JPEG and GIF, as their compression capabilities are adequate for Internet-based communication.

## Structured Messages

Structured messages are information originated by electronic mail (e-mails). The OLE technology allows everyone to create a structure for the content of these messages through the link with objects created in other applications.

## Text Documents

Text documents are fundamentally the A4, letter and legal standards (memos, letters, faxes, reports, etc.). A communication standard—SGML—was developed which originated the HTML format. Although the PDF Acrobat™ standard is largely used, mainly in the Internet (World Wide Web) in pages written using the HTML standard code.

## Database Transactions

Some information is not passed on through either drawings, messages or text documents, but through transactions triggered in the enterprise's database as, for instance, the possibility of one supplier getting into some tables of the database to see how much material must be delivered, for whom and when.

This concern with the information objects is justified as most of the models overlook the information that flows across the coordination mesh.

# CONCLUSIONS

One of the main challenges the integrator must face to coordinate and manage the dependencies and constraints among all the involved players in a major enterprise is based on its availability of increasing its embodiment and connectivity skills (Keen, 1991) through an open computational infrastructure that might "speak" with those of its partners. There are also challenges of transforming the right processes correctly, as says Keen (1997), through his worth/salience matrix.

The presented approach tries to overcome the normal barriers to represent productive flows (Wang, 1994), i.e.:
- Functional: the tasks of the macro-process are represented as well as the involved entities;
- Behavioral: the time factor is taken into account;
- Organizational: the involved organizations are clearly presented;
- Informational: the involved and exchanged information objects among the participants are shown explicitly.

The enterprise workflow is composed of several minor workflows, such as contract accomplishment, customer assistance, and contract management, just to name a few, which, by the same token, are compounded of other smaller workflows and so on. The detailed analysis of each one of these several workflows is tiresome work, incompatible with the purposes of this article.

But what must be stressed are the cultural issues derived from having so many companies and employees trying to work together. This "soft" side has been concluded to be the "hard" one. Nonetheless, it is important to have a logical and global taxonomy that leads to a model where the transactions and coordination issues can be well understood and can give a formal overview of the importance of the information technology in the enterprise.

Computational infrastructure without services is worthless. Service without processes is worthless. And processes that cannot be integrated in an overall one are useless. The links among all these levels and the possible paths for walking across the enterprise's coordination mesh are the actual purposes of this article.

As can be realized, more research needs to be undertaken as new ways for contracting and working, together with the technological innovations, have demanded a new *modus operandi* far different from the one still today practiced by the enterprises' integrators.

## ENDNOTE

1 We are using "Services" and "Systems" (see Nadler, 1997) as similar words.

## REFERENCES

Brown, S. L. & Eisenhardt, K. M. (1998). *Competing on the Edge: Strategy as Structured Chaos*. Boston: Harvard Business School Press.

Coase, R. (1993). The nature of the firm. In O. Williamson, and S. Winter (Eds.), *The Nature of the Firm: Origins, Evolution and Development* (chap. 2). New York: Oxford University Press.

Galbraith, J. (1973). *Designing Complex Organizations*. Reading, MA: Addison-Wesley.

Haeckel, S. & Nolan, R. (1993). Managing by wire. *Harvard Business Review*, September-October, 122-132.

Hammer, M. & Champy, J. (1993). *Reengineering the Corporation–A Manifesto for Business Revolution*. New York: HarperBusiness.

Hammer, M. & Stanton, S. (1999). How process enterprises really work. *Harvard Business Review*, November-December, 108-118.

Joia, L. A. (1995*). De Projetistas a Gerentes de Empreendimentos: Reengenharia de Larga-Escala e Tecnologia da Informação como Ferramentas de Mudança*. Unpublished doctoral thesis, COPPE / Federal University of Rio de Janeiro, Brazil.

Joia, L. A. (1998). Large-scale reengineering on project documentation at engineering consultancy companies. *International Journal of Information Management*, *18*(3), June, 215-224. New York: Elsevier Science Ltd.

Joia, L. A. (1999). An IT-based taxonomy model for enterprise engineering. *Information Strategy–The Executive's Journal*, 27-35. New York: Auerbach.

Keen, P. (1991). *Shaping the Future*. Boston, MA: Harvard Business School Press.

Keen, P. (1997). *The Process Edge*. Boston: Harvard Business School Press.

Korzeniowski, P. (1993). Workflow software automates processes. *Software Magazine*, February. Sentry Publishing Co.

Lefler, J. (1994). EW in the AEC industry. *Special Report on Enterprise Workflow Supplement of the A/E/C SYSTEMS Computer Solutions*, May-June.

Liles, D. H., Johnson, M., Meade, L. & Underdown, D. R. (1995). Enterprise engineering: A discipline? *Society for Enterprise Engineering Conference Proceedings*, June.

Liu, T. H. & Fischer, G. W. (1993). Developing feature-based manufacturing applications using PDES/STEP. *Concurrent Engineering–Research and Applications*, *1*(1), March, 39-50.

Loshin, P. (1997). *Extranet Design and Implementation*. San Francisco: Sybex Network Press.

Macomber, J. (1989). You can manage your construction risks. *Harvard Business Review*, March-April, 155-165.

Malone, T. & Crowston, K. (1993). The interdisciplinary study of coordination. *Working Paper 157, 3630-93*, Center for Coordination Science, Sloan School of Management, MIT, http://ccs.mit.edu/papers/CCSWP157.html.

Malone, T., Crowston, K., Lee, J. & Pentland, B. (1993). Tools for inventing organizations: Towards a handbook of organizational processes. *Working Paper 41, 3562-93*, Center for Coordination Science, Sloan School of Management, MIT, http://ccs.mit.edu/papers/CCSWP141.html.

Mathews, B. D. (1986). A merchant banker's contribution to successful international contracting. *World Summit for International Contractors*. Switzerland: Davos.

Moore, J. F. (1997). *The Death of Competition*. New York: HarperBusiness.

Nadler, D. A. & Tushman, M. L. (1997). *Competing by Design: The Power of Organizational Architecture*. New York: Oxford University Press.

Nonaka, I. & Takeuchi, H. (1995). *The Knowledge-Creating Company: How Japanese Companies Create the Dynamics of Innovation*. New York: Oxford University Press.

Polanyi, M. (1958). *Personal Knowledge*. London: Routledge.

Turban, E., Lee, J., King, D. & Chung, H. M. (1999). *Electronic Commerce: A Managerial Perspective*. Upper Saddle River, NJ: Prentice Hall.

von Krogh, G. & Roos, J. (1995). *Organizational Epistemology*. London: MacMillan.

Wang, S. (1994). OO modelling of business processes. *Information Systems Management, 11*(2), Spring.

Zangwill, W. (1992). Concurrent engineering: Concepts and implementation. *IEEE Engineering Management Review*, *20*(4), 40-52.

# Section III

# IT-Based Marketing and Retailing

## Chapter XI

# Contemporary IT-Assisted Retail Management

Herbert Kotzab
Copenhagen Business School, Denmark

Peter Schnedlitz
Vienna University of Economics and Business Administration, Austria

Kerstin Neumayer
Billa Warenhandel AG, Austria

## ABSTRACT

*The chapter describes the consequences of the use of IT in the field of retailing. We will discuss the area at matter beyond the perspective of retail marketing and logistics strategies. In particular we show, how IT is used to reengineer retail formats in order to allow customized shopping experience and how new retail channels such as Internet-based retail formats could be used to address new customer groups. IT in retail logistics help to implement just-in-time-oriented demand synchronized delivery systems. In such systems cross docking operations are performed to eliminate inventory in the channel. The basic notions of the presented ideas are applied to a case company, which is a leading retailer and belongs to the German Rewe Group.*

## INTRODUCTION

Retailing plays a major role in today's economy. Since the early 1990s, retailing has grown domestically and internationally. The 1.5 million retailers in the US and the 3.3 million wholesalers and 1.1 million retailers in Europe contribute about 10 % to the gross national product of their respective economies (EC, 1997). Every fifth employee is working in this sector, which makes wholesaling and retailing the second largest employer after manufacturing (Levy & Weitz, 1998, p. 11). Table 1 presents the world's leading retailers, where German, British, French, Dutch and Japanese retailers follow the US-based Wal-Mart Stores, Inc..

Although the majority of retail companies belong to the group of micro, small- and medium-sized companies—about 75% of all retailing companies are small to medium sized with sole proprietorships—the major dynamic in the retailing industry is mostly contributed by the "big retail players" like Metro, Aldi or Rewe (all German retailers), the Dutch Ahold, UK's Tesco or Sainsbury, and of course Wal-Mart, the world's biggest retailing company. However, the downturn in consumption and the increasingly international focus of relationships with suppliers have forced large retailers to adopt new strategies, taking the form of acquisitions, diversification or globalization. Successful retailers have to be flexible and have to simultaneously look for economies of scale. IT-based retail management helps retailers to gain competitive advantages. According to the scope of this book, this chapter presents how IT has created a new mandate for retail management and presents IT-based retail business models and frameworks. The following chapter discusses the subject from two perspectives and applies the introduced concepts to the Austrian BML-Group as a case company (see Table 2).

# BACKGROUND
## Retailing–Definition, Activities, and Channel Formats

Retailing is a set of business activities that add value to the products and services sold to end users (e.g., Berekoven, 1995; Levy & Weitz, 1998). This set of activities

*Table 1: The world's leading retailers in 2000 (Source: Anonymous, 2001, p. 6)*

|  | Company name | Country | Sales in Billion US $ | Profit in Billion US $ |
|---|---|---|---|---|
| 1 | Wal-Mart Stores Inc. | USA | 191.33 | 6.30 |
| 2 | Carrefour | France | 59.94 | 0.99 |
| 3 | The Kroger Co. | USA | 49.00 | 1.13 |
| 4 | Royal Ahold | Netherlands | 48.53 | 1.03 |
| 5 | Metro AG | Germany/Switzerland | 43.40 | - |
| 6 | Albertson's | USA | 36.80 | 0.87 |
| 7 | Rewe | Germany | 34.85 | - |
| 8 | Tesco | Great Britain | 32.90 | 0.65 |
| 9 | Costco Companies | USA | 32.17 | 0.63 |
| 10 | Aldi | Germany | 32.00 | - |
| 11 | Safeway Inc. | USA | 31.98 | 1.09 |
| 12 | ITM Enterprises (Intermarche) | France | 30.81 | - |
| 13 | Edeka/AVA | Germany | 29.80 | - |
| 14 | Ito Yokado | Japan | 28.66 | 0.42 |
| 15 | Tengelmann | Germany | 27.58 | - |
| 16 | J. Sainsbury | Great Britain | 26.31 | 0.56 |
| 17 | Daiei | Japan | 22.42 | 0.20 |
| 18 | Auchan | France | 24.10 | 0.35 |
| 19 | Jusco | Japan | 22.42 | 0.13 |
| 20 | E. Leclerc | France | 22.40 | - |

*Table 2: Discussion perspectives*

| IT-based retail marketing strategies, presenting | IT-based retail logistics systems, showing |
|---|---|
| • Reengineered IT-driven retail formats, allowing a customized shopping experience;<br><br>• Development of new retail channels, e.g., Internet-based retail formats to address new customer segments;<br><br>• Category management, in order to offer client-oriented sets of products, resulting from a joint-planning process with manufacturers based on real-time accessed client data. | • The implementation of just-in-time-oriented replenishment systems by connecting the electronic point-of-sale (EPOS) systems with the manufacturers' ERP systems;<br><br>• The execution of IT-driven distribution center operations with no-inventory-holding transit terminal structures;<br><br>• The realization of vendor-managed-inventory programs on a continuous replenishment basis to reduce inventory levels and to improve order cycles. |

can be considered to be different functions or processes that refer to retail marketing processes (such as assortment processes, which provide end users with a required assortment of products and services in terms of quantity as well as quality; advice, advertising and credit processes, which ease the purchase for end users, e.g., offering special payment modes or informing end users about the offers) and retail logistics processes (such as transportation, breaking bulk and inventory handling). The orchestration of these functions leads to the various types of retailing as presented in Figure 1.

In order to serve as many target groups as possible, the world's leading retailers follow a multichannel strategy, where stationary retailing has the most economic impact in today's retail life (Zentes & Schramm-Klein, 2001, p. 290). However, most of the stationary retailing institutions are considered to be either in the end of the growth-stage or in the maturity-stage of a retailing life cycle (PWC, 2000).

## Information Technology (IT)–Definition and Means

Dawe (1993) and Elliot and Starkings (1998) refer to IT as the hard- and software that collects, transmits, processes and circulates pictorial, vocal, textual and numerical data/information, such as:

- mobile data capturing terminals, light pens, bar code readers, bar code labels, disks, chip cards, sensors to collect information;
- database systems, tapes, CDs, optical disks, document retrieval systems to store information;
- PC's, information retrieval, decision support systems, expert systems: MIS, EIS, MSS, ESS to process information; and
- services (e.g., fax, email, EDI, telex, FTP, WAIS, WWW, SMTP, TCP/IP), networks (videoconferencing, teleconferencing, voicemail, ISDN, LAN, WAN, fiber-optic, intra-, Inter- and extranet) and devices (e.g., phones, TV, radio, fax machine, PC) to transmit information.

Many of these technologies can be combined into powerful retail solutions that can help to improve the interface between consumer and retailer, retailer and vendor, and even vendor and consumer (Kotzab, 1997).

*Figure 1: Retail channel formats*

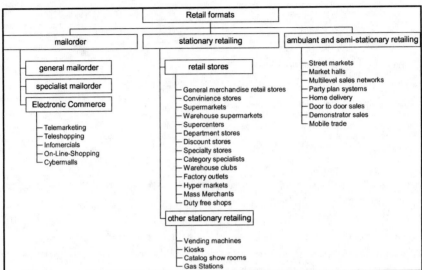

## Introduction of the Case Company BML[1]

The Austrian BML-Group was founded in 1953 by Karl Wlaschek, who started a little discount drugstore under the label of "BILLA" (a German abbreviation for cheap store). Today, the group has a market share of nearly 35 % of the total food and groceries retail market, has 43,500 employees, and is Austria's largest private employer (see Figure 2). Within the last 10 years, the average annual growth rate in BML's sales was + 12%, while the store network grew from 372 stores in 1980 to 2,260 stores in 2001. Since 1996, BML has been part of the German REWE-Group. The highly successful German REWE organization operates more than 11,500 outlets in the form of supermarkets, hypermarkets, discount markets, self-service department stores and various specialty markets all over Europe. REWE employs 162,000 people and generates a total sales volume of more than 32 billion Euro.

The different retail formats focus on different marketing strategies. While Billa targets local neighborhood coverage with a comprehensive assortment, the Merkur line offers the unique shopping experience of a modern hypermarket. With the Mondo-stores, BML competes in the difficult discount market, where ALDI/Hofer is the leading competitor. The Bipa stores operate as successful specialty markets offering cosmetics, beauty and health care products. Before joining the REWE group, BML also operated a bookstore format, LIBRO. The name BML refers to the combination of Billa, Merkur and Libro.

## IT-ASSISTED RETAIL MANAGEMENT
### Essential Elements of IT-Assisted Retailing

Beyond the recent developments of electronic business, Porter (2001) portrays the consequences for competitive strategy. The channel structure will change by

*Figure 2: The BML-Group: Store/channel formats and key numbers*

| Key numbers | BML store formats | | | | |
|---|---|---|---|---|---|
| channel format | Billa super-market | Merkur hyper-market | Emma neighbor-hood shop | Bipa category killer | Mondo discount market |
| Founded | 1953 | 1969 | 1988 | 1981 | 1983 |
| Turnover in billion Euro | 2.03 | 1.09 | 0.026 | 0.36 | 0.36 |
| Number of outlets | 900 | 86 | 31 | 380 | 190 |
| Number of employees | 10,000 | 5,500 | 140 | 1,200 | 730 |
| Number of articles per store | 6,000 | 25,000 | 2,600 | 7,000 | 940 |
| Average sales area in qm | 430 | 2,000 | 130 | 250 | 450 |
| Key numbers | Eurobilla store formats *) | | | | |
| | Italy | Czech Republic | Hungary | | Slovakia |
| Founded | 1990 | 1991 | 1993 | | 1993 |
| Turnover in billion Euro | 1.6 | 0.19 | .07 | | .07 |
| Number of outlets | 327 | 55 | 30 | 18 | |
| Number of employees | 7,000 | 2,000 | 800 | | 600 |
| Average sales area in qm | 1,000 | 1,000 | 1,000 | | 1,000 |

*) not including Rumania, Croatia, Ukraine and Bulgaria

compressing the layers, reducing the distances between the first and the last echelon of the supply chain. World-leading retailers are aware of these issues and use IT in their activities to gain the following competitive advantages (e.g., Keen, 1991):

- *Decreasing costs*: IT solutions help to reduce costs, e.g., administrative or inventory costs.
- *Speeding up time*: "Like a plane at mach speeds, a company must be able to respond to threats in real time" (Haeckel & Nolan 1993, p. 122). IT can help to reduce lead times of product and information flows within a channel. Companies can strategically use postponement strategies to shift the risk of producing not according to demand down the channel.
- *Increasing service*: IT can help to improve the dialogue between companies and their customers and consumers. Such systems allow one-to-one marketing possibilities and ensure individual solutions at lower price levels.

The Coca-Cola Retailing Research Group Europe (CCRRGE, 1996, p. 52) presents two fundamental issues for the food shopping process (see also Figure 3): a) the information exchange process between the customer and retailer ("The Interface"). In any case, retailers have to understand consumers' needs and wants; b) the physical fulfillment process of getting goods ("The Range") to where the customer is looking for them.

The IT-related interplay between variables of point of order, product and service range, pricing, fulfillment, service providers and the interface between customers and service providers consequently leads to new ways of performing retailing (CCRRGE, 1996, p. 55) such as:

- *Customized marketing strategies by using POS data*: Since more and more retailers have fully equipped their stores with electronic point-of-sale (EPOS) systems, they can easily capture accurate point-of-sale data on a daily basis.

*Figure 3: Essential elements of IT-based retailing*

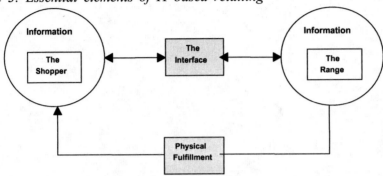

By linking the EPOS-system at store level with both the logistics information system at headquarters level and supplier level, retailers are better able to implement demand-synchronized delivery systems like quick response or continuous replenishment (Fisher, 1997).

- *Sophisticated logistics systems and processes*: With the success of mass merchants like Wal-Mart, retailers have been reminded of their powerful logistics capabilities. Since the presentation of the Wal-Mart logistics processes in the *Harvard Business Review* by Stalk, Evans, and Shulman (1992) and the first presentation of the efficient consumer models, e.g., the FMI-model (Salmon, 1993), more and more retailers, are recognizing the leverage potentials of different logistics solutions. Driven by sophisticated IT solutions, logistics can help decrease costs and increase services at the retail level, which has enormous savings effects for the total distribution pipeline (Mulhern, 1997).

## IT-Assisted Retail Marketing Processes
*General Application Fields of IT-Assisted Retail Marketing*

Business practice shows different approaches of IT-assisted retailing strategies (see, e.g., the Lebhar-Friedman Inc. Web site at www.lf.com; Table 3).

The common goal of all strategies is to obtain better information on consumer behavior in order to improve customer service. The examples also show that IT-assisted retailing affects all retail areas from the sales floor to the back offices.

## IT-Assisted Retail Format Layout
*General Contribution of the Store Layout to the Store Performance*

The layout of a retail format is one critical success factor which optimizes the link between sales productivity and consumers' excitement (Berekoven, 1995, p. 276). A store should offer an attractive atmosphere/layout considering that consumers postpone their purchase decision to the point-of-sale and seek orientation, friendly and helpful personnel, and short lines at the checkout. IT in the form of in-store media helps to achieve this prerequisite (Nymphenburg, 2001).

*Table 3: Recent examples of IT-assisted retail strategies*

| Retailer | Example | Description |
|---|---|---|
| Wal-Mart Stores Inc. | Merchandise Planning | Wal-Mart Stores will use online analytical processing (OLAP) technology from Sunnyvale, Calif.-based Hyperion under a deal unveiled today. The chain intends to build an advanced merchandise planning and reporting system with the Hyperion Essbase OLAP technology. |
| Sports Authority, Global Sports | Kiosk and Catalogue | In a move that augments its recent pairing with Global Sports, The Sports Authority Inc. says it will install interactive kiosks in 5 of its 198 stores. The specialty chain will also debut a catalogue during the fourth quarter of 2001. Global Sports, based in King of Prussia, Pa., will process and fulfil catalogue orders and provide customer service. It will also provide operational support for the kiosks. The Sports Authority does not plan to open any stores this year and instead is aiming to improve merchandising and control costs better. |
| Shoppers Drug Mart | ERP and Extranet | Shoppers Drug Mart signed a multiyear deal to license the SilverStream Application Server from SilverStream Software, Billerica, Mass. The 820-store Shoppers Drug Mart will use the product for core business functions, including a vendor extranet and store intranet, to improve online information access and interactions for company, employees and vendors. |
| Shaw's Supermarket | Self-Checkout | Shaw's Supermarkets will allow customers to scan, bag and pay for their groceries by themselves at 30 more stores. Installations of the NCR Corp. self-checkout systems are expected to be completed by February. The Shaw's and Star Market stores will use the latest system from Atlanta-based NCR—the A-Series, which includes a conveyor belt to help shoppers unload groceries. |
| Target Corp. | Smart Cards | Target Corp. is jumping on the smart-card bandwagon. The chain says it will issue Target smart Visa cards as part of its decision to roll out Target Visa cards on a national basis. It will also install point-of-sale terminals that accept smart-card payment in all stores next year. Like other smart Visas introduced last fall by major banks, the Target smart Visa will contain a computer chip—in addition to a magnetic stripe. The memory capabilities of the chips add the potential for more elaborate security and loyalty programs. |
| Home Depot | Checkout Systems | The Home Depot has installed Unleashed, a handheld wireless scanner that reduces checkout time, in about 700 of its stores. Unleashed enables associates to scan and record customers' purchases while they're in line. Home Depot said the application should be in all of its stores by the end of the year. |
| Kmart | Checkout Systems | Kmart announced a similar program titled Blue Lightning. During peak periods at checkouts, workers at Kmart stores will ring up customers' purchases while they wait in line and give them a card that the cashier can scan and process for payment. |
| Kroger | Theft Prevention | The Kroger Co. signed a 3-year agreement to install Sensormatic's UltraMax antitheft systems. The UltraMax system, already in place at the chain's Fred Meyer Stores division, is part of a chain-wide source-tagging program, under which consumer-goods manufacturers apply antitheft tags to their products at the point of origin or packaging. |

## In-Store Media

Karabateas, Barth and Wittmann (1999) or Silberer (1999) propose the following types of in-store media: audiovisual systems, such as in-store radio, in-store television and video animation; electronic price and information systems, e.g., displays, electronic price tags or electronic shopping carts or self-checkout systems; and multimedia systems, such as control systems, product information systems, customer service systems and olfactive systems, e.g., air circulation systems.

## In-Store Radio

In-store radio broadcasts radio programs for customers and employees of a certain store or a chain of stores during opening hours. The program can include promotion and advertising elements, which are customized even down to POS level. The radio programs are transmitted over satellites to the single stores. The retailers' investments into this media could be "refunded" by offering special advertising possibilities to manufacturers. Empirical tests showed that average sales increased from a range of 9 to 26% (Karabateas et al., 1999, p. 12).

## Electronic Shelf Labeling and Self-Checkout Systems

Stern, El-Ansary and Coughian (1996, p. 404) report about the possibilities of linking computer systems with the shelves and the checkout systems of retail stores. Using electronic price tags provides completely accurate pricing between shelves and checkout and helps to minimize administrative costs (because price labels are not replaced manually any more). Electronic shelf labels should be of such a size that enables the consumer to read the price information, but it should also allow flexible price management, smarter shelves management and improved promotion possibilities (Karabateas et al., 1999, p. 33; Figure 4). The technology is based on radio-frequency and infrared systems which link the master checkout with the shelves (NCR, 2001a, 2001b).

Giving the customer the possibility to self-register his/her purchases was already tested by Migros in 1969 (Gugelmann, 1988, p. 50). Then, the consumer punched in the data at the cash desk. Today, consumers get a handheld scanning device and can read the products' bar code information while walking around the aisles and can check out without waiting at the cash desk by putting the client card into the scanning device (Scanboy, 2001). This special connection can generate customized marketing approaches and allow one-to-one marketing and promotion activities. This approach is different than the self-checkout systems, e.g., developed by NCR, where the client scans the articles at the end of the shopping tour at the automated cash desk (NCR, 2001b; Figure 5).

A shopping cart could also be used as a IT-assisted retail marketing tool or promotion means (Karabateas et al., 1999, p. 37) The trolley can be equipped with

*Figure 4: Example of an electronic shelf label*

*Figure 5: Example of a self-checkout system*

*Figure 6: WATSON–The communicating shopping cart by Atlas New Media GmbH*

electronic displays, which can be used for product information, guiding customers through the store and providing promotion activities. The German Atlas New Media Group holds the worldwide patent for the "talking" or "communicating" shopping cart, WATSON. The communication devices are integrated at the grip of the cart (Figure 6), and based on radio frequency, the cart is linked with the shelves.

Whenever passing a "labeled" shelf, the cart announces a message to the shopper (Atlas New Media, 2001). Some pilot studies showed the enormous impact of WATSON on sales volume; sales increases of up to 250% for selected products have been realized (Atlas New Media, 2001).

## Multimedia Kiosks

Silberer (2000) outlines the possibilities of using information and presentation terminals (see also NCR, 2001b; Figure 7).

Such systems decrease burdens on personnel, increase sales possibilities and better inform consumers. Silberer (2000, p. 278) also points out the transformation of such systems from pure transaction-oriented kiosks to multimedia sales stations, combining ordering, payment and sales processes.

*Figure 7: Example of a Web kiosk*

## Europe's Most Modern Supermarket–Billa Supermarket in Purkersdorf

Billa launched a sophisticated store format in 2000, which includes many of the technologies described. With a size of only 800 square meters, the store offers a special shopping experience by concentrating on convenience and freshness by focusing on the categories vegetables and fruit, delicatessen, snack and salad bar, and coffee shop. In addition to these areas, the customer has the possibility to use free phones, have free access to the Internet, book a holiday by using online travel services, and seek health care information. In order to generate future customers, the supermarket offers also special child services like a special cinema and play station area, where children can play while their parents do their shopping. The children can be watched by a special video system. Also children-specific shopping carts are offered. Billa is one of the first supermarket chains using the WATSON technology and will expand its use to other stores (starting in October 2001 in Graz). All articles on the shelves are electronically price-tagged. The tags are directly linked with the EPOS system, which ensures a "right-price" guarantee. Also, price changes can be managed immediately without having problems with the central systems. In order to reduce the waiting time at the EPOS and increase the use of electronic payments, all shopping carts are equipped with self-scanning devices. While shopping, the customer scans articles immediately and knows at once not only the products' prices but also the value of his/her shopping basket. While checking out at the EPOS, the purchase is invoiced over the customer's payment card. All self-scanning customers receive a price reduction of 5%, which equals Billa's savings potential of not handling the articles by their personnel. Eighty percent of shoppers are choosing the self-scanning possibility and Billa is not experiencing higher inventory differences. In fact, sales went up 30% since the introduction of this technology. Another effect is given by installing a fountain spring inside the store, where clients can have a glass of water. A critical issue is the cleanness of the store.

In this store, cleaning activities are performed by a robot, which continuously cleans the floor and recognizes customers and other items. The shop also offers a 24-hour per day shopping possibility. By installing a special vending machine, which carries around 200 products, shoppers can shop outside the usual 66 weekly shopping hours. The prices are the same as in the store.

## Virtual or Internet-Based Retailing

*Integrating Internet-Based Retailing to the Wheel of Retailing*

Internet-based retailers, a new type of non-store-based type of retailing, are "attacking" stationary retailers' market position. "Dotcoms" or "virtual stores," like amazon.com, etoys.com, letsbuyit.com or webvan.com, have entered the market and tried to take serious market share from the existing players. The basic characteristic of these companies is that they do not have any physical stores and market direct to the consumers through the Internet (e.g., Green, 1999). As a result, electronic retailers are able to offer their products cheaper than their store-based competitors. A recent development showed the limits of pure Internet-based retailers. Webvan.com was not able to generate 3,000 customers/day and went bankrupt (Schnedlitz, 2001). According to Doherty, Ellis and Hart (1999), the adaptation of the Internet as a channel of distribution positively depends on the accessibility of consumers, the direct communication possibilities, and cost savings (especially transaction costs) of new markets. The negative impact is due to technical issues (e.g., interface problems and speed of data transfer), a heavily planned buying pattern, complex product differentiation and positioning.

*E-Consumer Typology*

Reitsma (2000) presents Internet shoppers as a critical group of buyers being very educated but not spending much time on the Net. These shoppers buy due to convenience of the channel, the unlimited shopping hours and the immediate order status information. Typical products bought over the Web are books, CDs or soft- and hardware. AC Nielsen Denmark presents the following Internet shopper typology and differentiates it in three groups: the critical user (approx. 25% of the population), who is reluctant towards the Internet; the goal-oriented user (approximately 31% of the population), who uses the Internet only for special purposes but generally has a positive attitude towards the technology; and the convenient user (approximately 21% of the population), who uses the Internet instead of catalogues (AC Nielsen Denmark, 2001).

## Evaluating the Channel Attractiveness of Virtual Retailing

*Market Volume*

Different empirical studies present different numbers for the global market volume of electronic commerce. Sanders and Temkin (2000) predict a US online sales volume for 2004 to be 3.2 trillion USD. Other studies are not that optimistic and deliver smaller numbers. The Nua Internet Surveys (2000) predict global online shopping revenues between 3.9 to 36.0 billion USD. According to this report, the United States is the area where electronic retailing is most developed. BCG (2000a) notes that the US-American standard should be reached in Europe within 2 years. According to the Forrester Group (2000), European online sales in 2005 will reach 55 billion Euro (!) or 5 % of total sales. Contrary to these optimistic numbers a Finish study by Kallio, Kemppainen, Tarkalla and Tinnila (2000) presents a future stagnation of online sales.

### Forms of Virtual Retailing

The electronic shopping world offers a lot of virtual store formats, e.g., intelligent agents, virtual malls, virtual auctions, portals, and virtual communities (Schnetkamp, 2000, p. 36). But similar to store-based retail formats, the electronic counterparts also have to deal with the strategic questions of attracting and satisfying customers (Paul & Runte, 1999; Garczorz & Krafft, 1999).

### Challenges of Virtual Retailing

Lancioni, Smith and Oliva (2000) present some challenges while using electronic distribution channels, such as shopping with no human contact but permanent client contact, improved customer service with improved flexibility (365 days a year, 7 days a week, 24 hours a day), and overall visibility of the order activities and status. However product requirements have to fit to a virtual retail concept as well as security issues because consumers are holding back on use of the Internet as a distribution channel due to lack of security (Cleven, 1999, p. 973).

### Consequences for Channel Adaptation

Kotzab and Madlberger (2001) and PriceWaterhouseCooper (2000) expect the top retailers and mail-order companies to adapt virtual store formats to their existing multichannel portfolios. The list of the Top 100 Internet retailers published by Stores Magazine already shows six "brick-and-mortar" companies with e-channels among the top 20 e-tailers. In order to serve future consumer groups, the leading retailers include more and more electronic distribution channels into their channel portfolios. It seems that these retailers have the financial resources which allow a long-term investment into this risky business.

## Billa's Virtual Distribution Channel: www.billa.at

### General Information on the Web Site and its Content

Billa started its online acitivities already in 1997 and was the first in the grocery retail industry offering a Web-site-related purchasing possibility. The goal of the Web approach is to position the Web site as a modern information, entertainment, and e-commerce platform. The Internet-based store format is seen as a promising future customer-relationship-management tool, with which clients can be addressed with individual one-to-one-marketing activities. Four years later, 1.8 million visitors per month click www.billa.at. The average usage time per visit is approximately 7 minutes. The growth rate compared to the previous months is on average 10%. The goal is to get 3 million clicks per month. The content is offered at 2,500 Web pages which are grouped in eight areas: company information, including corporate information and job offers; assortment, such as general information about products, promotions, and best buys; service, including recipes, advantage club, and photo online; store locator with virtual tours and information on new openings; magazine, including company-related news, weather reports, travel and tourist information and travel shop; fun, like games, chat possibilities, e-communities, e-cards and short messaging services; kids, such as virtual greeting cards, kid games and news; and the online shop, offering virtual shopping experiences.

### The Online Shop

The Billa online shop concentrates its service to 5,000 products for the geographic area of Vienna. Consumers can shop "365x24x7" and purchase the products at the same prices as in the store (including promotions). In case of any assistance, a special telephone hotline is offered. The order is confirmed by email and processed four hours after order receipt. The delivery is completed between 8 a.m. and 8 p.m. Monday through Friday and between 8 a.m. and 6 p.m. on Saturdays. The payment is cash or check when delivered. The minimum order is €22 and a fee of €7 for packages up to 99 kg is also charged. The orders are picked from one special store in the Vienna area.

## Category Management

Category management (CM) is a joint retailer and manufacturer process that involves managing product categories as business units and customizing them on a store-by-store basis to satisfy customer needs. Thus, a category is "a distinct, measurable and manageable group of products/services that consumers perceive to be interrelated and/or substitutable in meeting a consumer need" (ECRE, 1997).Category management differs from the traditional way of preparing an assortment for shoppers as follows: 1) The creation of categories is the result of a joint-planning process between retailers and manufacturers; 2) the definition of a category follows an end-user orientation rather than pure product characteristics; and 3) CM needs top management support. The purpose of CM is to determine the products that make up the category and its segmentation from the consumer's perspective. As most retailers offered different category-parts at different store locations, consumers got confused and lost in a store (ECR-Austria, 1997). Manufacturers instead focused on their brand management activities and did not consider the retail partner as an important source for their marketing success. CM allows now the creation of a commonly accepted language, common goals and achievements. Instead of arguing on prices and discounts, the two involved organizations work together on the fulfillment of consumer needs. The implementation of the CM organization within the European market allowed Procter & Gamble not only to reduce out-of-stocks on shelves by 26%, but also to increase its own market share within the category by 19%

and included a financial improvement for the retailer's turnover by + 11%. Total productivity could improve by + 45%. These results are very motivating for an industry where retailers usually obtain margins between -.5 and + 2% (Kotzab & Schnedlitz, 1999).

## IT-Assisted Retail Logistics Processes

*General Aspects to Retail Logistics Systems*

Logistics in a retailing context refers mostly to multi-echelon logistics systems, meaning that there are many nodes from the original supplier to the final store destination (Toporowski, 1996; Kotzab, 1998). As a consequence, retailing logistics presents itself as a very complex logistics system. The flows of goods and related information depend strongly on external factors such as vendors (size and structure), competitors and IT (able to use IT for logistics within the company and within the supply chain), and internal factors such as location (size and layout of the stores, logistics infrastructure at the locations), and range of products (how many different products in the store, how many facings at the shelves). Referring to the external factors, the structure of the vendors and the competitors mainly determines the quantitative input into a retailing logistics system, while IT determines the qualitative aspect of the input. As empirical studies are indicating, the interaction between retailers and their suppliers is crucial for the success of the retailers' logistics systems (Kotzab, 1998). A successful retail logistics system depends on the quality of the vendor's input. Furthermore, a growing number of retailers are increasingly evaluating their suppliers on their ability to communicate and cooperate with them. The internal factors can be interpreted as procurement and distribution instruments, which influence the quantity and quality of the output of the retailing logistics system. The location of the stores determines the number of delivery points within the system, while the "range of products" as well as the size of the store determine the "quantity scaffold" of the flow of goods. The overall flow of information is usually managed by integrated retail logistics information systems, which are defined, at least in the German area, as integrated merchandise information systems (Zentes, 1991).

## Combining IT into Just-In-Time-Oriented Retail Logistics Systems

*Electronic Data Interchange*

EDI is the meta-term for a multitude of different electronic standards allowing computerized and highly structured low-error communication (Kotzab, 1997). It is "the organization-to-organization, computer-to-computer exchange of business data in a structured, machine-pro-cessable format" (Emmelhainz, 1990). Within the European supermarket industry, the EDIFACT standard and its message subset EANCOM allows electronic communication between supply chain partners in the European consumer goods industry (e.g., Hildebrandt & Kamlage, 1995, p. 8). EANCOM considers three groups of standard messages—master data, commercial transactions, and report and planning—which should be primarily used for electronic information exchange between two supply chain partners (Deutsch, 1995). However, retailers and vendors in the various markets use so-called value-added networks (VANs) to allow multilateral communication within the supply chain. The VANs provide the participants with the necessary connection software, which enables the transmission of electronic information between numerous supply chain partners. Within Europe, several clearinghouses offer their services to the consumer goods industry, such as the German SEDAS Daten Service, the British TRADACOM (Trading Data Communication) or TRADANET (Trading Data Network), or the Austrian ECODEX (e.g., Colberg et al., 1995, p. 176). Beyond the imminent importance of the Internet, LiteEDI (EAN, 1998) combines the advantages of EDI with Internet technology and allows supply chain partners without EDI connections to communicate with EDI-using partners and vice versa.

*Bar codes and Scanning Devices*

Bar codes are the simplest form of optical character recognition by which information is encoded in printed bars of relative thickness and spacing (Colberg et al., 1995). The North American grocery industry relies on the UPC standard, while the European grocery industry applies the EAN standard. These bar codes refer as well as to symbolic requirements as well as to fields of application. UPC and EAN codes exist in three types (Kotzab, 1997): the UPC-7/EAN-8 for small volume items; the UPC-12/EAN-13 for retail units; and the UPC/EAN-128 for pallets (see Figure 8).

While UPC-7/EAN-8 and UPC-12/EAN-13 refer to an end-user-oriented identification of products, the UPC/EAN-128 can be used as a special logistical identification and labeling system for retail units (Frazelle & Apple, 1994, p. 595). Therefore special application identifiers (AI) were developed in order to allow a global use of this standard; e.g., the AI 00, which is the serial shipping container code and helps to identify the various shipping units and assists the automated management of the material and product flow as well as the customization of customer-oriented package units (Anonymous, 1994, p. 9). However, the bar codes need to be read and converted by scanners into a machine-readable form. The mechanisms that relay

*Figure 8: UPC/EAN bar codes*

| UPC/EAN-barcode standards | | |
|---|---|---|
| UPC-7/EAN-8 | UPC-12/EAN-13 | UCC/EAN-128 |
| 0 078349 | 0 12345 70054 | (00) 3 5412345 123456789 2 (420) 1000<br>AI — Kennzeichen f. Transporteinheit, undefiniert — BBN des Versenders — fortlaufende Nummer des Versenders — Prüfziffer — AI — Postleitzahl |

signals from bar codes are called scanners, which can be differentiated by their symbol recognition (fixed beam scanners which scan point-wise, moving beam scanners that scan line-wise, or fan scanners that scan area-wise); their field of application (stationary scanners, which are fixed installed and nonstationary = moveable scanners); and the handling (manual scanner or automatic scanner).

### Just-In-Time-Oriented Retail Logistics Systems

For retail logistics issues, EDI, bar codes and scanners can be used at the POS as EPOS systems (electronic point-of-sale systems), which read the bar code information of the purchased products, and in the distribution center for inbound and outbound logistics operations (Speh, Haley, Logan & West, 1992, p. 17). The channel-wide use of the described IT standards allows the integration with the involved ERP systems of both manufacturers and retailers and converts the former push-oriented logistics channels to pull-oriented supply chains like cross docking or continuous replenishment.

## IT-Assisted Flow-Through Distribution Center Operations–Cross Docking

### The Process of Cross Docking

Cross docking is the meta-term for all IT-related flow-through activities within a distribution center (see Table 4).

Table 4: Defining the concept of cross docking

| Author | Definition |
| --- | --- |
| Andel (1994, p. 93) | "Cross docking is the direct flow of merchandise/product from receiving to shipping, thus eliminating additional handling and storage steps in the distribution cycle." |
| Andersen Consulting (1994, p. 17) | "..the term refers to moving merchandise through a distribution facility from receiving to shipping without intermediate storage." |
| Cooke (1994, p. 35) | "In a cross dock operation, merchandise from an arriving truck is broken down into case- or pallet-loads upon arrival. Cases or pallets then are moved to the shipping dock, where they are placed onto trucks bound for individual stores. The speedy transfer of goods eliminates the need for warehouse storage." |
| Garry (1994, p. 63). | "The purpose of cross docking is to hasten the flow of products from the supplier to the store by removing storage and handling at the distribution center (DC) or warehous." |
| Lalonde & Masters (1994, p. 41) | "In a cross docking operation, shipments (normally of finished goods) move through a warehouse or distribution center without being held in storage." |
| Schwind (1995, p. 47) | ".. It is the expedited flow of goods from receiving to shipping. ... In cross docking, incoming loads are taken directly to shipping as part of the outbound flow." |
| Stalk et al. (1992, p. 58) | "In this system, goods are continuously delivered to Wal-Mart's warehouses, where they are selected, repacked, and then dispatched to stores, often without ever sitting in inventory. Instead of spending valuable time in the warehouse, goods just cross from one loading dock to another in 48 hours or less." |
| Wagar (1995, p. 29) | "Cross docking and flow-through have tended to be defined within the food industry as the simple movement of full pallets of merchandise across a distributor's dock to an outbound retail delivery truck." |

The main task of cross docking is to provide tailor-made deliveries on a just-in-time basis. The basic idea is to avoid inventory at the distribution center level. Therefore inventory building activities are replaced by sorting, transportation and handling activities, which are controlled by increased use of IT (e.g., bar codes, scanning devices and EDI connections; Kotzab, 1997; see Figure 9).

Different vendors deliver full truckloads of their goods to the transit terminal (a reengineered distribution center, also called a trans-shipment point) of the retail partners. There the goods are consolidated and/or broken into vendor-integrated POS-required smaller delivery units. The relevant literature offers various types of cross docking operations, which are presented in Table 5.

These forms show commonalities and differences which refer to the cooperation level between manufacturers and retailers, the electronic integration within the supply chain and the cross docking requirements for products and distribution centers. Of these forms, only complex cross docking and continuous movement cross docking are the most sophisticated forms of this operation and are operated only by a selected number of companies, e.g., Wal-Mart (Shulman, Stalk & Evans, 1992).

## Requirements for and Effects of Cross Docking Products and Facilities

Cross docking can be performed by anyone within the supply chain and does not refer to a retail-specific core competence. However, mainly retailers concentrate on such activities, especially within the grocery and/or fast-moving goods industry (Paché, 1998). The challenges and threats can be summarized as follows:

- *Challenges of cross docking*: speeds up the order cycle time; avoids duplication of costs; minimizes inventory levels and increases sales.
- *Threats of cross docking*: requires big investments in fully automated sorting and handling facilities and full electronic integration; requires changes in the organization within the company and specially trained human resources;

*Figure 9: Basic cross docking operation*

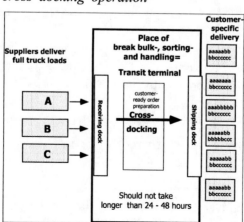

*Table 5: Types of cross docking operations*

| Types of cross docking operations | |
|---|---|
| **Differentiation by CCRRC (1992)** | |
| Complex cross docking (CCD) | The vendor delivers pre-labeled (according to store requirements) units to the retail DC. Pre-labeling is due to the exchange of POS data. |
| Intermediate cross docking (ICD) | The vendor delivers units, which are labeled and mixed for store destination at the retail DC. A store-specific ordering is not necessary. |
| Simple cross docking | Special cross docking operation for fast-moving items, which should be delivered to the stores within 24 to 48 hours. |
| **Differentiation by JIPOECR (1994b)** | |
| Pallet-level cross docking (PL-CD) | Full-pallet deliveries are directly loaded from vendors' to the retailers' trucks. |
| Case-level cross docking (CL-CD) | Break-bulk operations, where full pallets are transformed into smaller retail units. |
| **Differentiation by Andersen Consulting (1994)** | |
| Flow-through (continuous movement) cross docking (FT-CD) | Vendors deliver the right retail store mix to the retail DC, where it is directly loaded into the retailers' trucks. This process requires full electronic linkage of the supply chain. |
| Consolidated movement cross docking (CM-CD) | The mixing of the products is based on "traditional" methods of ordering, holding inventory and picking and packing. |
| Distributed movement cross docking (CM-CD) | Vendors deliver less-than-truckload units, which are mix to retail-customized full truckloads in the retailers' DCs. |

increases transportation costs and frequency; and requires reengineered inventory and warehouse systems.

The effects of cross docking can be seen in a flattened distribution structure and consequently in a speeding up of the delivery times within the channel. By reducing the costs of holding inventory, the total cost situation also improves. Cross docking is therefore one of these blueprints of successful distribution techniques where service improvements are fulfilled by lowering the costs (which is against traditional thinking of logistics). In order to run cross docking facilities, managers have to consider rather huge setup costs (e.g., highly automated distribution centers) and a vast number of items to be distributed. Both requirements are significantly related to the size of a company (Master & Lalonde, 1994).

# IT-Assisted Ordering Systems–Vendor-Managed Inventory Systems (VMI) or Continuous Replenishment Programs (CRP)

*The Process of VMI/CRP*

Vendor-managed inventory (VMI) or Continuous Replenishment (CRP) is a special cooperative form of an interfirm, automated replenishment program where the common goal is the automatic reinforcement of the supply of goods and the transfer of the burden of responsibility of storage from a retailer to a vendor (see Table 6).

Within a VMI/CRP setting, retailers retransfer the inventory competence back to their vendors by agreeing on certain average inventory levels on the distribution center level, service levels and/or other arrangements like the reduction or avoidance of out-of-stock situations. The VMI/CRP process helps to minimize the timely distance between the first and the following orders and consequently reduces the unnecessary security inventory levels at retail level (the bullwhip effect; Lee, Padmanabhan & Whang, 1997). To facilitate this goal, all parties have to be ready to exchange the necessary information at the time needed.

### Organizing the VMI/CRP Ordering Process

VMI/CRP changes the ordering process between retailers and vendors dramatically. In the past, a seller and a buyer who individually represent the goals of their companies drove the interaction. Within VMI/CRP this one-to-one relationship is replaced by interdepartmental, interorganizational teams which are responsible for the ordering process (Matthews, 1994, p. 44). These teams consist of representatives from marketing, logistics, sales, operations, finance and IT. Retailer and manufacturer teams cooperate closely and commonly develop VMI/CRP plans and actions (Golub, 1994, S. 13). According to JIPOECR (1994), these plans and operations refer to the determination of responsibilities (e.g., set up of teams, status quo reporting); promotion strategies (time plan, price setting); EDI strategies (e.g., EDI transaction sets); operative questions (e.g., routing plans); simulation processes

### Table 6: Defining the concept of VMI/CRP

| Author | Definition |
| --- | --- |
| Andraski (1994, p. 1) | "... A partnership which will transcend the basic interchange of electronic data interchange (EDI) to generate orders and manage inventory." |
| CCRRC (1992, p. 7) | "... Automated systems that enable distributors to stock and to reorder goods based on actual consumer sales (i.e., point-of-sale transactions)." |
| Crasper (1994, p. 76) | "... A mutual partnership, linking the distributor's business plans with the manufacturer's inventory replenishment and operations." |
| JIPOECR (1994, p. 111) | "The practice of partnering between distribution channel members that changes the traditional replenishment process from distributor-generated purchase orders, based on economic order quantities, to the replenishment of products based on actual and forecasted product deman." |
| Ricker & Sturtevant (1993, p. 527) | "... A mutual partnership, linking the distributor's business plans with the manufacturer's inventory replenishment and integrated operations. ... CRP is a vendor managed inventory control system." |
| Salmon (1993, p. 64) | "Continuous Replenishment Programs typically refer to the process by which warehouse inventory and movement is transmitted from distributor to supplier and the supplier generates the purchase order." |

(e.g., bar coding and ordering or EDI ordering processes); determination of common goals (e.g., fill rates, order cycles, reporting structures) and future strategies (e.g., time plan and follow-up).

### Requirements for and Effects of VMI/CRP

The continuous harmonizing of the activities of both partners is based on a steady information exchange and follows the goal of a reduction of the bullwhip effect between two levels of the supply chain. The challenges and threats can be seen as follows:

- *Challenges of VMI/CRP programs*: increases sales; reduces the number of slow-moving items; assists just-in-time-oriented inventory systems at the POS; reduces inventory holding and other administrative costs; and increases the quality of the cooperation between retailer and manufacturer.
- *Threats of VMI/CRP programs*: changes the organization within the supply chain and needs top-management support; needs other motivation and reward systems; is not applicable to all products, e.g., promotion items; needs high coordination between logistics and all other business units; its performance is difficult to measure; the profit is difficult to split among the partners; and needs specially trained human resources.

VMI/CRP requires high integration on organizational and technological levels from both vendor and retailer. The setup of interorganizational working groups to overcome functional silos and interfirm barriers is required in order to reengineer the total order process within the supply chain. Another important issue for success with VMI/CRP is product suitability. Some categories might not be appropriate to be managed on a VMI/CRP basis. It might also be a question of the critical mass. The VMI/CRP volume in certain retail sectors is estimated to be 1 to 2 percent of total products (Kotzab, 1997).

## Billa Logistics and IT Services

### Defining Competency Fields

Billa recognized early that their logistics and IT management capabilities as core competencies centralized their IT and administrative activities to the Billa Management Support Systems business unit (finance, IT and software development, engineering and advertising). The logistics and supply chain activities of all store formats are managed by the Warehouse and Transport profit center. This division operates a truck fleet of over 330 trucks, which deliver dry and packaged goods 6 times a week within 24 hours from one central distribution center in Wr. Neudorf. Fruit, vegetables and other perishable goods are delivered daily from five local fresh goods distribution centers (Wr. Neudorf, Ansfelden, Maria Saal, Kalsdorf and Hallein). Beverages are logistically managed by the Billa Beverage Distribution Department. All beverages come in returnable glass bottles. They are picked up by BML's trucks at the manufacturers' sites and then delivered directly to the stores. The empty bottles are returned to the BML central empty bottle sorting plant.

*The Automated Central Distribution Center (CDC), Wr. Neudorf*

BML opened one of the world's most modern central grocery distribution centers in 1995. All dry and packaged goods sold in the total store network (including Billa, Mondo, Emma, Merkur and Bipa) are delivered from the CDC. The CDC has a storage capacity for 38,000 pallets and operates 16 hours/day with an average daily outbound throughput of 250,000 cartons (7,000 roll cages) and inbound throughput of 4,000 pallets/day (3,000 from trucks and 1,000 from railways). Nearly all operations within the CDC are fully automated and based on EAN-128 and RTF technology. All vendors have to equip their pallets with EAN-128 transport labels and have to follow strict loading rules for their pallets and time windows for their delivery. The storage area is divided into sections for fast movers (2,000 articles, which are already prepared for store destination during receipt from the vendors), slow movers (2,500 low-volume articles, which are prepared for traditional pick to belt operations), and storage goods (automatic storage and retrieval system for a daily picking volume of 9,000 full pallets). The robots in the storage goods area operate 24 hours a day by a first-in-first-out principle and follow chaotic rules for locating the inventory location. The RTF-controlled picking area allows paperless picking and packing of 3,500 articles. The picked items are moved by conveyor belts to the sorter area. High-speed scanners can read the information from the bar code labels and direct the items to one of the 192 chutes by using flip-shells. This allows immediate order fulfillment for 96 store deliveries. Table 7 summarizes the dimensions of the Billa CDC, which can be seen as a benchmark for Austria as well as for Europe.

# FUTURE TRENDS

## General Retail Trends

Looking ahead, a number of other changes will affect retailing operations (Table 8).

It is predicted that these issues will affect existing retail strategies. Many retailers will correct their existing multiple format strategy and try either to reduce the number of retail formats or relaunch selected formats.

*Table 7: Technical key numbers of Billa's distribution center*

| Technical key numbers of the Billa Distribution Center Wr. Neudorf | |
|---|---|
| Number of articles managed | 6,000 items |
| Technical equipment; storage and throughput performance: | 10 ASRS robots |
| | inbound 3,000 pallets/day by truck |
| | inbound 1,000 pallets/day by train |
| | storage of 30,000 pallets |
| | outbound 250,000 cases/day |
| Additional information | setup costs of over 70 million Euro |
| | total area of 50,000 sqm |
| | 16 hours/day on operation |

*Table 8: General retail trends (PwC, 2000)*

| | |
|---|---|
| The transformation from the industrial age to the information age, | where more and more people will work for the service industries, will be entrepreneurial, self-employed and more independent. Regarding consumer behavior, consumers should show more iconoclastic shopping patterns. |
| Shoppers will be more and more time-constrained, | which means more focused shopping behavior and less leisure. Restrictive shopping hours will be replaced by Internet shopping, which will allow 24 hours shopping on 7 days a week. |
| Less frequent, more large transaction shopping behavior, | which supports hypermarket structures offering products for the basic needs at reasonable prices. |
| Increasing importance of "best-value-shoppers" | due to the ageing population, much more emphasis will be given to value pricing than to fashion. This supports hard-discount retailers, hypermarkets and category killers. |

## Special IT-Assisted Retail Trend–Efficient Consumer Response

ECR is a strategy of "how partners in the supply chain can best synchronize the flow of product through the distribution pipeline from point of manufacture to point to final sale" (Martin, 1994, p. 377). Various attempts to define ECR show that ECR is primarily related to strategic partnerships in the distribution channels of the grocery industry to increase the performance to the consumers (Salmon, 1993; JIPOECR, 1996a; ECRE, 1996, 1997). The vision of ECR is to set up a consumer-driven distribution system in which the production is permanently managed by the consumers' POS activities (according to Salmon, 1993). The realization of this strategy is based originally on four pillars (efficient store assortment; efficient promotion; efficient replenishment and efficient new product introduction), which had been "customized" to two strategy blocks for the European market (demand and supply side). As a result, ECR leads to increased productivity. The optimal combination of these areas leads to a benefit for the members of the supply chains of USD 30 billion in the US and DM 50 billion within Europe (according to Salmon, 1993, p. 4; ECRE, 1996). The savings result mostly from total-chain reduction of inventory by speeding up cycle time. These results had been documented in a lot of series published by the various ECR-working groups and other organizations. The studies include rules and case studies, which can be used as benchmarks (FMI, 2000; ECR-Scorecard, 2000). ECR's basics are quite simple and refer to harmonization and cooperative adaptation of commonly agreed business processes and standards that can help to avoid duplications of costs. ECR's originality might be seen in the request towards common endeavors to harmonize the business relationships of the market partners (Table 9).

*Table 9: General characteristics of efficient consumer response*

| Characteristic | Description |
|---|---|
| Centralization and standardization | Centralizing the flow of goods eliminates unnecessary inventory levels and thus leads to increased profits. Implementing supply-chain-wide IT and organizational standards reduces insecurity in the marketplace, reduces inventory and leads to a steady flow of goods and related information. |
| Cooperation/integration and systems thinking | The realization of ECR depends on common approaches. Suboptimization does not lead to improvements; the total system has to be optimized. |
| End-user orientation by postponement | The design and the optimization by ECR are controlled by the end user (meaning the POS data). Bullwhip effects can be reduced and out-of-stock situations at the POS can be avoided if an integrated access to this data is guaranteed. The assortment of end-user-oriented categories has to be done in close conjunction between retailers and manufacturers. |

# CONCLUSION AND OUTLOOK

IT-assisted retailing needs visionary leaders. Kotzab (1997, p. 207) names Sam Walton as one example:

Sam Walton started his operation in the 1950s as a "Five and Dime Shop," knowing about the power of IT to run his retail company. In 1978, Wal-Mart started with cross docking operations, using bar codes and scanners. In 1983, all stores were equipped with EPOS systems, which were linked with the central headquarters and the distribution centers. In 1987, Wal-Mart started a CRP/VMI partnership with Procter & Gamble, which set benchmarks for any retailer and manufacturer. Today, all Wal-Mart's information flows are managed by satellite technology. All sales information is kept on a database, which can be accessed by all Wal-Mart vendors. The database keeps track on all sales and offers a sales history of up to 65 weeks. However, it took Wal-Mart more than 30 years to become the most efficient IT-based retailer of the world. The managers of our case company BML-Austria also showed leadership by recognizing very early the power of IT-assisted retail management. BML introduced the first EPOS system, the first fully automated distribution center, and the first grocery online shop in Austria in 1982. It is mainly the grocery and fast-moving goods industries which introduce many of the IT-based innovations. These solutions enable retailers to find more sophisticated ways to integrate data quantities and quality (see Figure 10) and make retail operations more efficient (doing more with less). Retail managers who would like to use IT-assisted retailing should consider four areas as crucial: sales planning, assortment structure planning, visual merchandising, and space management (Management Horizons, 2001).

The combination of these fields will lead to new alternative store formats that combine convenience and excitement for the consumer with mass customized and profitable operations for retailers and manufacturers.

*Figure 10: Crucial IT-assisted retail tools*

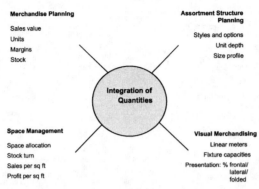

## ACKNOWLEDGMENT

The authors gratefully thank Mr. David Grant (the University of Edinburgh), whose comments and suggestions considerably improved this paper, and Prof. Luiz Antonio Joia for his patience and recommendations.

## ENDNOTE

1 This section and the sections titled *Europe's Most Modern Supermarket– Billa Supermarket in Purkersdorf, Billa's Virtual Distribution Channel: www.billa.at, and Billa Logistics and IT Services* refer to Billa (2001a), Billa (2001b), Billa (2001c) and Billa (2001d).

## REFERENCES

AC Nielsen Denmark. (2001). *Future Web*. http://www.acnielsen.aim.dk/produkter/ kommunikation_og_media/future_web/future_web.htm. Accessed February 3, 2001.

Andel, T. (1994). Define cross-docking before you do it. *Transportation & Distribution, 11*, 93-98.

Andraski, J. (1994). Foundations for successful continuous replenishment programs. *The International Journal of Logistics Management, 5*(1), 1-8.

Anonymous. (1994). *Der Serial Shipping Container Code* [The serial shipping container code]. EAN-Austria: Wien.

Anonymous. (2001). Die weltweit größten einzelhändler (retailers of the world). *LP-International, 15*, 6.

Atlas New Media. (2001). *Watson, der sprechende Einkaufswagen* (Watson, the talking shopping cart). Hamburg.

Berekoven, L. (1995). *Erfolgreiches Einzelhandelsmarketing. Grundlagen und Entscheidungshilfen* (2. Auflage) (Successful retail marketing, basics and decision aid). München: C.H. Beck.

Billa. (2001a). *BML Corporation*.

Billa. (2001b). www.billa.at. Accessed September 9, 2001.

Billa. (2001c). *Billa Purkersdorf, der modernste Supermarkt Europas* (Billa Purkersdorf, Europe's most modern supermarket).

Billa. (2001d). *Das Zentrallager in Biedermannsdorf (The Central Distribution Center in Biedermannsdorf)*.

Cleven, H. D. (1999). Entwicklungspfade und leistungsperspektiven des electronic commerce (Developments in electronic commerce). In O. Beisheim (Ed.), *Distribution im Aufbruch. Bestandsaufnahme und Perspektiven (Changing Distribution. State of the Art and Future Perspectives)*, pp. 967-986. München: Vahlen.

Coca-Cola Retail Research Group Europe (CCRRGE). (1996). *The Future for the Food Store–Challenges And Alternatives*. London.

Coca-Cola-Retailing-Research-Council (CCRRC). (1992). *New Ways to Take Costs Out of the Retail Food Pipeline*. Atlanta.

Colberg, T., Willenz Gardner, N., Horan, K., McGinnis, D., McLauchlin, P. & Yuk-Ho, S. (1995). *The Price Waterhouse EDI Handbook*. New York: John Wiley & Sons.

Cooke, J. (1994). Beyond quality. *Traffic Management, 6*, 33-37.

Crasper, S. (1994). The next strategic weapon. Continuous replenishment. *Hospital Material Management, 16*(8), 76-79.

Dawe, R. (1993). *The Impact of Information Technology on Materials Logistics in the 1990's*. Cleveland, OH: Penton.

Deutsch, M. (1995). *Unternehmenserfolg mit EDI. Strategie und Realisierung des elektronischen Datenaustausches (Profits with EDI. Strategy and Realization of Electronic Data Interchange)*. Braunschweig: Wiesbaden.

Doherty, N., Ellis, C. & Hart, C. (1999). Cyber retailing in the UK: The potential of the Internet as a retail channel. *International Journal of Retailing and Distribution Management, 27*(1), 22-36.

EAN. (1998). Position paper on *Lite EDI*. Brussels: EAN.

European Commission (EC) (Ed.). (1997). *Green Paper on Commerce and Distribution*. Brussels: European Commission.

ECR Europe (ECRE). (1996). *European Value Chain Analysis Study–Final Report*.

ECR Europe (ECRE). (1997). *CEO Overview–Efficient Consumer Response*.

ECR-Scorecard. (2000). *ECR Global Scorecard*. http.//216.247.25.35/Default.asp. Accessed May 27, 2000.

Elliot, G. & Starkings, S. (1998). *Business Information Technology: Systems, Theory and Practice*. New York & London: Longman.

Fisher, M. (1997). What is the right supply chain for your product. *Harvard Business Review, 2*, 105-116.

Food Marketing Institute (FMI). (2000). http.//www.fmi.org/pub/Pubs_searchresults.cfm. Accessed May 27, 2000.

Forrester Group (2000). *Northern Europe Will Close The Ecommerce Gap With The US.* http.//www.forrester.com/ER/Press/Release/0,1769,196,FF.htm. Accessed January 11, 2000.

Frazelle, E. & Apple, J. (1994). Materials handling technologies. In J. Robeson and W. Copacino (Eds.), *The Logistics Handbook*, 547-603. Toronto et. al.:Free Press.

Garczorz, I. & Krafft, M. (1999). Wie halte ich Kunden? Kundenbindung. (Customer relationship management). In A. Sönke, M. Clement, K. Peters and B. Skiera (Eds.), *eCommerce. Einstieg, Strategie und Umsetzung im Unternehmen, (eCommerce, Strategy and Realization within the Firm)*, 135-147. Frankfurt/Main/FAZ.

Garry, M. (1994). A blueprint for the future. *Progressive Grocer, 10*, 63-66.

Golub, J. (1994). Preparing a partnership. *Progressive Grocer, 1*, 12-13.

Green, D. (1999). *How will the traditional retailer compete with e-commerce retailers evolving in today's marketplace. The supply chain perspective.* Paper presented at the *Annual Conference of the Council of Logistics Management*, October, Toronto, Canada.

Gugelmann, E. (1988). Marktbearbeitung mit gesellschaftlichem Anspruch (marketing beyond social requirements). *Dynamik im Handel, Sonderausgabe, 10*, 48-58.

Haeckel, S. & Nolan, R. (1993). Managing by wire. *Harvard Business Review, 5*, 122-132.

Hildebrandt, L. & Kamlage, K. (1995). EDIFACT. Die Normung des elektronischen Datenaustauschs (EDIFACT, norming electronic data interchange). In V. Trommsdorff (Ed.), *Handelsforschung 1995/96. Informationsmanagement im Handel. Jahrbuch der Forschungstelle für den Handel (FfH) (Retail Research 1995/96, Information Management and Retailing. Annual Yearbook of the Retail Research Council)*, pp. 3-18. Berlin: Physica.

Joint Industry Project on Efficient Consumer Response (JIPOECR). (1994). *Continuous Replenishment. An ECR Best Practices Report.* Washington, DC: Grocery Manufacturers of America.

Joint Industry Project on Efficient Consumer Response (JIPOECR). (1996a). *ECR 1995 Progress Report.* Grocery Manufacturers of America.

Joint Industry Project on Efficient Consumer Response (JIPOECR). (1996b). *The ECR Scorecard.* Grocery Manufacturers of America.

Joint Industry Project on Efficient Consumer Response (JIPOECR). (1998). *1997 ECR Industry Benchmarking Survey.* Grocery Manufacturers of America.

Kallio, J., Kemppainen, K., Tarkalla, M. & Tinnilä, M. (2000). New distribution models for grocery shopping. In A. Thorstenson and P. Østergaard (Eds.), *Logistics Changes in the New Century. Proceedings of the 12th NOFOMA Conference*, 74-91. Handelshojskolen i Aarhus, Aarhus.

Karabateas, K., Barth, S. & Wittmann, N. (1999). *Instore Medien & Multimedien am POS (Instore Media and Multimedia at the P.O.S.).* Köln: EHI.

Keen, P. (1991). Redesigning the organization through information technology. *Planning Review, 19*(3), 4-9.

Kotzab, H. (1997). Neue Konzepte der Distributionslogistik von Handelsunternehmen (Recent concepts for retail logistics). Wiesbaden: Deutscher Universtitätsverlag.

Kotzab, H. (1998). Handelslogistik (retail logistics). In W. Krieger and P. Klaus (Eds.), *Gablers Logistik-Lexikon (Gablers Logistics Encyclopedia)*, pp. 169-175. Wiesbaden:Gabler.

Kotzab, H. & Madlberger, M. (2001). European retailing in e-transition? An empirical evaluation of Web-based retailing–Indications from Austria. *International Journal of Physical Distribution & Logistics Management, 31*(6), 440-462.

Kotzab, H. & Schnedlitz, P. (1999). The integration of retailing to the general concept of supply chain management concept. *Journal für Betriebswirtschaft, 4*, 140-153.

Lalonde, B. & Masters, J. (1994). Emerging logistics strategies. Blueprints for the next century. *International Journal of Physical Distribution and Logistics Management, 24*(7), 35-47.

Lancioni, R., Smith, Mi. & Oliva, T. (2000). The role of the Internet in supply chain management. *Industrial Marketing Management, 1*, 45-56.

Lebhar-Friedman, Inc. (2001). http://www.lf.com.

Lee, H., Padmanabhan, V. & Whang, S. (1997). The bullwhip effect in supply chains. *Sloan Management Review*, Spring, 93-102.

Levy, M. & Weitz, B. (1998). *Retailing Management* (3rd ed.). Boston: Irwin/McGraw-Hill.

The Logistics Strategy Group, Andersen Consulting (1994). *The Mass Merchant Distribution Channel. Challenges and Opportunities*. Oak Brook, IL: Warehousing Education and Research Council.

Management Horizons. (Eds.). (2000). *Category Management. Profit through Customer Focus. Retail Best Practice*. London.

Martin, A. (1994). The ultimate ECR strategy. In Council of Logistics Management (CLM). (Ed.), *Annual Conference Proceedings*, 375-391, October 16-19. Cincinatti, Ohio. Chicago, IL: CLM.

Mathews, R. (1994). CRP moves toward reality. *Progressive Grocer, 7*, 43-46.

NCR Corporation. (NCR). (2001a). *NCR Takes Electronic Shelf Labels from Novelty to Necessity*. http.//www.ncr.com/media_information/2001/jun/pr062501.htm. Accessed September 09, 2001.

NCR Corporation (NCR). (2001b). http://www.ncr.com/media_information/photos_sa.htm. Accessed September 27, 2001.

Nua Internet Surveys. (2000). Online shopping revenue estimates. *Marketing News*, July 3, 20.

Nymphenburg. (2001). *Elektronische Medien Erobern den Handel (Electronic Media "Conquer" Retail)*. www.nymphenburg.de. Accessed August 14, 2001.

Paché, G. (1998). Retail logistics in France: The coming of vertical disintegration.

*International Journal of Logistics Management, 9*(1), 85-93.

Paul, C. & Runte, M. (1999). Wie ziehe ich kunden an–Virtuelle communities. In A. Sönke, M. Clement, K. Peters, and B. Skiera (Eds.), *eCommerce. Einstieg, Strategie und Umsetzung im Unternehmen (eCommerce, Strategy and Realization within the Firm)*, pp. 121-134. Frankfurt/Main:FAZ.

Porter, M. (2001). Strategy and the Internet. *Harvard Business Review*, March, 63-78.

PriceWaterhouseCooper (PwC). (2000). *Europan Retailing 2010*. http.//www.ideabeat.com/ResLib/pricewaterhouse/euroretail2010/page1.htm. Accessed June 24, 2000.

Reitsma, R. (2000). eCommerce enters Europe. *Presentation of Forrester Research Inc.*

Ricker, F. & Sturtevant, P. (1993). Continuous replenishment planning (CRP). The driving force in the healthcare industry. In Council of Logistics Management (Ed.), *Annual Conference Proceedings*, 525-533, October 3-6. Washington, D. C. Chicago, IL: CLM.

Salmon, K. (1993). Efficient consumer response. *Enhancing Consumer Value in the Grocery Industry*. Washington: FMI.

Sanders, M. & Temkin, B. (2000). *Global eCommerce Approaches Hypergrowth*. http.//www.forrester.com/ER/Research/Brief/0,1317,9229,FF.html. Accessed October 4, 2000.

Scanboy (2001). *Handscanner im Vormarsch.[Manual Scanners on the Way]*. Retrieved on September 9, 2001 from http://www.scanboy.de/news/fachpresse/meldung116133852.htm.

Schnedlitz, P. (2001). Internet-shopping. Rechnung ohne die menschen (Internet-shopping without considering people). *Die Presse*, 2.

Schnetkamp, G. (2000). Aktuelle und zukünftige erfolgsfaktoren des electronic shopping. In D. Ahlert (Ed.), *Internet & Co. im Handel (Internet & Co and Retail)*, pp. 29-50. Berlin et al:Springer.

Schwind, G. (1995). Considerations for cross docking. *Material Handling Engineering, 11*, 47-51.

Silberer, G. (1999). Handelsmarketing mit neuen medien. Herausforderungen für den klassischen und den elektronischen handel. In O. Beisheim (Ed.), *Distribution im Aufbruch. Bestandsaufnahme und Perspektiven (Changing Distribution. State of the Art and Future Perspectives)*, 1035-1048). München: Vahlen.

Silberer, G. (2000). Neue medien im handel. In T. Foscht, G. Jungwirth and P. Schnedlitz (Eds.), *Zukunftsperspektiven für das Handelsmanagement. Konzepte–Instrumente–Trends (Future Perspectives in Retailing. Concepts, Tools and Trends*, pp. 273-288. Frankfurt/Main:Deutscher Fachverlag, Studien für die Praxis Band XIV.

Speh, T., Haley, J., Logan, K. & West, M. (1992). *A Guide for Evaluating and Implementing a Warehouse Bar Code System*. Oak Brook, IL: Warehousing

Education and Research Council.

Stalk, G., Evans, P. & Shulman, L. (1992). Competing on capabilities–The new rules of corporate strategy. *Harvard Business Review, 2*, 57-69.

Stern, L., El-Ansary, A. & Coughlan, A. (1996). *Marketing Channels* (5th ed.). Upper Saddle River, NJ: Prentice Hall.

Toporowski, W. (1996). *Logistik im Handel. Optimale Lagerstruktur und Bestellpolitik einer Filialunternehmung (Retail Logistics. Optimal Inventory and Order Policies)*. Heidelberg: Physica.

Wagar, K. (1995). The logic of flow-through logistics. *Supermarket Business, 6*, 29-35.

Zentes, J. (1991). Computer integrated merchandising–Neuorientierung der distributionskonzepte im handel und in der konsumgüterindustrie (Computer integrated merchandising–Re-orientation of retail distribution). In J. Zentes (Ed.), *Moderne Distributionskonzepte in der Konsumgüterwirtschaft (Modern Distribution in the Grocery Industry)*, 1-15. Stuttgart.

Zentes, J. & Schramm-Klein, H. (2001). Multi-channel retailing–Ausprägungen und trends (Multi-channel retailing–Forms and trends). In B. Hallier (Ed.), *Praxisorientierte Handelsforschung (Empirical Retail Research)*, pp. 290-296. Köln: EHI.

**Chapter XII**

# Evolution and Revolution of Retailing Through IT

Marcel Cohen
Imperial College Management School, UK

## ABSTRACT

*This chapter examines the impact that IT has had on retailing under two headings–evolutionary and revolutionary changes. The evolutionary changes described focus on the electronic identification of products, the improved communication links between retailers and their suppliers, and the introduction of electronic payment. The revolutionary changes considered are those stemming from e-commerce. The thrust of the discussion is that whilst IT has revolutionised product associated with the physical transfer (delivery or pickup) of goods to customers. This has opened up an opportunity for a new form of retailer that may be the result of an alliance between companies with IT skills (e.g., Microsoft), delivery capability (e.g., DHL) and distributed physical assets (e.g., Exxon).*

## INTRODUCTION

The classical distribution chain from manufacturer to end user is essentially a break bulk process. Manufacturers supply a small number of wholesalers with large/bulk quantities (for example, truckloads) of the same product. Wholesalers supply a larger number of intermediaries/retailers with a variety of products but smaller quantities (for example, boxes containing dozens of items) of each. Retailing describes the final link in the distribution chain that deals with the supply to end users (or consumers). It is characterised by supplying a very large number of people with small, often single items, with a large variety of products.

The retail shop has remained largely unchanged for centuries as the final stage of a break bulk distribution operation. In the last 30 years however certain societal trends (see Henley Centre for Forecasting, 1984) have caused fundamental changes in the food retailing landscape. The fundamental driver to change is the consumers' willingness and ability to hold stocks of food products in their own home rather than depend on retailers to hold the entire inventory. This in turn is driven largely by the availability of storage devices, such as refrigerators, in peoples' homes, the ability to transport large quantities of goods through the availability of cars, and finally having the ability to finance the stock held through regular salaries and other credit facilities. This has led naturally to a change of buying habits from daily small purchases to less frequent larger purchases. The latter became so major an event that they justified a purposeful expedition, called a "mission shop" to a suitable retailer rather than a chance purchase on the way to or from work. That was the motivation for the birth of out-of-town large food superstores, also called hypermarkets.

The out-of-town hypermarkets were focused initially on functional products such as grocery and other domestic requirements. This left the less functional (and possibly more enjoyable) purchases in the high street. Thus a polarisation occurred with high-touch/pleasurable purchases, from clothes to cameras, in the high street and functional purchases, from canned foods to detergents, in out-of-town centres. Each of these facilities developed at its own pace. For instance the out-of-town centres grew in size and diversity in range, most notably offering petrol for sale. High street shops became more aesthetically pleasing by the use of interesting displays and lighting. Indeed the very nature of the high street has evolved from a long line of shops to malls or precincts. Some suggest (see Popcorn, 1998) that the birth of such precincts is driven by the societal trend of fear and mistrust of others. The precincts provide secure environments to allow retailers to vet customers before serving them.

The important fact remains that retailing has undergone major changes as a result of societal changes. However we argue here that this change in retailing, large as it is, is surpassed by the impact that IT has had on retailing.

The impact of information technology (IT) in causing change to retailing has taken two basic forms—evolution and revolution. Historically IT has helped the *evolution* of retailing but more recently it has begun to cause a *revolution* in retailing. We shall visit each of these two roles of IT in turn.

Whilst IT in its broadest definition has helped retailing evolve in many ways—including security systems, edge-of-shelf displays showing computer-controlled prices, and the like—we shall focus on the three most significant developments. We shall consider product identification, linkages with suppliers and lastly electronic payment. These three contributions from IT have had a fundamental impact in the evolution of the retailing process.

The main focus of this chapter however is not to describe how IT has merely helped the *evolution* of retailing but rather to examine how the development of IT might contribute to the *revolution* of retailing. We are specifically concerned with electronic trading, otherwise known as e-commerce. In a sense this is an attempt to grapple with the future and we will have to speculate to a large extent on the way the world will change. We shall also discuss whether the advent of e-commerce requires the retailing rule book to be rewritten.

## *Evolution* Through IT

### *Product Identification*

A typical retail store offers for sale a large number of products—commonly the range will encompass hundreds of products and sometimes thousands of products. Knowing which products sell well and which do not is at the heart of retailing. Yet until recently knowing what sells was a matter of guesswork and such understanding was attributed to the "art" of retailing. Good retailers were credited with having a "feel" for what might sell and having "a finger on the pulse" in adapting the range of products on offer to meet customer expectations and requirements.

For example, a typical decorating shop will stock amongst other items a number of brands of decorative paints of different colours, sizes and finishes (emulsion, gloss, vinyl matt, vinyl silk) and also wall coverings with different patterns (e.g., geometric, floral, plain), colours, textures (embossed, smooth), properties (washable, vinyl, paper) and so on. The product buyer for such a store has traditionally been valued for his flair and ability to track market trends. These qualities were valued simply because, other than the annual or biannual stock-take, there were no direct mechanisms for establishing the level and mix of products that were actually being sold. Whilst the annual (or biannual) stock-take did provide an indication of the sales mix, this was long after the event and it was not frequent enough to direct buying decisions. Its only useful purpose was as an audit process for a trading period that had been completed. The same audit also revealed the gross profit achieved during the trading period. This overall gross profit is of course extremely important and must be monitored week by week. It is clearly made up of the individual gross profit contributions of individual items being sold. Since the individual gross profit contributions can vary widely between one product and another, estimating the overall gross profit on a weekly basis requires knowledge of the mix of products being sold. Again since the identity of products being sold was known only in vague terms, the daily or weekly gross profit being generated was largely a matter of speculation. This made managing and monitoring the performance of a retail business a matter of guesswork—likened to a game of football where the score was withheld from the players!

IT's major contribution was in providing the mechanism by which the identity of individual products sold could be recorded. One mechanism used mostly in the clothing trade was the "Kimbel" tag. These tags were essentially small punch cards that recorded information according to the arrangement of holes perforated on the card. When a garment was sold, the card attached to the garment was collected by the retailer and later read by a special card reader. This was the first development in automated product identity and proved very useful in identifying styles and colours of garments that were being purchased. Indeed, it also helps provide a better estimate of the gross profit being achieved. However the cost of each card was substantial and whilst it was negligible relative to a cost of a garment it was not so negligible when compared to lower priced items, to say nothing of the difficulties of attaching such cards to products of awkward size and material.

The successor to "Kimbel" tags was the introduction of bar codes—essentially a combination of parallel lines—whose positioning could be used to store information readable by a relatively inexpensive infrared reader. Bar codes first appeared on a restricted number of products, but eventually European legislation forced their introduction at the point of manufacture for almost all product categories. Bar codes are now a fundamental part of every retailing operation and have been a tremendous success in identifying products as they pass through the distribution chain. Sales trends and margins achieved are now no longer an art but have been transformed into a science. Some would say taking the agony (and fun) out of retailing.  Indeed it has been argued that the knowledge that bar codes provide retailers concerning trends in product purchase and consumption have strengthened their negotiating power when facing manufacturers. The knowledge gained about the preference of consumers has made retailers the consumer's representative in negotiations and empowered them.  When a negotiation between retailer and supplier takes place, it is the retailer now that has the power to dictate the terms under which trade will take place.  This is in effect a dramatic shift in the balance of power from manufacturer to retailer (Kadiyali, Chintagunta & Vilcassim, 2000) and has had profound consequences for the supply chain infrastructure and competition in general. Note for example the power wielded by European grocery supermarkets who can demand side payments from their suppliers (Kim & Staelin, 1999). It is the supermarkets that specify profit margins, payment terms and delivery schedules. This has transformed the European grocery distribution landscape—supermarket retailers have effectively absorbed the role of wholesaling, and through their own-label products they are effectively becoming suppliers too (Bontems, Monier-Dilham & Requillart, 1999). IT can claim a key role in this and such transformation.

## Relationships with Suppliers

In the past individual links in the distribution chain—e.g., manufacturers, wholesalers, retailers—were regarded as stand-alone entities who traded with suppliers and customers in such a way as to optimise their own performance and the return to their shareholders. It soon became evident that strong relationships with other entities in the distribution chain could unleash additional benefits (both social and economic) which could be shared amongst the parties concerned. This is at the heart of "relationship marketing," which plays down the value of an individual transaction and emphasises longer term relationships.

The introduction of a closer relationship between supplier and retailer through IT leads to two business benefits—low inventory and the ability to offer "mass customisation."

A retailer must hold inventory to cover for the variability in his sales and also the variability in the supply time from the manufacturer. The retailer must hold inventory because he cannot perfectly predict when customers will be entering his store and what products they might buy. Even if the retailer knew exactly when customers would enter his store and what they would buy he would still need to hold stock to cater for possible delay in supply from the manufacturer. Inventory is in effect the cost of poor information. The manufacturer has analogous problems. He must hold stock to cater for the variability in orders from the retailer and also delays in delivery from his (raw material) suppliers. It is clear from this simple example that if the manufacturer was given access to information on the retailer's daily sales then he could predict more accurately and sooner what orders the retailer is likely to place on him. This means that the manufacturer's inventory can be reduced (since he has forewarning of variability in demand) and so can the inventory of the retailer be reduced (because he will experience a smaller and less variable lead time of supply). Therefore there is a direct inventory benefit to both parties (Ganeshan, 1999).

Initially IT helped the achievement of inventory benefits through electronic data interchange (EDI)—essentially one mainframe computer talking to the other—but this is now being overtaken by Internet-based information exchange. This exchange of information is key to the reduction of inventory. Sears, one of the world's largest retailers, chooses to work closely with its suppliers and has been reported to have rationalised the number of suppliers that it deals with in order to facilitate the achievement of this inventory benefit.

Another benefit that results from the presence of a close relationship between supplier and retailer is that commonly known as "mass customisation." Ever since the 1920s, the era of Henry Ford's model T car, the buzz notion for manufacturing was mass production. However, to the consumer of today standing out from the crowd and expressing his/her individuality has become paramount. This has largely knocked on the head the notion of mass production and by implication mass marketing. The key to marketing today is to tailor product manufacture to the specific requirements of individual customers. However the challenge is to do so without a cost penalty.

IT has come to the rescue here too in enabling customer preferences to be taken into account at the time of manufacture, tailoring products to individual customer requirements (demand-pull) rather than making products for stock in the hope that someone will want to buy them (supply-push). A good example of such IT facilities being used in practice is the case of Dell computers. The customer specifies what features he wants in his PC prior to the computer being assembled.

Inventory reduction and mass customisation have been pioneered by car manufacturers but many other industries are seeking to derive the benefits from close relationships between supplier and retailer (Economist, 2001).

IT has played a major role in creating relationships between parties. Whilst relationships are about people getting together, an important component of a relationship is the exchange of information. IT has of course provided the technology by which such information exchanges can take place. There are also intangible benefits from such relationships. Trust and understanding between the two parties can also lead to efficiencies that can ultimately be translated into economic benefits. Whether the benefits are tangible or intangible, the key point is there are significant benefits to be had from information exchange between supplier and retailer and it is IT that has made this possible.

## Electronic Payment

A major contribution of IT to retailing is in the introduction and enabling of electronic payment.

Electronic payment breaks down into three component parts – the issue of cards or other forms of consumer identification (and authorisation), the transfer of transaction data from the retailer's premises to the financial institutions and the account clearing process. IT has played a major role in all three of these areas. The consumer identification and authorisation is mostly via magnetic-striped cards (although there are some smart cards in use—see later) which carry relevant consumer data and point-of-sale devices that can read this information. The transfer of transaction details is communicated via polling mechanisms or dedicated telecommunication lines between retailers and financial institutions. The clearing process is handled by specialised computer software.

The financial institutions have attempted to control each of these processes as they have felt that they were an integral part of their business—dealing with payment.   Retailers have in the main acquiesced to this but some of the larger retailers have been concerned at the power and profit this gave the financial institutions. In particular, some retailers (e.g., Marks & Spencer) initially refused to accept "bank cards" and only accepted their own store payment cards. Other retailers (in particular, petrol companies) have placed their own point-of-sale terminals and polled their own transactions. In this way they retained ownership of their transaction data and then "wholesaled" it on to financial institutions for clearing. This, they felt, gave them greater control of their own fate and avoided the possibility of "the (financial institution) tail wagging the (petrol business) dog."

Such electronic payment is geared to largish transactions—say a minimum of $5. Their impact on retailing to both the consumer and the retailer has nevertheless been quite significant.

To the consumer it provides the following:
- An *easy way* of making payments without the need to carry large sums of money
- A *secure* way of "carrying" money
- The possibility of obtaining *credit*
- A *record* of transactions made
- A *guarantee* from the card issuer, who in law is considered to be the supplier of the goods or services purchased.

It is interesting to note that market research often shows that "enabling a record of transactions to be kept" features as one of the (if not *the*) most important of these benefits.

To the retailer, the benefits include:
- Guaranteeing that payments will be received
- Customers always have access to funds

- Desensitisation of the pain felt by consumers when parting with their money (by distancing the purchase process from the commitment it entails)
- Permitting remote shopping. For example:
  o   mail order (catalogues, insurance, utilities)
  o   telephone booking (theatres and travel)
  o   tele-shopping (see later).

More recently, an alternative to the magnetic stripe as the mechanism for recording information has been introduced—namely, the smart chip. This is essentially a tiny computer that can be communicated with either via contact to certain points or by induction via an aerial mechanism so removing the necessity of making contact. The latter is commonly known as the "contact-less" smart chip. The main advantage of the smart chip (whether contact or contact-less) is the security with which it stores data and increasingly the capacity of data that it can hold. These advantages make it possible to use such a medium for performing financial transactions and become effectively an "electronic purse." Experiments have been carried out in university campuses and even some towns in the UK where money has been totally bypassed by "electronic money." This opens up the way, it is said, to do away with cash altogether and extend the benefits outlined above to all purchasing transactions, however small.

A parallel development in telecommunications, in particular the third generation Universal Mobile Telecommunications Systems (UMTS), allows the mobile telephone to also serve as an electronic purse. Again challenging the use of money for small transactions.

So it seems that IT has totally changed the payment process—for large transactions via payment cards and for smaller transactions by changing the nature of money to an electronic counterpart. The changes in the way consumers pay for transactions have implications, as we have seen, for both the customer and the retailer. In summary the impact of IT on payment has evolved and continues to evolve the retailing process.

## *Revolution* Through IT

We now turn to how IT is causing a *revolution* in retailing. We shall focus on the advent of e-commerce and consider whether the retailing rule book must be rewritten.

Any purchase consists of four distinct stages:

- **Selection** – this is the process of "choosing." Customers compare and contrast alternative products and eventually make a decision on what model, style, size, etc. is right for them.
- **Ordering** – this is the process of communicating to the vendor the identity of the product to be purchased. In retail purchases this is often simply removing a product from a shelf and placing it on a counter or shopping trolley or just telephoning the vendor.
- **Payment** – the handing over to the vendor funds to cover the purchase. In a retail environment this is often at the checkout or pay desk.

- **Transfer** – this refers to the physical transfer of goods from vendor to customer. This can be via home delivery but for small items it often involves the customer simply picking the goods up and placing them in their car.

It is interesting to note that e-commerce (and the Internet in particular) facilitates and focuses on only the first three processes. These have been revolutionised through the formation of "virtual stores"—the electronic counterpart of the physical stores in common use. However, whereas in the physical store the customer can take his purchase away with him/her, in the virtual store this is not possible. To overcome this difficulty most operators of virtual stores offer "home delivery." Indeed all sorts of new "delivery" companies have emerged—for example, Kosmo and Urban-fetch—with mottos such as "from mouse to house" and falling over each other in claiming speedier delivery. However, speed is not the fundamental issue. The real issue is that home delivery is far from convenient to the customer. It is true that in the days when women were tied to the house and there was someone at home to receive the delivery, home delivery could be said to be convenient. But, in today's world where both partners are working, special arrangements have to be made for someone to be at home to receive the delivery. This is most inconvenient, particularly as delivery times cannot be very precise. Home delivery is forcing an old solution to address a new problem. Therefore it seems that whilst the full thrust of development in IT has targeted the selection and ordering processes in a purchase, the transfer process has remained in the "Stone-Age" and retailers are only now beginning to realise that.

It is true that the Internet has made amazing changes to the process of selection and ordering, particularly through the use of sophisticated search algorithms. In order to assess the progress being made we shall consider more deeply the nature of products. Conventionally products have been classified according to their usage—for example, fast-moving consumer goods (FMCG), consumables vs. durables, etc. As we shall see, such a view of products is inadequate if we are to understand the workings of virtual stores.

It is worth summarising here the nature of products as described by Evans and Wurster (1999). According to these researchers, we can distinguish between the information content of a product and its physical content. They illustrate this by citing the *Encyclopaedia Britannica*—it has valuable information carried physically in beautifully bound books. The point of emphasising this split is that the economics of information differs greatly from the economics of things. In particular the marginal cost of making the information available to one more customer is close to zero, whereas the marginal cost of the beautifully bound volume is finite. In today's world retailers have to compromise between the two forms of economics—that of information and that of things. For example, in the case of a grocer, the compromise is made in favour of information. The grocery shop might offer wide ranges of products because the cost of "things" is generally small and it would rather customers were informed of the wide choice available. Conversely, for a bookseller the compromise is made in favour of things. The cost of things (the books) is substantial and therefore he cannot afford to offer a large variety of books. That *was* true of course until Amazon.com came unto the scene because they could offer the wide choice (information) without having to incur the penalty of the high cost of books (things). More generally, Evans and Wurster claim that e-commerce untangles the economics of things from the economics of information and in so doing it unleashes enormous economic potential. It is this unleashed economic potential which drives Amazon.com.

From the above, it is clear that the information content of a product variety matters in deciding whether they can be successfully sold through a virtual store. For example share prices would be ideal but perfume would not be ideal. These examples touch on another but related aspect of the nature of products and that is whether selection depends on logic. For example, to buy a flight to a far away destination, one needs factual information such as times of departure and arrival, whether there are intermediate stops, the price, etc. and a comparison can be made on that basis. We refer to these as logical triggers. In contrast, sensory triggers like the fragrance of a perfume and how tactile is the container influence the purchase decision. Most products fall somewhere in between these two extremes.

When products have high information content and also rely almost entirely on logical triggers then comparisons between alternatives can easily be made. This is especially so with technological advances such as "personal intelligent agents" which essentially do the searching on behalf of the consumer. Such multiagent systems will have a dramatic effect on competition (Cohen & Stathis, 2001). When comparisons become so easy (and thorough), there will be no room for inferior products that try to pass themselves off as similar to superior alternatives. Inferior products will ultimately be found out and will have to face the choice of either improving their quality or else charging lower prices that are commensurate with their inferior quality.

Because of this last point, prices for almost identical products will have to be very similar—or as economists might put it, there will be narrow price dispersion. This is of no surprise since the availability to the customer of so much information and the facilitation of searching through the variety of products are a close approximation to the economist's ideal of a perfect market.

In the new virtual stores, the price a customer is prepared to pay is an input to the deal to be struck rather than price being established by the retailer. We therefore come across the notion of "price-based costing" to replace the antiquated approach of "cost-based pricing." In a sense we return to the primitive basis of trading, which is still used in many flea markets, of the customer stating what he is prepared to pay and the retailer then responds either with a counteroffer or finds a product that can fit that specification. This is in essence the business of Priceline.com. The customer states (and commits) to what he is prepared to pay and Priceline.com finds him an airline prepared to meet his requirements. In many ways this marks the beginning of the notion of a "reverse market" described below.

The examples just given describe the notion of a reverse market as it relates to pricing—that is, customers name the price they are willing to pay and suppliers try to match it rather than simply posting a "take it or leave it" price. The notion of a reverse market can be broadened to include the other marketing variables. For instance, customers may wish to specify the product attributes they require and suppliers attempt to match that specification rather than simply presenting the customer with a range of products from which to choose. Another example is that customers may wish to specify the information they require about the supplier or his products rather than the supplier deciding what information to provide through advertising. Finally, it is customers that might like to decide whether they wish to visit the supplier's premises, whether they would like someone to call on them, or whether they will carry out their purchasing remotely—catalogues, tele-shopping, etc.

The reverse market is, in effect, progressing the shift in the balance of power. The power had moved from manufacturer to retailer but now it can reach its ultimate destination, the customer. This shift in power to customers is made possible because the Internet unites customers into a force that has to be reckoned with. The Internet allows the formation of what Hagle and Armstrong (2000) describe as virtual communities. The formation of communities of people that are similar is not new. Physical communities are quite common. People like to congregate with other people that are similar to them. For example, people live in an area of the country where similar people live—hence the presence of professional districts, worker districts, student districts, large family districts, etc. The Internet simply allows like-minded people to congregate in a virtual way, without the necessity of physically congregating—for instance, communities of a particular religion, special interest groups, and the like. When people congregate they can pool their energies together to create significant power that has to be considered. Thus the Internet has enabled the formation of virtual communities, which in turn have enabled the voice of the customer to be heard, thus forming the reverse market.

An important point in purchases over the Internet is trust. Of course trust is fundamental in all forms of trading, but none more so than in e-tailing simply because buyer and seller are remote from each other. Customers cannot examine the goods about to be purchased nor are able to make judgements on the reliability of the supplier. Will the supplier deliver the goods? Can he be trusted with credit card details? All such concerns make trust a crucial issue in e-tailing. It is for this reason that dotcom companies spend enormous amounts of money brand building to promote trust. As important are third-party accreditations—the views of journalists or even past customers are opinions valued by potential customers. That is why customer-to-customer forums are so important.

Retailers have addressed the challenge of e-commerce in different ways. The most dramatic developments have come from new entrants—and with barriers to entry being so low there have been quite a number. These had little or nothing to lose—other than the cheap money from venture capital. Accordingly they have been rather daring and ambitious—for example, Boo.com, the designer clothes retailer, and Amazon.com, the book e-tailer. These examples can be contrasted in many ways. Boo.com decided to launch internationally without first establishing a domestic market whereas Amazon.com developed the US market first and then used it as a springboard for international access. Another major difference is in the product category on offer. Using our earlier classifications, Boo.com had a high touch product category, which relies on sensory triggers (look and feel) whereas Amazon.com's product category could be said to be low touch, relying on logical triggers. There are a number of other differences but the end result is that Amazon.com has so far survived, although not yet profitable, whilst Boo.com has not or, as some commentators put it, has become "Boo-hoo.com." The important point we make here is that both were extremely daring and could take high risks. This is in great contrast to incumbents.

Incumbents in the book business, like Barnes & Noble and WHSmith, had to tread very carefully in fear of cannibalising their existing businesses and/or tarnishing their reputation. They were dragged into the world of e-commerce as a defensive measure rather than an opportunistic move. More generally, the single greatest disadvantage to incumbents is that they are saddled with legacy systems that must be dismantled if they are to succeed in the world of e-commerce. Their reluctance to dismantle and throw away what used to be valuable is understandable, but if they do not grasp the nettle then competitors may dismantle their business for them—and by the way, the competitors will be ruthless!

The approach of incumbents has in the main been to replicate their physical offering unto the electronic medium. So a supermarket virtual store displays its cold meats adjacent to its cheeses—as it does in its physical store. However the physical store layout accounts for the need to refrigerate/chill both of these products and this is not relevant to a virtual layout. Similarly in a physical layout, products are displayed only once in the store since duplicate displays mean more (costly) inventory. Again this is not relevant to a virtual display. Lastly the entire shopping process assumes no change in the way the consumer will go about his/her shopping. That is, it is assumed that consumers compile a list that at some point in time has to be acted upon. It could be that with Internet retailing consumers might like to communicate their shopping requirements as and when they occur (for example, as products run out)— or some other fundamental change in behaviour. So it seems that the approach to e-tailing does not fully exploit the potential of the new medium and instead simply replicates the physical concept with an electronic version of it. In so doing the real benefit of e-tailing is largely missed.

To return to the question of whether the retailing rule book needs to change, it seems that the fundamental objectives of retailing such as "satisfying customer needs better than competitors" remain in tact. Where change must take place is in the way such objectives are achieved. We have suggested a number of problem areas so far—namely, that the nature of the product affects the likely success of the e-tailing, the need to exploit and react to the concept of a reverse market and finally to deal with the problem of product transfer, a problem that has not yet been properly addressed by technology.

The mantra that the three most important factors in retailing are "location, location and location" stems from the importance and difficulties associated with access to the retail offer. With the Internet, access has been made relatively easy— indeed, consumers need not leave their armchairs. What matters then is not access but content (in the form of the choice of products on offer) and product transfer, which itself is dependent on the product characteristics. Therefore the new mantra in the e-tailing environment may well be "content, content and content."

# CONCLUSION/SUMMARY

It is undoubtedly true that retailing has undergone tremendous change in the last 30 years or so. The important drivers to change have been largely societal trends (such as change in shopping patterns), but a major contributor to change has been IT, which has helped the evolution of retailing. In particular, IT's contribution to product identification has helped transform the retailing operation from an art to a well-defined science. The improvement in the relationship between supplier and retailer brought about by information exchange has allowed the retailing operation to become far more efficient. Lastly the contribution of IT to payment mechanisms has stimulated the retailing business in facilitating payment for the consumer. However the largest contribution of IT to retailing is only just beginning and the contribution will be revolutionary.

The revolution in retailing is of course through the development of e-commerce. However, whilst suppliers have begun to flirt with this new concept it seems that there is lots to be learned if its true potential is to be exploited.

Firstly, the developments in IT have focused only on the first stages of "shopping." In addition the application of these developments have failed to recognise and exploit some fundamental differences between traditional retailing and the new forms of retailing—namely, the recognition of potential behavioural changes in the consumer and reclassification of products according to their information content and nature.

The last stage of shopping, that of product transfer, has largely been ignored and is still in the Stone-Age. It is interesting to note that the few successes in e-tailing circumvent this issue—for example, Amazon's use of postage. The break-bulk model of retailing needs to be superseded by a new model which allows the consumer to purchase small items from a variety of suppliers. Home delivery from a number of suppliers clearly makes no economic sense. We suggest that there is room for a new "build-bulk" operation which integrates supplies from different sources but destined for one consumer. Since home delivery is hardly convenient, it is possible that consumers will wish to pickup from this build-bulk facility. That is the real challenge of product transfer and not simply faster and faster home delivery. Perhaps such a build-bulk facility defines the new role of retailing—only time will tell.

The new role of retailing will involve the ability to integrate products from various suppliers not, as now through stock held in shops but the integration will be in response to customer preorders. This will necessitate sophisticated software that can track products from different suppliers destined for the same customer and route these to the customer's most convenient pickup location. It follows that the new retailer will need a geographical network of physical sites as well as delivery capabilities. To fulfil this new role, we anticipate interesting alliances between companies that have IT skills (e.g., Microsoft), those involved in delivery (e.g., DHL) and those with distributed physical assets (e.g., Exxon). Such an alliance may seem curious at present but makes perfect sense in the future.

In this way IT will no longer just support the retailing operation but becomes the prime driver to change and cause a revolution in retailing.

# REFERENCES

Bontems, P., Monier-Dilhan, S., & Requillart, V. (1999). Strategic effects of private labels. *European Review of Agricultural Economics, 26*(2), 147-165.

Cohen, M. & Stathis, K. (2001). Strategic change stemming from e-commerce. *Strategic Change, 10*(3).

Economist. (2001). A long march–Special report on mass customisation. *The Economist,* July, 79-81.

Evans, P. & Wurster, T. S. (1999). *Blown to Bits: How the New Economy Transforms Strategy.* Boston: Harvard Business Press.

Ganeshan, R. (1999). Managing supply chain inventories: A multiple retailer, one warehouse, multiple supplier model. *International Journal of Production Economics, 59*(1-3), 341-54.

Hagle, J., III, & Armstrong, T. S. (1997). *Net Gain.* Boston: Harvard Business Press.

Henley Centre for Forecasting. (1984). *Full Circle into the Future: Britain in the 21st Century.* London: Henley Centre.

Kadiyali, V., Chintagunta, P. & Vilcassim, N. (2000). Manufacturer-retailer channel interactions and implications. *Marketing Science, 19*(2), 127-148.

Kim, S. Y., & Staelin, R. (1999). Manufacturer allowances and retailer pass-through rates in a competitive environment. *Marketing Science, 18*(1), 59-76.

Popcorn, F. (1991). *The Popcorn Report.* London: Doubleday.

**Chapter XIII**

# IT-Enabled Strategic Marketing Management

Xianzhong Mark Xu
University of Portsmouth, UK

Yanqing Duan and Yu Li
University of Luton, UK

## ABSTRACT

*This chapter examines the applications of information systems in supporting marketing operational and strategic functions. It reviews the important role of marketing strategic function and reveals the current practice of database marketing, decision support systems, expert systems and Internet marketing through a number of studies conducted in the UK. It suggests that marketing executives tend to perceive the importance of the strategic role of marketing in shaping corporate strategy, but information technologies have not yet been fully applied to support the strategic function. It is proposed that a hybrid system that is capable of incorporating with executives vision and knowledge needs to be developed in order to systematically scan marketing environment, refine data into meaningful intelligence, and provide marketing executives with personalized strategic information. The problems for implementing the system are discussed.*

## INTRODUCTION

Marketing information systems has been discussed since the 1960s (Kotler, 1966; Cox & Good, 1967; Brien & Stafford, 1968; Fletcher, Buttery & Deans, 1988; Proctor, 1991). However, it is until the last decade that the marketing function has been increasingly supported or reshaped by information technology, for example, from database marketing to Internet marketing. This chapter aims to examine how the marketing functions at both operational and strategic levels has been supported by traditional and emerging information technologies, e.g., database technology, decision support systems (DSS), expert systems (ES) and Internet technology. It will reveal the practical application of IT for marketing operations and management with a focus on the strategic application of marketing information systems (MkIS). It identifies and highlights the problems associated with the application by drawing evidence from both the literature and the empirical studies conducted by the authors in the UK. A hybrid strategic-oriented MkIS model for support marketing, strategic information scanning, and strategic decision making has been developed. The new configuration of the model and the challenges for implementing the model are discussed. An insight into the future role of IT-enabled strategic marketing is provided.

# THE DUAL FUNCTION OF MARKETING

Marketing typically includes activities such as direct selling, sales promotion, advertising campaign, distribution, new product development and marketing research. According to Kotler (1997), in order to meet changing customers' needs, organisations prepare an "offering mix" of products, services, and prices and utilise a "promotion mix" of sales promotion, advertising, sales forces, public relations, direct mail, telemarketing, and Internet to reach the trade channels and the target customers. Typically, organisations need to strategically make changes on their prices, sales forces, and advertising expenditure to match their business objectives. Winning organisations will be those who can meet customer needs economically and conveniently and with effective communication. The most common tool used by marketing managers is known as the 4Ps, i.e., the mix of product, price, place and promotion strategies. It is used as a tactical and strategic marketing tool manipulated by most marketing practitioners (Dibb, Simkin, Pride & Ferrell, 1997). Successful marketing activity relies as much on interaction and synergy between marketing mix elements. Frances et al. (1997) state that achieving that mix has to be an outcome of a wide framework of strategic marketing planning, implementation and control. Marketing activities must be looked at within the context of a coherent and consistent marketing mix.

However, when an organisation operates in a highly competitive market, the function-oriented marketing view exhibits its limitations on developing a capability to anticipate changing market needs and to respond to the changes rapidly via increased innovation. Criticism over the traditional "4Ps" has emerged. Mitchell (1993) argues that marketing has traditionally demonstrated a tendency to functional self-absorption that renders it increasingly irrelevant to the new environment and lacks sufficient responsiveness. Gronroos (1994) stresses that the marketing mix and its 4Ps constitute a production-oriented definition. The adoption of the marketing concept and the marketing orientation does not create nor bring into existence new business function, but it does call for a change in both focus and emphasis. Lynch (1994) argues that marketing functional focus is a very narrow perspective. It ignores the crucial fact that the most significant contribution which marketing brings to an organisation is not functional but attitudinal. He suggests that marketing should be an organisational orientation that transcends narrow functional activities, as well as informs and illuminates every aspect of organisational strategy and operations. At the same time, marketing should be essentially concerned with the development and maintenance of an external orientation and sensitivity rather than an internal orientation.

It is suggested that proper appreciation of marketing's dual role has been a key factor in organisational success. Marketing can only operate effectively unless it is rooted in a clear sense of corporate purpose that reflects internal capability as well as external reality (Hooley & Lynch, 1985). The essential dual role that marketing occupies is described by Lynch (1995) as follows:

> First and foremost, at the strategic level, marketing is conceived as an external orientation or philosophy that should permeate the decision processes and operations of the whole organisation. Additionally, but at a secondary level, marketing is also conceptualised as a series of specific functional activities (such as advertising, market research and new product development) which are traditionally provide of a specialist marketing department.

A marketing orientation requires an organisation to monitor and continuously learn about the environments that comprise those influential forces so as to adjust its offerings (strength and weakness; Palmer & Hartley, 1999). With a strategic orientation, the formula "segmentation- targeting- positioning (STP)" is the essence of strategic marketing, which seeks to understand the changes of the dynamic market environments and illuminate organisational strategy in order to achieve effective responses.

# THE APPLICATION OF IT IN MARKETING – SOME EMPIRICAL EVIDENCE

With rapid development and application of sales and marketing information systems since the 1990s, a few studies have been carried out to examine the current status of MkIS (Rogers, Williams & McLeod, 1990; Higby & Farah, 1991; Jones & Arnett, 1993; Li, Kinman, Duan & Edwards, 1998; Xu, 1999). This section reviews and summarises some of the key findings.

## Database-Centred IS Application for Marketing

In the early '90s, the application of IS in marketing concentrated on customer-facing activities, which including sales activities support and customer service support. According to UK AiMS's (Association for Information Systems in Marketing and Sales) 1993 survey, information systems application in marketing shows a greatest rise in the areas of call logging, contact management, consumer support (customer database, mail shot database), and direct marketing/telesales for sales activities. Shaw (1993) reports that the top 10 packaged application systems used to support sales and marketing activities in the UK are: 1. word processing; 2. spreadsheets; 3. general purpose database; 4. enquiry processing; 5. sales order processing;  6. direct marketing;  7. sales/marketing database;  8. contact manage-ment; 9. decision support/EIS;    and 10. market research.

A typical database-centred marketing system is examined and depicted in Figure 1. The system is centred on seven databases, i.e., the company database, the contact database, the address database, the action database, the project database, the product database, and the contract database. Each database has its own function but interacts with others. The system also embodies query, call analysis, report generator and remote communication tools. This enables the system to be able to support and facilitate marketing contact management, campaign management, lead tracking, project management and document management. A close examination of the system suggests that the databases contain mostly internal transactional data and activities; little external information such as competitors, prospective customers and suppliers are held to support marketing strategic activities.

In the middle '90s, sales and marketing information systems have been widespread in most of the UK organisations. However, most of the applications are routine and operational rather than strategic (Wilson & McDonald, 1994). A comprehensive study on the MkIS has been conducted by Hewson and Hewson (1994). The study adopted both questionnaire survey and interview approaches within 41 UK-based companies that have applied some sales and marketing systems and found that:

- 80% of the companies use some forms of packaged sales and marketing systems. Most systems support sales management (93%), sales productivity (85%), and direct mail (85%). Few systems support market analysis, competi-tor intelligence and campaign management.
- Many companies implement purchased sales and marketing information system packages with some customisation; many systems exhibit common traits but some differences exist between type of data they hold and the business processes they support.

*Figure 1: A database-centred marketing information system (adopted from Pro-Action, 1996)*

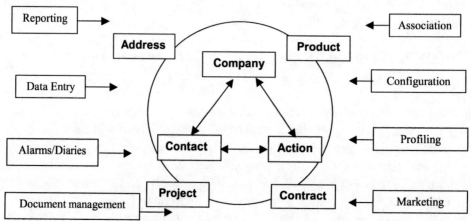

- The use of sales and marketing systems is dominated by field sales force and sales and marketing support staff.
- In terms of systems applied, customer/prospective database, which holding details of historical transaction data and events, appears to be the central system.
- The majority of companies view the use of sales and marketing systems as of strategic importance. But most companies appear to be impelled by the need to solve a specific problem or problems.
- Users are least satisfied with the level of support offered for competitor intelligence, market analysis and campaign management.

This finding was akin to that of Wilson and McDonald's (1994) study that marketing and sales productivity tools are often based on general purpose database systems, which provide specific facilities such as lead tracking, order taking and mail shots. However, decision support systems are little used to support marketing planning and intelligence provision.

In summary, the research suggests that information systems used for sales and marketing are implemented primarily to solve specific and operational marketing problems. External intelligence and strategic issues such as position mapping and strategic opportunities/threats analysis have received little support from the application.

## Strategic Application of IT in Marketing

The author (Xu, 1999) examined the current status of IS for marketing strategic function through a questionnaire survey. The study was based on 55 UK companies in the finance and computer industries. It reports that although some of the marketing strategic functions have been performed by most of the companies surveyed, marketing strategic function has received very limited support from current information systems. Table 1 presents the data.

The data shows that 80% of the companies conduct "competition and competitor analysis" as marketing function, and 69.1% of the marketing managers engage in "market segmentation and targeting." Over 60% of the respondents indicate that "market/industry analysis" and "corporate strategic planning" are their primary marketing activities. About 70% of the respondents describe "managing sales and sales promotion," "managing customer relationship," and "advertising campaign" as the primary marketing activity. However, "direct selling" (54.5%), "determine price strategy" (49.1%), "product R&D" (43.6%) have been less emphasised as the primary marketing activities in computer and financial industries.

It reveals that computer-based information systems have been highly used for "managing sales and sales promotion" (67.3%), "direct selling" (61.8%), and "managing customer relationship" (50.9%). Marketing managers are also found to be highly satisfied with the systems' support of these operational functions. Other operational activities such as "advertising campaign," "pricing strategy," and "product design" are not well-supported by MkIS. The support for the strategic function is rather limited in "market segmentation and targeting" (47.3%), and "competition analysis" (45.5%). Other strategic functions such as "opportunities/

*Table 1: The current practice of marketing function and MkIS support*

| Marketing Operational Function | Supported by MkIS | Percent n = 55 | Perform the function | Percent n = 55 |
|---|---|---|---|---|
| Managing sales and sales promotion | 37 | 67.3% | 39 | 70.9% |
| Direct selling | 34 | 61.8% | 30 | 54.5% |
| Managing customer relationship | 28 | 50.9% | 38 | 69.1% |
| Determine price strategy | 17 | 30.9% | 27 | 49.1% |
| Advertising campaign | 13 | 23.6% | 36 | 65.5% |
| New product R&D | 13 | 23.6% | 24 | 43.6% |
| **Marketing Strategic Function** | | | | |
| Market segmentation and targeting | 26 | 47.3% | 38 | 69.1% |
| Competition analysis | 25 | 45.5% | 44 | 80.0% |
| Market/industry analysis | 20 | 36.4% | 36 | 65.5% |
| Corporate strategic planning | 16 | 29.1% | 34 | 61.8% |
| Opportunities/threats analysis | 12 | 21.8% | 30 | 54.5% |

threats analysis," and "strategic planning" received little support from the MkIS.

Managers' views on the barriers of implementing a strategic-oriented MkIS are explored and summarised as follows:

- Lack of a strategic sense and vision by some marketing managers and professionals, i.e., fail to understand the benefit and the strategic role of marketing. Marketing in some companies is still sales/technology driven, rather than customer- and strategic-oriented.
- Lack of a strategic marketing culture and organisational support that enable the company to gear towards strategic marketing, i.e., the politics, limited resources in costs, staff, and mistrust of the value of investing in marketing strategic functions.
- Lack of knowledge, experience and tools to diminish overwhelmed data from the marketing daily operations and to base the development of strategic-oriented marketing information systems.

## DSS and ES in Marketing Strategic Planning

Decision support systems (DSSs) and expert systems (ESs) are two growing areas of computer applications for management. Both of the systems share the same aim of supporting decision making and problem solving. Some researchers have made comparisons between them. Ford (1985) found that the objective of a DSS is to support the user in the decision making process by providing access to data and models while an ES is to provide the user with a conclusion or decision significantly better, and more often correct, than the user could reach otherwise. Turban and

Watkins (1986) argue that the problem area tackled by a DSS is broad and complex, while an ES is restricted to a much more structured and narrow domain. ESs have been applied to a variety of domains, and marketing has been one of these. Several systems have been developed with the aim to support marketing decisions; some examples of the systems are drawn from literature and listed in Table 2.

A typical marketing DSS provides managers with analytic techniques, mathematical models, presentation tools, report generators, and networked communication protocols to enable the users to carry out a number of tasks during the decision making process. Compared with the extensive literature on general DSS applications, the use of DSSs in marketing has been limited. Some researchers have attempted to tackle the marketing domain with ES techniques (McDonald & Wilson, 1990; Borch & Hartvigsen, 1991; Moutinho, Curry & Davies., 1993; Duan & Burrell, 1995, 1997). There are reports on using artificial neural networks (Poh, 1994) and fuzzy logic (Levy & Yoon, 1995) to handle the imprecision and fuzziness in developing marketing strategy and modelling market entry decisions. However, despite the availability of sophisticated programming tools, ESs has proven to be difficult and time-consuming (Burke, 1991). Most of the reported marketing ESs are either prototype or experimental (Duan & Burrell, 1995).

# Internet Application in Marketing

The Internet as an emerging technology prevails and affects social and business life at an unexpected scale since the late '90s. Although numerous commentaries

*Table 2: DSSs and ESs in marketing*

| Decision Support Systems for Marketing | | Expert Systems for Marketing | |
|---|---|---|---|
| **Name** | **Description** | **Name** | **Description** |
| STRATPORT | a DSS for strategic planning (Larreche & Srinivasan, 1988) | HYMS | a prototype system which combines DSS and ES to support marketing strategic planning (Duan & Burrell, 1995, 1997) |
| Advia | a DSS for small business planning and decision making (Sterling & Stubblefield, 1994) | STRATEX | a knowledge-based system supporting the choice of marketing segments (Borch & Hartvigsen, 1991) |
| SLIM | a Strategic Logistics Integrative Modelling system (Shapiro, 1992) | COMSTRAT | a system for strategic marketing decisions with a special emphasis on competitive positioning (Curry et al., 1992; Moutinho et al., 1993) |
| MKDSS | a system to support the production planner's strategy for marketing the company's central product by aiding in the selection of a suitable marketing mix (Arinze, 1990) | ADCAD | ADvertising Communication Approach Design: a system designed to assist advertisers of consumer products in the formulation of advertising objectives, copy strategy, and the selection of communication approaches (Burke et al., 1990) |
| Pro-Action | an integrated database marketing and analytical tools for support marketing management and decision analysis (1996) | ADDUCE | a frame-based system for reasoning about consumer response to advertising by searching for relevant past advertising experiments (Burke, 1991) |

highlight the benefits of conducting business over the Internet, most early online presenters failed to generate enough sales to survive. Despite the optimistic tone of prediction, this is not a guarantee of success to any business that adopts the Internet. Bell and Tang (1998) argue that since the Internet is such a recent development, conducting selling on the Internet or any other profits aimed Internet activity is still in the embryonic phase. Such efforts as have been made still exhibit a disappointing degree of success.

## Internet Marketing

The ever-increasing user base of the Internet has a great potential for marketing. It is revealed that Web spending on advertising grows nationwide by an estimated $22 million every three months (Breitenbach & Van Doren, 1998). E-commerce conducted over the Internet market will grow to $184 billion by 2004 (Forrester Research, 1999). Some recent reports (Cohen, 2000; Stanley, 2000) emphasis that it is important for retailers and other companies using the Internet to recognise that the commercial use of the Internet is not restricted to its merchandising opportunities. It is more important to achieve a competitive advantage by using the Internet without ever making a sale. Rowley (1998) argues that the Internet can function well as a strategic tool on these market elements: product, price, place, and promotion. The most exciting aspect of the Internet is that it provides two of the most important aspects of modern marketing philosophies—the ability to target select groups of buyers and to open interactive dialog. Unlike traditional marketing channels, which is a one-way communication between a vendor who wants to sell and the buyer, the Internet provides a means of communication that is a more intimate relationship between buyer and seller. The Web offers companies an easy, inexpensive, fast, and technologically sophisticated tool for advertising goods and services, taking and placing orders, promoting their philosophy and policy, and communicating with their customers all over the world. Even smaller companies can provide their own information on a global scale through the Web.

Internet marketing is defined as the process of creating awareness and brand recognition for a company's goods and services over the Web. Evidence suggests that current Internet applications focus on marketing functional activities such as conducting online selling, advertising and product promotion. Very few studies are concerned with using the Internet for marketing strategic function, i.e., to support external environmental analysis, corporate strategy, market positioning, and strength/weakness/opportunity/threat (SWOT) analysis. Ranchhod, Gurau and Hackney (2000) report that most activities on the Internet sites are restricted to the simplest activities, selling-buying or join research, without integration of these activities in a structured strategic portfolio. Hart, Doherty and Ellis-Chadwick (2000) reviewed UK retailer Internet activities and report that the majority of retail organisations surveyed have not yet registered a Web site address, and even the vast majority of those who have Web sites are using them primarily as a communication tool to promote product information.

# Empirical Evidence of Internet Marketing in the UK

A survey was conducted by the authors to examine the current application of the Internet for marketing function. The study aims to explore to what extent the marketing function, in particular, marketing strategic function, has been supported by the Internet. The study is based in four industries in the UK, i.e., retailing, entertainment and leisure, financial and banking services, and hotel and tourism. All the companies selected have Web site presence on the World Wide Web through "surfing" the Internet. A number of 30 companies with employees over 200 were drawn from each industrial sector. Thus, a total of 120 companies are surveyed. Both e-mail and postal mailing are used to collect data; a total of 39 valid responses (83 total responses) are received, which represents a 32.5% response rate. It is worthy to note that the results should be interpreted with caution because of this relatively small sample size.

The study firstly examined marketing managers' perceptions on the importance of using the Internet for marketing strategic function. It reveals that managers perceive the importance of using the Internet to support marketing strategic function; in particular, in support of "market segmentation, product positioning," which has the highest mean score, 3.8, as shown in Table 3. The other two items, "market research and consumer behaviours analysis" and "competitors analysis and competition strategies," are also perceived as important, as the mean score is above average.

It is surprising to note that managers tend not to see the importance of using the Internet to conduct SWOT analysis. This is further evident from a manager's remarks that "overall the Internet is used as a marketing tool. It is hard to assess if the Internet can specifically or deeply support these analysis, and it depends on what the SWOT is about." The study further revealed that the Internet is highly used on some of the key marketing activities, as shown in Table 4.

The data shows that 79% of organisations conduct "managing advertising, sales promotion and public relations" through the internet, i.e., to use the Internet as a media to enhance traditional marketing and 54% of the companies use the Internet to carry out e-commerce, i.e., "online product selling." There are relatively small numbers of companies that use the Internet for "managing customer service" (46%) and "developing market research and new offering"(38%). It appears that marketing operational function has been largely supported by Internet technology. The data

*Table 3: Managers' perceptions on the importance of the Internet for marketing strategic function*

| Item | Mean score (n=39) | Standard deviation |
| --- | --- | --- |
| Marketing segmentation, product positioning | 3.8 | 1.12 |
| Market research and consumer behaviours analysis | 3.4 | 1.18 |
| Competitors analysis and competition strategies | 3.3 | 1.24 |
| Strength/weakness/opportunity/threat (SWOT) analysis | 2.8 | 1.14 |

*Scale: 1 means "not important," 5 means "very important."*

*Table 4: Current Internet application on marketing function*

| Operational Function | Frequency (%) | Strategic Function | Frequency (%) |
|---|---|---|---|
| Online product selling | 62 | Analysing buyer's behaviours, collecting consumer information | 51 |
| Managing advertising, sales promotion, public relations | 79 | Identifying market segments and selecting target market | 49 |
| Design price strategies | 21 | Positioning in market | 28 |
| Managing customer service | 46 | Managing competition | 46 |
| Developing market research | 38 | Scanning the whole marketing environment | 38 |

shows that about half of the companies indicate that Internet is used to support marketing strategic function, i.e., 51% of organisations use the Internet for "analysing buyers' behaviours." 49% of organisations use the Internet to conduct "market segmentation" and 46% conduct "competition analysis." However, "scanning external information" and "market positioning" have received less support. This reaffirms Hoffman, Novak and Chatterjee's (1996) earlier finding that most UK retailers are unsure of how to employ the Internet strategically to support their overall marketing strategies. Many of them have simply adopted a reactive approach by inserting company brochures on their Web sites, without a clear strategic vision.

# A MODEL OF A HYBRID STRATEGIC MKIS

## The Basis for Developing the Model

Li et al. (1998) summarised some key considerations for developing an information system to support marketing strategic planning. These considerations are valuable for proposing a strategic-oriented MkIS. A system to support marketing strategic function should be able to:

- Provide and interpret strategic information for the process of developing strategy (McDonald & Wilson, 1990).
- Provide strategic analysis assistance and organised methods of strategy development to guide the strategy formulation process (Curry et al., 1992).
- Offer domain expert knowledge at key aspects of key stages of strategy formulation (McDonald & Wilson, 1990; Duan & Burrell, 1995).
- Make recommendations for managers in selecting marketing strategy (Duan & Burrell, 1997).
- Help managers cope with uncertainty and ambiguity in the process of developing marketing strategy.
- Help managers understand marketing strategy factors and how they interact.
- Provide mechanisms to couple systematic analysis with managers' judgment (Mintzberg, 1994).

As revealed from this study, part of the reason for not using IT to support marketing strategic function is that current MkIS do not have the functionality to support marketing strategic activities. One of the key features of strategic marketing is the interaction with the external environment by capturing the significant signals (Ahituv, Zif & Machlin, 1998). Systematically gaining understanding of the changes in the marketplace can enable a company to promptly and appropriately adjust its market position and strategy to maximise customer satisfaction while maintaining a sustainable and competitive posture in the environment. Although internal information on sales and marketing is important for monitoring current performance, it is not a substitute for managers' identification of opportunities and threats from the changing environment. This suggests that the MkIS needs to be embodied with the market environmental scanning function through which an external orientation is maintained. The systems should be designed to systematically collect, filter, decode, and transmit market information throughout the organisation.

Because of the complexity of strategic analysis and the intuitive nature of executives' work, the information captured through the scanning mechanism needs to be filtered, synthesised, interpreted, personalised and presented to the marketing executives. Computer-based systems can hardly perform all these tasks that require human knowledge and judgment. Thus a hybrid intelligent system that integrates different systems, components, and human interaction would be more appropriate in tackling this complex domain. A hybrid intelligent system represents not only the combination of different intelligent techniques—e.g., the scanning agent, the analysis agent, the report agent—but also the integration with conventional systems such as DSSs, spreadsheets, databases, and the Internet (Goonatilake & Khebbal, 1995). The central driving force for using a hybrid intelligent system are to incorporate the strengths of the diverse support techniques and technologies and to integrate the advantages of various strategic analysis models to avoid the limitations of a particular one. It also incorporates managers' experience and judgment into the system or allows managers to directly intervene the system.

## The Components and Function of the Model

Current MkIS could be improved by embedding strategic marketing information scanning and refining components and the Internet-enhanced communication functions. The system will also incorporate managers' strategic vision and knowledge to maximise the IT potential. Figure 2 depicts a hybrid strategic-oriented MkIS model for support marketing strategic management. The function of the system is discussed next.

### Strategic Marketing Information Scanning

The environmental scanning function will support external information collection, filtering and synthesising and enlarge marketing managers' vision of the external environment, from which strategic marketing signals and opportunities can be captured. This is akin to the marketing audit stage of marketing strategic planning as described by McDonald (1992), who suggests that a marketing audit is a structured approach to the collection and analysis of information and data on the internal and external environment, including information on the business and economic climate, the market, competition, major competitors and the company's operating performance. The audit is an essential prerequisite to marketing strategy formulation. The scanning and refining function can be implemented by incorporating the latest intelligent agent technology that has been widely used for conducting intelligent information processing tasks, e.g., a data watch agent for reading and selecting relevant data according to a set of criteria.

## Strategic Analytical Function

This study reveals that SWOT analysis has been rarely supported by MkIS and one of the reasons for dissatisfaction with the MkIS is that the system is incapable of providing effective decision analysis and support. The purpose of conducting a SWOT analysis is to capitalise on company strengths, minimise any weaknesses, exploit market opportunities as they arise and avoid, as far as possible, any threats (Brooksbank, 1990). The proposed MkIS should be enhanced by strategic decision analysis and modeling function. A number of marketing strategic models such as SWOT analysis, key success factors matrix, opportunities matrix, threats matrix, and Porter's five-force model (McDonald, 1992) could be used to develop a strategic decision support function. Expert systems technology can be employed together with DSS to offer expert knowledge and advice.

*Figure 2: A hybrid strategic-oriented MkIS*

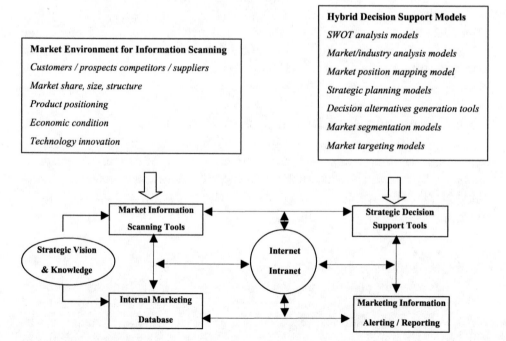

## Portfolio and Trends Mapping

It is strategically important for marketing managers to foresee the trends and the dynamic positioning of the company in the competitive market. As revealed from this study, most of the current MkIS can provide some basic forecast, analytical functions that are based on the company's internal historical data, but lack monitoring of the company's positioning and the dynamic trends of competitors. It is thus proposed that the system should be able to continuously generate trends of the company and the market and map out the market/product positioning (portfolio) of the company in the industry. It is suggested that the strategic positioning model, animated simulation techniques, and multimedia graphic presentation technology can be used to develop this function.

## Internet-Based Personalised Information Reporting

With the prevailing of Internet technology in marketing, it is envisaged that the Internet will play an increasing role not only for marketing operation, but also for marketing strategic management. Marketing managers need to be instantly informed/alerted with the emerging strategic issues, events, news, and even rumors and gossip (soft information as described by Watson, Houdeshel & Rainer, 1997). Current MkIS is not capable to deal with strategic marketing information provision, alerting and reporting. It is proposed that systems should be able to tailor the information to the individual manager's needs and present it to the manager in the way that fits his/her managerial pattern and style, i.e., personalized strategic information provision. With the advance of Internet technology, the marketing manager should be able to receive/query information wherever he is, and whenever he needs it.

In summary, the proposed MkIS will help marketing managers analyse market conditions, identify problems, foresee future trends, map out market position, benchmark competitors and be alerted with emerging strategic intelligence. These functions should not be isolated from other internal and external subsystems. For example, the MkIS includes an internal marketing records system, which enables marketing managers to draw data from the operational systems. The scanning and the reporting system are essential parts of the strategic-oriented MkIS, as marketing managers need to be proactively, instantly informed about the changes in the marketplace in order to appropriately react to the changes, rather than solicit information after a problem occurred. It also needs to address that managers' knowledge, intuition, vision and judgment are important factors in determining strategic decision making. Even the proposed MkIS attempts to incorporate these factors in order to deal with uncertainty and complex situations. Because of the tacit nature of managerial knowledge, it has been a great challenge to elicit this type of knowledge and to make it explicit for computerisation. This is why a hybrid system solution is proposed, that is, to allow managers to use their managerial experience and judgment in strategic decision making while using IT to enhance managers' learning through information provision and knowledge sharing.

# IMPLEMENTING THE MODEL

## Identify the Most Influential Market Environment Factors for Scanning

This study shows that some companies engaged in competitors' intelligence. However, scanning market environment does not mean only collecting competitors' information. Market environmental factors such as market size, market share, brand loyalty, competitors, concentration of the industry, barriers to entry, and market trends should be selectively identified. In addition, far environmental factors such as changes in economic conditions, political climate and legal regulations, social and cultural patterns, and technology innovation and proliferation should be selectively monitored, as they may significantly affect a company's long-term strategy and direction. A company should differentiate these environmental factors according to their immediate and potential impact on the company's market and future direction, based on which to identify what environmental factors are more strategically important in affecting its marketing than others. It becomes apparent that a company's strategic capability and sensibility can be weakened by the ignorance of scanning the external environments.

## Enhancing MkIS With Data Filtering and Position Mapping Function

It should be noted that increasing the capability and the coverage of MkIS to conduct external environmental information scanning runs the risk of worsening the data overload problem. Some marketing managers are not inclined to strategic-oriented MkIS simply because they are overwhelmed with the sheer volume of data from the current MkIS. It thus suggests that strategic-oriented MkIS should incorporate a data filtering and synthesising function and analytical tools. The system should be able to help marketing managers make sense of data, map out the company's position in the marketplace, and benchmark the industry best.

## Creating a Visionary Leadership and Champion

Corporate political conflict has been seen as one of the barriers to strategic marketing. Stacey (1990) stated that an agenda for strategic action is implicit and dynamic; simply putting matters into a formal plan does not make them issues. Thus, a champion with political clout and influence is needed in order to lobby others, to obtain support and to fight to get the strategic MkIS into the management agenda. Implementing the system needs management support through articulating the grand concepts of the strategic function of marketing and the strategic significance of marketing—i.e., the nose and ear of a viable organisation in the competitive and uncertain business environment—to the company's top management; in particular, to the non-marketing executives.

## New Configuration of Marketing Department

As a result of the implementation of the strategic-oriented MkIS and the spread of Internet marketing, some duplicated functions across the whole organization may need to be evaluated and restructured. For example, the traditional marketing-information-related functions, such as the market research department, market intelligence unit, corporate strategic planning unit, etc., need to be restructured in order to enhance effective information processing and provision. It also needs to empower marketing managers with strategic responsibility and reengineer the corporate strategic planning and decision process with an emphasis on marketing strategic function and the involvement of marketing managers. It is envisaged that the strategic-centred MkIS integrated with the Internet and the internal systems would enable managers to make informed decisions and to turn the organization into a viable, interactive and learning organization in the increasingly competitive market.

# CONCLUSION

The applications of computer-based information systems (e.g., database marketing and Internet marketing) have significantly altered the way of traditional marketing. However, studies reveal that the application is far from reaching marketing managerial level; i.e., current MkIS focus on support marketing routine function rather than strategic function, in particular, using information systems to scan strategic marketing information and to support strategic decision analysis (SWOT analysis) has been rare. Such systems if implemented, in most instances, are found to be less than satisfactory. A hybrid strategic-oriented MkIS could be an effective means to support the strategic marketing function. The system would support: strategic marketing information scanning, strategic decision modelling, and personalised strategic marketing information reporting. The system would embody the latest information technology such as the Internet and the intelligent agent, but also incorporate current DSS and ES systems and managerial knowledge and judgment, and integrate with internal and external subsystems. Implementing the system relies on not only technology innovation (e.g., intelligent data watch, reasoning, etc.), but, more importantly, on the change of the organization. It is envisaged that information technology will gradually penetrate into the marketing management level, and the strategic-oriented MkIS will be imperative for modern marketing management.

# REFERENCES

Ahituv, N., Zif, J. & Machlin, I. (1998). Environmental scanning and information systems in relation to success in introducing new products. *Information & Management, 33*(4), 201-211.

AiMS. (1993). Softworld in sales & marketing. *Softworld Report & Directory for Sales & Marketing Information Systems*. London

Alpar, P. (1991). Knowledge-based modelling of marketing managers' problem solving behaviour. *International Journal of Research in Marketing, 8*, 5-16.

Arinze, B. (1990). Market planning with computer models: a case study in the software industry. *Industrial Marketing Management*, 19(2), pp. 117-29.

Bell, H. & Tang, N. K. H. (1998). The effectiveness of commercial Internet Web sites: A user's perspective. *Internet Research: Electronic Networking Applications and Policy*, 8(3).

Borch, O. J. & Hartvigsen, G. (1991). Knowledge-based systems for strategic market planning in small firms. *Decision Support Systems*, 7(2), 145-157.

Breitenbach, C. S. & Van Doren, D. C. (1998). Value-added marketing in the digital domain: Enhancing the utility of the Internet. *Journal of Consumer Marketing*, 15(6).

Brien & Stafford. (1968). Marketing information systems: A new dimension for marketing research. *Journal of Marketing*, 23(3), Fall, 19-23.

Brooksbank, R. W. (1990). Marketing planning: A seven-stage process. *Marketing Intelligence & Planning*, 8(7), 21-28.

Brownlie, D. & Spender, J. C. (1995). Managerial judgment in strategic marketing: Some preliminary thoughts. *Management Decision*, 33(6), 39-50.

Burke, R. R. (1991). Reasoning with empirical marketing knowledge. *International Journal of Research in Marketing*, 8(1), 75-90.

Burke, R.R., Rangaswamy, A., Wind, J. and Eliashberg, J. (1990). A knowledge-based system for advertising design. *Marketing Science*, 9(3), pp. 212-29.

Cohen, A. (2000). Why online advertising is failing. *Sales and Marketing Management*, 152(11).

Cox & Good. (1967). How to build a marketing information system. *Harvard Business Review*, 45(3), May-June, 145-154.

Curry, B., Moutinho, L. and Davies, F. (1992). Constructing a knowledge base for a marketing expert system. *Marketing Intelligence & Planning*, 10(11), pp. 12-20.

Dibb, S., Simkin, L., Pride, W. & Ferrell, O. (1997). *Marketing: Concepts and Strategies* (European ed.). London: Houghton Mifflin.

Duan, Y. & Burrell, P. (1995). A hybrid system for strategic marketing planning. *Marketing Intelligence & Planning*, 13(11), 5-12.

Duan, Y. & Burrell, P. (1997). Some issues in developing expert marketing systems. *Journal of Business & Industrial Marketing*, 12(2), 149-162.

Ernst & Young. (1999). *The Second Annual Ernst and Young Internet Shopping Study*. New York

Fletcher, F., Buttery, A. & Deans, K. (1988). The structure and content of the marketing information system: A guide for management. *Marketing Intelligence & Planning*, 6(4), 27-35.

Ford, F. N. (1985). Decision support systems and expert systems: A comparison. *Information & Management*, 8(1), 21-26.

Forrester Research. (1999). *Online retail to reach $184 billion by 2004 as post-Web retail era unfolds*. Retrieved on September 28 from http// www.forrester.com/ER/Press/Release/0,1769,164,FF.html.

Goonatilake, S. & Khebbal, S. (1995). Intelligent hybrid systems: Issues, classifications and future directions. In S. Goonatilake and S. Khebbal (Eds), *Intelligent*

*Hybrid Systems* (pp. 1-15). New York: John Wiley & Sons.

Gronroos, C. (1994). From marketing mix to relationship marketing towards a paradigm shift in marketing. *Management Decision, 32*(2).

Hart, C., Doherty, N. & Ellis-Chadwick, F. (2000). Retailer adoption of the Internet: Implication for retail marketing. *European Journal of Marketing, 34*(8), 954-974.

Hewson, N. & Hewson, W. (Ed.). (1994). *The Impact of Computerised Sales and Marketing Systems in the UK* (4th ed.). *A Practical Research Study into the Successful Use of Sales and Marketing Systems.* Buckinghamshire: HCG.

Higby, M. & Farah, B. (1991). The status of marketing in information systems, decision support systems and expert systems in the marketing function of US. firms. *Information Management, 20*, 29-35.

Hoffman, D. L., Novak, T. P. & Chatterjee, C. (1996). Commercial scenarios for the Web: Opportunities and challenges. *Journal of Computer-Mediated Communication, 1*(3). Retrieved from http://www.usc.edu/dept/annenberg/journal.html.

Hooley, G. J. & Lynch, J. E. (1985). Marketing lessons from the UK's high flying companies. *Journal of Marketing Management, 1*, 65-74.

Jones, M. & Arnett, K. (1993). Current practices in management information systems. *Information & Management, 24*, 61-69.

Kotler, P. (1966). A design for the firm's marketing Nerve Centre. *Business Horizons, 9*(3), 63-74.

Kotler, P. (1997). *Marketing Management: Analysis, Implementation and Control* (9th ed.). Englewood Cliffs, NJ: Prentice Hall.

Larreche, J. and Srinivasan, V. (1988). STRATPORT: a decision support system for strategic planning. In B. A. Weitz and R. Wensley (Eds), *Readings in Strategic Marketing: Analysis, Planning, and Implementation*, San Diego, CA: The Dryden Press, pp. 257-80.

Levy, J. B. & Yoon, E. (1995). Modelling global market entry decision by fuzzy logic with an application to country risk assessment. *European Journal of Operational Research, 82*(1), 53-78.

Li, S., Kinman, R., Duan, Y. & Edwards, J. (1998). Computer-based support for marketing strategy development. *European Journal of Marketing, 34*(5/6), 551-575.

Lynch, E. J. (1994). Only connect: The role of marketing and strategic management in the modern organisation. *Journal of Marketing Management, 10*, 527-542.

Lynch, E. J. (1995). *Marketing and business process re-engineering* (Working paper). University of Leeds, School of Business & Economic Studies.

Marshall, K. & Lamotte, S. (1992). Marketing information systems: A marriage of systems analysis and marketing management. *Journal of Applied Business Research, 8*, 61-73.

McDonald, M. (1992). Strategic marketing planning: A state-of-the-art review. *Marketing Intelligence & Planning, 10*(4), 4-22.

McDonald, M. H. B. & Wilson, H. N. (1990). State-of-the-art development in expert systems and strategic marketing planning. *British Journal of Management,* *1*(3), 159-170.

Mintzberg, H. (1994). Rethinking strategic planning. Part 2: New role for planners. *Long Range Planning, 27*(3), 22-33.

Mitchell, A. (1993). The transformation of marketing. *Marketing Business,* November, 9-14.

Moutinho, L., Curry, B. & Davies, F. (1993). The COMSTRAT model: Development of an expert system in strategic marketing. *Journal of General Management, 19*(1), 32-47.

Palmer, A. & Hartley, B. (1999). *The Business and Marketing Environment* (3rd ed.). New York: McGraw-Hill.

Poh, H. L. (1994). A neural network approach for decision support. *International Journal of Applied Expert Systems, 2*(3), 196-216.

Pro-Action. (1996). *Software developed by F1 Computer Systems Ltd.* London.

Proctor, R. (1991). Marketing information systems. *Management Decision, 29*(4), 55-60.

Ranchhod, A., Gurau, C. & Hackney, R. (2000). Marketing on the Internet observation within the biotechnology sector. *International Journal of Physical Distribution & Logistics Management, 30*(7/8), 697-709.

Rogers, J., Williams, T. & McLeod, R., Jr. (1990). Microcomputer usage in marketing departments of Fortune 500 firms: What should marketing students study? *Journal of Marketing Education, 12,* 18-23.

Rowley, J. (1998). Retailing and shopping on the Internet. *International Journal of Retail & Distribution Management, 24*(3).

Shapiro, J.F. (1992). Integrated logistics management, total cost analysis and optimization modelling. *International Journal of Physical Distribution & Logistics Management,* 22(3), pp. 33-6.

Shaw, R. (1993). *Technology in Sales and Marketing Consultants' Conspectus–A Management Consultants News Publication,* December, London.

Stacey, R. (1990). *Dynamic Strategic Management for the 1990s.* Kogan Page Ltd.

Stanley, J. (2000). New tools of the trade. *Chain Store Age, 76*(11).

Sterling, J.W. and Stubblefield, A. (1994). Advia: planning and decision support for smaller businesses. *Planning Review,* 22(1), pp. 50-4.

Turban, E. & Watkins, P.R. (1986). Integrating expert systems and decision support systems. *MIS Quarterly,* June, 121-136.

Watson, H., Houdeshel, G. & Rainer, R., Jr. (1997). *Building Executive Information Systems and other Decision Support Applications,* 219. New York: John Wiley & Sons.

Wilson, M. & McDonald, M. (1994). Critical problems in marketing planning: The potential of decision support systems. *Journal of Strategic Marketing, 2,* 249-269.

Xu. (1999). The strategic orientation of marketing information systems–An empirical study. *Marketing Intelligence & Planing, 17*(6), 262-271.

## Chapter XIV

# Diffusion of Information Technology Innovations within Retail Banking: An Historical Review

Bernardo Bátiz-Lazo
Open University Business School, UK

Douglas Wood
Manchester Business School, UK

## ABSTRACT

*Technological innovation in general and information technology (IT) applications in particular have had a major effect in banking and finance. Following Garbade and Silber (1978), this research reviews the effects on banking organisations with reference to front office or external changes as described by the nature of product and service offerings. Following Morris (1986), Quintás (1991) and Fincham et al. (1994), the research also considers innovations in the back office or internal (operational function) changes brought about to banking organisations. Outstanding IT-based innovations are considered and grouped into four distinct periods: early adoption (1864-1945), specific application (1945-1965), emergence (1965-1980) and diffusion (1980-1995). The research then discusses the potential impact of more recent innovations (i.e., electronic purses, digital cash and Internet banking). As a result, the research provides an historical perspective on the main drivers determining the adoption of technological innovation in retail banking.*

# INTRODUCTION

Table 1 summarises two dimensions of technological progress. These dimensions describe the nature of change brought about by technological innovation externally (product or service offerings) and internally (operational function) to banking organisations. Other dimensions might offer a more comprehensive treatment of innovation in financial services. However, the dimensions portrayed here suffice to provide an historical perspective on the adoption of technological innovation in retail bank markets. Initially, change induced by innovations in information and communications technologies (IT) reduced price differentials in geographically distant markets. The next stage saw the emergence of specific IT markets and then specific IT applications modifying the relations between previously isolated departments of banking organisations. Over time, IT applications produced alterations throughout the whole organisational structure in terms of internal operations and with respect to bank-client relationships. In brief, Table 1 outlines key technological innovations in retail finance as grouped into four distinct periods: early adoptions, specific application, emergence and diffusion.

The dimensions of technological innovation in retail banking portray the internal structure of banks as being determined by a combination of changes in banks' external environment and advances in information technology. Pugh (1973, p. 28) was one of the first contributions to document widespread empirical support on the effect the external environment had on individual organisations, relative to competitors' size and technology. According to this view, managers are passive in the adoption of the boundaries drawn around their organisation, while the rate of adoption of new technology is contingent on the organisation's circumstances. However, empirical studies suggested that despite the limitations imposed by the context in which organisations perform, managers have plenty of leeway to make their influence felt in the pursuit of competitive advantage (Pugh, 1973). Based on these

*Table 1: Dimensions of IT innovation in retail banking*

| Impact on the Provision of Retail Finance | Use of Technology in the Organisation | | | |
|---|---|---|---|---|
| | Early Adoption (1846-1945) | Specific Application (1945-1968) | Emergence (1968-1980) | Diffusion (1980-1998) |
| Innovation in Service Offering | • Reduce inter-market price differentials. | • Conversion from branch to bank relationships. <br> • Automated bank statements. <br> • Cheque guaranty cards. | • Growth of cross-border payment. <br> • ATM introduced. | • Supply of non-payment products like insurance, mortgages and pensions. |
| Operational Function Innovation | • Increased co-ordination between head office and branches. | • Reduce cost of labour-intensive activities (i.e. clearing system). | • Automation of branch accounting. <br> • Real-time control begins. | • Growth of alternative distribution channels, such as phone banking and EFTPOS. |

studies, the current research considered that managers of banks have little influence over the development of technological innovation while, simultaneously, the actions (or omissions) of managers in banking organisations in adopting technology are considered critical to determine how technological innovations modify competition in bank markets.

In what follows, the discussion of technological innovation that altered the provision of financial services will cover external changes over methods of undertaking transactions (between customers and bank) and changes up to the point at which customers enter the banking system. The discussion will also cover technology-induced changes in internal procedures. In particular, changes over operational functions and process innovations are explored. These changes and innovations will be identified as changes in:

- national payment systems (i.e., distribution of cash and coins between the central bank and individuals rather than bank assets as substitutes for cash balances);
- the delivery of deposit lending and settlement transactions; and
- the storage and retrieval of accounting information.

The research, therefore, presents a summary of major IT-based innovations and an analytical framework with which to structure an historical review of how IT innovations were adopted in retail bank markets. The discussion will focus on how the performance of retail banks changed through the applications of new information and telecommunications technologies and resulted in product and operational (process) improvements. This historical review defines participants in bank markets following Klein (1971, p. 206), Baltensperger (1980, p. 1), Swank (1996, p. 193) and Radecki (1998, p. 4). In order words, throughout the research, commercial banks are defined as financial intermediaries that accept deposits without explicit payment of interest (sight accounts) and which create assets that are generally acceptable means of exchange (paper and electronic payment instruments).

Alongside the general review of the absorption of IT innovations in banking, particular attention will be given to IT innovation in the United Kingdom's (UK) bank markets. The UK and England in particular are used as the benchmark because they have had large and highly competitive wholesale banking markets and have preceded other developed countries in the introduction of changes regulating financial markets (Bank of England, 1991). UK participants in bank markets also seem to have adopted key technology innovations before counterparts in North America (Bátiz-Lazo, 1998, p. 277). Focus on the UK bank markets will also provide an opportunity to explore whether technological change has enhanced the importance of computer systems within the strategic compass of commercial banks. Specifically, this research will determine whether the introduction of IT applications supported changes in banks' strategic goals and modified the principal-agent relationship between bank and customer, so that client-bank relations depended less on subjective loyalty or service quality considerations (approached as idiosyncratic investments) and more on current and prospective levels of financial margin.

The document proceeds as follows. The second section considers the effects of outstanding IT-based technical innovations as grouped into four distinct periods defined as early adoptions (1864-1945), specific application (1945-65), emergence (1965-80) and diffusion (1980-98). In the third section the discussion turns to the potential impact of more recent innovations in payment systems, the so-called "electronic purses" and Internet banking, as well as their likely effects on competition within bank markets. The fourth and final section discusses the implications of IT-based change for the corporate strategy of commercial banks.

# INFORMATION TECHNOLOGY INNOVATION AND BANKING

## Early Adoption Period[1]

The introduction of telecommunications into bank markets dates to 1846 when the telegraph reduced stock price differentials between New York and regional stock markets (Garbade & Silber, 1978, p. 823). The 1866 introduction of the trans-Atlantic cable equally enabled greater integration of securities trading in New York and London (Garbade & Silber, 1978, p. 827). Greater integration took place as the completion of the cable reduced the time delay to execute a trade in New York which had been initiated in London from six weeks to only one day. According to Garbade and Silber (1978), early innovations such as the trans-Atlantic cable were accompanied by statistically significant evidence that the introduction of primitive forms of telecommunication substantially reduced or even eliminated foreign exchange and security price differentials between geographically distinct markets.

However, evidence has yet to develop and support the possibility that market integration increased or continued during the years that followed the emergence of individual new communication innovations. Evidence in Garbade and Silber (1978) suggests that new communication innovations represented (proportionally) smaller reductions in price differentials. This evidence suggests that the adoption of telegraph or telephone facilities primarily produced the same kind of information asymmetry amongst market participants. However, greater use of telegraph or telephone facilities also resulted in price-related information becoming homogeneous by linking the head office with branches in different domestic and international locations or by providing dealers and banks with the same price information in a timely manner. It is no surprise, then, that the statistical significance of the enhanced market integration was greatest for early developments, that is, those financial transactions where information delays were greatest prior to the introduction of telecommunication applications (Garbade & Silber, 1978, p. 831).

The early introduction of telecommunications into bank markets did little to modify front office procedures, the way in which the methods of conducting transactions between customers and bank. For instance, the amalgamation process that swept UK banking after the introduction of limited liability banking during the late 19th century resulted in financial intermediaries with nationwide retail branch networks. However, it was not until the 1950s that UK commercial banks actively pursued the aim of becoming depository institutions for excess funds or began to develop non-deposit products for mid-income customers (more below).

During the early adoption period, bank customers entered the banking system directly through retail bank branches or indirectly through agency representatives (such as savings banks, mortgage specialists and even retail outlets). Telephone conversations between bank managers and customers have been recorded in use as early as the 1890s, but, in spite of this, service remained largely unaffected by technology with the front office relationship unchanged and controlled locally though asynchronous, analogue systems such as paper-based records and passbook control.

At the time, financial intermediaries observed little in the way of systematic product and customer group diversification. The main function of the head office was to manage and provide services such as cheque clearing and relations with the central bank and to manage the bank's liquidity and balance sheet through treasury operations. Head office was also in charge of policing performance through financial control and draconian inspection methods. Long-term relations of individual customers with the bank retail branch were needed to secure services such as loans or establish credit ratings, and as a result, managers of retail bank branches were persons of independent authority and standing in their local communities. Meanwhile, individual banks performed international transactions such as clearing bills of exchange through networks of correspondent banks abroad rather than through open markets.

During the late 1930s the first tabulating machines were purchased to address the growing volume of transactions and enhance working conditions and productivity of senior staff (Wardley, 2000, pp. 83-89). This trend was reinforced through the purchase of additional adding and listing machines that supported the growing network of branches and agents. However, the potential of these machines, as well as punch-hole "accounting" machines, as mechanisms for recording and updating transactions was not fully exploited until after the post-war recovery years. Increasing the size of the branch network and divesting under-performing agents then became a priority. Performance indicators primarily measured growth in size (such as assets per employee and investment referrals) rather than efficiency or effectiveness (such as financial profitability and credit risk exposure). Moreover, during this period, financial performance of the branch network and individual retail branches was examined only at random and when specifically commissioned by the Board or the Finance Committee.

The characteristic provision of financial services in retail markets was to change with the commercial use of computer power. According to Locke (1999, p. 5) and Leslie (2000, p. 49), the most important IT applications had their origins in US-government-sponsored research in the first half of the 20th century. Interactive IT applications would never have existed without a long and expensive gestation period in which computer power and telecommunication applications were devoted to help the US gain the initiative in science and technology. Indeed, the British experience with computer hardware development would tend to confirm Leslie's and Locke's view of a defence-based technology push. The first stored-program computer in the world was developed in 1948 by academics at Manchester University (Anonymous, 1998). However, lack of funding resulted in Freddie Williams and Tom Kilburn being unable to continue with their project. Government-sponsored research in the US was therefore the force behind the development of highly sophisticated hardware and software as well as the networks which linked computers together.

In brief, early adoptions of telecommunications and computer applications had greatest impact in organised high value wholesale bank markets, that is, those activities that had traditionally been further away from volume transactions through retail bank branches. Banks absorbed the new technology on the back of a growing market for retail bank services, which expanded as middle-income individuals became a growing proportion of the population. However, it was government-sponsored research in the US rather than bank initiatives that provided the force behind the original innovations that would result in interactive IT applications during the 1970s.

## Specific Application Period

The second wave of IT innovation in retail finance begins in the late 1950s and lasted up to the late 1960s. Banks introduced computers to keep up with growth in business volume while, at the same time, solve very specific problems and automate existing practices of specific departments (see further Seeger, Lorsch & Gibson, 1974; Morris, 1986; BBC, 1995). The introduction of computer power relied on US-based suppliers of accounting machines such as IBM, Xerox and Burroughs (later Univac and Unisys). Initially, computer manufacturers responded quickly to the demand for hardware but failed to make much concession to users' software requirements (Fincham et al., 1994, p. 153) or to recognise the new strategic possibilities reduced information costs provided. The lack of ready-made software products forced user organisations to devise their own solutions to this problem until the emergence of high-level programming languages emerged from joint collaboration of users and computer manufacturers (Fincham et al., 1994).

At the time, banks aimed to develop the capacity to handle more complex and higher level service tasks with their existing "high street" skills and resources. This resulted in the branch network quickly turning into the main point of contact with retail customers while, internally, there was a growing need to supply top management with prompt (i.e., quarterly) financial information. A process-directed automation thrust dominated the specific application period and aimed at undercutting the cost of administrative tasks such as the labour-intensive cheque clearing system. During this period, the typical financial sector computer installation consisted of a central mainframe (Fincham et al., 1994, p. 154) dedicated to sequential batch processing of computer readable instructions dealing with separate processes, such as providing a service for handling customer transactions, standing orders and other clerical procedures. Computer applications were therefore concentrated on back office operations (Morris, 1986, p. 77) because controlling a growing mountain of paperwork provided the potential for economies of scale. There was also an incentive to automate at the individual branch bank level and to improve market-wide processes.

As above mentioned, US-based providers of hardware solutions had achieved a position of advantage from their head start in the development of the first digital computer in the 1940s. This was maintained throughout the technological competition with the then Soviet Union during the 1950s and 1960s.

By 1965, most major banks in the US and UK had been introduced to electronic data processing and many of them had seen the arrival of their first computer installation. Towards the end of the decade, with the introduction of a second or third computer, a major redistribution of organisational responsibilities followed. Organisational change tried to solve the apparent paradox between greater efficiency associated with automation (i.e., greater centralisation) and enhanced service offerings to customers associated with devolution of discretion to customer-facing staff at retail branches (i.e., greater decentralisation). Greater automation and improved communications, such as automatic internal switchboards, resulted in the establishment of central accounting units and in centralisation of customer account control so that regional and branch managers lost autonomy to centralised senior managers. Centralisation on the back of computer applications, therefore, created a space for a standardisation of service offering and the potential to reduce cost structures of traditional activities.

The increasing complexity and volume of financial transactions eventually led to the development of database management systems, or DBMS (Fincham et al., 1994, p. 154). The role of the DBMS was to overcome the limitations of conventional filing systems by providing a generalised, structured and integrated body of data that could be read and updated in a controlled, efficient, and reliable way (Fincham et al., 1994). Two key applications built on DBMS and took place in 1968. First came an interbank voucher-less payment facility called the Bankers' Automated Clearing System, or BACS (Morris, 1986). The second innovation involved the installation of the National Girobank, the automation of retail national and international money transfer through forms handled by Post Office outlets (Thomson, 1968).

A payment clearing system known as the Banker's Clearing House had existed in London since the 1770s (Bank of England, 1987, p. 392). The system emerged as representatives of note-issuing banks met informally to exchange cheques drawn on their various banks and to settle up by netting their positions and transferring money between accounts at different branches and banks or from their account at the central bank (e.g., Perry, 1975, p. 63). The system grew organically into a limited liability company known as the Bankers' Clearing House Ltd. (established in 1864). The company was owned and controlled by a group of banks called the "Committee of London Clearing Banks" and built upon banks that regarded the provision of current account facilities and money transmission services as their core business (Cooper, 1984, p. 50). In 1960, the system of clearing was extended to credit transfers and standing orders of payment (Perry, 1975, p. 75). Non-members could also provide current account and other facilities but required members (known as clearing banks) to act as agents to settle their cheques, transfers and standing orders.

In 1968 clearing banks established the first intra-organisational network while aiming to exploit the cost advantages of electronic data interchange (EDI). This network emerged in the form of an electronic transfer system of payments (called BACS) to which non-clearing banks could subscribe but, again, only through a clearing member acting as agent. The BACS system grew to be the world's largest automated clearing house, with a total staff of approximately 200 handling 262 million items by 1976 (Cooper, 1984, p. 53). The development of BACS created an interbank facility in an attempt to bring under control rising costs associated with the huge growth of cheque transactions during economic life-style improvement in the post-war recovery years (Gardener & Molyneux, 1990, p. 84). In 1967, the National Board for Prices and Income reported on bank changes and recommended various ways for increased competition. Following legislation introduced after the 1967 review of banking, from 1972 onwards BACS also aimed to create new sources of bank business by moving wage payment away from cash and into bank accounts (Price Commission, 1978, p. 33).

A second key development in the UK during the specific application period was the establishment of the National Giro Centre (later Girobank) in 1968. Girobank introduced another important innovation in the British money transmission system. Girobank was the first full computer-centred financial intermediary (Thomson, 1968, p. ix). Its original purpose was to help update the Post Office by making them the distribution channel for low-cost transactions (Girobank, 1993), that is, offering a money transmission service through 21,000 post offices in the UK.

Internationally, the UK was a latecomer to this service. Austria pioneered postal giro in 1883 and automated giro systems in 1962 (Thomson, 1968, p. 209). The UK version of the giro system envisioned maintaining current accounts. By 1977 Girobank attracted 580,000 customers, all but 30,000 of whom were individuals, representing about 3% of the personal account banking market (Price Commission, 1978, p. 45). Developments in the UK, however, were below expectations. It was readily recognised that external factors had little influence on Girobank's slow penetration of the personal market (Price Commission, 1978, p. 46). This was because Girobank tended to rely on recruiting Post Office personnel, most lacking the professional skills of the banking sector. A complex system that resulted in higher than average tariffs for money transmission was also a mentioned contributor. Nonetheless, the UK's Girobank was a sign of things to come with regards to:

- being a specialised institution in terms of activity (money transfer) and market segment (low-income banking and benefit payment);
- introducing an alternative retail money transfer system utilising an existing non-dedicated distribution channel already in place (Post Office counters);
- posing a competitive challenge to established providers as it offered a standard service through focussed operations and at lower costs (internal allocation to process postal payment orders and bank cheques was 12 and 20%, respectively).

Succinctly, during the specific application period, computer-based applications emerge and take place in isolated departments of the banking firm. During this period the first IT applications in the bank-client transactions were introduced. Enhanced computer power allowed banks to process the growing volume of paper-based transactions in central locations with the added effect of modified labour costs. This would suggest that greater use of IT applications in banking reinforced the hierarchical and volume-driven ethos of financial intermediaries serving retail markets while promising product diversification on the back of standardised service offerings and reduced cost structures. At the same time, computer power enabled managers of banks to look for more standardised (and cheaper) labour while a new set of IT-related capabilities began to emerge as a necessary condition for competition in bank markets.

## Emergence Period

The third wave of IT innovations in retail finance emerged hand in hand with advances in telecommunications. During the emergence period, banks became one of the world's dominant customers for computer-based applications, far exceeding other sectors such as capital goods manufacturers or transportation (Scherer, 1982; Quintás, 1991). Between 1968 and 1980 banks emerged as major customers of software and hardware as they became involved in applications which delivered significant cost reductions as well as increased business volume and variety. The main difference between this and the specific application period was that the impact of computers was felt throughout the organisation rather than in specific departments. The ability to achieve higher quality and lower cost in an unprecedented way established large-scale economies in banking which were not offset by organisational discontinuities (Walker, 1978).

Developments in hardware and software that found their applications in the private sector in general and in banking in particular were further enhanced with the reduction of government expenditure that had supported the space exploration project. As a result, throughout the 1970s many highly qualified individuals formerly working at NASA found employment in investment banks and the treasury operations of US-based commercial banks. Changes were also observed in the recruitment strategies of banks outside of North America. In the UK, highly skilled university graduates were attracted and prepared for future responsibilities as senior staff at banks and non-bank financial intermediaries. This was a departure from the traditional practice of "internal job markets" developed in the 1920s, that is, the recruitment and in-house training of low-skilled and risk-adverse individuals, who had few ambitions beyond the security of job "for life" employment offered by banks and would require little motivation (Parker, 1981, p. 147; Wardley, 2000, pp.81-83).

Other distinctive characteristics for banking organisations during the emergence period included the introduction of full automation to branch accounting, real-time operation and control of branches by the central office. In the UK, Clydesdale Bank was the first to network every teller and cashier position (Fincham et al., 1994, pp. 154-155), thus providing Clydesdale's customers the possibility for each transaction to have direct access to the bank's online transaction-processing services. Concisely, the immediate result of innovations during this period was that customers were able to bank at any point in the retail branch network while the previous arrangement limited several transactions to the customer's own branch. Indeed, the regional manager for a major UK provider reported at the time that:

> The [bank's] computer will provide to all branches an "online" enquiry service. Account balances and redemption figures will be immediately available ensuring a much speedier service to members and professional contacts.[2]

Table 2 illustrates the growth of one of the most successful applications that emerged during this period. It took place in 1967 when Barclays Bank (UK) introduced the first automated teller machine (ATM) in the world (Barclays, 1982), while IBM introduced the magnetic-stripe plastic cards in 1969 (Bátiz-Lazo, Wonlimpiyarat & Wood, 2001, p. 867). Together these innovations marked the birth of electronic banking.

Barclays introduced credit cards to the UK by importing systems (including computer applications) from Bank of America (US) at the end of 1965 (Bátiz-Lazo et al., 2002, p. 865). Barclay's early adoption of ATMs was no coincidence because cash withdrawal through ATMs is a major use for credit cards. Indeed, the emergence of the ATM marked the beginning of self-service banking as services provided by the bank teller could be performed on a 24-hour schedule and at the customers' convenience rather than during banking hours. ATMs expanded rapidly as other institutions followed Barclays' lead. By 1974 there were 3,140 cash-dispensing machines in the US, owned by 534 banks (Walker, 1978, p. 68). More recently, according to 1990 figures, the UK had some 294 ATMs per million inhabitants (Maudos & Pastor, 1995, p. 8).

Noticeable changes in bank internal organisation started to take place alongside the growth in ATM adoption complementing retail bank branch distribution. Initially the heavy investment required to build an ATM network was seen as a major source of competitive advantage for large banks, so interconnection was slow to develop. However, managers of banks eventually realised that few organisations had access to the financial resources and IT skills to develop widespread ATM networks. Banks then increasingly sought critical mass through strategic alliances. For example, the Co-operative Bank was notoriously slow to introduce "online" systems. Only in 1987 was the bank able to offer online banking rather than the passbook system through its agencies in Co-operative stores. To solve the IT problem, the Co-operative Bank pursued several collaborative solutions. One was to become a founding member of the LINK Group in 1984. The bank had 50 ATMs in its 78 branches but, through LINK, bank customers could access around 400 ATMs. This number grew to 1,000 in 1988 and then to 3,500 when the Matrix Group joined LINK (also in 1988). By 1995, LINK allowed access to over 8,500 ATMs in the UK alone, with the Co-operative Bank contributing 119 ATMs (managed by IBM under a £13 million outsourcing contract signed in 1994). Hence, 30 years after the introduction of the first ATM, the

*Table 2: Growth of ATMs in the UK and elsewhere, 1974-1995*

**Panel A: Bank Branches and ATMs in the UK, 1974-1995**

| Year | Branches | ATMs |
|------|----------|------|
| 1974 | 14,908 | N/A |
| 1984 | 14,058 | 6,106 |
| 1989 | 13,131 | 12,253 |
| 1994 | 10,724 | 15,180 |

Source: Collet and Maher (1997)

**Panel B: Cash Dispensers and ATMs in Four OCDE Countries, 1988-1995**

| | 1988 | 1989 | 1990 | 1991 | 1992 | 1993 | 1994 | 1995 |
|---|------|------|------|------|------|------|------|------|
| *Number of machines per million inhabitants:* | | | | | | | | |
| Belgium | 85 | 92 | 94 | 105 | 109 | 119 | 313 | 360 |
| France | 206 | 231 | 255 | 284 | 305 | 325 | 356 | 395 |
| UK | 245 | 275 | 296 | 314 | 324 | 328 | 342 | 358 |
| US | 296 | 306 | 321 | 331 | 342 | 367 | 418 | 467 |
| *Number of transactions per inhabitant:* | | | | | | | | |
| Belgium | 5.7 | 6.8 | 7.1 | 8.1 | 8.8 | 9.1 | 11.9 | 14.2 |
| France | 8.0 | 9.0 | 10.0 | 11.0 | 12.0 | 13.3 | 14.2 | 15.7 |
| UK | 13.2 | 15.4 | 17.3 | 18.8 | 20.2 | 21.3 | 22.9 | 25.2 |
| US | 18.4 | 20.6 | 23.2 | 25.3 | 28.2 | 29.8 | 31.8 | 36.9 |
| *Average value of transactions (USD):* [*] | | | | | | | | |
| Belgium | 94.4 | 94.2 | 113.2 | 117.4 | 113.2 | 110.3 | 125.2 | 137.5 |
| France | 75.3 | 72.3 | 81.4 | 83.4 | 95.5 | 77.0 | 76.5 | 81.3 |
| UK | 68.0 | 65.0 | 77.0 | 81.0 | 84.6 | 72.5 | 74.6 | 77.3 |
| US | 66.0 | 64.7 | 66.0 | 67.0 | 66.9 | 68.2 | 67.2 | 67.7 |

*Sources:* Bank for International Settlements (1989, 1996)

\* Converted at yearly average exchange areas

absurdity of terminals connected to different networks located side by side and long after terminal density had reached saturation point eventually resulted in a single interconnected network in 1999 for the UK (Bátiz-Lazo et al., 2002, p. 865).

Another interesting innovation during the emergence period was the introduction of management information systems, or MIS (Fincham et al., 1994, p. 155). These systems initially aimed to use the computational power of transaction-processing capabilities to provide regular reports and analyses of business activity. In this way MIS offered managers of banks the possibility to increase the scope for monitoring, controlling and planning of operational procedures. Although MIS increased line management productivity, MIS systems proliferated throughout the organisation but without any fundamental change in the nature of managers' activities (Fincham et al., 1994).

In summary, during the emergence period, technological change spread to many internal aspects of the banking organisation and permeated bank-client relationships.

These changes started to modify how, when and where customers could enter the banking system but banks had yet to be considered multi-delivery channel organisations in their service offering or in their ability to direct all their information to any point of customer contact. It is during this period that the convergence of telecommunications and computer power resulted in true IT applications as the emphasis of technological innovations shifted from data processing to communications. At the same time, cost effective supply of financial services rather than customer value creation continued to predominate the design of banks' internal organisation and strategy development.

## Diffusion Period

The diffusion period of the information revolution in commercial banking saw the spread of IT to all aspects of banks' internal organisation and market relationships thanks to the introduction of personal computers (PCs) in clerical and managerial roles. During this period, consumer-oriented innovations were widespread as information technology provided support to all points of contact between customers and bank. PCs offered a flexible way of providing and enhancing computer resources for a wide range of applications. Simultaneously, widely available packaged software reduced the need to devote in-house resources for the development of general application systems. Incorporating, standardising and exploiting IT-based innovations became a key issue in banks' long-term strategies. Moreover, IT applications offered banks greater anticipated advantage thanks to expectations of enhanced control of financial and strategic resources.

The most important consequence of the drive towards mass delivery of retail financial services was that banks effectively moved from being places of decentralised personal relationships to ones run by institutional managers.[3] During the diffusion period, banks began to create relationship databases instead of using skilled personnel at all points of contact with customers (BBC, 1995). For example, Lesley Taylor (head of direct banking, Royal Bank of Scotland) claimed that current technology allowed one person to develop in 3 or 4 weeks the skills that previously required 5 years in the job (BBC, 1995; Morris, 1986, p. 97). Information technology applications, therefore, promised higher organisational flexibility to those banks that could effectively implement technical changes.

The second effect of technical innovations on banks' approach to business during the diffusion period pertained to distribution capabilities. The branch network reduced its importance as the point of sale for financial services. This development was facilitated with the advent of digital communications technologies and networks, which allowed the performance and reliability required for organisation-wide integration of data resources as well as more effective extra-organisational networks.

The integration of services around digital networks (ISDN) and greater use of electronic data interchange (EDI) protocols were at the heart of new distribution channels such as electronic fund at point-of-sale terminals (EFTPOS), telephone transfer systems and smart cards. Card technology evolved to provide individual

*Table 3: Growth of EFTPOS terminals in four OCDE countries, 1988-1995*

(Number of terminals per million inhabitants)

| Country | 1988 | 1989 | 1990 | 1991 | 1992 | 1993 | 1994 | 1995 |
|---|---|---|---|---|---|---|---|---|
| Belgium | 1,925 | 2,477 | 2,828 | 3,213 | 4,034 | 5,246 | 6,294 | 7,174 |
| France | 2,154 | 2,842 | 3,180 | 3,568 | 5,594 | 7,435 | 7,574 | 9,394 |
| UK | 426 | 1,311 | 1,916 | 3,299 | 3,806 | 4,639 | 5,993 | 8,647 |
| US | 183 | 200 | 240 | 348 | 450 | 759 | 1,440 | 2,107 |

*Source*: Bank for International Settlements (1989, 1996)

customers with border-less services, primarily under the trademarks of VISA and MasterCard International networks. Table 3 illustrates the growth in the adoption of point-of-sale terminals, and in turn, this growth reflects how IT applications were used instead of cash registers and telephone credit authorisations. Other innovations included cheque verification terminals and fund transfer terminals.

Nevertheless, not all substitutes of the bank branch enjoyed the same success (McNamara & Bromley, 1997). For example, growth of the most sophisticated EFTPOS terminals was hampered by conflicts between retailers and banks about the inadequacy of cash and cheques. A related issue was who should receive the "lion's share" of the profit. As a result, by the end of the 1980s, EFTPOS had yet to fulfil its potential and develop into a major new source of profit for banks' fee income (e.g., Channon, 1988, p. 317; Wood, 1989, p. 3).

All types of financial institutions invested heavily in the integration and standardisation of internal systems during the 1980s. Progress, however, was uneven because banks had traditionally operated through their own closely controlled retail branch networks while the use of second and third parties as distributors was more popular in the building society or insurance sectors. At the same time, high transaction costs resulted in low international interconnectivity of payment systems. The established framework handled urgent high value payment well, but achieving potential economies of scale in small payments was deterred by some countries lagging in the use of automated clearing systems, regulation or concentration in bank markets (Wood & Erturk, 1996, pp. 15-16).

In brief, during the diffusion period, IT applications resulted in customers acquiring several options when engaging in financial transactions with their main bank but also with competing banks. Together with regulatory change and theoretical advances to price risk, technological innovations put a premium on financial information rather than on banking on a set of transaction-processing capabilities. Developments in IT were instrumental in lowering entry barriers to bank markets by providing scale benefits to the smallest providers. Applications of information technology also threatened to turn retail bank branch networks into sunk (i.e., irrecoverable) strategic costs. During this period IT developments augmented the range of financial services and product availability by increasing the threat of substitution and by lowering the cost of imitation. Moreover, during the diffusion period, digitisation and standardisation of IT applications helped to explain the development of markets for second- and third-party processing. Unfortunately, most potential opportunities opened by technology were slow to develop because, although technology allowed new entrants to contest markets for financial services, these challenges took place only in the most profitable segments of bank markets (such as credit cards or unsecured lending).

# HISTORICAL EXPERIENCE AND THE MOST RECENT APPLICATIONS

Table 4 summarises some of the most important recent IT applications in retail finance markets, namely, ATMs, telephone banking and "electronic" banking. Partial success of most of these applications questions whether technological change in the Digital Age[4] (as opposed to those in the Information Age[5]) offers new forms of competition and business models in bank markets. On the one hand, commercial banks have coped with technological innovation and accomplished managers' intended objectives with varying success. Technology has opened the way for banks to improve their cost structures provided they could induce customers to change their behaviour according to banks' expectations. At the same time, there have been uneven effects from the same technological innovation across distinct geography.

On the other hand, as noted by Pennings and Harianto (1992), the propensity of banking organisations to adopt technological innovation evolves around the match between the new application and the resources, capacities and capabilities that organisations have accumulated over time. Banks have had no proprietary hold on most of their technology and this has been notably the case with the technology fuelling the growth of the latest applications (such as Internet banking or middle-ware solutions). Some established participants in bank markets have responded by offering nontraditional services like holiday travel (e.g., Midland and Thomas Cook) and real estate agencies (Lloyds' Black Horse Agencies). However, the vast majority responded through new service offerings in core areas and by increasing the diversity in their products in terms of markets and customer groups. A reduced number of banking organisations (such as HSBC, BBVA, BSCH, ABNAmro, Deutsche Bank and Citigroup) also increased their geographical scope, but most other banks found little joy in cross-border and foreign operations that failed to match the returns available in home markets. Participants in bank markets have thus tried to use technological applications and IT in particular to integrate retail and financial services into "one-stop" shopping, support volume-oriented sales, and strengthen their brand name and corporate culture.

As suggested by empirical research documented in Bátiz-Lazo and Wood (1999, p. 25), focus on traditional markets and the creation of new customer groups within geographical markets reflects commercial bank managers' preference to accept a degree of cross-subsidisation because of its associated stability. Although managers of banks expect software and hardware developments to enable close

*Table 4: Key technological innovations in electronic retail finance, 1979-2001*

| Year | Name | Characteristic | Contribution |
|------|------|----------------|--------------|
| 1979-1985 | Telephone banking (US, UK) | Branch-less retail intermediaries | Multichannel distribution system for banks based on an integrated customer account and information system. |
| 1988-1996 | Mondex cards (UK) | Debit card with re-writable microchip | Facilitate small-value retail transactions with the potential to substitute central bank issued notes and coins. Formalise ways to collect broad array of information from customers. |
| 1989-1998 | DigiCash (NL) | Electronic only medium of exchange and unit of account | Payment systems and products that depend exclusively upon high-speed communications done through computers. |
| 1995-2001 | Security First Network Bank (US) | First intermediary working through the Internet | Technology opens new opportunities for bank growth and offers managers of banks possibilities to achieve high organisational flexibility. |

control of their bank's main profit drivers (Bátiz-Lazo and Wood, 1999, p. 25), only a handful of participants in the world have developed IT applications that provided detailed and reliable profitability reports. Diversification and greater asset size, therefore, are solutions to managers' inability to track key economic drivers for individual distribution channels, service/product offerings, customer groups and individual customers.

Concluding that greater diversification and scale are the way forward for financial service organisations in general and banks in particular is reasonable, given that managers of banks have failed to take full advantage of opportunities created by IT innovations. However, there is an apparent paradox when greater diversity and asset size are pervasive despite technological change, because of the expectation that IT innovation should result in greater specialisation being the typical business model for participants in bank markets.

The successful use of digital media by wholesale payment systems and the potential for retail transactions to follow suit led many (e.g., Taylor, 1998; Browne & Cronin; 1999; Zimmermann & Koerner, 1999; Koerner & Zimmermann, 2000) to conclude that the *virtual bank* would be the typical organisational form for financial intermediaries. Although the *virtual bank* is still a broadly defined concept, there is some general assumption for *virtual* to reflect a tendency towards the prominence of nonproprietary networks so that nonfinance providers would acquire a low sunk (i.e., irrecoverable) cost capability that enables the mediation of financial transactions (i.e., total disintermediation of established participants in bank markets).

Some elements which explain the apparent inability of IT innovations to result in greater specialisation have already been discussed throughout this paper and include:

- each new technological innovation accounting for (proportionally) smaller reductions in price differentials;
- possibilities of observing network economies, that is, suggesting that activities which are critical to develop a competitive advantage in bank markets will be very hard to match for potential innovations because once some players get started building proprietary payment networks it will be impossible to catch up, even with technically better systems.
- trials with smart cards and digital cash showing that bank customers are unwilling to pay for interfaces for the new technology, while merchants expect to share the revenue of new payment media through lower commission charges. In other words, the latest innovations have done little to modify the methods of conducting transactions between customers and banks.

There are two other arguments to conclude that it is unlikely that the *virtual bank* will be the typical organisational form for financial intermediaries. These relate to, first, the transferability of skills within banking and second, regulation. Transferability of skills refers to banks' proven expertise and ability to control losses from payment activities efficiently (Radecki, 1998, p. 21). Losses from payment activities emerge from fraud, bankruptcy and operational errors (unique to a bank or system-wide). The control of these losses involves their prevention as well as recovering funds in the event of a loss. In other words, skills and capabilities associated with managing payment systems seem readily transferable to lending and would explain why banks provide both lending and payment services.

According to empirical evidence documented in McNamara and Bromley (1997), IT applications enabled standardisation of activities in payment and lending services. However, the same report suggests that superior financial performance could be achieved when managers were allowed to make discretionary judgements on lending decisions based on a combination of software-driven risk assessments, emerging from elaborate algorithms and other computer applications, with experience and skill-based judgement. This suggests the continued importance of contextual elements to assess risk as a core capability to compete in retail bank markets and also that few banks (or non-banks) could engage in volume transactions making indiscriminate use of technology in core activities.

Secondly, the potential for fraud, money laundering and systemic failure requires supervision, regulation and minimum capital requirement for organisations supplying wholesale and retail bank services through electronic media (e.g., Group of Ten, 1997). In the literature, regulation has been viewed as mitigating competition as well as hindering the adoption of technological innovation (Baumol, Panzar & Willig, 1982). Hence, the result of regulation limiting the potential of non-banks to contest bank markets indicates a lengthy move to retail and wholesale electronic-only payment systems.

In brief, payment systems still rely on bank deposit transfers and central bank issued money as a medium of exchange. This suggests that in the foreseeable future the complete substitution of notes and coins issued by central banks by digital systems running in high capacity communications media through computers is unlikely. Transactions involving e-commerce, m-commerce or WebTV have the potential of reintroducing privately issued currency, but generally banks are strongly positioned as administrators of local and international payment systems. However, the expected growth in the volume of payment and banks' lack of proprietary control of technology suggest that potential threats of entry to bank markets will persist.

# DISCUSSION

This review set out to determine whether technological change enhanced the importance of computer systems in the strategy of commercial banks. One early expectation was that banks' strategic goals would evolve and look to modify the principal-agent relationship between bank and customer, so the client-bank relations depend less on loyalty and service quality (i.e., idiosyncratic investments) and more on financial margin. There is evidence to suggest that, on an historical perspective, technological innovation and, in particular, increasing applications of telecommunications in bank markets, such as telephone banking, electronic cross-border payment systems or wholesale payment systems, have effectively modified the external and internal nature of the banking organisation.

However, the way in which future technological innovation is likely to modify the banking organisations, both externally (product or service) and internally (operational function), is at best uncertain. Externally banks are challenged to service the growth in the volume of payments through e-commerce, m-commerce and WebTV, but historical evidence suggests that very few IT applications have had an immediate effect and transform business practice in bank markets. Indeed, some of the most promising innovations have failed significantly. Smart new software applications and innovative hardware interfaces which link new ways of making payments (e.g., Mondex or VISA Cash) with conventional payment systems are likely to coexist and influence the way customers enter the banking system. Banks will continue to be pressed to resolve operational issues in terms of individual customer risk and individual customer profitability while, at the same time, continuing to increase size and diversity. The preeminence of conservatism in consumption patterns for retail financial services will continue to limit the success of the most promising technological developments.

Internally, technological innovations have increased the leverage of superior processing relative to capital and other physical resources. Changes in technology have lowered transaction costs for processing financial transactions and some banks have been very effective in implementing those innovations. In the future, hardware and software are expected to provide the platform that will improve banks' multi-channel management while reducing the cost of coordination. But at present, it is uncertain whether the solution to banks' operational problem will result in a) no change for the banking organisation; b) the creation of networks of stand-alone product/service groups, stand-alone distribution channels and stand-alone treasury operations; or c) a combination that allows product/service and channel managers to negotiate deals independently.

Throughout the technology innovation process, banks have shown that they lack full proprietary knowledge and capabilities to successfully develop new technological solutions. This suggests that alliances between banks and technology providers have greater chances of success than efforts unique to commercial banks or unique to technology providers. Managers of banks are thus challenged to excel in the implementation of these IT-based strategies. Otherwise, poor execution will result in few *ex post* options and low sustainability of competitive advantage.

On the other hand, technology has helped non-bank providers to enter banking by reducing price differentials and increasing transparency in organised markets and creating new customer segments through relationship databases. Technology has also allowed managers of banks and non-banks to segment relationships by profitability as well as providing the basis for the development of new distribution channels (e.g., customer group diversification). However, the possibility to transfer capabilities between lending and managing payment systems encourages managers of non-banks who wish to take advantage of the growth in the volume of payments to create new capabilities as a way to gain entry in bank markets.

In brief, the full move away from the branch-centred organisation into *virtual banking* will require new IT applications, new managerial practices and new consumption patterns within the banks' most profitable market segments. Managers of banks (and non-banks wishing to enter bank markets) are now challenged to design internal systems that provide greater control of the profitability drivers and which enable their organisations to capture new synergy.

# ACKNOWLEDGMENTS

Dr. Bátiz-Lazo benefited from the financial support of Conacyt (Num. 82619) in the early stages of this research. Comments and suggestions from Sally Aisbitt (Open), Jacky Fry (Open), Chris Holland (MBS), Robert Locke (Hawaii, Manoa), participants at the Financial Information and Systems Annual Conference, Twelfth Accounting, Business and Financial History Conference and anonymous referees are gratefully acknowledged. The usual caveats do apply.

# ENDNOTES

1 Unless otherwise stated, this section borrows freely from Cassell (1984, pp. 62-87) and archival search of the Board Meeting Minutes (1941 to 1965), Minutes

of the Finance and General Purpose Committee (1941 to 1965), Minutes of the Annual General Meeting (1923 to 1962) and Notes to Meetings of the Board (1962 to 1976) from the Co-operative Permanent Building Society.

2 Notes to Meetings of the Board from the Co-operative Permanent Building Society, 19 August 1976.

3 With the effect that "The banker as a man of stature had been lost." (Interview with senior executive of Lloyds Bank Group, 3 March 1995).

4 Starting in 1977, with the introduction of the Apple personal computer.

5 Starting in 1948, with the invention of the first programmable computer.

# REFERENCES

Anonymous. (1998). *The Birth of the Baby*. Retrieved on October 18, 1999 from http://www.man.ac.uk/news/april20/baby.html.

Baltensperger, E. (1980). Alternative approaches to the theory of the banking firm. *Journal of Monetary Economics*, *6*, 1-37.

Bank for International Settlements. (1989, 1996). *Statistics on Payment Systems*. The Group of Ten Countries, Basle.

Bank of England. (1987). Recent developments in UK payment clearing systems. *Bank of England Quarterly Bulletin*, *27*, 392-394.

Bank of England. (1991). The performance of British banks. *Bank of England Quarterly Bulletin*, *31*, 508-515.

Barclays. (1982). *Barclays: A Story of Money and Banking*. London: Barclays Bank.

Bátiz-Lazo, B. (1998). *Internal and External Influences on Innovations in Commercial Banking*. Unpublished doctoral dissertation. Faculty of Business Administration, University of Manchester.

Bátiz-Lazo, B. & Wood, D. (1999). Management of core capabilities in Mexican and European banks. *International Service Industry Management Journal* (Special issue, Service Management in Latin America), *10*(5), 430-48.

Bátiz-Lazo, B., Wonlimpiyarat, J. & Wood, D. (2002). Barclaycard. In Johnson, G. and Scholes, K. (Eds.), *Exploring Corporate Strategy: Text and Cases* (sixth edition), 864-879. Harlow, England: Prentice Hall.

Baumol, W. J., Panzar, J. C. & Willig, R. D. (1982). *Contestable Markets and the Theory of Industry Structure*. New York: Harcourt Brace Jovanovich.

BBC. (1995). *The Money Programme Special: Uncertain Times. News and Current Affairs Department*, September 23 & 30. London, England: British Broadcasting Corporation.

Browne, F. X. & Cronin, D. (1999). Payment technologies, financial innovation, and Laissez-Faire banking. *Cato Journal*, *15*(1), 1-12.

Cassell, M. (1984). *Inside Nationwide*. London, England: Nationwide Building Society.

Channon, D. F. (1988). *Global Banking Strategy*. New York: John Wiley & Sons.

Collett, N. J. & Maher, P. (1997). *A Dark Horse Merger – Lloyds TSB Case Study, mimeo*. Manchester, England: Manchester Business School.

Cooper, J. (1984). *The Management and Regulation of Banks*. London: Macmillan.

Fincham, R., Fleck, J., Procter, R., Scarbrough, H., Tierney, M. & Williams, R. (1994). *Expertise and Innovation: Information Technology Strategies in the Financial Services Sector*. Oxford, England: Oxford University Press.

Garbade, K. D. & Silber, W. L. (1978). Technology, communications and the performance of financial markets: 1840-1975. *Journal of Finance, 33*(3), 819-832.

Gardener, E. P. M. & Molyneux, P. (1990). *Changes in Western European Banking*. London: Unwin Hyman.

Girobank. (1993). Developments of Girobank. *Archives-Library Unit*. London: National Girobank.

Group of Ten. (1997). *Electronic Money: Consumer Protection, Law Enforcement, Supervision and Cross-border Issues*. Basle: Bank for International Settlements.

Klein, M. A. (1971). A theory of the banking firm. *Journal of Money Credit and Banking, 3*(2), 205-18.

Koerner, V. & Zimmermann, H. D. (2000). Management of customer relationship in business media–The case of the financial industry. *Proceedings of the 33rd Hawaii International Conference On System Science (HICSS)*, January 4-7. Maui, Hawaii. http://www.electronicmarkets.org/netacademy/publications.nsf/all_print_pk/1388. Accessed July 7, 2000.

Leslie, S. W. (2000). The biggest "angel" of them all: The military and the making of Silicon Valley. In M. Kenney (Ed.), *Understanding Silicon Valley*, pp. 48-67. Stanford, CA: Stanford University Press.

Locke, R. (1999). Factoring American business school education into the revolution in interactive information technology. In P. Jeffcutt (Ed.), *The Foundations of Management Knowledge*. London, England: Routledge.

Maudos, J. & Pastor, J. M. (1995). Prestación de servicios bancarios en las cajas de ahorro españolas: Cajeros automáticos versus oficinas. *Valenecia, Institut Valencià d'Investigacions Econòmicas*, WP 95-14.

McNamara, G. & Philip, B. (1997). Decision making in an organizational setting: Cognitive and organizational influences on risk assessment in commercial lending. *Academy of Management Journal, 40*(5), 1063-1088.

Morris, T. (1986). *Innovations in Banking*. London: Croom Helm.

Parker, G. G. C. (1981). Now management will make or break the bank. *Harvard Business Review*, November-December, 140-148.

Pennings, J. M. & Harianto, F. (1992). The diffusion of technological innovation in the commercial banking industry. *Strategic Management Journal, 13*(2), 29-46.

Perry, E. F. (1975). *The Elements of Banking* (4th ed.). London, England: The Institute of Bankers.

Price Commission. (1978). *Banks: Charges for Money Transmission Services*. London: H. M. Stationery Office.

Pugh, D. S. (1973). The measurement of organisation structures: Does context determine form? *Organizational Dynamics*, Spring, 19-34. Reprinted (1971) *Organisation Theory* (4th ed.), 16-35. Pugh, D. S. (Ed.), (1997). London: Penguin Books.

Quintás Seoane, J. R. (1991). Tecnología y banca minorista en la década de los noventa. *Papeles de Economía Española, 47*, 72-86.

Radecki, L. J. (1998). *Banks' Payment-Driven Revenues. Research and Market Analysis Group*. New York: Federal Reserve Bank of New York.

Scherer, F. M. (1982). Inter-industry technology flows in the United States. *Research Policy, 11*, 227-245.

Seeger, J. A., Lorsch, J. W. & Gibson, C. F. (1974). *First National Citibank Operating Group (A)*. Cambridge, MA: Harvard Business School (ref. 9-474-165, rev. 5 May 1995).

Swank, J. (1996). Theories of the banking firm: A review of the literature. *Bulletin of Economic Research, 48*(3), 173-207.

Taylor, B. (1998). The Darwinian shakeout in financial services–An interim report. *Long Range Planning, 31*(1), 82-92.

Thomson, F. P. (1968). *Money in the Computer Age*. Oxford, England: Pergamon Press.

Walker, D. A. (1978). Economies of scale in electronic funds transfer systems. *Journal of Banking and Finance, 2*, 65-78.

Wardley, P. (2000). The commercial banking industry and its part in the emergence and consolidation of the corporate economy in Britain before 1940. *Journal of Industrial History, 3*(2), 71-97.

White, L. H. (1999). *The Theory of Monetary Institutions*. Oxford, England: Basil Blackwell.

Wood, D. (1989). The IT Impact of 1992 strategies. In D. Wood (Ed.), *Financial Service Strategies for 1992*. Manchester, England: Manchester Business School.

Wood, D. & Erturk, I. (1996). *European Payment Systems, in Payments–Past, Present and Future*, 7-26. London: Association for Payment Clearing.

Zimmermann, H. D. & Koerner, V. (1999). New emerging industrial structures in the digital economy–The case of the financial industry. In W. D. Haseman, and D. L. Nazareth (Ed.), *Proceedings of the Fifth Americas Conference on Information Systems (AMCIS'99)*, 115-117. Milwaukee, http://www.electronicmarkets.org/netacademy/publications.nsf/all_pk/1299. Accessed July 7, 2000.

# Section IV

# IT-Based Logistics
# and Accounting

Chapter XV

# Logistics, Information Technology, and Retail Internationalisation: The Formation of International Strategic Retail Networks

Constantine A. Bourlakis
Athens University of Economics and Business, Greece

Michael A. Bourlakis
University of Newcastle upon Tyne, UK

## ABSTRACT

*In the present work we suggest the notion of the strategic information technology competitive advantage and its potential strategic impact upon a retailer's organisational supply chain coordination. The existence of a logistics strategy and an information technology strategy constitute two functions that offer the platform for retail firms to "internalise" the effective management of the supply chain by converting it to a coordination competitive advantage. The latter depends upon the ability of the retail firms to transform a logistics strategy and an information technology strategy into what the authors call strategic logistics and strategic information technology. We also argue that logistics and information technology can assist a retailer to form a "logistics network" with third-party firms in the supply chain, with the aim to capture and to protect to the full the differential returns generated via the internalisation of the supply chain activities. The coordination competitive advantage owned by the retailer enhances retail change in domestic and in international markets, as the retailer enters foreign markets via a similar network of third party and its own account logistics operations, giving rise to new retail organisation schemes, such as the international strategic retail network.*

# INTRODUCTION

In the present work the authors argue for the potential of retail evolution across national boundaries in the dawn of the 21st century. Dominant retailers that possess an "ownership" competitive advantage at their home territory are in a favourable position to expand abroad. Logistics and information technology provide the infrastructure for the management of information and have been gradually elevated to be powerful tools of coordination of retail supply channel management. Logistics and information technology offer the platform for the "internalisation" of the retailer's competitive advantage, something that can strategically enhance the internationalisation of retail firms via a significant impact upon a retailer's organisational supply chain structure in domestic and in international markets. Logistics and information technology can assist a retailer to form a "strategic retail network" in the supply chain at home and in foreign markets with the aim to capture and to protect to the full "ownership" specific competitive advantage differential returns.

At the early stages of the competitive process, logistics and information technology can be part of cost-cutting operations for the retail firm. Retail firms foresee the competitive benefits that can accrue to them by the use of logistics and information technology, so retail firms spend heavily upon crafting and implementing a logistics strategy and an information technology strategy. In particular, dominant retailers with a large volume of profits are in a favourable position to invest proportionally more on information technology, logistics, advertising campaigns, as well as on the production of their own brand items in an effort to sustain and enhance their market position and their competitive advantage. In turn, if successful over time, such investments will cause an increase in profits and will potentially lower the overall cost to the company. Higher profits will be ploughed back to successfully implemented investments with the company expecting further beneficial feedback effects on profits, as apparently, a number of factors influence simultaneously retail change and innovation. In the course of the competitive process, logistics becomes strategic logistics and information technology becomes strategic information technology, and the firm is rewarded with a unique and fully owned competitive advantage.

In terms of strategy the latter means that the new practices become part of the competitive advantage to the retailer as emergent practices/strategies turn into deliberate actions/strategies. The impact on retail change could be dramatic, ranging from going international to further enhancing the internalisation of domestic and/or international operations. We argue that it is the relevant switch of an activity from emergent to deliberate that changes the nature of the core competitive advantage of the retailer and pushes the company to undertake the form of an innovative new format. For that reason, a simultaneous equations framework is also formulated that includes as exogenous variables retailer's practices related to deliberate and / or emergent strategies. Traditional retail evolution may not continue beyond the point where emergent strategies can not be successfully converted into a fully owned competitive advantage in the shape of deliberate strategies.

The relevant "ownership"—coordination competitive advantage propagates retail change in domestic and in international markets. Retailers expand initially at home ground via the creation of a network of third party and their own logistic operations. A natural step for a retailer that possesses a dominant position at home is to expand abroad. In the course of entry in foreign markets, the retailer creates a similar network of third party and its own account logistics operations in the international arena. At the end of the retailer's internationalisation process, new retail organisation schemes may arrive, such as the international strategic retail network.

# RETAIL NETWORKS

There are three theoretical perspectives related to the decision of firm integration. The first theoretical perspective is rooted in the industrial organisation approach developed by Porter (1980), who suggests that integration is a powerful tool for the company to create and to sustain competitive advantages by exploiting opportunities in imperfect markets. The strategic motives behind the integration are associated with economies of stable relationship, economies of combined operations, economies of internal control and coordination, economies of avoiding the market, and economies of information (Porter, 1980).

The second theoretical approach is the transaction cost approach proposed initially by Coase (1937) and expanded further by Williamson (1971, 1975, 1985), and defined by Arrow (1969) as being "the cost of organising the economic system." The transaction cost approach states that in the presence of transaction-specific investments and uncertainty the firm must decide on the form of its organisational arrangements of economic exchanges in such a way as to minimise costs. In the light of the above, the firm chooses either to internalise (integrate) operations or to mediate through the market (externalise) its exposure to low information (uncertain) transactions with recurring transaction-specific investments. The firm will internalise its production when the costs of market transactions are in excess of the internal costs of the organisation of production (Levy, 1985).

The third theoretical approach is linked with the sustainability of the company's competitive advantage, and it is commonly known as the resource-based view of the firm. The heart of the argument of the resource-based view of the firm is that some firms have the ability to organise production in a way that it is difficult (if not possible) to be imitated by other firms. This unique company ability to combine available heterogeneous resources effectively may give rise to a sustained competitive advantage (see, for example, *inter alia*, Ramanujam & Varadarajan, 1989).

We can assess the approach taken by the three theoretical perspectives upon a firm's integration as follows: The industrial organisation approach regards the industry-specific environment that the firm operates as important in following an integration strategy in order to achieve competitive advantage. The transaction cost approach emphasises that the motive behind the internalisation of production is associated with the case where the costs of externalising production outweigh the costs of internalising production. The resource-based view of the firm suggests that the internalisation of production is a complex strategy, but once achieved by a firm it is very difficult to be imitated by rival companies.

Logistics and information technology offer the platform for the "internalisation" of the retailer's competitive advantage, something that can strategically enhance the internalisation process for the retail firm via a significant impact upon a retailer's organisational supply chain structure in domestic and in international markets. A network, by definition, encompasses a company's set of relationships, both vertical and horizontal, with other organisations, including relationships across industries and countries (Jarillo, 1988). There is a growing body of research in retail strategy that is coming to terms with the performance consequences of firms participating in strategic supplier networks. Following the resource-based view of the firm, a firm's network of ties represents a valuable resource that can yield differential returns in the same manner as other intangible and tangible assets contribute. Logistics and information technology can assist a retailer to form a "logistics network" in the supply chain at home and in foreign markets with the aim to capture and to protect to the full such differential returns. Under the "network" mode, a retailer can manage its logistics operations via its information technology capabilities (e.g., specialised warehousing and transportation systems), while specific logistics functions such as transportation and warehousing are externalised or semi-externalised to third-party logistics firms.

## DELIBERATE AND EMERGENT STRATEGIES

Changes in strategic direction require changes in the organisational structure of a company. A diversification or a vertical integration strategy demands that the company must adopt a new organisational structure. Chandler (1962) studied 70 large US corporations and concluded that changes in strategy led to changes in the organisational structure of those corporations. Following Chandler (1962), when a new strategy is formulated new administrative problems emerge, so the organisational performance declines. Following such an organisational performance decline, a new organisational structure is established that improves organisational performance. Chandler's (1962) classic study proposes that a company's organisational structure seems to be not important in the absence of strategy, and more importantly, it should be designed in such a manner as to facilitate the company's strategic actions.

Recent developments in strategy include, *inter alia,* work by Brown and Eisenhardt (1998), who suggest that for those organisations "competing on the edge of order and chaos" there is a platform to survive. The platform to survive and to thrive in such volatile conditions is to plot a delicate strategic path between anarchy and order in a manner that will sustain a continuous competitive advantage. Although such a strategy may seem inefficient against standard survival strategies, it offers a credible alternative. The company may remain in its current business, but actions are shaped by future opportunities by constantly reshaping the firm's competitive advantage.

The "classical school" of strategic thinking (Whittington, 1993) envisages strategy as a deliberate one and views corporations as hierarchies that are directed from the top. Strategy is a rational process designed to achieve a competitive advantage of one organisation over another in the long term. On the contrary, strategy can emerge from a combination of influences within the organisation, and strategy is an emergent rather than a deliberate action (Mintzberg, 1987). Strategies that are imposed top-down, without incorporating other organisational constituencies, are unlikely to be effective, realised strategies. Mintzberg and Waters (1998) state that "comparing intended strategy with realised strategy has allowed us to distinguish deliberate strategies (realised as intended) from emergent strategies (patterns or consistencies realised despite, or in the absence of, intentions)" (see Figure 1).

Although retailing is an evolving and a cut-throat competition market there is little to suggest that a "retail revolution" has taken place (Dawson, 2000). We will try to propose a different perspective on retail change, as it seems to us that changes in retailing emanate from strategic changes starting within a retail company and eventually imitated by other rival retail firms.

# LOGISTICS AND RETAIL STRATEGY

The effective use of a logistics strategy is of primary importance for the implementation and support of a retailing company's strategy. The most common

*Figure 1: Emergent and deliberate strategy*

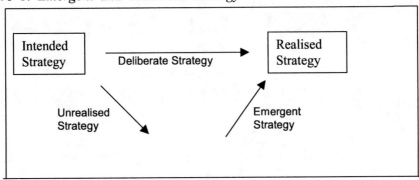

Source: Mintzberg and Waters (1998)

approach to formulate a logistics strategy consists of designing the firm's overall strategy and then defining the logistics strategy that will enable the firm to reach its objectives. Logistics is thus conceived as a functional support system and a tool for assisting the success of the company's domestic and/or international strategy. However, logistics like other functions may open new paths of strategic lines of action, and in order to visualise these new lines it is imperative to convert a logistics strategy into strategic logistics (Fabbe-Costes & Colin, 1999). Strategic logistics is the development of strategic actions that could not be implemented without acquired core logistics competencies after the conversion of logistics from a key factor for success into a fully owned competitive advantage. Table 1 illustrates the above by depicting the different perceptions given to the retail logistics function.

The change of a strategy from an emergent to a deliberate one will also create some sort of internal organisational conflict within the company. The strategic switch from a retail logistics strategy to retail strategic logistics, attributed largely to the rise of logistics competencies into the sphere of a complete competitive advantage for the retail firm, may face "resistance from within." The forthcoming organisational change will not go unnoticed by other divisional managers, as it will lower the importance of their own divisions and their personal influence upon the company's strategy.

# INFORMATION TECHNOLOGY AND RETAIL STRATEGY

Information technology provides the infrastructure for the management of information, and in the area of retailing, it is gradually utilised within food retail logistics as a powerful tool of coordination in the retail channel. Information technology can drive a firm towards domestic expansion and eventually towards internationalisation and also plays a central part in the evolution of retailers' organisational structure.

*Table 1: Retail logistics strategy and retail strategic logistics*

|  | Retail Logistics Strategy | Retail Strategic Logistics |
|---|---|---|
| Perception of logistics | Strategy support | Strategy foundation |
| Effects on organisation | Improvement, evolution | Change, transmutation |
| Major benefit of logistics | Tool to control/reduce costs | Competitive advantage |
| Followed approach | Non-intended, emergent | Intended, deliberate |
| Time sequence of the approach | Reactive | Proactive |
| Logistics' role during retailer's domestic and/or international expansion | Supporting function | Primary importance |

Source: Bourlakis (1997) and Fabbe-Costes and Colin (1999)

The facilitating role of information technology for a retailer acts as a catalyst for domestic expansion and for the transition to an internationally coordinated and managed organisation. Ives, Jarvenpaa, and Mason (1993) mentioned that information technology can drive a firm towards globalisation in a number of ways, and they point out the implementation of many worldwide strategic systems in areas such as procurement, logistics, financial planning, demand forecast and inventory management.

Another area of concern is the broad question of whether information technology is making a contribution to corporate strategy. This contribution can be in the form of three types of relationships, as Lucas and Turner (1987) have argued, depending on the level of integration within strategy formulation (see Table 2).

In the first row of Table 2 we meet the case of independent information systems that help the firm implement strategy by creating greater operational efficiency. These systems are not directly linked to the strategy formulation process or integrated with a strategic plan. A more direct contribution to strategy comes from policy support systems, which are designed to aid the planning process. In this case, the system helps in the formulation of the strategic plan, but offers no platform for strategy foundation in its own right. That is, the system is not part of an end product or service produced by the firm but it is an administrative device to interface the various components of the planning system. The most exciting version takes place when the technology itself becomes a fully integrated element in strategy formulation, as it expands the range of strategic alternatives considered by the firm. In this case, technology bears an integral relation to a company's strategic thinking by helping to define the range of possibilities.

In addition, Ives, Jarvenpaa, and Mason (1993) discuss the global business driver approach, with an objective to provide a close alignment between the firm's global vision and the firm's information technology strategy. The global business drivers are those entities that benefit from global economies of scale and scope and thus contributing to the global business strategy. Once global business drivers are agreed upon, they form the basis for the information technology strategy. In the case of retailing, we contend that global business drivers are the global own brands,

*Table 2: Information technology and corporate strategy*

| Level of Integration with Strategy Formulation | Primary Objective | Secondary Effect |
|---|---|---|
| Independent | Operational efficiency | Managerial information |
| Policy support | Aid repetitive decision making | Better understanding of problem dynamics |
| Fully integrated | Open new products, markets, directions | Change decision making process; alternatives considered; evaluation criteria |

Source: Lucas and Turner (1987)

global customers, global retail formats, and global distribution-logistics. All the above lead to the establishment of an information technology strategy as a facilitating factor (see Figure 2). Dawson (1994) supports the latter and states that "it is hard to imagine how the European hypermarket (business driver) could have become an established form of retailing without information technology." Ives, Jarvenpaa, and Mason (1993) suggest that the most successful prescription for global implementation of business application is a "shared common information-tion technology/data model" with data successfully passed from node to node within a communication network of an electronically wired organisation (see Figure 2).

In an extension to the work carried out by Lucas and Turner (1987) by the authors, we provide in Table 3 the evolution of information technology integration within the logistics and retail logistics strategy formulation. Table 3 presents the three levels that exist in the process of the relevant integration and with examples provided for a retail firm's logistics strategy formulation in the fourth column of Table 3.

Based upon the work of Lucas and Turner (1987), we argue that for the 1st level of integration, independent information technology systems assist the firm to implement its logistics strategy by enhancing operational efficiency. These systems are not directly linked to the logistics strategy formulation process and in our view,

*Figure 2: Global drivers, information technology and the network organisation*

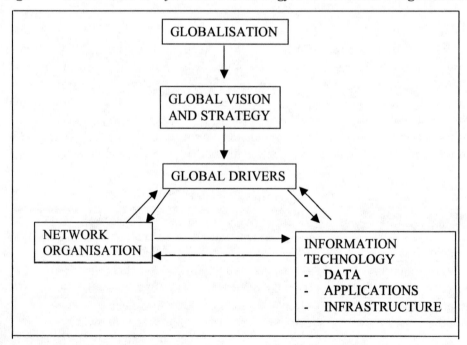

Source : Ives, Jarvenpaa and Mason (1993)

*Table 3: The evolution of information technology systems integration within logistics strategy*

| Level of IT System's Integration within Logistics Strategy Formulation | Primary Objective | Secondary Effect | Examples for Level of IT System's Integration within Retailer's Logistics Strategy Formulation |
|---|---|---|---|
| 1st Level – Independent information technology systems | Increase operational efficiency | Managerial information | Warehouse control systems (e.g., Denver) |
| 2nd Level – Policy support information technology systems | Aid the logistics planning process | Better understanding of logistics problem dynamics | Business planning applications (e.g., accounting systems such as activity-based costing systems dealing with logistics-related activities) |
| 3rd Level – Fully integrated information technology systems | To open new logistics-supported strategic options and to provide the company with a competitive advantage | To change the logistics decision-making process; strategic alternatives considered | EDI, Internet technology |

Table 3 is based on Lucas and Turner (1987) for the first three columns.

most information systems fall into this category. At the 2nd level of integration, policy support systems are designed to aid the logistics planning process and to help management to construct a strategic plan for logistical activities.

At the 3rd level of integration, information technology is fully incorporated within the company's logistics strategy and provides the company with a unique differential competitive advantage. At this stage, information technology facilitates the management of the company to define the range of logistics-supported strategic options open for exploitation. This is the case for EDI that transformed retail logistics operations, as its early users enjoyed a competitive advantage over rival companies (McKinnon, 1990). It is possible that a similar competitive advantage will be bestowed upon the companies that are early movers in the use of the Internet service. It is worth pointing out that according to Roche (1992), information technology started to play a greater part in the strategic expansion plan of the firm from the 1970s onwards, a time when the necessary information technology systems were in place. Roche (1992) argues that due to the weak state of information technology this function followed the firm's overall strategy, although Roche (1992) questions if this is still the case.

# INFORMATION TECHNOLOGY AND THE STRATEGIC RETAIL NETWORK

Information technology has repeatedly played a role in the evolution of organisational structure, largely helped by the fact that the cost of information technology has been steadily falling in recent years. With reference to the network structure, we mean a collection of separate units that create value by virtue of the fact that they are interconnected, so that transactions can take place between them. Networks are not new to the information and the relevant structure is presented in terms of a hierarchy of five levels of business reconfigurations. These configurations levels are presented in Figure 3 and show a framework through which companies assimilate the consequences and benefits of information technology (see Venkatraman, 1991).

The first stage of development is described in Figure 3 as the localised exploitation of information technology and this involves using information technology to help solve a single logistics business problem. This might be the installation of a warehouse control computer or perhaps a vehicle routing program. The second stage of development, the internal integration of information technology, is perhaps best described as the installation of a company-wide database/systems from which all reports are generated. As a result, the internal business process is improved and the

*Figure 3: The five levels of information-technology-induced business reconfiguration*

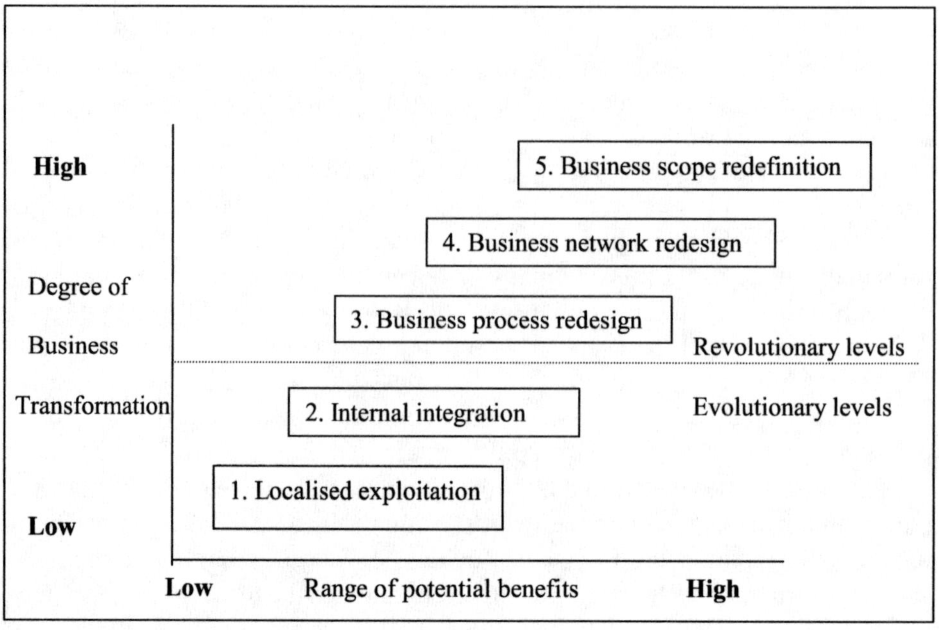

Source : Venkatraman (1991)

same happens for the rest of the business functions. These two levels are viewed as evolutionary, requiring relatively incremental changes in the existing organisational processes. We can name the first two evolutionary levels as information technology strategy levels if we are to make a corresponding configuration to logistics strategy.

In contrast, the other three levels in Figure 3 are conceptualised as revolutionary levels, requiring fundamental changes in the nature of business processes. Following the level of internal integration of their systems, many companies enter stage three, or the "business process redesign" level. At this point the introduction of a major information technology project should enable a company to operate in a new manner. For example, the use of EDI has enabled retail companies to manage stocks and data on a 24-hour basis, instead of being restricted to their normal working hours. In our view, the majority of European retailers fall into the level three category, with the exception of very few retailers that fall into the level four category, described as the "business network redesign" level. This stage is concerned with the reconfiguration of the scope and tasks of the business network and includes the business tasks within and outside the formal boundaries of a focal organisation and the consequent redesign of this "virtual business network" through information technology capabilities.

The final development stage is defined as the "business scope redefinition" stage where the retailer will manage everything via an information technology network and will subcontract most of its operations (e.g., to open retail outlets under a franchising agreement or to assign its logistics operations to third-party companies). Therefore, levels three, four and five are classified as revolutionary ones and can be named as strategic information technology levels, where the emergent information technology strategies from levels one and two have matured into deliberate strategies in levels three, four and five.

# THE PROPOSED SIMULTANEOUS EQUATIONS FRAMEWORK

In the present section the authors argue that a *simultaneity* issue is embedded within the retail change process based upon their work carried in Bourlakis and Bourlakis (2000). Consider, for example, the dominant retailers with a large volume of profits (PROFIT) and market share (MS). Dominant retailers are in a favourable position to invest proportionally more on information technology and logistics, as well as to sustain intensive advertising campaigns in an effort to retain and enhance their market position and to protect their competitive advantage. A large market share alongside the production of a range of its own brand items may also reward the retailer with higher pecuniary economies in its negotiations with suppliers and credit organizations. In turn, if successful over time, logistics and information technology related spending by a large retailers would cause a further increase in profits by lowering the cost of operations. Higher profits will be ploughed back to successfully implemented deliberate strategies as the retailer expects further beneficial feedback effects on profits and market share from such an investment (see Figure 4).

Figure 4 shows that potential correlations found between large market shares and the profits for retailers are spurious, because of the potential inter-relationships among market share, profits, information technology, and logistics, and information technology strategies. That is, market share and profits for retailers are simultaneously determined by the successful implementation of logistics and information technology deliberate strategies as shown graphically in Figure 4.

We argue that it is the relevant switch of an activity from emergent to deliberate that changes the nature of the core competitive advantage of the retailer. For that reason, a simultaneous equations framework is formulated that includes as endogenous variables retailers' characteristics related to their current retail format and as exogenous variables those variables related to the increase of the competive advantage such as information technology and logistics. The influence of an *emergent strategy* should have no significant impact upon a retailer's market share and profits. A *deliberate strategy,* however, should significantly raise both profits and market share for retailers. If an information technology strategy and a logistics strategy turn into strategic information technology and strategic logistics, then the core competitive advantage of the retail firm has been changed and they should have a significant impact upon market share and profits. In turn, however, the portfolio of deliberate strategies becomes endogenous to the system as large retailers with high profits spend proportionally more on information technology and logistics. Over time, other emergent strategies that have been successfully switched into deliberate strategies will also become endogenous to the system by inducing retail change.

The retail change process can be represented by a series of simultaneous interdependent equations where a company's performance and market share are simultaneously determined by the interaction of logistics and information technology. From this point of view we consider the retail change as consisting of a series of equations, each equation serving to explain one variable as a function of a portfolio of emergent strategies.

*Figure 4: Simultaneity within the process of retail change*

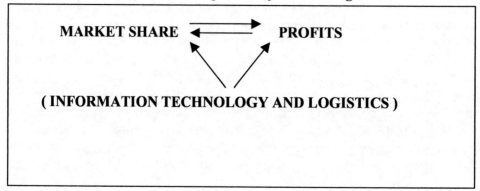

MARKET SHARE (MS) EQUATION:

$$MS = A_0 + A_1 \, PROFIT + A_2 \, INFORMATION \, TECHNOLOGY + A_3 \, LOGISTICS + U_{MS}$$

PROFITABILITY EQUATION (PROFIT):

$$PROFIT = B_0 + B_1 \, MS + B_2 \, INFORMATION \, TECHNOLOGY + B_3 \, LOGISTICS + U_{PROFIT}$$

where $U_{MS}$ and $U_{PROFIT}$ are the stochastic disturbance terms.

The variables LOGISTICS and INFORMATION TECHNOLOGY are exogenous variables as they are determined within the system of equations, while the PROFIT and MARKET SHARE variables are endogenously determined within the system of equations.

It should be noted again that over time one of the independent variables will become endogenous to the system as a fully embedded competitive advantage within the retailer's organisational structure, so it can be included as a separate equation within the simultaneous equations framework. For example, if we suppose that the LOGISTICS variable has switched from an emergent strategy to a deliberate strategy, we obtain a third equation with logistics as the dependent variable as follows:

$$LOGISTICS = C_0 + C_1 \, MS + C_2 \, PROFIT + C_3 \, INFORMATION \, TECHNOLOGY + U_{LOGISTICS}$$

where $U_{LOGISTICS}$ is the relevant stochastic disturbance term.

# LOGISTICS, INFORMATION TECHNOLOGY AND RETAIL STRATEGY

Armed with all the previously exposed theoretical background, we are well-placed to round up our argument in the section that follows. At an early stage logistics is a competitive advantage that is "available for buying it" (it is internal) to all firms in the retail sector, but it is not incorporated (it is external) into the retail firms' strategy process. At this stage retail firms envisage the potential benefits that can be derived from logistics, and they start developing a logistics strategy by investing in logistical operations. In terms of the strategy process, retail firms are getting involved in an (emergent) logistics strategy. In the course of the competitive process, information technology at its early stage is also a competitive advantage that is internal to the retail sector, but it is external to the retail firms' strategy process. In a similar strategic context, retail firms foresee the potential competitive benefits than can accrue to them by the use of information technology, so retail firms spend heavily upon crafting and implementing an (emergent) information technology strategy. The appearance of the newly arrived (emergent) information technology strategy should have an inter-temporal "side effect" upon the existing (emergent) logistics strategy. The "side effect" of the information technology strategy upon the existing logistics strategy gives rise to a "new combined emergent strategy" that is gradually absorbed (internalised) within the retailer's overall strategy process. Upon the completion of the internalisation process, logistics and information technology become internal to the retailer's strategy process, and a realised (deliberate) *logistics-information technology strategy* emerges for the retailer. In strategic terms, logistics and information technology are no more cost-reduction functions but have been transformed to fully fledged strategic supply chain coordination weapons. The strategy process has entered the phase where the logistics strategy has been switched to *strategic logistics* and the information technology strategy has been converted to *strategic information technology*, and the retail firm is rewarded with a unique and fully owned supply chain coordination competitive advantage. The retailer is now in a position to use in a fully fledged *deliberate* strategic manner, the unique and fully owned *logistics-information technology strategy* against rival retail firms.

We can clarify the argument in "a step by step" manner in Figure 5. Firms formulate their overall strategy in a manner that the logistics strategy can fit in and in order to enable the firm to reach its objectives. Following this reasoning, Fabbe-Costes and Colin (1999) argued that logistics is usually conceived as a supporting function that facilitates a firm's domestic and international expansion (the logistics strategy approach). However, in the course of the strategy process, logistics can become the platform of a firm's strategic action. Logistics, from being a major supporting factor in its early days, can be the source of a firm's competitive advantage in the longer run (the strategic logistics approach) as Figure 5 depicts.

*Figure 5: Information technology strategy and strategic information technology*

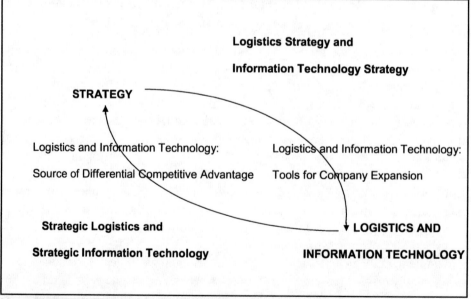

Note: Figure 5 is based upon the work carried out by Fabbe-Costes and Colin (1999) to distinguish between a company's logistics strategy and a company's strategic logistics.

We incorporate in the present work the important part played by information technology upon the competitive process described above. Companies formulate their strategy in such a way that—at an initial stage—the logistics strategy and the information technology strategy can fit in together as cost-reducing supporting functions (the logistics strategy and the information technology strategy approach). In a similar fashion, in the course of the strategy process, information technology and logistics interact with each other and switch from being major supporting factors to a differential competitive advantage (the strategic logistics and the strategic information technology approach), as illustrated in Figure 5.

In Bourlakis and Bourlakis (2001) the argument cited above was examined for the retail sector as far as the logistics function is concerned. The authors identified the differences between retail logistics strategy and retail strategic logistics based upon specific parameters that represent a wide spectrum of organisational, strategic and other issues (see Table 4). We must point out that the first two parameters in Table 4, namely, the "perception of logistics" and the "effects on organisation", are based on the work carried out by Fabbe-Costes and Colin (1999). In Table 4 (final row), the strategic approach followed by retailers in their information technology and logistics operations is also illustrated.

This approach can be the outcome of an intended/deliberate strategy, directed from a firm's headquarters. This is in line with the "classical" school of thinking (Chandler, 1962; Whittington, 1993) where the focus of strategies (including the information technology strategy and the logistics strategy) is seen as deliberate and rational, directed towards profit maximisation, and it is, therefore, in the restricted

*Table 4: From retail logistics strategy and retail information technology strategy to retail strategic logistics and retail strategic information technology*

| Parameters | Retail Logistics Strategy and Retail Information Technology Strategy | Retail Strategic Logistics and Retail Strategic Information Technology |
|---|---|---|
| Perception of logistics and information technology | Strategy support | Strategy foundation |
| Effects on organisation | Improvement, evolution | Change, transmutation |
| Major benefit of logistics and information technology | Tool to control/reduce Costs | Source of firm's competitive advantage |
| Logistics' and information technology's roles in retail strategy | Secondary importance | Primary importance |
| Time sequence of the approach | Reactive | Proactive |
| Strategic approach | Non-intended, emergent | Intended, deliberate |

Note: Table 4 is an extension of the work carried out in Bourlakis (1997) and in Bourlakis and Bourlakis (2001) to distinguish between logistics strategy and strategic logistics.

domain of top management. On the other hand, the information technology strategy and the logistics strategy can be seen as nonrational processes that emerge from a combination of influences within the organisation. As we mentioned before, from this perspective, Mintzberg's (1987) and Mintzberg's and Water's (1998) views are the best known. According to Mintzberg (1987) and Mintzberg and Waters (1998), the information technology strategy and the logistics strategy are regarded as being emergent, rather than deliberate strategies, as those strategies which are imposed top-down, without incorporating other organisational constituencies, are unlikely to be effective, realised strategies.

As stated above, upon the completion of the competitive advantage internalisation process, the logistics strategy and the information technology strategy become internal to the retailer's strategy process and they have been transformed to *strategic logistics* and *strategic information technology* company devices. The retail firm is now in a supply chain management "captaincy" position to create a retail network, either in the form of third-party logistics, and/or in the form of the retailer running their own logistics operations. The retail firm is also in a good position to expand in and to penetrate foreign markets by carrying its unique competitive advantage of strategic logistics and strategic information technology abroad.

# THE FORMATION OF INTERNATIONAL STRATEGIC RETAIL NETWORKS

At this stage we can bring into our analysis the integration-transaction costs framework suggested in Bourlakis (1998) and presented in Figure 6. The strategic retail network in Figure 6 is the recommended organisational mode in the case where (internal) organisation and transactions costs are especially high.

During internationalisation, a company faces the same choices in terms of how to coordinate its activities in the local market and so the whole issue of externalise/internalise across borders becomes of strategic importance. It can be argued that organisational costs across borders tend to be higher than domestically—it is the traditional concept of the "extra expense of doing business abroad." For example communication, transportation and monitoring activities tend to be more expensive when compared to organising domestically. In addition, transaction costs are also higher across borders due to, for instance, the high cost of information gathering and creation of specific assets. For food retailing, it can be argued that if retail logistics-related transaction costs are high and integration-organisation costs are low, internalisation through their own account distribution will take place, provided that the retailer has an advantage in operating its own distribution abroad (see Figure 6).

On the other hand, if organisation costs are high and transaction costs low, a contract distribution (externalisation) is more appropriate. Furthermore, with both low transaction costs and low organisation costs, the final choice will depend on reasons such as the company's history, its financial status, the existence of logistics service providers abroad and the general cost efficiency of such choices. The

*Figure 6: Organisational modes for food multiples, depending on the level of transaction costs/integration costs and the externalise/internalise decision*

| | | **Organisation–Integration Costs** | |
| --- | --- | --- | --- |
| | | **High** | **Low** |
| **Transaction Costs** | **High** | International Strategic Retail Network | Own Account Distribution |
| | **Low** | Contract Distribution | Own Account or Contract Distribution or Both |

Note: Figure 6 is based upon the work carried out in Bourlakis (1998) on organisational modes for national and international food multiples depending on the level of transaction costs/ integration costs and the externalise/internalise decision.

choices can be either the own account distribution or the contract distribution or both. The international strategic retail network (Figure 6), which is an attempt by the authors to apply the "network approach" within retailing, is the optimal organisational mode in the case where both costs (internal organisation and transactions) are especially high across borders, and there is an advantage from coordinating worldwide operations closely. This mode is also able to capture the main advantages of organisations considered as autonomous units, and according to Jarillo (1988) "strategic networks are long-term, purposeful arrangements among distinct but related for-profit organisations that allow those firms in them to gain or sustain competitive advantage vis-à-vis their competitors outside the network." Within the international strategic retail network, one company (e.g., a food retail multiple) takes the role of "central controller" and organises the flow of products and information among itself and the service providers (e.g., logistics service providers), which are independent companies. A very close relationship is being gradually formed then which is based on the achievement of the same goals and understanding that there will be more to gain when working closely. The latter will be greatly enhanced if the retailer possesses the strategic information technology and the strategic logistics competitive advantages.

Using the framework in Figure 6, Bourlakis (1998) examined the formation of the retail network mode between a food retail multiple and third-party logistics firms based on the examination of transaction and organisation costs accruing during the retailer's domestic and international expansion. Bourlakis (1998) argued that this mode was followed when both organisation and transaction costs are high and stressed Marks and Spencer as a primary example of a food multiple pursuing the "strategic retail network" path. In Bourlakis (2001) it was found that DIA, the international food discounter owned by Carrefour/Promodès, has been following a "deliberate" international logistics strategy and a "deliberate" information technology strategy in its supply chain operations. DIA followed two distinctly different strategic routes in its logistics operations by externalising its transportation operations to third-party logistics firms all over Europe while at the same time internalising its warehousing operations. DIA has developed a European retail network controlled and managed by the firm's own information technology capabilities.

However, third-party firms can challenge the supply chain management "captaincy" status of a retailer within the retail network if they possess a superior information technology advantage or if they possess logistics-related specific assets that are prohibitively high for retailers to own. For example, the ownership of a heavy transportation fleet by third-party companies may prove to be a "sunk costs" asset for the retailer if the retailer is not in a position to use it for its full line of products.

## CONCLUDING REMARKS

The authors' objective was to introduce the concept of strategic information technology and to associate it with the formation of the "international strategic retail network." Undoubtedly, we live in an era in which retailers reconsider their overall strategic positioning, either in terms of vertical integration (see, for example, Jennings, 2001, on "Thornton's" strategy), or in terms of subcontracting networks as an alternative to internalisation (see, Cox, Mowatt & Prevezer, 1999). The authors hope that the strategic information technology route in conjunction with the strategic logistics approach may offer further insight into the strategic management of the supply chain.

Finally, and by discussing the relevant issue in a rather philosophical mood at this point in time, we suggest that traditional manufacturing activity may be completely wiped out by retailers' advance in international markets. Traditional manufacturers nowadays face a credible threat by the commitment of the retailers to integrate backwards and to control the supply chain in order to extract maximum upstream profits. The international expansion of retailers will undoubtedly rise their degree of oligopsonistic power against manufacturers, and in the course of the retailers' international expansion, we may experience in parallel a strategic upstream retail integration at home and abroad with the ultimate task to replace manufacturers in the 21st century.

## REFERENCES

Arrow, K. J. (1969). The organisation of economic activity. In *The Analysis and Evaluation of Public Expenditure: The PPB System*. Joint Economic Committee, 91st Congress, 1st Session, Washington, DC: U.S. Government Printing Office.

Bourlakis, M. (1997). Transaction costs, internationalisation and logistics: The case of European food retailing. Paper presented at the *9th International Conference on Research in the Distributive Trades,* July, Leuven, Belgium.

Bourlakis, M. (1998). Transaction costs, internationalisation and logistics: The case of European food retailing. *International Journal of Logistics: Research and Applications, 1*(3), 251–264.

Bourlakis, M. (2001). *Logistics strategies in domestic and international expansion: The case of the Greek food multiple retail sector. Unpublished doctoral thesis,* University of Edinburgh, United Kingdom.

Bourlakis, M. & Bourlakis, C. (2000). A simultaneous equations framework of retail change. Paper presented at the *International Conference on Research in the Distributive Trades on Retail Innovation, ESADE,* July, Ramon Llull University, Barcelona, Spain.

Bourlakis, M. & Bourlakis, C. (2001). Deliberate and emergent logistics strategies in food retailing: A case study of the Greek multiple food retail sector. *Supply Chain Management: An International Journal, 6*(4), 189-200.

Brown, S. L. & Eisenhardt, K. M. (1998). *Competing on the edge, strategy as structured chaos.* Boston: Harvard Business School Press.

Chandler, A. D. (1962). *Strategy and Structure.* Cambridge, MA: MIT Press.

Coase, R. H. (1937). The nature of the firm. *Economica, 4,* November, 386-405.

Cox, H., Mowatt, S. & Prevezer, M. (1999). The management of subcontracted networks as an alternative to internalisation: The shift from the standardised to the specialised in frozen and chilled foods. *Research Papers in International Business, Paper Number 16–99,* South Bank University.

Dawson, J. A. (1994). Applications of information management in European retailing. *The International Review of Retail, Distribution and Consumer Research, 4*(2), 219-238.

Dawson, J. A. (2000). Retailing at century end: Some challenges for management and research. *The International Review of Retail, Distribution and Consumer Research, 10*(2), 119-148.

Fabbe-Costes, N. & Colin, J. (1999). Formulating logistics strategy. In D. Waters (Ed.), *Global Logistics and Distribution Planning* (3rd ed., pp.63-84). London: Kogan Page.

Ives, B., Jarvenpaa, S. L. & Mason, R .O. (1993). Global business drivers: Aligning information technology to global business strategy. *IBM Systems Journal, 32*(1), 132-156.

Jarillo, J. C. (1988). On strategic networks. *Strategic Management Journal, 9*(1), 31-41.

Jennings, D. (2001). Thorntons: The vertically integrated retailer, questioning the strategy. *International Journal of Retail and Distribution Management, 29*(4), 176-187.

Levy, D. T. (1985). The transaction cost approach to vertical integration: An empirical examination. *Review of Economics and Statistics, 67,* August, 438-445.

Lucas, H. C., Jr., & Turner, J .A. (1987). A corporate strategy for the control of information processing. In S. E. Madnick (Ed.), *The Strategic Use of Information Technology,* Oxford, England: Oxford University Press.

McKinnon, A. C. (1990). Electronic data interchange in the retail supply chain. *International Journal of Retail and Distribution Management, 18*(2), 39-42.

Mintzberg, H. (1987). Crafting strategy. *Harvard Business Review, 65*(1), 65-75.

Mintzberg, H. & Waters, J. A. (1998). Of strategies, deliberate and emergent. In S. Segal-Horn (Ed.), *The Strategy Reader,* 20-34. Oxford: Blackwell.

Porter, M. E. (1980). *Competitive Strategy.* New York: The Free Press.

Ramanujam, V. & Varadarajan, P. (1989). Research on corporate diversification: a synthesis. *Strategic Management Journal, 10,* 523-551.

Roche, E. M. (1992). *Managing Information Technology in Multinational Corporations.* London: Macmillan.

Venkatraman, N. (1991). Information technology induced business reconfiguration. In M. S. Morton (Ed.), *The Corporation of the 1990s,* 116-135. Oxford: Oxford University Press.

Whittington, R. (1993). *What is Strategy–And Does it Matter?* London: Routledge.

Williamson, O. E. (1971). On the vertical integration of production: Market failure considerations. *American Economic Review, 61*(2), 112-123.

Williamson, O. E. (1975). *Markets and Hierarchies: Analysis and Antitrust Implications.* New York: Free Press.

Williamson, O. E. (1985). *The Economic Institutions of Capitalism.* New York: Free Press.

## Chapter XVI

# Managing Data Quality in Accounting Information Systems

Hongjiang Xu, Andy Koronios and Noel Brown
University of Southern Queensland, Australia

## ABSTRACT

*Information is the key resource of today's organizations, and therefore, quality information is critical to organizations' success. Accounting information systems (AIS) in particular, requires high quality information. This chapter discusses critical success factors for data quality in accounting information systems. A model for factors that impact on data quality in AIS was proposed, and then examined in seven Australian case studies. The detailed discussion of each factor was included, and it was found that* education and training, nature of AIS, *and* top management commitment *are the most critical factors. The findings of the study would help organizations to focus on important factors to obtain better benefit from less effort. Top management, IT and accounting professionals should be able to gain the better understanding of accounting information systems' data quality management from the discussion of this chapter.*

# INTRODUCTION

Today's organizations are operating and competing in an information age. Information has become a key resource of most organizations, economies, and societies. Indeed, an organization's basis for competition has changed from tangible products to intangible information. More and more organizations are realising that quality information is critical to their success; however, not many of them have turned this realisation into effective actions. Poor quality information can have significant social and business impacts (Strong, Lee & Wang, 1997). There is strong evidence that data quality problems are becoming increasingly prevalent in practice (Redman, 1998; Wand & Wang, 1996). Many organizations have experienced the adverse effects of decisions based on information of inferior quality (Huang, Lee & Wang, 1999). It is likely that some data stakeholders are not satisfied in the quality of the information delivered in their organizations. In brief, information quality issues have become critical for organizations that want to perform well, obtain competitive advantage, or even just survive in the 21st century.

Accounting information systems (AIS) maintain and produce the data used by organizations to plan, evaluate, and diagnose the dynamics of operations and financial circumstances (Anthony, Reese & Herrenstein, 1994). AIS's data quality is concerned with detecting the presence or absence of target error classes in the accounts (Kaplan, Krishnan, Padman & Peters, 1998). Providing and assuring quality data is an objective of accounting. With the advent of AIS, the traditional focus on the input and recording of data needs to be offset with recognition that the systems themselves may affect the quality of data (Fedorowicz & Lee, 1998). Indeed, empirical evidence suggests that data quality is problematic in AIS (Johnson, Leitch, & Neter, 1981).

Thus, knowledge of the critical factors that influence data quality in AIS will assist organizations to improve their accounting information systems' data quality. While many AIS studies have looked at internal control and audit, data quality (DQ) studies focused on measurement of DQ outcomes. It appears that very few attempts to identify the critical success factors (CSF) for improving data quality in AIS. Thus, there is a need for research to identify the critical success factors that affect organizations' AIS DQ.

Information technology has changed the way in which traditional accounting systems work. There is more and more electronically captured information that needs to be processed, stored, and distributed through IT-based accounting systems. Advanced IT has dramatically increased the ability and capability of processing accounting information. At the same time, however, it also brings some issues that the traditional accounting systems have not experienced. One critical issue is the data quality in the AIS. When data quality issues have not been addressed properly, the IT advantages can sometimes create problems rather than benefit the organization. Information overload as an example; do we really need the quantity of information generated by the systems to make the right decision? Equally, in e-commence settings, can the quality of data captured online be trusted?

Data quality has become crucial for the AIS's success in today's IT age. Therefore, knowledge of those factors that are important in ensuring the data quality in accounting information systems is desirable, because those factors can increase the operating efficiency of the AIS and contribute to the effectiveness of management decision making.

The objectives of this chapter are:
- define data and information quality,
- discuss the critical success factors (CSF) of data quality in accounting information systems (AIS),
- propose a model for factors that impact on data quality in AIS, and
- conclude and summarize the important factors for data quality in AIS from the case studies analysis.

# BACKGROUND

## Data Quality (DQ)

There appears to be no single standard definition of data quality accepted within the field (Klein, 1998). Traditionally, data quality has been described from the perspective of accuracy. Nowadays, research and practice indicate that data quality should be defined beyond accuracy and is identified as encompassing multiple dimensions (Huang et al., 1999). Commonly identified data quality dimensions include:

- *accuracy*, which occurs when the recorded value is in conformity with the actual value;
- *timeliness*, which occurs when the recorded value is not out-of-date;
- *completeness*, which occurs when all values for a certain variable are recorded; and
- *consistency*, which occurs when the representation of the data values is the same in all cases (Ballou, Belardo & Klein, 1987; Ballou & Pazer, 1982, 1985, 1987; Ballou, Wang, Pazer & Tayi, 1993).

Four other data quality dimensions have been identified (Wang & Strong, 1996) and are also widely accepted. They are:

- *Intrinsic* dimensions, which define the quality of data in its own right;
- *contextual* dimensions, which define data quality within the context of the task at hand;
- *accessibility* dimensions, which emphasize the role of information systems in providing data; and
- *representational* dimensions, which define data quality in terms of the presentation and delivery of data.

Sometimes, data quality and information quality are treated as different terms. For example, traditionally, data is treated as a collection of symbols which signify real-world system states and are brought together because they are considered relevant to some purposeful activity; while information is considered to be *processed* data. However, in our discussion, data quality and information quality will be used synonymously.

## Accounting Information Systems (AIS)

In order to understand data quality issues in AIS in particular, it is important to define the term of AIS. Accounting information system process both financial and nonfinancial records that directly affect the processing of financial transactions. An accounting information system comprises four major subsystems:

1.   the *transaction processing system*, which supports daily business operations with numerous documents and messages for users throughout the organization;
2.   the *general ledger/financial reporting system*, which produces the traditional financial statements, such as the income statement, balance sheet, statement of cash flows, tax return, and other reports required by law;
3.   the *fixed asset system*, which processes transactions pertaining to the acquisition, maintenance, and disposal of fixed assets; and
4.   the *management reporting system*, which provides internal management with special purpose financial reports and information needed for decision making, such as budgets, variance reports, and responsibility reports (Hall, 1998).

## Data Quality within Accounting Information Systems

Within accounting and auditing, where internal control systems require maximum reliability with minimum cost, the key data quality dimension used is *accuracy*—defined in terms of the frequency, size, and distribution of errors in data (Wang, Storey & Firth, 1995). In assessing the value of accounting information, researchers have also identified *relevance* and *timeliness* as desirable attributes (Feltham, 1968). The focus in this chapter will be on the dimensions of accuracy, timeliness, completeness, and consistency of data.

## Stakeholder Groups in Data Quality within Accounting Information Systems

In order to understand how stakeholder groups may impact on accounting information quality, it is essential to identify their relationships with accounting information systems. The framework for understanding stakeholders in accounting information systems proposed in Figure 1 combines the stakeholder concepts from data quality, data warehouse, accounting information systems and quality management areas.

In data quality and data warehouse areas, four stakeholder groups who are responsible for creating, maintaining, using, and managing data have been identified. These groups are: data producers, data custodians, data consumers, and data managers (Strong et al., 1997; Wang, 1998; Shanks & Darke, 1998). In the accounting information systems area, auditors are recognized as fulfilling the role of monitoring how the accounting information systems work and the quality of the information generated by the systems (Gay, Schelluch & Baines, 1998; Pae & Yoo,

*Figure 1: A framework for the understanding of relationships between stakeholder groups and data quality in accounting information systems*

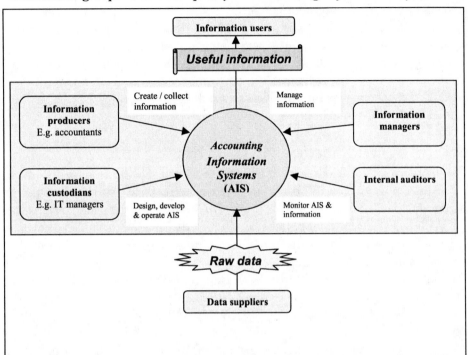

2001). Internal auditors normally perform the internal policing and quality advising roles within the organization. While data quality research focussed on the processing, and accounting management focussed on the results checking and monitoring, the quality management area, the source where raw data originates, was also addressed. In the quality management literature, supplier quality management has been highlighted as the important aspect of the total quality management (Saraph, Benson & Schroeder, 1989; Badri, Davis & Davis, 1995).

In summary and combined with the above-mentioned areas, the stakeholder groups in accounting information systems have now been identified as follows:

- *Information producers*: create or collect information for the AIS;
- *Information custodians*: design, develop and operate the AIS;
- *Information users*: use the accounting information in their work;
- *Information managers*: are responsible for managing the information quality in the AIS;
- *Internal auditors*: monitor the AIS and its data quality and check internal controls in the AIS; and
- *Data suppliers*: provide the unorganized raw data to the AIS.

In accounting information systems, different stakeholders have different functional roles in relation to the quality of the information. The framework that is provided in Figure 1 relates all the stakeholders to accounting information systems at three different levels. The lowest level contains only one stakeholder group, the data suppliers who provide unorganized raw data to the AIS. It represents the input stage, at which raw data is entered into the AIS. In the middle level, there exist four stakeholder groups, namely, information producers, information custodians, information managers, and internal auditors, who are responsible for creating and collecting the information and for designing, developing and operating the AIS, as well as managing information and monitoring the AIS and information. In addition, this middle level contains the processing, storing, maintaining, and monitoring stages. The highest level contains the information users and serves to distribute the organized, useful information to the information users; i.e., it is the output stage.

## Critical Success Factors for Data Quality in AIS

In order to ensure data quality in AIS, it is important to understand the underlying factors that influence the AIS's data quality. Knowledge of the critical success factors that constitute an AIS having high data quality is desirable but is still unclear at this time.

Although the critical success factors for high data quality in AIS have not been addressed, there have been many studies of critical success factors in quality management such as total quality management (TQM) and just-in-time (JIT) (Saraph et al, 1989; Porter & Parker, 1993; Black & Porter, 1996; Badri et al., 1995; Yusof & Aspinwall, 1999). Some of the data quality literature has addressed the critical points and steps for DQ (Firth, 1996; Segev, 1996; Huang et al., 1999; English, 1999).

Table 1 indicates the related research efforts and reflects whether these research efforts addressed certain issues or elements of critical success factors of quality or data quality management.

# ISSUES AND MODELS

It is important to identify the critical success factors for data quality in accounting information systems as this will enhance the AIS ability in gathering data, processing information and preparing reports. It also assists the organization's management, accountants, and IT managers to better safeguard the data resources of the organization. A model is proposed in Figure 2 which will assist in gaining an understanding of the critical factors that constitute data quality.

It is useful to group the critical success factors into different categories in order to have a broader overview of their effect on data quality in accounting information systems in both organizational and external environments. These categories are:
- AIS characteristics,
- DQ characteristics,
- external factors,
- organizational factors, and
- stakeholders' related factors.

The model represents five constructs at three levels. The first level is the external environment, which consists external factors; the second level is the

*Table 1: Summary of literature review identifying factors influencing data quality*

| Factor | Saraph (1989) | English (1999) | Firth (1996) | Wang (1998, 1999) | Segev (1996) | Zhu (1995) | Birkett (1986) | Yu (1973) Cushing (1974) Fields (1986) Nichols (1987) | Johnson (1981) Groomer (1989) | Bowen (1993) |
|---|---|---|---|---|---|---|---|---|---|---|
| Role of top management | ✔ | ✔ | ✔ | ✔ | ✔ | ✔ | | | | |
| (Data) quality polices & standards | | | ✔ | ✔ | ✔ | | | | | |
| Role of (data) quality & (data) quality manager | ✔ | ✔ | ✔ | ✔ | ✔ | ✔ | | | | |
| Training | ✔ | ✔ | | ✔ | | ✔ | | | | |
| Organizational structure | | ✔ | | | | ✔ | | | | |
| Nature of the system Product/service design | ✔ | | | | ✔ | | | | | |
| Approaches (control & improvement) Process management | ✔ | ✔ | | ✔ | ✔ | | | | | |
| Employee/ personnel relations | ✔ | | ✔ | | | ✔ | | | | |
| Supplier quality management | ✔ | | | ✔ | | ✔ | | | | |
| Performance evaluation and rewards (responsibility for DQ) | | ✔ | | ✔ | | | ✔ | | | |
| Manage change | | ✔ | | | | | | | | |
| External factors | | | | | | | ✔ | | | |
| Evaluate cost/benefit tradeoffs | | | | | ✔ | ✔ | | | | |
| Audits | | | | | | | | | ✔ | |
| Internal control (systems, process) | | | | | | | | ✔ | | |
| Input control | | | | | | | | | | ✔ |
| Customer focus | | | ✔ | | | | | | | |
| Continuous improvement | | ✔ | | | | | | | | |

organizational environment, which consists of organizational factors; and the third level is the accounting information systems, which both have AIS and DQ characteristics.

The stockholders' categories exist in all the above-mentioned levels. The distribution of stakeholder groups is shown in Table 2. They could exist within and outside the AIS as well as within and outside the organization. For example, AIS could have both internal and external information suppliers and customers.

# DATA QUALITY IN AIS CASE STUDIES

Multiple case studies were conducted in seven Australian organizations; four of them were chosen from large organizations, and three from small to medium organizations (SMEs). Table 3 summarizes the different groupings interviewed in the seven cases.

*Figure 2: Categories of factors that impact on data quality in accounting information systems*

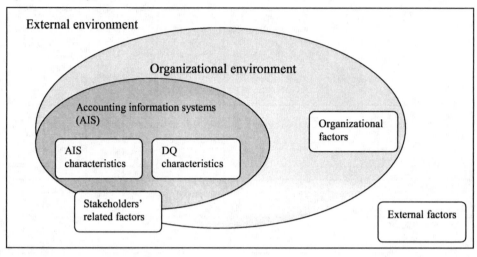

*Table 2: Distributions of the stakeholder groups*

|                     | **Within the Organization** | **Outside the Organization** |
|---------------------|:---------------------------:|:----------------------------:|
| **Within the AIS**  | X                           | X                            |
| **Outside the AIS** | X                           | -                            |

*Table 3: Summary of case study interviews*

| Stakeholders Category | Position within the organization | | | | | | |
|---|---|---|---|---|---|---|---|
|  | **Large organizations** | | | | **SMEs** | | |
|  | **A** | **B** | **C** | **D** | **E** | **F** | **G** |
| **Data producers** | Financial manager | System accountant manager | Director of finance | Accountants | CFO & Accounting officer | CFO | System accountant |
| **Data custodians** | IT manager | IT manager | IT manager | IT manager | IT manager | IT manager | IS manager |
| **Data consumers** | Senior manager | Senior manager | Senior manager | Users | General user | User | N/A |
| **Data / database managers** | Data manager & DA | DBA | DBA | DA | N/A | N/A | N/A |
| **Internal auditors** | Internal auditors | Internal auditor | Director of internal audit | Internal auditors | N/A | N/A | Internal auditor |

The cases included an educational enterprise, a government-funded research institution, a public utility, a private national agricultural enterprise and a government department. The large organizations included all the categories of stakeholders while the small to medium-sized enterprises only included a few of the stakeholder groupings. These were: data producers, data custodians and data consumers. The findings of those seven case studies are summarized in the Table 4.

# IMPORTANT FACTORS THAT IMPACT ON DATA QUALITY IN ACCOUNTING INFORMATION SYSTEMS

Following the cross-stakeholders and cross-case analyses, a set of factors was derived. Some of those factors were similar to the previous literature, while some other factors were "new." Each of these factors will be discussed, commencing with the "new" factors identified by the case studies and which have not appeared in the current literature.

## New Factors

- Teamwork (communication)
- Risk management
- Middle management's commitment to DQ
- Personnel competency
- Physical environment
- Organizational culture of focusing on DQ
- Understanding of the systems and DQ

### Teamwork

Working means working as a team and having sufficient communication, and is not only within the department, but also between different departments. More often, people in different sections within the organization lack sufficient communication to be able to work as a whole team, rather than only working within their own small area. Furthermore, it is also an issue between different professionals, such as accounting and IT. It is often heard that accounting professionals complain about the new technology and could not obtain enough support from IT professionals. Conversely, IT people complain that businesspeople do not know what they really need and request something that is not worth doing or is already provided by the system. This lack of teamwork effort could potentially cause data quality problems.

### Risk Management

Risk management can be defined as the awareness of and level of commitment to the reduction of the consequences of poor DQ on AIS. Awareness of risk would enable the organisation to identify the key areas and critical factors to ensure DQ in AIS.

*Table 4: Summary of case studies findings*

| Cases / Factors | Large organizations | | | | SMEs | | |
|---|---|---|---|---|---|---|---|
| | A | B | C | D | E | F | G |
| Top management commitment to DQ | ✔ | ✔ | ✔ | ✔ | ✔ | ✔ | ? |
| Middle management commitment | ✔ | ? | ✔ | ✔ | ✘ | ✔ | ✔ |
| Education and training | ✔ | ✔ | ✔ | ✔ | ✔ | ✔ | ✔ |
| Clear DQ vision | ✔ | ? | ✔ | ? | ? | ✔ | ? |
| Establish DQ manager position | ✘ | ✘ | ✘ | ✘ | ✘ | ✘ | ✘ |
| Appropriate organizational structure | ✘ | ✘ | ? | ✔ | ? | ✘ | ✔ |
| DQ policies and standards | ✔ | ✘ | ✔ | ✔ | ? | ✘ | ✘ |
| Organizational culture | ✔ | ✔ | ✔ | ✔ | ✔ | ✔ | ✔ |
| DQ controls | - | ✔ | ✔ | ✔ | ✔ | - | - |
| Input controls | ✔ | ✔ | ✔ | ✔ | ✔ | ✔ | ✔ |
| User focus | ✔ | ? | ✔ | ✔ | ✔ | ✔ | ✔ |
| Nature of the AIS | ✔ | ✔ | ✔ | ✔ | ✔ | ✔ | ✔ |
| Effective employee relations | ✔ | ? | - | ✔ | ? | ✘ | ✔ |
| Management of changes | ✔ | ✔ | ? | - | ✔ | ✔ | - |
| Performance evaluation (measurement and reporting) | ✘ | ✘ | ? | ✘ | ✔ | ✘ | ✘ |
| Data supplier quality management | ✔ | ✔ | ✔ | ✔ | ✔ | ✘ | ✔ |
| Continuous improvement | ✔ | ? | ✔ | ✔ | ✔ | - | - |
| Teamwork (communication) | ✔ | - | - | ✔ | ✔ | ✔ | - |
| Evaluate cost/benefit tradeoffs | ? | ✔ | ✔ | ✔ | ? | - | - |
| Understanding of the systems and DQ | ✔ | ✔ | ✔ | ✔ | ✔ | ✔ | ✔ |
| Risk management | ✔ | ✔ | - | ? | - | ✔ | ✔ |
| Personnel competency | ✔ | ✔ | ✔ | ✔ | ✔ | ✔ | ✔ |
| Physical environment | - | - | ? | ✔ | - | ✔ | ✔ |
| Audit and reviews | ✔ | ? | ✔ | ? | ✔ | ✔ | ? |
| Internal controls | ✔ | ✔ | ✔ | ✔ | ✔ | ✔ | ✔ |
| External factors | ? | ? | ? | ? | ? | ✘ | ? |

Legend:   ✔ = factors supported by the case study

✘ = factors not supported by the case study

? = conflict findings of the factors from different stakeholders within the case

- = N/A

*"We made the decision not to have external links. We set risk assessment based on our information needs. And the risk of having the external link somewhere in the network is greater than the risk that we are willing to accept of having our core business corrupted."*

CFO (Case E)

*"One of the things they need to keep in mind these days and particularly in the Public Service organization is cost effectiveness and risk management. Just because there is a risk doesn't mean you go and spend a $1,000,000 to fix it. You have to do things like risk analysis to determine the level of risk that the organization is willing to wear if you like, and those risks impact on the quality of information being processed, quality of the decisions that are made by the system and all those sorts of things."*

IT Auditor (Case A)

### Middle Management's Commitment to Data Quality

It is quite interesting to find that middle management plays a very important role in ensuring data quality. To be able to have high quality data, there have to be effective procedures at the middle management level because they are the people who report to top management and supervise the day-to-day employees in relation to data quality. Acceptance of responsibility of data quality performance by middle managers is essential in the organization hierarchal level to ensure the quality of data.

### Personnel Competency

Competency of individual personnel that are responsible for the AIS is particularly important, for instance, highly skilled and knowledgeable employees in both technical and business areas. The organization has to employ well-trained, experienced and qualified individual personnel at all levels, from top and middle management to employees.

*"Let's gets down to an understanding of the system and individual, the qualifications and the experience of the people. I have come from a very wide background, which means that I can see the auditor perspective, the user perspective, the financial accounting perspective, and the system perspective."*

CFO (Case F)

*"That comes back to the things we said before, to have the right staff at the right job, appropriately rewarded, and they understand what their role is in the total process."*

Internal Auditor (Case G)

## Physical Environment

This essentially means a pleasant physical working environment, such as a modern environment with air-conditioning and sufficient office space. Management theories certainly explain the need for employees in general to have adequate working conditions (Hawthorne studies). Previous studies in the areas of data quality and accounting information systems have not identified the physical environment as being an important factor that may impact upon the data quality.

This factor was initially identified in one of the early case studies but was later verified by some of the other case studies. For example, lack of air-conditioning facilities in warm climates impacts upon the efficiency of an employee and therefore may further impact upon the degree of care taken into the quality of the data.

*"No air-conditioning in hot weather? I think that will be terrible. It will be terrible to sit there and perform functional accounting, reporting to the group or something, with no air-conditioning."*

User (Case F)

*"Yeah, look, I think certainly if people don't have a good environment to work then they're not happy, they're less motivated; all those sorts of things."*

Director of Finance (Case C)

## Organizational Culture of Focusing on DQ

Whether the organization has a culture to promote the DQ, i.e., there must be high quality data in accounting information systems, it could have a significant impact on its data quality outcomes. Within a good data quality focused organizational culture, it is likely that the commitment from the top management would lead to an allocation of more resources, and the organization is likely to have more controls in place. In addition, employees working within an organization that has embraced such culture will likely put more effort in ensuring data quality than those who work in an organisation that doesn't focus on data quality issues. Therefore, organizational culture of focussing on data quality is likely to lead to high quality of information output.

## Understanding of the Systems and DQ

The understanding of how the system functions and the importance of data quality by personnel that are involved in accounting information systems is considered to be an essential factor.

1.  Understand how the systems work (technical competence)
2.  Understand the importance of data quality and its relationship to business objectives (perception of importance)
3.  Understand the usefulness and usage of information (the right information to the right people at the right time in the right format—4Rs)

*"Whether we understand what systems can do. With my job now, if I have to put this piece of information in, it doesn't give me any benefits, but it*

*gives the benefits to someone else. But if I don't understand in my little job here, I don't really care, I don't have to write organization drivers to put that information in the first place, to put it in accurately in the second place, and put it in consistently in the third place."*

IS Manager (Case G)

## Old Factors Confirmed by the Case Studies

Other factors that exist in the current relevant parent literature in some similar terms and specified by the case studies as particularly important for data quality in accounting information systems are:

- Top management commitment to DQ
- Education and training
- Clear DQ vision for entire organisation
- Organizational structure
- DQ policies and standards
- DQ controls
- Input controls
- Customer focus
- Nature of the AIS
- Employee relations
- Change management
- Data supplier quality management
- Continuous improvement
- Evaluate cost/benefit trade-offs
- Audit and reviews
- Internal controls

### Top Management Commitment to DQ

Top management recognizes the importance of data quality in accounting information systems and supports data quality activities.

### Education and Training

Providing effective and adequate training for staff to be able to understand and efficiently use AIS in order to obtain quality information.
1. Initial training – new personnel, new/upgrade systems
2. Ongoing training – regular training to employees and managers

### Clear DQ Vision for Entire Organization

Allocate sufficient funds, technical tools, expertise, and skilled personnel to ensure data quality, i.e., data quality is seen as a top priority.

### Organizational Structure

It is accepted that the suitable organizational structure could help to produce high quality information. For example, centralized organizational structure is likely have better DQ controls. However, in large organizations which have divisions located in different geographical areas, it is difficult to have centralized responsibility for DQ because parts of their AIS functions are performed by the individual divisions. Therefore, organizations should incorporate different DQ control approaches in accordance with their organizational structures to obtain better DQ outcomes.

### DQ Policies and Standards

The organization should have in place data quality policies and standards that are simple, relevant and consistent. It consists of two main components:
1.   Establishment of appropriate and specific data quality goals and standards
2.   Implementation/enforcement of policies and standards

However, guidelines and standards sometimes are seen only in the general sense.

*"Probably not what is written down—it is probably in people's mind how people are told to work as opposed to a proper quality document as such."*

IT Manager (Case E)

### DQ Controls

This is one of the primary factors to ensure high quality information, because without active and adequate DQ controls in place, many other factors would not have too much direct effect on the overall DQ outcomes. This is achieved by having appropriate DQ controls, approaches, and adequate processes for DQ improvement activities.

### Input Controls

Get the information right in its initial phase, i.e. input, so as to prevent input errors (Garbage-In-Garbage-Out).

*"It is at the input stage. When we look at the reports, we can tell if there has been an error just by the scale of a certain number. After all I will look at and say that seems unusual, I will just go back and check the input. Typically we try and pick that up at the input stage."*

CFO (Case E)

### Customer Focus

Focus on information users' needs and their quality requirements. Enable active participation from users to ensure and improve data quality.

### Nature of the AIS

This means to have suitable systems/packages for the accounting information systems and includes the following elements:
1.   Intuitive and easy to use

2.  Automatically performs as much validation of data as possible (base upon business rules, etc.)
3.  Adequate and sufficient documentation for people to follow
4.  Ease of modification/upgrade
5.  The system is mature (stable)
6.  The system is up-to-date (adopt new technology)
7.  Level of the integration and system interpretability
8.  Effective data management approach, such as centralized database and data warehouse

### Employee Relations

High employee self-satisfaction, job security, and career development. "Happy, fulfilled employees produce higher quality work."

### Management of Changes

It is the organization's ability and skill to manage internal and external changes. Internal changes include things like organizational restructure, introducing new technology, and personnel changes. External changes include things such as government regulations, technology, economy, and market changes.

*"Yes it [management changes] will influence data quality. I mean if there is a change I guess everyone has to be on board with the change or at least know what their responsibilities are and what they need to do. So things need to be well-planned and well-documented."*

System Accountant Manger (Case B)

### Data Supplier Quality Management

Data suppliers are those who provide raw, unorganized data to the accounting systems, including both internal and external, such as, other departments within the organization (internal) and trading partners (external). Data supplier quality management means to have an effective data quality management relationship with raw data suppliers, which has two important parts:

1.  To have agreement about the acceptable level of quality of raw data to be supplied, such as the requirements of availability, timeliness, accuracy, and completeness.
2.  To provide regular data quality reports and technical assistance to data suppliers

*"I think another external factor impacting on data quality is the fact that no matter how much we try with our data quality, some of our poor data quality is a result of external organizations we deal with as well. So the poor data quality of some of our suppliers and inconsistency there leads us to have poor quality too."*

Senior Manager (Case B)

### Continuous Improvement

The internal and external environments of the organization are always changing. In particular, new information technology is developed and upgraded very rapidly. In addition, accounting regulations are constantly changing. These all require the continuous focus and improvement on DQ to retain the long-term competitive advantages of the organization. Therefore, there is a need for continuous and consistent improvement of system and human data quality controls.

### Evaluate Cost/Benefit Trade-offs

This means having systematic cost/benefit analysis of data quality controls and activities in order to maximize benefits at minimum cost.

*"Which is based on the idea that rather than saying what have we got, does it do the job? The first question is, what's new and what can we get to replace what we have got? Sometimes it may be driven by user requirements, which is fine, but you have to trade that off. How important is that compared to the cost and all these sorts of things? Cost/benefits need to be done."*

DBA (Case B)

### Audit and Reviews

Have independent internal and external audits of the systems and the data quality to ensure appropriate controls are in place, and have regular reviews on data quality.

### Internal Controls

Have adequate internal system and process controls, which includes:
1.  Systems controls, such as access control and security
2.  Human and process controls, such as segregation of duties

*"The biggest human element that I found is trust. I've been the auditor, I used to audit against all these controls, and after many many years, I realized that the most important control is trust. Because I can break any payment system, I can break any control systems that you give me. And on that basis, the control systems although is fantastic, if you don't have good people who you trust ..."*

CFO (Case F)

*"Oh, thousands of them. There are a lot of internal controls right across the whole organization. Segregation of duties is one of the best ones. Polices that are reported against regularly; therefore we are monitoring variance critical positions. Really I think the strength comes from having defined what risks are, having defined how to do best control. A lot of segregation of conscience, and the independence of reporting, and lines of reporting."*

Internal Auditor (Case E)

# Factors That Are Not Supported by the Case Studies

There are also a few factors that are not supported by the case studies, and they are:

- External factors
- DQ manager
- Performance evaluation and rewards

## *External Factors*

*"I don't think it (change of legislation) will impact much. No, it shouldn't really. It might make it a tiny bit better because you want to try to become more comfortable with the data, because you want to get your 10% back from the government. You want to keep it accurate, otherwise you are not going to get it."*

IT Manager (Case F)

*"I'll put them (external factors) neutral. I mean if you've got everything else in place, change your culture, you should be able to handle those external factors."*

IS Manager (Case G)

## *DQ Manager*

From the data quality literature, it is suggested that a data quality manager position be established to manage the overall data quality. This means appointing a skilled person or a group of people as data quality manager(s) to manage information flow: from input to process to output. However, all the case studies didn't support the establishment of such a position. The most frequently mentioned reasons for rejection were:

*"Data quality is everybody's responsibility."*
*"It is very hard to have one person to be responsible for the whole system's data quality."*

All case studies were conducted in Australian organizations, and the literature that supports the DQ manager position was all from USA. It is quite interesting to find such common rejection of a DQ manager from Australian organizations. It could be because some USA organizations were bigger and more advanced than most of Australian organizations, or it might be because of the different organizational culture between US and Australian organizations.

## *Performance Evaluation and Rewards*

This includes measurement and reporting. On the one hand, DQ results need to be measured, which is performance evaluation, to evaluate employees, management and relevant sections/department's DQ performance. On the other hand, there is also a need to establish DQ reporting systems. It should include both appropriate formal and informal reports and reward/penalty systems for DQ positive/negative incentives.

In theory, performance evaluation should be crucial to ensure DQ; however, in the real world, it is not always the case. First of all, it is very hard to measure data quality; different people have different perspectives as to what high quality information is, which makes it harder to evaluate the data quality. Second, it had been found that it was also not easy to establish a good rewards/penalty system for data quality, which is due to a variety of reasons, such as lack of resources and lack of management awareness and support. Sometimes, it is just impossible to establish data quality positive/negative incentives.

*"Difficult question really because it is often one part of their functions. It is difficult because what do you need to do to evaluate their accuracy of the data they are entering, and how do you evaluate and say, yes, this person is 88% accurate, and how intrusive or how much time does it take evaluating what they are doing and is that taking up more time away from the things they do.  It becomes very difficult."*

DBA (Case B)

## Critical Factors

The factors that are considered to be most critical are:

- Education and training
- Nature of the accounting information systems
- Top management commitment

All the case study interview participants were also asked to rate the factors. The factors that are considered to be most critical are:

In summarizing the discussion, Figure 3 provides the comparison of the factors identified by the existing literature and the case studies. It highlights the similarities and the differences between the two sets of factors from the literature and the case studies.

The two components of Figure 3 are the factors identified by the existing literature and the factors identified by the case studies. The overlap part in the middle of the figure includes the factors identified by the relevant literature and confirmed by the case studies. However, there were two factors (6, 19) that had conflicting findings from case studies; they were supported by some cases but not by others. They were also put in the middle part of the figure, enclosed in brackets. The part that did not overlap in the case study factors means that those factors are discovered by the case study, and they are "new" factors that haven't appeared in the existing literature. There are also a few factors (5, 15, 26) from the relevant literature that were not supported by case studies.

## SOLUTIONS AND RECOMMENDATIONS

Based on the above discussions a model for factors that impact on data quality in AIS has been proposed to aid the understanding of the issues and is shown in Figure 4.

*Figure 3: Factors identified by the existing literature and case studies (inclusive & exclusive)*

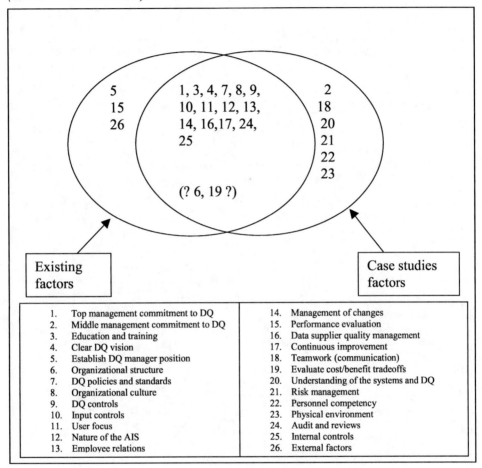

## FUTURE TRENDS

The AIS has many stakeholders, and different stakeholders may have different perspectives of critical success factors impacting on its data quality. This chapter only includes the major stakeholders in AIS: accounting professionals, IT professionals, internal auditors, information users, and data managers, because the key stakeholder's perspective of CSF in data quality is critical. However, other minor stakeholders' perspectives may also be important, and therefore, further research should be conducted.

The study was confined to Australian organizations; therefore, the conclusions drawn from this chapter may have a potential problem on generalisability. However, there is some evidence suggesting that the differences of data quality issues among Australia, USA, and other Western countries are likely to be minor. Although the

*Figure 4: A model for factors that impact on data quailty in accounting information systems*

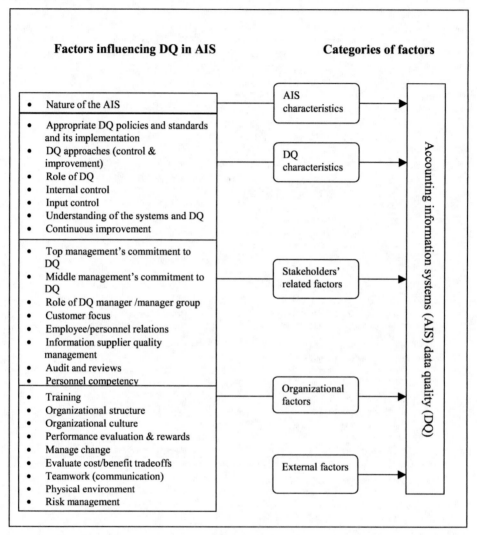

results of this chapter only are drawn from Australian organizations, it is predicted that there would be similar results even if a study was conducted in other cities and other Western countries. It is acknowledged that cultural differences may impact upon the results but are beyond the scope of this chapter, and those issues could be addressed by further research.

Future research could investigate the relationship between the CSF implementation with the DQ outcomes in organizations' AIS as well as cross-cultures and cross-countries research in this topic.

# CONCLUSION

Given that little research has been conducted to investigate CSF for data quality in AIS, this chapter is likely to make both theoretical and practical contributions to the field of data quality and accounting information systems in the following ways:

1.  It will make a contribution to the body of knowledge of data quality and AIS by identifying the critical success factors for AIS data quality. The finding of the research assists in finding what factors are more important than others. It will fill the research gap on critical success factors of data quality for AIS and provide knowledge of AIS data quality in practice.

2.  The study would make a contribution to practice as well. The research could help organizations focus on only the important factors, therefore obtaining greater benefit from less effort. Such outcomes will be helpful to both accounting and IT professionals in obtaining a better understanding of data quality issues in AIS.

    2.1. A recommended model of critical success factors that constitute the successful AIS DQ was developed for managers and accounting professionals who currently have no guidelines.

    2.2. It provides IT professionals with the knowledge on specific sets of factors that would impact on AIS data quality, and it would lead to a deeper understanding of accounting information systems data quality issues. Such knowledge could assist them in developing, maintaining and improving accounting information systems and aid their communication with accounting professionals during those processes.

A high-level data quality management practice could be a key to success for many organizations. Specification of the critical success factors of DQ management in AIS permits managers to obtain a better understanding of accounting information systems data quality management practices. If organizations focus on those critical success factors, they may be able to evaluate the perception of data quality management in their organizations' AIS and ensure the quality of the accounting information. In addition, they will be able to identify those areas of AIS data quality management where improvements should be made and improve the overall data quality in the future.

# REFERENCES

Anthony, R. S., Reese, J. S. & Herrenstein, J. H. (1994). *Accounting Text and Cases*. New York: Irwin.

Badri, M. A., Davis, D. & Davis, D. (1995). A study of measuring the critical factors of quality management. *International Journal of Quality and Reliability Management, 12*(2), 36-53.

Ballou, D. P. & Pazer, H. L. (1982). The impact of inspector fallibility on the inspection policy serial production system. *Management Science, 28*(4), 387-399.

Ballou, D. P. & Pazer, H. L. (1987). Cost/quality tradeoffs of control procedures in information systems. *OMEGA: International Journal of Management Science, 15*(6), 509-521.

Ballou, D. P. & Pazer, H. L. (1985). Modelling data and process quality in multi-input, multi-output information systems. *Management Science, 31*(2), 150-162.

Ballou, D. P., Belardo, S. & Klein B. (1987). Implication of data quality for spreadsheet analysis. *DataBase, 18*(3), 13-19.

Ballou, D. P., Wang, R. Y., Pazer, H. L. & Tayi, K. G. (1993). Modeling data manufacturing systems to determine data product quality. (No. TDQM-93-09). Cambridge, MA: *Total Data Quality Management Research Program*, MIT Sloan School of Management.

Black, S. A. & Porter, L. J. (1996). Identification of critical factors of TQM. *Decision Sciences, 27*, 1-21.

Bowen, P. (1993). *Managing data quality accounting information systems: A stochastic clearing system approach.* Unpublished doctoral dissertation, Univ. of Tennessee.

Cushing, B. E. (1974). A mathematical approach to the analysis and design of internal control systems. *The Accounting Review, 49*(1), 24-41.

English, L. P. (1999). *Improving Data Warehouse and Business Information Quality: Methods for Reducing Costs and Increasing Profits.* New York: John Wiley & Sons.

Fedorowicz, J. & Lee, Y. W. (1998). Accounting information quality: Reconciling Hierarchical and dimensional contexts. *Proceedings of Association of Information Systems (AIS) Conference*, February.

Feltham, G. (1968). The value of information. *The Accounting Review, 43*(4), 684-696.

Fields, K. T., Sami, H. & Sumners, G. E. (1986). Quantification of the auditor's evaluation of internal control in data base systems. *The Journal of Information Systems, 1*(1), 24-77.

Firth, C. (1996). *Data quality in practice: Experience from the frontline.* Paper presented to the Conference of Information Quality, October 25-26.

Gay, G., Schelluch, P. & Baines, A. (1998). Perceptions of messages conveyed by review and audit reports. *Accounting Auditing & Accountability Journal, 11*(4), 472-494.

Groomer, S. M. & Murthy, U. S. (1989). Continuous auditing of database applications: An embedded audit module approach. *The Journal of Information Systems, 3*(2), 53-69.

Hall, J. A. (1998). *Accounting Information Systems* (2nd ed.). South-Western College.

Huang, H.-T., Lee, Y. W. & Wang, R. Y. (1999). *Quality Information and Knowledge.* Englewood Cliffs, NJ: Prentice Hall.

Johnson, J. R., Leitch, R. A. & Neter, J. (1981). Characteristics of errors in accounts receivable and inventory audits. *The Accounting Review, 56*(2), 270-293.

Kaplan, D., Krishnan, R., Padman, R. & Peters, J. (1998). Assessing data quality in accounting information systems. *Communications of the ACM, 41*(2), 72-78.

Klein, B. D. (1998). Data quality in the practice of consumer product management: Evidence from the field. *Data Quality, 4*(1).

Nichols, D. R. (1987). A model of auditor's preliminary evaluations of internal control from audit data. *The Accounting Review, 62*, 183-190.

Pae, S. & Yoo, S. (2001). Strategic interaction in auditing: An analysis of auditors' legal liability, internal control system quality, and audit effort. *The Accounting Review, 76*(3), 333-356.

Porter, L. J. & Parker, A. J. (1993). Total quality management—The critical success factors. *Total Quality Management, 4*, 13-22.

Redman, T. C. (1998). The impact of poor data quality on the typical enterprise. *Communications of the ACM, 41*(2).

Saraph, J. V., Benson, P. G. & Schroeder, R. G. (1989). An instrument for measuring the critical factors of quality management. *Decision Sciences, 20*(4), 810-829.

Segev, A. (1996). *On information quality and the WWW impact a position paper.* Paper presented at Conference of Information Quality, October 25-26.

Shanks, G. & Darke, P. (1998). Understanding data quality in data warehousing A semiotic approach. Proceeding of the *1998 Conference on Information Quality, Boston, Massachusetts*, October.

Strong, D. M., Lee, Y. W. & Wang, R. Y. (1997). Data quality in context. *Communications of the ACM, 40*(5), 103-110.

Wand, Y. & Wang, R. Y. (1996). Anchoring data quality dimensions in ontological foundations. *Communications of the ACM, 39*(11), 86-95.

Wang, R. Y. (1998). A product perspective on total data quality management. *Communications of the ACM, 41*(2), 58-65.

Wang, R. Y., Lee, Y. L., Pipino, L. & Strong, D. M. (1998). Manage your information as a product. *Sloan Management Review, 39*(4), 95-105.

Wang, R. Y., Storey, V. C. & Firth, C. P. (1995). A framework for analysis of data quality research. *IEEE Transactions on Knowledge and Data Engineering, 7*(4), 623-640.

Yu, S. & Neter, J. (1973). A stochastic model of the internal control system. *Journal of Accounting Research, 11*(3), 273-295.

Zhu, Z. & Meredith, P. H. (1995). Defining critical elements in JIT implementation: A survey. *Industrial Management & Data Systems, 95*(8), 21-29.

# About the Authors

**Luiz Antonio Joia** is an associate professor and academic coordinator of the MBA Program at Brazilian School of Public and Business Administration, Getulio Vargas Foundation, in Rio de Janeiro, Brazil, and also an adjunct professor of Rio de Janeiro State University. He has an BSc in Engineering from the Militar Institute of Engineering, Rio de Janeiro, Brazil, and an MSc and DSc in Production Engineering from Federal University of Rio de Janeiro and post-graduated in Management Studies at Oxford University. He has published widely in international journals like: *Internet Research, Journal of Workplace Learning, International Journal of Information Management, Journal of Intellectual Capital,* and *Journal of Knowledge Management.* He serves as a member of the Editorial Advisory Board of the *Journal of Intellectual Capital*, MCB University Press. He consulted with the World Bank from 1999 to 2000.

* * *

**Bernardo Bátiz-Lazo**, Lic. Econ., M. Applied Econ., PhD is a lecturer in management at Open University Business School (UK). After studying economics in Mexico City and Barcelona, Mr. Bátiz was awarded his PhD in Business Administration at Manchester University. He then joined the School of Management of the Queen's University of Belfast and later on the Open University Business School. Prior to university life he worked as trader and research analyst in capital and derivatives markets in both the US and Mexico. Since 1991 he has been active in teaching and researching financial markets and financial institutions. He lectures regularly on comparative financial markets and the strategic management of banking organisations to graduates and specialists in Germany, Portugal, Spain and Sweden.

**David W. Birchall** is the Director of the Centre for Business in the Digital Economy at Henley Management College in the UK. The Centre carries out applied research into innovation management, future work, knowledge management, organizational and personal learning and e-business. Dr. Birchall's research and consulting interests are in strategic response to the digital economy.

**Constantine A. Bourlakis** is a senior lecturer in Microeconomics in the Department of Business Administration, Athens University of Economics and Business, Greece. Dr. Bourlakis obtained his first degree in Economics and Statistics in the Department of Economics, Athens University of Economics and Business, Greece. Subsequently, Dr. Bourlakis completed an MA in Economic Studies at the University of Newcastle upon Tyne (UK) and a PhD at the University of East Anglia (UK). Dr. Bourlakis worked as a research associate at the University of Warwick (UK) and as a lecturer at the University of Leeds (UK), the University of Edinburgh (UK) and the University of Leicester (UK).

**Michael A. Bourlakis** is a lecturer in Food Marketing in the Department of Agricultural Economics and Food Marketing, University of Newcastle upon Tyne (UK). He graduated in Business Administration from the Department of Business Administration, Athens University of Economics and Business, Greece, and obtained an MBA and a PhD at the Department of Business Studies, University of Edinburgh (UK). He worked as a sales manager for the largest dairy company in Greece and as a research associate at the Management Centre, University of Leicester (UK) and at the Oxford Institute of Retail Management, University of Oxford (UK).

**Naomi J. Brookes** received a PhD in Manufacturing Engineering from Imperial College (UK). She worked for Rolls Royce plc as a manufacturing engineer, operations manager and corporate controller. Her primary research interests are the impact of organisation on business performance, especially during product development, and the development of tools and techniques to improve product development performance. She currently works as a lecturer in the Department of Manufacturing Engineering of Loughborough University (UK). She is the co-editor of a book about concurrent engineering: *Concurrent Engineering, What's Working Where*. Articles authored by Naomi Brookes have appeared in journals such as the *International Journal of Advanced Manufacturing Technology*, the *Journal of Science Measurement and Technology, Manufacturing Engineer,* the *International Journal of Production Research,* and the *Journal of Engineering Manufacture*.

**Noel Brown** is a senior lecturer in electronic commerce at the University of Southern Queensland, Toowoomba, Australia. Prior to his academic career, he was a corporate accountant within the mining and transport industries. He has been involved with developing and teaching courses in the area of accounting information systems for over a decade. His current research interests are in the area of electronic commerce, and he is the foundation editor for the *Australian Journal of Electronic Commerce*.

**Mari W. Buche** is a doctoral candidate in Information Systems at the University of Kansas. Her primary research interests include management information systems, IS strategy, technology change agents, behavioral decision making, and knowledge management. She is currently investigating issues of transition in IT organizations, specifically the phenomenon of changing IT professional work identity. She focuses on cross-disciplinary research designs that combine qualitative and quantitative methodologies. Her work has been published in the *Journal of Information Technology and Management*.

**Ting Yee Chang**, an honours graduate, Bachelor of Business (Business Administration), of the Department of Management, Monash University, Australia, is currently working as the human resource and administration executive at Netrust Private Limited in Singapore. Her previous research and publications were concerned with understanding the relationship between telecommuters (teleworkers) and their teams in Australia and with the management of people engaged in this IT-enabled flexible work. In this current research, she was able to combine her former research interest with her current Singapore employment area of technology and human resource management. Ting Yee Chang may be contacted by email: tingyee.chang@netrust.net.

**Marcel Cohen** has spent over 20 years in industry – mostly in retailing. After graduating in Physics and gaining an MSc in management at Imperial College, his very first job was running his own stall in a street market selling children's clothes. This marked his introduction to retailing and marketing in general. He was later recruited by Fads, the paint and wallpaper retail chain as general manager of its DIY chain. Following this post, he joined Shell UK and was soon promoted to a senior management position in their petrol station retailing operation where he was responsible for marketing, planning and investment for a retail business whose turnover was over £2.5 billion. After 10 years he left Shell to join the faculty of Imperial College Management School. It was 1990 that Marcel Cohen joined the Management School of Imperial College, where he gained his PhD at the same time as lecturing. He is a dynamic lecturer and is also an active researcher. He regularly contributes to professional journals such as *Strategic Change* and *Applied Economics*. He has also written a number of papers on the subject of petrol competition and has just completed a book on petrol, co-authored with an old colleague.

**Yanqing Duan** is principal research fellow at Luton Business School, University of Luton, UK. She obtained her PhD from Aston University. She received a number of research fundings from European Commission. Her research interests are the development and use of intelligent systems and decision support systems for decision-making, and the development of computer-based training and support systems for SMEs. She supervises a number of PhD projects and has publications in leading international journals and conferences.

**Marjorie A. Jerrard** lectures in the Department of Management, Monash University, Melbourne, Australia, teaching in the areas of strategic management, industrial and employee relations, and human resource management. Her research interests cover strategic industrial and employee relations and human resource management and she is a member of Monash's REACH Unit. Recent publications and international conference presentations have covered the strategic management of flexible work, including teleworking (with Ting Yee Chang), and critical assessment of IT-enabled work practices. Her current research project is concerned with the contribution made by women to stages of the supply chain in the Australian and New Zealand meat industries. She may be contacted by email: marjorie.jerrard@BusEco.monash.edu.au.

**Benedict Kemmerer** is a doctoral student in Strategic Management at the University of Kansas School of Business. His primary research interests focus on cognitive aspects of strategic management. Current research includes the social construction of capabilities, managerial decision processes with respect to resources and capabilities, and venture capital decision making.

**Andy Koronios** is associate professor of Information Systems and head of the Division of Information Systems at the University of Southern Queensland, Australia. He has degrees in Electrical Engineering and Education as well as a master's degree from the University of New England and a PhD degree from the University of Queensland. He has extensive computing experience in the commercial environment, especially in small to medium-sized enterprises. He has also taught at undergraduate, postgraduate and executive levels and has received the USQ Award for Excellence in Teaching. His research interests are in the area of electronic commerce, strategy and technologies as well as data quality, security and computer-facilitated learning.

**Herbert Kotzab**, born in 1965 in Vienna, Austria, is an associate professor at the Department of Operations Management at the Copenhagen Business School (CBS), Denmark. He received his doctorate degree from the Vienna University of Economics and Business Administration (WU-Wien; Prof. Schnedlitz). Before his assignment at CBS, he was assistant to the CEO of Velux-Austria and senior lecturer at the Department for Retail Marketing at the Vienna University of Economics and Business Administration at WU-Wien. His research is carried out in close cooperation with major Austrian and Danish companies. In 1998, he was visiting scholar at the Center for Transportation Studies at the Massachusetts Institute of Technology. He also was an invited lecturer at the Kellogg's Graduate School of Management, Northwestern University; INSEAD; Hochschule St. Gallen; and Händelshogskolen i Göteborg. He received the Vienna Award for Research in Retailing and the 1999 NOFOMA Best Paper Award.

**Michel J. Leseure** received a PhD in Manufacturing Management from the University of Sheffield (UK), an MBA from the Eastern Washington University (USA), and an engineering diploma from ENSMM (France). He started his career as a mechanical engineer in the customized capital goods industry. He is now an assistant professor in the School of Business Administration at Al Akhawayn University, a Moroccan university based on the American pedagogical model. Articles authored by Michel Leseure have appeared in journals such as the *International Journal of Operations and Production Management*, the *Interna-*

*tional Journal of Technology Management, Omega  (the International Journal of Management Science),* and the *International Journal of Business Performance Management.*

**Reuven R. Levary** is a professor of Decision Sciences at Saint Louis University. He received an MSc and a PhD in operations research from Case Western Reserve University. Dr. Levary has held visiting positions at MIT, Princeton University, Rensselaer Polytechnic Institute, Yale University, Washington University and Caltech's Jet Propulsion Laboratory. His research, teaching and consulting activities are in the areas of computer-integrated supply chains, computer simulation, manufacturing systems, and mathematical programming models to financial planning. Dr. Levary has published widely in a variety of professional journals. He serves on the editorial boards of several journals. He is a fellow of AAAS and a member of INFORMS, IEEE and Society for Computer Simulation.

**Mingfang Li** is a professor of Management in the College of Business and Economics, California State University, Northridge, USA. He received his PhD in Strategic Management from Virginia Polytechnic Institute and State University. His research focuses on company strategy and performance, top management, global strategies, and application of technology in strategic management. His work has appeared in a variety of management outlets including *Strategic Management Journal, Advances in International Marketing, Advances in Competitiveness Research, Asia Pacific Journal of Management, Journal of Applied Management Studies,* and *Information & Management.* He currently serves as an assistant editor at *International Journal of Organizational Analysis.*

**Yu Li** is developing her research interests in the impact of Information Technology on marketing management. She gained her first degree from Colorado University at Denver and master degree in Marketing Management from University of Luton, UK.

**James McCalman** is Director of MBA Programmes at Ashridge Management College, UK, and a reader in Organizational Behaviour at Brunel University and visiting professor at the University of North Carolina. A senior management academic with business experience and a research and publishing record, he has wide experience of teaching, research and consulting in the UK, Europe, Southeast Asia and the United States. He also worked as Director of Education and Training for a healthcare firm, and most of his consultancy work is on change management and teams. Dr. McCalman is the author of six books and numerous academic and management journal articles. His current research interests concern the management and politics of change—what factors account for the successful and unsuccessful introduction of change and how do change managers "manage" the political issues that arise?

**V. K. Narayanan** is the Stubbs professor of Strategy and Entrepreneurship at Drexel University, Philadelphia. He was previously the Fulbright-FLAD chair in Management of Technology at the University of Aveiro, the associate dean for Academic Affairs, and the director of the Center for Management of Technology in Kansas University School of Business. Dr. Narayanan's most recent book, *Managing Technology and Innovation for Competitive Advantage*, was published by Prentice Hall in 2001. He has published numerous articles in professional journals such as *Academy of Management Journal, Academy of Management Review, Management Information Systems Quarterly,* and *Strategic Management Journal.* He serves on the editorial board of *Organization Science.*

**Kerstin Neumayer,** born in 1969 in Salzburg, Austria, is managing director of Marketing of the Billa Warenhandel AG, the largest Austrian retailer. She received her Master of Science (Advertising) at the Vienna University of Economics and Business Administration (WU-Wien) and was ranked as the fourth best student of her graduation year. The topic of her master's thesis dealt with "Advertising Regulations in the United States of America, Austria, Saudi Arabia and The European Community at the Supranational Level—With Special Emphasis on Case Studies." As managing director, Kerstin Neumayer is responsible for the strategic branding of the firm and Billa's total advertising and media strategy (including classical advertising as well as POS strategies and promotion activities). (In the year 2000, Billa spent 33 million Euro on advertising and was the largest client in Austria.) She is also responsible for Billa's customer relationship management program and Internet strategy.

**Fred Niederman** is currently serving as Shaughnessy associate professor of MIS at Saint Louis University. He holds a doctoral degree from the University of Minnesota. He currently serves as chair of the ACM special interest group on computer personnel research and as area editor for the *Journal of Global Information Management.* He has published in *MIS Quarterly, Decision Sciences, Communications of the ACM, Journal of Global Information Management, Journal of Strategic Information Systems, Decision Support Systems, DATABASE, Computer Personnel, Group Decision and Negotiation, Small Group Research,* and the *Journal of Business Communications.* His primary areas of research are virtual groups and organizations, computer personnel, and global information systems.

**Theodorou Petros** has an HBSc in Economics, MSc in Informatics, a PhD in Applied Informatics, and a post. doct. in Strategy of Information Systems. He is a member of the New York Academy, the Economic Chamber of Greece, the Management of Technology Organization, and the Who's Who Marquis. His work experience includes the Public Power Corporation, Astron/PEP, and Computer Logic. He has taught at Aristotle's University, the University of Macedonia, Sheffield/City College, the Technological Educational Institution, the College of Advanced Education, etc. He has published in various sources like University Publications of Crete, the *International Journal of Production Economics,* etc.

He has spoken at many conferences about strategy matters and IT. He has done further work as a free-lance consultant in various firms.

**Peter Schnedlitz**, born in 1954 in Murau, Austria, has been a professor of Retailing and Marketing and head of the Department of Retailing and Marketing at the Vienna University of Economics and Business Administration (WU-Wien), Austria, since 1992. He was previously a professor of Marketing in Trier, Germany; Innsbruck, Austria; and Graz, Austria; and Maribor, Slovenia. He graduated from University of Graz, Austria, from which he got both his doctorate degree and his habilitation degree in Business Administration (major Retailing and Marketing). Furthermore, he was a visiting scholar at the Sloan School of Management (Massachusetts Institute of Technology). He is executive president of the WU-Wien Alumni Club, with more than 20,000 alumni. Austria's President Dr. Thomas Klestil and many CEOs in Austria and Germany are graduates of that university. Prof. Schnedlitz is editor and/ or author of some 100 publications, and he is also owner of a marketing consulting company and has undertaken consulting and executive education for most major retailing companies in Austria and Germany.

**Bernd Carsten Stahl**, born in 1968, Dipl.-Wi.-Ing., MA, DEA; studied mechanical engineering and commerce at the University of the German Armed Forces in Hamburg from 1990 to 1994 (degree: Diplom-Wirtschaftsingenieur). From 1994 to 1998 he studied philosophy and economics at the University of Hagen (degree: Magister Artium). From 1999 to 2000 he studied philosophy in Bordeaux, France, where he graduated with a Diplôme d'Etudes Approfondies. From 1987 to 1997 he was an officer of the German Armed Forces, his latest assignment was that of a deputy company commander in the artillery regiment 7 in Dülmen. From 1998 to 2000 he was a research assistant at the University Witten/Herdecke at the Institute of Economics and Philosophy. Since September 2000 he has been a lecturer at the Department of Management Information Systems at the University College Dublin, Ireland. He works on questions of the relationship of ethics and business with a particular emphasis on the notion of responsibility. His other field of research is normative problems arising from the use of information technology in business.

**George Tovstiga** leads the "Leadership & People Management" consulting practice within ABB's Process & Business Consulting, based in Switzerland. He is a member of the Associate Faculty at Henley Management College (UK) and visiting professor of management at the International Graduate School of Management of the Technical University of St. Petersburg, Russia. Dr. Tovstiga's research and practice interests are in managing organizational competencies and change in knowledge-intensive organizations.

**Douglas Wood**, M.Comm., Ph.D., is a National Westminster Bank professor of Banking and Finance at Manchester Business School (UK). After studying at Birmingham, Oxford and MIT, Prof. Wood was awarded his PhD at Manchester

University, after which he joined Manchester Business School, where he is the National Westminster professor of Banking and Financial Services. His main interest is in financial and business forecasting and he has written/edited six books in the area including *International Business Finance,* published by Macmillan in 1981, and *Neural Network Solutions for Trading in Financial Markets,* published by Pitman/Financial Times in 1994. He is editor of the finance volume of Blackwell's New Encyclopaedia of Management and also contributed to *Project and Infrastructure Finance in Asia,* published by Asia Law and Practice.

**Hongjiang Xu** is a PhD candidate and part-time lecturer at Division of Information Systems, University of Southern Queensland, Australia. She has a master's degree in Information Systems from the University of Queensland, Australia. Prior to coming to Australia, she was a supervisor accountant-accounting general in a Sino – Hong Kong joint venture company for many years. She holds several accounting qualifications from China and also is a member of CPA Australia. Her research interests are in the area of data and information quality, accounting information systems, ERP systems, and electronic commerce.

**Xianzhong Mark Xu** is a senior lecturer at University of Portsmouth, UK. He gained his PhD in MIS from Open University Business School, UK. He is a journal reviewer and PhD supervisor. His specialist interests are in strategic information systems with a focus on information scanning, information support and executives' information behaviour. He has published widely in international journals and conferences such as *International Journal of Information Management*, and *Marketing Intelligence & Planning*.

# Index

# The International Journal of IT Standards and Standardization Research(JITSR)

**NEW!**   **NEW!**

## The International Source for Advances in IT Standards and Standardization Research

**ISSN:** 1539-3062
**eISSN:** 1539-3054

**Subscription:** Annual fee per volume (2 issues):
Individual US $85
Institutional US $145

**Editor:** Kai Jakobs
Technical University
of Aachen, Germany

## Mission

The primary mission of *The International Journal of IT Standards & Standardization Research* is to publish research findings to advance knowledge and research in all aspects of IT standards and standardization in modern organizations. Furthermore, *The International Journal of IT Standards & Standardization Research* will be considered as an authoritative source and information outlet for the diverse community of IT standards researchers. JITSR is targeted towards researchers, scholars, policymakers, IT managers, and IT standards associations and organizations.

## Coverage

JITSR will include contibutions from disciplines in computer science, information systems, management, business, social sciences, economics, engineering, political science, and communications. Potential topics include: Technological innovation and standarization; Standards for information infrastructures; standardization and economic development; open source and standardization; intellectual property rights; economics of standardization; emerging roles of standards organizations and consortia; conformity assessment; standards strategies; standarization and regulation; standardization in the public sphere; standardization in public policy; tools and services related to standardiztion; and other relevant issues related to standards and standardization.

For subscription information, contact:

**Idea Group Publishing**
**701 E Chocolate Ave., Ste 200**
**Hershey PA 17033-1240, USA**
cust@idea-group.com

For paper submission information:

**Dr. Kai Jakobs**
**Technical University of Aachen, Germany**
**Kai.Jakobs@i4mail.informatik.rwth-aachen.de**